SuSE

SuSE Linux

Administration Guide

Fifth edition 2003

Please direct suggestions and comments to documentation@suse.de

Authors:	Frank Bodammer, Stefan Dirsch, Olaf Donjak, Torsten Duwe, Roman Drahtmüller, Thorsten Dubiel, Karl Eichwalder, Thomas Fehr, Stefan Fent, Werner Fink, Kurt Garloff, Carsten Groß, Andreas Grünbacher, Franz Hassels, Hendrik Vogelsang, Klaus Kämpf, Hubert Mantel, Anas Nashif, Johannes Meixner, Lars Müller, Matthias Nagorni, Peter Pöml, Siegfried Olschner, Heiko Rommel, Marcus Schaefer, Klaus Singvogel, Klaus G. Wagner, Christian Zoz
Translators:	Daniel Pisano, Tino Tanner
Editors:	Jörg Arndt, Antje Faber, Berthold Gunreben Roland Haidl, Jana Jaeger, Edith Parzefall, Peter Reinhart, Thomas Rölz Marc Rührschneck, Thomas Schraitle, Rebecca Walter
Layout:	Manuela Piotrowski, Thomas Schraitle
Setting:	LaTeX

This book has been printed on 100 % chlorine-free bleached paper.

Contents

II Configuration 63

Preface

The *Administration Guide* offers an introduction to the technology of SuSE Linux, providing details about the installation, system administration, and the configuration of special system components. It also introduces the theoretical basics of certain properties of Linux and especially of SuSE Linux, including background information about the X window system, the boot concept, printing, and the Linux kernel.

Working with and in networks has always been one of the main strengths of Linux. Therefore, a large portion of the book is dedicated to the theory, configuration, and administration of networks and their various services. Learn about various protocols, routing, NFS and NIS, heterogeneous networks with Samba and Netatalk, and proxies. The final chapter extensively covers the issue of security in networks.

We are confident that the Open Source policy, the boot concept, the easy installation, the stable and secure network operation, and the extremely flexible X11 environment will do their part to convince you that that your SuSE Linux is the superior operating system! The digital versions of both SuSE Linux manuals can be accessed by way of the SuSE Help System under SuSE Linux.

New Features in the Administration Guide

This section lists the changes to the documentation from the last version to the current:

- The Kerberos chapter was expanded to include installation and configuration (see *Installing and Administering Kerberos* on page 462).
- Additional information about power management is available in *APM and ACPI — Power Management* on page 238.
- Information about the configuration of the Emacs editor is provided in *Settings for GNU Emacs* on page 272.
- Many other sections were updated in line with the new features in SuSE Linux 8.2.
- The YaST configuration chapter was omitted. The information was shifted to the *User Guide* or to the respective chapters in the *Administration Guide*.

The following are new in this release:

- A chapter about *Access Control Lists* in Linux (*Access Control Lists in Linux* on page 505)
- Information about "smpppd" in *The smpppd as Dial-up Assistant* on page 422
- Information about the installation of patch RPMs in *RPM and Patches* on page 59
- Information on the file synchronization in *File Synchronization* on page 381

Illustrations of the SuSE 8.2 Distributions

Personal Edition

The illustration for the Personal Edition shows a surface constructed by Werner Boy in 1901, which represents an immersion of the real projective plane in the three-dimensional real space. The image was calculated with the help of the `surf` application (see `http://surf.sourceforge.net`), using the following equation:

$$\begin{aligned} 36zy^4 + 36x^2z^4 + 36x^4z - 243x^4y^2 - 243x^2y^4 + 36z^4y^2 + 72x^2zy^2 \\ -48\sqrt{2}z^3y^3 + 72\sqrt{2}y^2z^3x - 90y^4z^2 - 16y^2z^2 - 16z^2x^2 - 90z^2x^4 \\ -81y^6 - 24z^6 + 48z^5 - 32z^4 + 64/9z^3 - 81x^6 - 180y^2z^2x^2 \\ -24\sqrt{2}z^3x^3 + 48\sqrt{2}y^3z^2 - 144\sqrt{2}yz^2x^2 - 324\sqrt{2}y^4zx \\ -216\sqrt{2}y^2zx^3 + 108\sqrt{2}zx^5 + 144\sqrt{2}x^2z^3y &= 0 \end{aligned}$$

Refer to `http://www.OliverLabs.net/suse/` for more information. The `surf` file used for drawing the image is available for download.

Professional Edition

The illustration for the Professional Edition is a quintic surface with four higher-order double points. To be able to draw the projective equation

$$\begin{aligned} (x+z)^2(y^3+w^3) + (y+w)^2(x^3+z^3) \\ +(8yzw + 8xzw + 8xyw + 8xyz)(y+w)(x+z) \\ +4y^2w^2(x+z) + 4x^2z^2(y+w) &= 0 \end{aligned}$$

of the tetrahedron-symmetrical surface with the `surf` application (see `http://surf.sourceforge.net`), the tetrahedral coordinates

$$x' = z-1+\sqrt{2}x, \quad y' = z-1-\sqrt{2}x, \quad z' = -(z+1+\sqrt{2}y), \quad w' = -(z+1-\sqrt{2}y)$$

were used. Refer to `http://www.OliverLabs.net/suse/` for more information. The `surf` file used for drawing the image is available for download.

Typographical Conventions

The following typographical conventions are used in this book:

Text layout	Meaning
YaST	programs
/etc/passwd	file or directory names
⟨*parameter*⟩	when entering a command, parameter should be replaced by the actual value, excluding the angle brackets.
PATH	the environment variable PATH
192.168.1.2	the value of a variable. In this case, 192.168.1.2
ls	the command ls
news	the user news
earth:~ # **ls**	Input of ls in the command shell of the user root in his home directory of the host "Earth"
newbie@earth:~ > **ls**	Input of ls in the command shell of user newbie in his home directory on the host "Earth"
C:\> **fdisk**	DOS prompt with the command input fdisk
(Alt)	A key to press. Keys to press sequentially are separated by spaces.
(Ctrl) + (Alt) + (Del)	Keys to press simultaneously are grouped with the '+' sign.
"Permission denied"	System messages
'System Update'	Menu items, buttons, labels

A Word of Thanks

The list of all people who contributed to the success of this distribution would exceed the scope of this book. We would like to express our gratitude to all who worked tirelessly to present this quality SuSE Linux release.

With their voluntary commitment, the developers of Linux cooperate on a global scale to promote the development of Linux. We thank them for their efforts — this distribution would not exist without them. Furthermore, we want to thank Frank Zappa and Pawar. Last but not least, special thanks to Linus Torvalds.

Have a lot of fun!

Your SuSE Team

Part I

Installation

1 The Installation

SuSE Linux can installed in a flexible way according to the local circumstances. The various methods range from a graphical "quick installation" to a text-based installation that allows manual intervention. The following sections cover various installation methods, such as the text-based installation with YaST2 and the use of various installation sources (CD-ROM, NFS). A comprehensive description of the graphical standard installation can be found in the User Guide. This chapter also offers troubleshooting tips for problems with the installation. The concluding section provides detailed information on partitioning.

Text-Based Installation with YaST2

In addition to installing with the assistance of a graphical interface, SuSE Linux can also be installed with the help of the YaST2 text menus (console mode). All YaST2 modules are also available in this text mode. The text mode is especially useful if you do not need a graphical interface (e.g., for server systems) or if the graphics card is not supported by the X Window System.

The Start Screen

Insert CD 1 into the drive and restart the computer. If the computer does not boot the CD, reset the boot sequence in the BIOS to `CDROM, C, A`. The start screen will be displayed after a few moments.

Use the (↑) and (↓) keys to select 'Manual Installation' within ten seconds to prevent YaST2 from being started automatically. In case your hardware requires special parameters (which is usually not the case), these can be entered in the line Boot Options. The parameter textmode=1 can be used to run YaST2 in full-screen text mode.

The keys (F2) to (F5) can be used to determine the screen resolution for the installation. Press (F2) to enter the text-only mode. Then press (↵). Now, a box will appear with the progress display "Loading Linux kernel". The kernel boots and linuxrc is started. Subsequently, proceed with the installation using the menus of linuxrc.

Troubleshooting

- Other boot problems can usually be circumvented with kernel parameters. If DMA causes difficulties, use the start option 'Installation – Safe Settings'.

- If your CD-ROM drive (ATAPI) crashes when booting the system, refer to *ATAPI CD-ROM Hangs While Reading* on page 25.

- CD 1, which features an optimized kernel for Pentium processors, is not recognized as a boot medium. Try the "boot floppy" or CD 2. See *Booting from Disk (SYSLINUX)* on page 23 or *Using CD 2 for Booting* on page 24.

- The graphical mode cannot be used for graphics cards like FireGL 1, 2, and 3. In this case, the installation must be performed in text mode. In this case, select (F2) in the boot menu.

- If unexplainable errors occur when the kernel is loaded or during the installation, select 'Memory Test' in the boot menu to check the memory. Linux requires the hardware to meet high standards, which means the memory and its timing must be set correctly. More information is available at `http://sdb.suse.de/sdb/html/thallma_memtest86.html`. If possible, run the memory test overnight.

The Basis: linuxrc

The linuxrc program can be used to specify settings for the installation and load needed drivers as kernel modules. Finally, linuxrc will launch YaST2, starting the actual installation of the system software and other applications.

Use ↑ or ↓ to choose menu items. Use ← or → to select a command such as 'Ok' or 'Cancel'. Execute the command by pressing ↵.

A detailed description of linuxrc is provided in *linuxrc* on page 278.

Settings

The linuxrc application automatically begins with the language and keyboard selection.

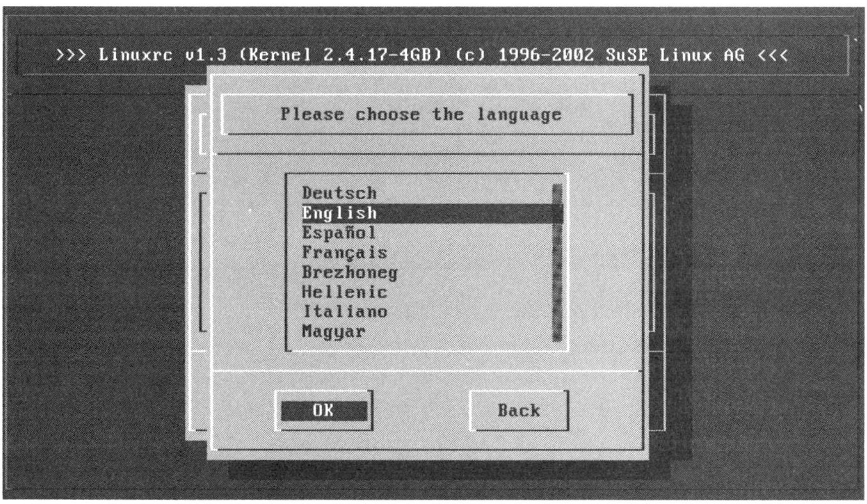

Figure 1.1: Language Selection

- Select the installation language (e.g., 'English') and confirm with (↵).
- Next, select the keyboard layout (e.g., 'English').

Possible Problems

- If linuxrc does not offer the desired keyboard layout, select an alternative layout. Once the installation is completed, the layout can be changed with YaST2.

Main Menu of linuxrc

Now, you will find yourself in the main menu in linuxrc (Figure 1.2). The

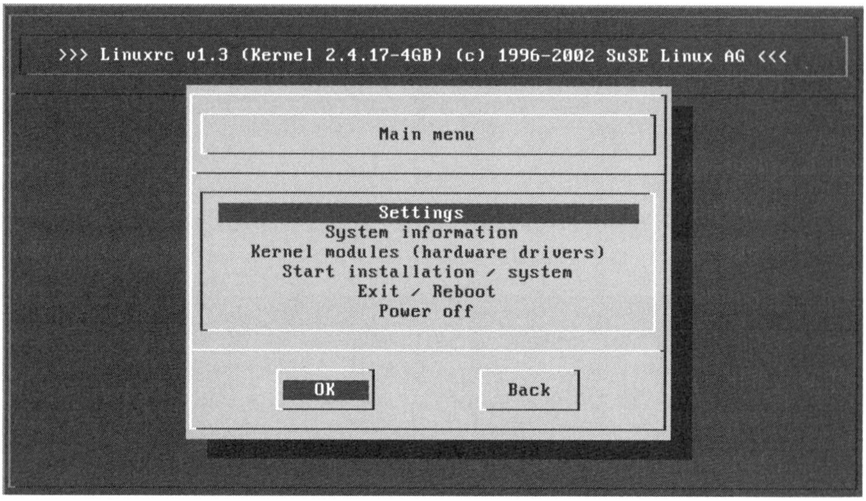

Figure 1.2: The Main Menu of linuxrc

following options are offered here:

'Settings' Here, select the language, screen, and keyboard. This subject is covered above.

'System Information' Find information about the hardware as detected by the kernel or activated by loaded modules.

'Kernel modules (hardware drivers)' Here, load any modules needed for your hardware. Also use this to load modules for additional file systems, such as ReiserFS.

Normally, you do *not* need to use this menu item if both your hard disks and the CD drive (ATAPI) are connected to an (E)IDE controller, as (E)IDE support is integrated in the kernel. Details for module selection are presented in the following paragraph.

'Start installation/system' Continues installation.

'Cancel/reboot' Cancels the installation.

'Power off' Halts the system and switches the power off.

Hardware Integration with Modules

Select loading of kernel modules with 'Kernel module' only if you need support for SCSI or for PCMCIA or if you do *not* have an ATAPI drive. At present, other components are also be swapped out as modules (e.g., IDE) or added (e.g., USB, FireWire, or file systems). Read about how modules are loaded in *linuxrc* on page 278. In the following submenu, choose which modules to load. Possible choices are:

A SCSI Module Use this if you have a SCSI hard disk or SCSI CD-ROM drive.

A CD-ROM Module This is required if your CD-ROM drive is *not* connected to the (E)IDE controller or the SCSI controller. This especially applies to older CD-ROM drives connected to the computer by way of a proprietary controller.

A Network Module Use this if you want to install via NFS or FTP. Refer to *Installation from a Network Source* on page 18 for information.

One or More File Systems Required to add file systems, such as ReiserFS or ext3.

Tip

If you cannot find any support for your installation medium (proprietary CD-ROM drive, parallel port CD-ROM drive, network cards, PCMCIA) among the standard modules, you may find what you need on a module floppy disk, which contains additional drivers. To do this, go to the end of the list and select the item '-- More modules --'. In this case, linuxrc will prompt you to insert the module disk.

Tip

Starting Installation

Because 'Start installation/system' is usually preselected, normally just press ↵ to proceed with the installation.

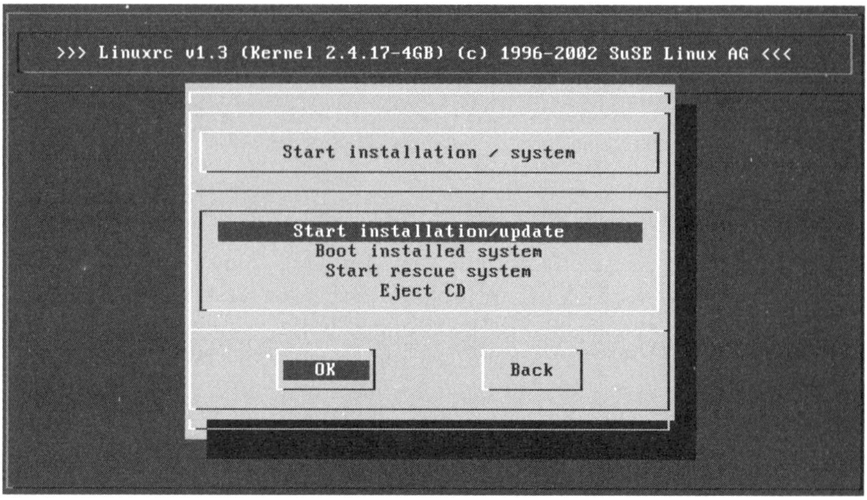

Figure 1.3: linuxrc *Installation Menu*

The following items are available:

'Start installation/update' Install a new system or update an existing installation.

'Boot installed system' Boot an already installed system.

'Boot rescue system' Start the rescue system, which can be used if an installed system is damaged.

'Eject CD' Eject CD.

To begin the installation, press ↵ to access the menu item 'Start installation/update'. Then select the source medium. Usually, the cursor can be left at the default selection: 'CD-ROM'.

Now press ↵. The installation environment will be loaded directly from CD 1.

As soon as this procedure is completed, YaST2 starts in the text-based (ncurses) version. The installation will then continue as described in **?**, chapter *Installation*.

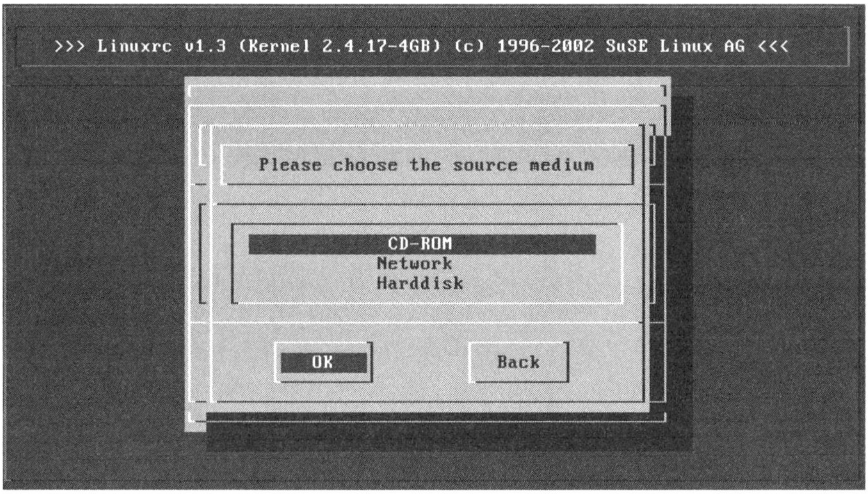

Figure 1.4: Selecting the Source Medium in linuxrc

Possible Problems

- The SCSI adapter is not detected:

  ▷ Try loading a module for a compatible driver.

  ▷ Use a kernel with the appropriate integrated SCSI driver. This kernel would need to be custom-built.

- The ATAPI CD-ROM drive hangs when reading the data. See *ATAPI CD-ROM Hangs While Reading* on page 25.

- For reasons still unknown, sometimes problems occur when loading data to the RAM disk so YaST2 cannot be started.

  If this situation arises, the following procedure can often lead to efficient results:

  Select 'Settings' → 'Debug (Experts)' in the linuxrc main menu. There, select `no` in 'Force root image'. Then return to the main menu and restart installation.

Starting SuSE Linux

Following the installation, decide how to boot Linux for daily operations. The following overview introduces various alternatives for booting Linux. The most suitable method depends on the intended purpose.

Boot Disk You can boot Linux from a *boot disk*. This approach will always work and is easy. The boot disk can be created with YaST. See User Guide (2003), *YaST2— Configuration: Creating a Boot, Rescue, or Module Disk.*

The boot disk is a useful interim solution if you have difficulties configuring the other possibilities or if you want to postpone the decision regarding the final boot mechanism. A boot disk may also be a suitable solution in connection with OS/2 or Windows NT.

Linux Boot Loader The most versatile and technically elegant solution for booting your system is the use of a Linux boot manager like GRUB (GRand Unified Bootloader) or LILO (LInux LOader), which both allow selection from different operating systems prior to booting. The boot loader can either be configured during installation or later with the help of YaST.

Caution

There are BIOS variants that check the structure of the boot sector (MBR) and erroneously display a virus warning after the installation of GRUB or LILO. This problem can be easily solved by entering the BIOS and looking for corresponding adjustable settings. For example, you should switch off 'virus protection'. You can switch this option back on again later. It is unnecessary, however, if Linux is the only operating system you use.

Caution

A detailed discussion of various boot methods, especially of GRUB and LILO, can be found in *Booting and Boot Managers* on page 71.

The Graphical SuSE Screen

Starting with SuSE Linux 7.2, the graphical SuSE screen is displayed on the first console, if the option "vga=771" is active as kernel parameter. If you install using YaST2, this option is automatically activated in accordance with the selected resolution and the graphics card.

Disabling the SuSE Screen

Basically there are three ways to achieve this:

- Disabling SuSE screen on an as-needed basis:

  Enter the command `echo 0 >/proc/splash` to disable the graphical screen. `echo 0x0f01 >/proc/splash` activates the screen again.

- Disabling the SuSE screen by default:

  Add the kernel parameter `splash=0` to your boot loader configuration. *Booting and Boot Managers* on page 71 offers more information about this. However, if you prefer the old text mode anyway (which was the default with previous versions), set this to `"vga=normal"` .

- Completely disabling the SuSE screen:

  Compile a new kernel after disabling the option `Use splash screen instead of boot logo` in the menu 'framebuffer support'.

Tip

Removing the framebuffer support from the kernel will automatically disable the splash screen as well. SuSE cannot not provide any support for your system if you run it with a custom kernel.

Tip

Special Installation Procedures

Installation Without CD-ROM Support

What if a standard installation via CD-ROM drive is not possible? For example, your CD-ROM may not be supported because it is an older proprietary drive. A secondary machine, like a notebook, might not have any CD-ROM drive at all, only an ethernet adapter. SuSE Linux offers the possibility of performing the installation on machines without a CD-ROM drive over a network connection. Usually this is done by means of NFS or FTP over ethernet. The following section describes the procedure.

Installation from a Network Source

No installation support is available for this approach. Therefore, the following procedure should only be applied by experienced computer users.

To install SuSE Linux from a network source, two steps are necessary:

1. The data required for the installation (CDs, DVD) must be made available on a machine that will serve as the installation source.
2. The system to install must be booted from floppy disk or CD and the network must be configured.

Configuring a Network Installation Source

Prepare the network share by copying the installation CDs to individual directories and make these available on a system with NFS server functionality. For example, on an existing SuSE Linux machine, copy the individual CDs with the following command:

```
earth:/ #  cp -a /mnt/cdrom /suse-share/
```

Then rename the directory, for example, to "CD1":

```
earth:/ #  mv /suse-share/cdrom /suse-share/CD1
```

Repeat this procedure for the other CDs. Then export the `/suse-share` directory via NFS. For information, see *NFS — Shared File Systems* on page 371.

Booting for the Network Installation

Insert the boot medium in the drive. The creation of the boot disk is described in *Creating a Boot Disk in DOS* on page 21 and *Creating a Boot Disk in a UNIX-Type System* on page 22. The boot menu will appear after a short time. Select 'Manual Installation'. You can also specify additional kernel parameters. Confirm the selection with (Enter). The kernel will be loaded and you will be prompted to insert the first module disk.

After a short while, linuxrc will appear and ask you to enter a number of parameters:

1. Select the language and the keyboard layout in linuxrc.
2. Select 'Kernel modules (hardware drivers)'.
3. Load the IDE, RAID, or SCSI drivers required for your system.
4. Select 'Load network card modules' and load the needed network card driver (e.g., `eepro100`).
5. Select 'Load file system driver' and load the needed drivers (e.g., `reiserfs`).
6. Select 'Back' then 'Start installation / system'.
7. Select 'Start installation/update'.
8. Select 'Network' then the network protocol (e.g., `NFS`).
9. Select the network card to use.
10. Specify the IP addresses and other network information.
11. Specify the IP address of the NFS server providing the installation data.
12. Enter the path of the NFS share (e.g., `/suse-share/CD1`).

Now linuxrc will load the installation environment from the network source and start YaST2. Proceed with the installation as described in User Guide (2003), Chapter *Installation*.

Troubleshooting

- The installation is terminated before it actually starts. The installation directory of the "other" machine was not exported with `exec` permissions. Do this now.

- The server does not recognize the host on which to install SuSE Linux. Enter the name and IP address of the host to install in the `/etc/hosts` file of the server.

Tips and Tricks

Creating a Boot Disk in DOS

The requirements for this are a formatted 3.5" floppy disk and a bootable 3.5" floppy drive.

Additional Information

The directory `boot` on CD 1 contains a number of disk images. Such an image can be copied to a disk with the help of a suitable utility. A floppy disk prepared in this way is called boot disk.

These disk images also include the "loader", SYSLINUX, and the program linuxrc. SYSLINUX allows the selection of the desired kernel during the boot process and the specification of parameters for the hardware used, if necessary. The program linuxrc supports the loading of kernel modules for your hardware and subsequently starts the installation.

Procedure

The DOS application rawrite.exe (CD 1, directory `\dosutils\rawrite`) is useful for generating the SuSE boot and module disks. Requirements for this are a machine with a DOS (e.g., FreeDOS) or Windows.

The procedure described in the following is for working with Windows:

1. Insert the SuSE Linux CD 1.

2. Open a DOS window (in the start menu under 'Applications' → 'MS-DOS Prompt').

3. Start the rawrite.exe application by giving the correct path name for the CD drive. The following example takes place on the `C:` drive in the `Windows` directory and your CD drive is `D:`.

   ```
   C:\Windows> d:\dosutils\rawrite\rawrite
   ```

4. After starting the application, it will prompt you for the source and destination of the file to copy. The image of the boot disk is stored on CD 1 under `\boot`. The file is simply named `bootdisk`. Remember to include the path to the CD.

   ```
   C:\Windows> d:\dosutils\rawrite\rawrite
   RaWrite 1.2 -- Write disk file to raw floppy diskette
   ```

```
Enter source file name:  d:\boot\bootdisk
Enter destination drive:  a:
```

After entering the destination drive `a:`, insert a formatted disk as requested then press ↵. rawrite then shows the copy progress. This process can be terminated with Ctrl + C.

In this manner, you can also create the other floppy images, `modules1`, `modules2`, `modules3`, and `modules4`. These are required if you have USB or SCSI devices or a network or PCMCIA card that you want to address during the installation. A module disk may also be needed if you want to start using a special file system during the installation.

Creating a Boot Disk in a UNIX-Type System

This requires access to a Unix or Linux system with a CD-ROM drive and a formatted disk.

To create a boot disk:

1. If you need to format the disks first:

   ```
   earth:~ #  fdformat /dev/fd0u1440
   ```

2. Mount CD 1, for example, to `/media/cdrom`:

   ```
   earth:~ #  mount -tiso9660 /dev/cdrom /media/cdrom
   ```

3. Change to the `boot` directory on the CD:

   ```
   earth:~ #  cd /media/cdrom/boot
   ```

4. Create the boot disk with

   ```
   earth:~ #  dd if=/media/cdrom/boot/bootdisk of=/dev/fd0
       bs=8k
   ```

   The `README` file in the `boot` directory provides details about the floppy disk images. Read the files with `more` or `less`.

In this manner, you can also create the other floppy images, `modules1`, `modules2`, `modules3`, and `modules4` . These are required if you have USB or SCSI devices or a network or PCMCIA card that you want to address during the installation. A module disk may also be needed if you want to start using a special file system during the installation.

The procedure is little bit more complicated if you want to use a self-compiled kernel during the installation. In this case, first write the default image (`bootdisk`) to the floppy disk then overwrite the actual kernel (`linux`) with your own kernel (see *Compiling the Kernel* on page 262):

```
earth:~ #  dd if=/media/cdrom/boot/bootdisk of=/dev/fd0 bs=8k
earth:~ #  mount -t msdos /dev/fd0 /mnt
earth:~ #  cp /usr/src/linux/arch/i386/boot/vmlinuz /mnt/linux
earth:~ #  umount /mnt
```

Booting from Disk (SYSLINUX)

The "boot disk" can be used if you have to deal with special installation requirements (e.g., CD-ROM drive not available). For more information about creating the boot disk, read *Creating a Boot Disk in DOS* on page 21 or *Creating a Boot Disk in a UNIX-Type System* on the facing page.

The boot process is initiated by the boot loader SYSLINUX (package `syslinux`). SYSLINUX is configured to perform a minimum hardware detection when the system is booted. Basically this includes the following steps:

- The programs checks whether the BIOS provides VESA 2.0 compliant framebuffer support and makes sure the kernel is booted accordingly.
- The monitor information (DDC info) is read.
- The first sector of the first hard disk ("MBR") is read to be able to map BIOS IDs to Linux device names later during the boot loader configuration. The program attempts to read the block with the lba32 functions of the BIOS to find out if the BIOS supports these functions.

Tip

If you keep ⇧ Shift pressed when SYSLINUX is started, all these steps will be skipped.

For troubleshooting: You can insert the following line In `syslinux.cfg`:

```
verbose 1
```

to prompt the boot loader to tell you which action is currently being performed.

Tip

Possible Problems

- If the machine does not boot from the floppy disk, change the boot sequence in the BIOS to `A,C,CDROM`

Using CD 2 for Booting

As well as CD 1, the second CD is bootable. However, while CD 1 uses a bootable ISO image, CD 2 is booted by means of a 2.88 MB disk image. Use CD 2 if you are sure that you can boot from CD but it does work with CD 1 (fallback solution).

Supported CD-ROM Drives

Generally, most CD-ROM drives are supported.

- ATAPI drives should not cause any problems.
- A key issue for SCSI CD-ROM drives is whether the SCSI controller to which the CD-ROM drive is connected is supported. The supported SCSI controllers are listed under `http://cdb.suse.de/`. If your SCSI controller is not supported and your hard drive is also connected to it, you have a problem.
- Many proprietary CD-ROM drives are supported under Linux. Nevertheless, problems may be encountered with this type of drive. If your drive is not explicitly listed, you can still try to use a similar type from the same manufacturer.

- USB CD-ROM drives are also supported. If the BIOS of your machine does not yet support booting from USB devices, start the installation via the boot disks. For details, refer to *Booting from Disk (SYSLINUX)* on page 23. Before booting from the floppy disk, make sure all required USB devices are connected and powered on.

ATAPI CD-ROM Hangs While Reading

If your ATAPI CD-ROM is not recognized or it hangs while reading, this is most frequently due to incorrectly installed hardware. All devices must be connected to the EIDE controller in the correct order. The first device is master on the first controller. The second device is slave on the first controller. The third device should be master on the second controller, and so forth.

It often occurs that there is only a CD-ROM besides the first device. The CD--ROM drive is sometimes connected as master to the second controller (secondary IDE controller). This is wrong and can cause Linux not to know what to do with this "gap". Try to fix this by passing the appropriate parameter to the kernel (`hdc=cdrom`).

Sometimes one of the devices is just "misjumpered". This means it is jumpered as slave, but is connected as master, or vice versa. When in doubt, check your hardware settings and correct them where necessary.

In addition, there is a series of faulty EIDE chipsets, most of which have now been identified. There is a special kernel to handle such cases. See the `README` in `/boot` of the installation CD-ROM.

If booting does not work immediately, try using the following kernel parameters:

hd⟨*x*⟩=cdrom ⟨*x*⟩ stands for `a`, `b`, `c`, `d`, etc., and is interpreted as follows:

- `a` — Master on the first IDE controller
- `b` — Slave on the first IDE controller
- `c` — Master on the second IDE controller
- ...

An example of ⟨*parameter to enter*⟩ is `hdb=cdrom`. With this parameter, specify the CD-ROM drive to the kernel, if it cannot find it itself and you have an ATAPI CD-ROM drive.

ide⟨*x*⟩=noautotune ⟨*x*⟩ stands for `0`, `1`, `2`, `3`, etc., and is interpreted as follows:

- `0` — First IDE controller
- `1` — Second IDE controller
- ...

An example of ⟨*parameter to enter*⟩ is `ide0=noautotune` This parameter is often useful for (E)IDE hard disks.

Partitioning for Experts

This section provides detailed information for tailoring a system to your needs. This section is mainly of interest for those who want a system optimized system for security and performance and are prepared to reinstall the complete system where necessary. It is absolutely essential that you have extensive knowledge of the functions of a UNIX file system. You should be familiar with mount points and physical, extended, and logical partitions.

There is *no* golden rule for everything, but many rules for each situation. However, you will find concrete figures in this section to help you.

First, consider the following:

- What is the purpose of the machine (file server, compute server, standalone machine)?
- How many people are going to work with this machine (simultaneous logins)?
- How many hard disks are installed? How big are they and what kind (EIDE, SCSI, or even RAID controllers)?

Size of Swap Partition

Quite often you will read, "Swap should be at least twice as large as the main memory". This is a relic of times when 8 MB was regarded as a lot of RAM. Today, a new computer should not have less than 64 MB RAM. In the past, the aim was to equip the machine with about 30 to 40 MB of virtual memory, meaning RAM plus swap.

Modern memory-consuming applications require even more memory. Usually 128 MB of virtual memory should be sufficient. If you want to compile a kernel in KDE, look at the help pages with Netscape while emacs is running somewhere, not much will be left of your 128 MB of virtual memory.

Installation	Required Disk Space
minimum	180 MB to 400 MB
small	400 MB to 1500 MB
medium	1500 MB to 4 GB
large	more than 4 GB

Table 1.1: *Estimated Disk Space Requirements for Different Installations*

As a normal user, 256 MB of virtual memory is currently a reasonable value. Never do without any swap memory. A swap partition should be available even on a machine with 256 MB RAM. However, in this case 64 MB of swap space will be adequate to fill the basic need. The reasons for this are outlined in *Processing Speed and Size of Main Memory* on page 30.

If you want to run extensive simulations with a memory requirement of several gigabytes, you may need a large swap memory. If you are not sure if Linux has sufficient reserves for your application, refer to *As a Compute Server* on the next page.

Utilization of the Computer

As a Stand-Alone Machine

The most common use for a Linux machine is as a stand-alone computer. Table 1.1 is an overview of size requirements for different Linux systems.

The recommended partitioning depends on the size used. The following are only examples that should be modified to your needs.

Small Stand-Alone Machine With a 500 MB spare hard disk to hold Linux, use a 64 MB swap partition and the rest for / (root partition).

Average Stand-Alone Machine If you have 1.5 GB available for Linux, use a small boot partition `/boot` (5–10 MB or 1 cylinder), 128 MB for swap, 800 MB for `/`, and the rest for a separate `/home` partition.

Deluxe Stand-Alone Machine If you have more than 1.5 GB available, there is no standard way to partition. Read *Optimizations* on the next page.

As a File Server

Here, hard disk performance is crucial. You should use SCSI devices if possible. Keep in mind the performance of the disk and the controller. A file server is used to save data centrally. This data might be home directories, a database, or other archives. The advantage of this is that administration of the data is simple.

If the file server will serve a huge net (twenty users and more), optimizing hard disk access is essential. Suppose you want to provide a file server for 25 users (their home directories). If the average user requires 100–150 MB for personal space, a 4 GB partition mounted under `home` will probably do.

If there are fifty users, you will need an 8 GB partition. In this case, it would be better to split `home` into two 4 GB hard disks, as they would then share the load (and access time).

Tip

The web browser cache should absolutely be stored locally on the user's hard disk.

Tip

As a Compute Server

A compute server is generally a powerful machine that carries out extensive calculations over the net. Normally, such a machine is equipped with extensive main memory (512 RAM or greater). The only point where fast disks are needed is for the swap space. If you have a number of hard disks, you can spread swap partitions across them.

Optimizations

The disks are normally the limiting factor. To avoid this bottleneck, there are two possibilities that should be used together:

- separate the load onto multiple disks
- use an optimized file system (e.g., `reiserfs`).
- equip your file server with enough memory (at least 256 MB)

Parallel Use of Multiple Disks

This needs some further discussion. The total amount of time needed for transferring data can be separated into five parts:

- time elapsed until the request reaches the controller
- time elapsed until this request is send to the disk
- time elapsed until the hard disk positions its head
- time elapsed until the media has turned to the relevant sector
- time elapsed for transferring data

The first item depends on the network connection and must be regulated there. This subject is not covered here. Item two is a relatively insignificant period that depends on the hard disk controller itself. Items three and four are the main parts. The positioning time is measured in ms.Compared to the access times of the main memory, which are measured in ns,this represents a factor of 1 million. Item four depends on the disk rotation speed, which is usually several ms.Item five depends on the rotation speed, the number of heads, and the current position of the head (inside or outside).

To optimize the performance, the third item should be improved. In SCSI devices, the "disconnect" feature comes into play. If this feature is used: The controller sends the command (in this case to the hard disk) "Go to track x, sector y" to the device. Now the disk motor must start. If this is an intelligent disk (if it supports disconnect) and the driver itself is also able to do disconnect, the controller sends a disconnect and the disk separates itself from the SCSI bus. Now other SCSI devices can do work. After a time (depending on the strategy or load on the SCSI bus), a connection to the disk is reestablished. Normally, the device has now reached the requested track.

On a multitasking, multiuser system like Linux, there are lots of optimizations that can be done here. Look at an output of the command `df` (see Output 1).

```
Filesystem            Size  Used Avail Use% Mounted on
/dev/sda5             1.8G  1.6G  201M  89% /
/dev/sda1              23M  3.9M   17M  18% /boot
/dev/sdb1             2.9G  2.1G  677M  76% /usr
/dev/sdc1             1.9G  958M  941M  51% /usr/lib
shmfs                 185M     0  184M   0% /dev/shm
```

Output 1: *Example of df Command Output*

To demonstate the advantages, consider what happens if `root` enters the following in `/usr/src`:

```
root@earth:/usr/src/ >  tar xzf package.tgz -C /usr/lib
```

`package.tgz` will be untarred into `/usr/lib/package`. To do so, the shell launches tar and gzip (located in `/bin`, so on `/dev/sda`) then package.tgz in `/usr/src` is read (on `/dev/sdb`). Last, the extracted data is written to `/usr/lib` (on `/dev/sdc`). With parallel disks, positioning as well as read and write of the disks' internal buffers can be activated at the same time.

This is only one example. There are many more. If this example were a frequent processing requirement and if there are many disks (with the same speed), as a rule of thumb, `/usr` and `/usr/lib` should physically be placed on different disks. Here `/usr/lib` should have approximately seventy percent of the capacity of `/usr`. `/`, due to its access, should be placed on the disk containing `/usr/lib`.

From a certain number of SCSI disks onwards (4–5), consider buying a RAID controller. Thus, operations on the disks are not merely semiparallel but parallel. Fault tolerance is one of its famous by-products.

Processing Speed and Size of Main Memory

The size of main memory is more important in Linux than the processor itself. One reason, if not the main reason, is Linux's ability to dynamically create buffers of hard disk data. Here, Linux uses lots of tricks, such as "read ahead" (getting sectors in advance) and "delayed write" (saving writes until there is a bundle to write). The latter is the reason why you should not switch off your Linux machine. Both factors contribute to the fact that the main memory seems to fill up over time as well as to Linux's high speed. See also *The free Command* on page 271.

LVM Configuration with YaST

This professional partitioning tool enables you to edit and delete existing partitions and create new ones. Access the Soft RAID and LVM configuration from here.

Note

Background information and partitioning tips can be found in *Partitioning for Experts* on page 26.

Note

In normal circumstances, partitions are specified during installation. However, it is possible to integrate a second hard disk in an existing Linux system. First, the new hard disk must be partitioned. Then it must be mounted and entered into the /etc/fstab file. It may be necessary to copy some of the data to move an /opt partition from the old hard disk to the new one.

Use caution if you want to repartition the hard disk in use — this is essentially possible, but you will have to reboot the system right afterwards. It is a bit safer to boot from CD then repartition it.

'Experts...' opens a pop-up menu containing the following commands:

Reread Partition Table Rereads the partitioning from disk. For example, you will need this for manual partitioning in the text console.

Adopt Mount Points from Existing /etc/fstab This will only be relevant during installation. Reading the old fstab is useful for completely reinstalling your system rather than just updating it. In this case, it is not necessary to enter the mount points by hand.

Delete Partition Table and Disk Label This completely overwrites the old partition table. For example, this can be helpful if you have problems with unconventional disk labels. Using this method, all data on the hard disk will be lost.

Logical Volume Manager (LVM)

The Logical Volume Manager (LVM) enables flexible distribution of hard disk space over several file systems. As it is difficult to modify partitions on a running system, LVM was developed. It provides a virtual pool (Volume Group — VG for short) of memory space from which logical volumes (LV) can be generated if needed. The operating system will access these instead of the physical partitions.

Features:

- Several hard disks or partitions can be combined into a large logical partition.
- Provided the configuration is suitable, a LV (e. g., /usr) can be enlarged when the free space is exhausted.
- With the LVM, append hard disks or LVs in a running system. However, hot-swappable hardware, designed for these types of interventions, is required for this.

Implementing LVM already makes sense for heavily used home PCs or small servers. If you have a growing data stock, as in the case of databases, MP3 archives, or user directories, the Logical Volume Manager is just the right thing for you. This would allow you file systems that are larger than physical hard disk. Another advantage of the LVM is up to 256 LVs can be added. Keep in mind that working with the LVM is very different than working with conventional partitions.

Instructions and further information about configuring the Logical Volume Manager (LVM) can be found in the official LVM HOWTO and the SuSE documentation:

- `http://www.sistina.com/lvm/Pages/howto.html`
- `http://www.suse.com/us/support/oracle/`

LVM Configuration with YaST

Prepare the LVM configuration in YaST2 by creating an LVM partition when installing. To do this, click 'Partitioning' in the suggestion window then 'Discard' or 'Change' in the screen that follows. Next, create a partition for LVM by first clicking 'Add' → 'Do not format' in the Partitioner then clicking '0x8e Linux LVM'. Continue partitioning with LVM immediately afterwards or wait until after the system is completely installed. To do this, highlight the LVM partition in the partitioner then click 'LVM...'.

LVM — Partitioning

After you select 'LVM...' in the partitioning section, continue automatically to a dialog in which you can repartition your hard disks. Delete or modify existing partitions here or add new ones. A partition to use for LVM must have the partition label `8E`. These partitions are indicated by "Linux LVM" in the partition list.

> **Tip**
>
> **Repartitioning Logical Volumes**
>
> At the beginning of the PVs, information about the volume is written to the partition. In this way, a PV "knows" to which Volume Group it belongs. If you want to repartition, it is advisable to delete the beginning of this volume. In a Volume Group "system" and a Physical Volume "/dev/sda2", this can be done with the command `dd if=/dev/zero of=/dev/sda2 bs=512 count=1`
>
> **Tip**

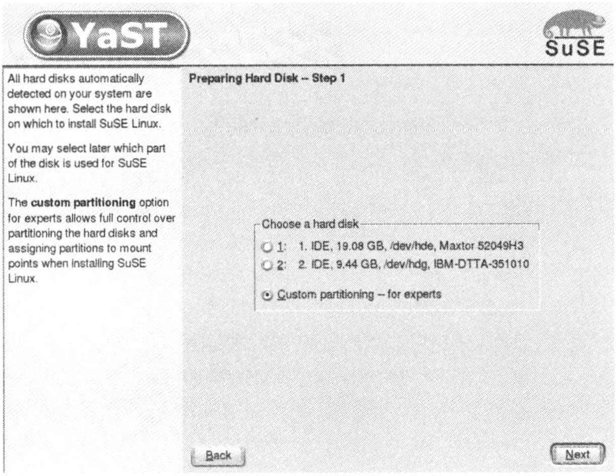

Figure 1.5: Activating LVM During Installation

You do not need to individually set the 8E label for all partitions designated for LVM. If needed, YaST2 will automatically set the partition label of a partition assigned to an LVM Volume Group to 8E. For any unpartitioned areas on your disks, create LVM partitions in this dialog. These partitions should then be designated the partition label 8E. They do not have to be formatted and no mount point can be entered.

If a working LVM configuration already exists on your system, it will be automatically activated as soon as you begin configuring the LVM. If this is successfully activated, any disks containing a partition belonging to an activated volume group can no longer be repartitioned. The Linux kernel will refuse to read the modified partitioning of a hard disk as long as only one partition on this disk is used. Repartitioning disks not belonging to an LVM volume group is not a problem at all. If you already have a functioning LVM configuration on your system, repartitioning is usually not necessary. In this screen, configure all mount points not located on LVM Logical Volumes. The root file system in YaST2 must be stored on a normal partition. Select this partition from the list and specify this as root file system using the 'Edit' button. To ensure LVM's optimal flexibility, it is recommended to pool all additional file systems onto LVM logical volumes. After specifying the root partition, exit this dialog.

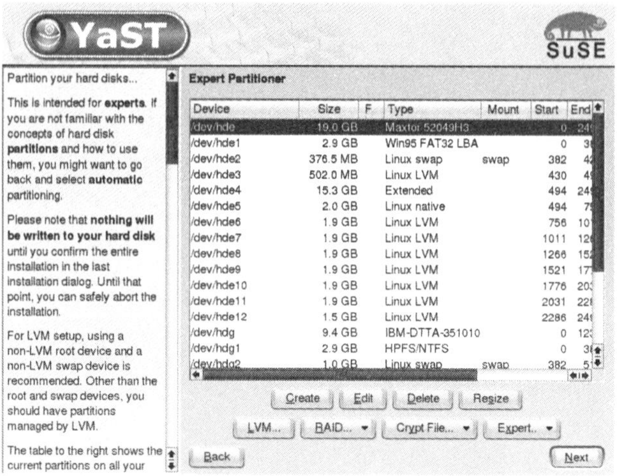

Figure 1.6: YaST2: LVM Partitioner

LVM — Configuring Physical Volumes

In the dialog 'LVM', the LVM volume groups (often indicated by "VG") are managed. If no volume group exists on your system yet, you will be prompted to add one. `system` is suggested as a name for the volume group where the SuSE Linux system files are located. Physical Extent Size (PE Size) defines the maximum size of a physical and logical volume in this volume group. This value is normally set to 4 megabytes. This allows for a maximum size of 256 gigabytes for physical and logical volumes. The physical extent size should only be increased if you need larger logical volumes than 256 gigabytes (e. g., to 8, 16, or 32 megabytes).

The following dialog lists all partitions with either the "Linux LVM" or "Linux native" type. Therefore, no swap and DOS partitions will be shown. If a partition is already assigned to a volume group, the name of the volume group will be shown in the list. Unassigned partitions are indicated by "--".

The volume group currently being edited can be modified in the selection box to the upper left. The buttons in the upper right enable creation of additional volume groups and deletion of existing volume groups. Only volume groups to which no other partitions are assigned can be deleted. No more than one volume group needs to be created for a normally installed SuSE Linux system. A partition assigned to a volume group is also referred to as a physical volume (often indicated by PV).

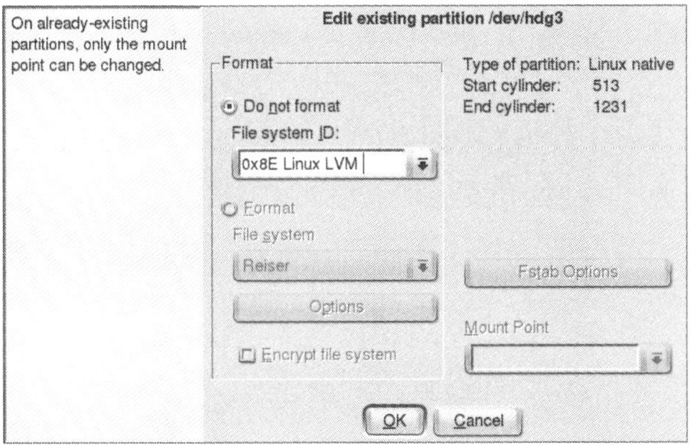

Figure 1.7: Creating LVM Partitions

To add a previously unassigned partition to the selected volume group, first click the partition then the 'Add Volume' button below the selection list. At this point, the name of the volume group is entered next to the selected partition. Assign all partitions reserved for LVM to a volume group. Otherwise, the space on the partition will remain unused. Before exiting the dialog, every volume group must be assigned at least one physical volume.

Logical Volumes

This dialog is responsible for managing logical volumes (often indicated by just "LV").

Logical volumes are assigned, one to each volume group, and have a particular given size. To create a striping array when you create the logical volumes, first create the LV with the largest number of stripes. A striping LV with n stripes can only be created correctly if the hard disk space required by the LV can still be distributed evenly to n Physical Volumes. If only PVs are available, an LV with three stripes is impossible.

Normally, a file system is created on a logical volume (e. g., reiserfs, ext2) and is then designated a mount point. The files stored on this logical volume can be found at this mount point on the installed system. All normal Linux partitions to which a mount point is assigned, all swap partitions, and all already existing logical volumes are listed here.

If you have already configured LVM on your system, the existing logical volumes must be entered now. Before you proceed, assign the appropriate

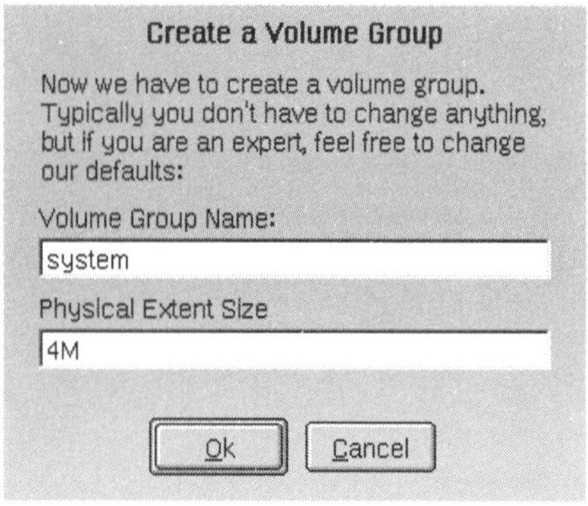

Figure 1.8: Adding a Volume Group

mount point to these logical volumes. If you are configuring LVM on a system for the first time, no logical volumes will be displayed in this screen yet. A logical volume must be generated for each mount point (using the 'Add' button). You will also need to specify the size, the file system type (e. g., reiserfs or ext2), and the mount point (e. g., `/var`, `/usr`, `/home`).

If you have created several volume groups, switch between the different volume groups in the selection list to the upper left. The added logical volumes are listed in the volume group displayed there. Once you have created all the logical volumes as required, exit the dialog and go on to software selection if you are still in the installation process.

Caution

Using LVM might be associated with increased risk factors, such as data loss. Risks also include application crashes, power outage, and faulty commands. Save your data before implementing LVM or reconfiguring volumes — never work without a backup.

Caution

Soft RAID

The purpose of RAID (Redundant Array of Inexpensive Disks) is to combine several hard disk partitions into one large "virtual" hard disk for the optimization of performance and data security. Using this method, however, one

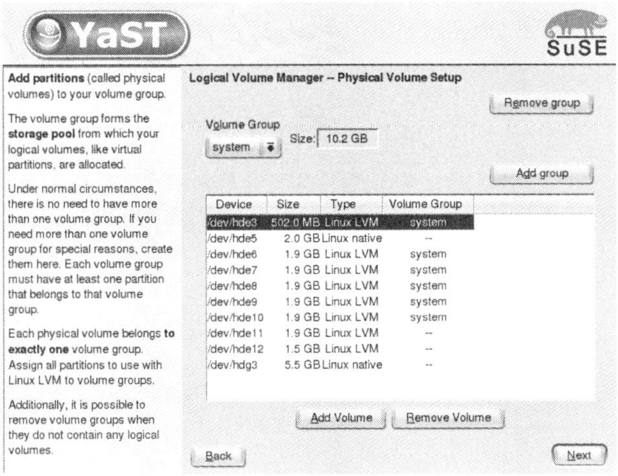

Figure 1.9: Partition List

advantage is sacrificed for another. "RAID level" defines the pool and common triggering device of the all hard disks, the RAID controller. A RAID controller mostly uses the SCSI protocol, because it can drive more hard disks better than the IDE protocol. It is also better able to process parallel running commands.

Instead of a RAID controller, which can often be quite expensive, soft RAID is also able to take on these tasks. SuSE Linux offers the option of combining several hard disks into one soft RAID system with the help of YaST2 — a very reasonable alternative to Hardware RAID.

Common RAID Levels

RAID 0 This level improves the performance of your data access. Actually, this is not really a RAID, because it does not provide data backup, but the name "RAID 0" for this type of system has become the norm. With RAID 0, two hard disks are pooled together. The performance is very good — although the RAID system will be destroyed and your data lost, even if just one of the many remaining hard disks fails.

RAID 1 This level provides more than adequate backup for your data, because the data is copied to another hard disk 1:1. This is known as "hard disk mirroring" — if a disk is destroyed, a copy of its contents

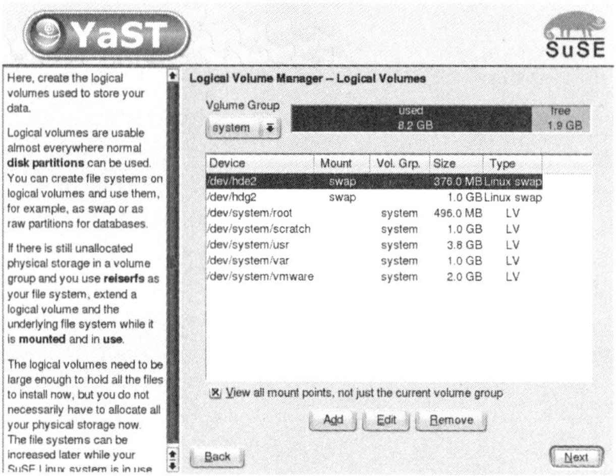

Figure 1.10: *Logical Volume Management*

is located on another one. All of them except one could be damaged without endangering your data. The writing performance suffers a little in the copying process when using RAID 1 (ten to twenty percent slower), but read access is significantly faster in comparison to any one of the normal physical hard disks, because the data is duplicated so can be parallel scanned.

RAID 5 RAID 5 is an optimized compromise between the two other levels in terms of performance and redundancy. The hard disk potential equals the number of disks used minus one. The data is distributed over the hard disks as with RAID 0. "Parity blocks", created on one of the partitions, are there for security reasons. They are linked to each other with XOR — thus enabling the contents, via XDR, to be reconstructed by the corresponding parity block in case of system failure. With RAID 5, no more than one hard disk can fail at the same time. If one is destroyed, it must be replaced as soon as possible to save the data.

Soft RAID Configuration with YaST

Access Soft RAID configuration by way of the 'RAID' module under 'System' or via the partitioning module under 'Hardware'.

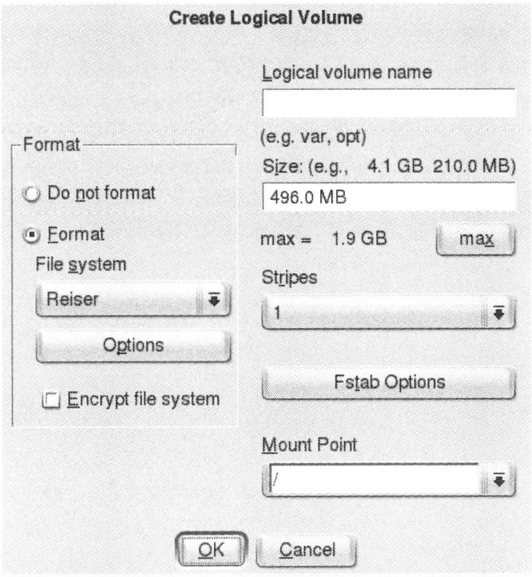

Figure 1.11: Creating Logical Volumes

First Step: Partitioning

First, see a list of your partitions under 'Expert Settings' in the partitioning tool. If the Soft RAID partitions have already been set up, they will appear here. Otherwise, set them up from scratch. For RAID 0 and RAID 1, at least two partitions are needed — usually for RAID 1, exactly two and no more. If RAID 5 is used, at least three partitions will be required. It is recommended to only take partitions of the same size. The RAID partitions should be stored on various hard disks to insure against the risk of losing data if one is defective (RAID 1 and to optimize the performance of RAID 0.

Second Step: Setting Up RAID

Click 'RAID' to open a dialog in which to choose between RAID levels 0, 1, and 5. In the following screen, assign the partition to the new RAID. 'Expert Options' opens the settings options for the "chunk size" — for fine-tuning the performance. Checking 'Persistent Superblock' ensures that the RAID partitions will be recognized as such when booting.

After completing the configuration, you will then see the `/dev/md0` device and others indicated on the expert page in the partitioning module by "RAID".

Troubleshooting

Find out whether a RAID partition has been destroyed by the file contents `/proc/mdstats`. The basic procedure in case of system failure is to shut down your Linux system and replace the defective hard disk with a new one partitioned the same way. Then restart your system and give the `raidhotadd /dev/mdX /dev/sdX` command. This will enable the hard disk to be integrated automatically into the RAID system and be fully reconstructed.

Configuration instructions and more details for Soft RAID can be found in the HOWTOs at:

- `/usr/share/doc/packages/raidtools/Software-RAID-HOWTO.html`
- `http://www.LinuxDoc.org/HOWTO/Software-RAID-HOWTO.html`

Linux RAID mailing lists are also available, such as `http://www.mail-archive.com/linux-raid@vger.rutgers.edu`.

Updating the System and Package Management

SuSE Linux provides the option of updating an existing system without completely reinstalling it. There are two types of updates: *updating individual software packages* and *updating the entire system*. Packages can also be installed by hand using the package manager RPM.

Updating SuSE Linux

Software tends to "grow" from version to version. Therefore, we recommend first taking a look at the available partition space with `df` *before* updating. If you suspect you are running short of disk space, secure your data before updating and repartition your system. There is no general rule of thumb regarding how much space each partition should have. Space requirements depend on your particular partitioning profile, the software selected, and the version numbers of SuSE Linux 8.2.

Note

It is recommended to read the `README` and, in DOS and Windows, `README.DOS` file on your CD. Find notes there regarding any additional changes made *after* this manual went to print.

Note

Preparations

Before you begin your update, copy the old configuration files to a separate medium just to be on the safe side. Such media can include streamers, removable disks, floppy drives, ZIP drives. This primarily applies to files stored in `/etc`. Also, review the configuration files in `/var/lib`. Furthermore, it cannot hurt to write the current user data in `/home` (the `HOME` directories) to a backup medium. Back up this data as `root`. Only `root` has read permission for all local files.

Before starting your update, make note of the root partition. The command `df /` lists the device name of the root partition. According to the Output 2, the root partition to write down is `/dev/hda7`.

```
Filesystem            Size  Used Avail Use% Mounted on
/dev/hda1             1.9G  189M  1.7G  10% /dos
/dev/hda7             3.0G  1.1G  1.7G  38% /
/dev/hda5              15M  2.4M   12M  17% /boot
shmfs                 141M     0  141M   0% /dev/shm
```

***Output 2:** List with df -h*

The root partition can be recognized as the one mounted as `/`.

Possible Problems

PostgreSQL

Before updating PostgreSQL (package postgres), it is usually best to "dump" the databases. See the man page for pg_dump (man pg_dump). This is, of course, only necessary if you actually *used* PostgreSQL prior to your update.

Promise Controller The hard disk controller manufactured by Promise is currently found on high-end motherboards in numerous computer models, either as a pure IDE controller (for UDMA 100) or as an IDE-RAID controller. As of SuSE Linux 8.0, these controllers are directly supported by the kernel and treated as a standard controller for IDE hard disks. The additional kernel module pdcraid is required before you can aquire RAID functionality.

For some updates, hard disks on the Promise controller may be detected before disks on the standard IDE controller. If so, the system will no longer boot following a kernel update and usually exit with "Kernel panic: VFS: unable to mount root fs". In this case, the kernel parameter ide=reverse must be passed when booting to reverse this disk detection process. See *The Start Screen* on page 10. To apply this parameter universally when using YaST, enter it in the boot configuration. See User Guide (2003), chapter *YaST2, Boot Mode.*

Caution

Only the controllers activated in the BIOS are detectable. In particular, subsequently activating or deactivating the controllers in the BIOS has a direct effect on the device names. Use caution or risk being unable to boot the system.

Caution

Technical Explanation

The controller sequence depends on the motherboard. Each manufacturer wires its supplementary controllers differently. The lspci shows this sequence. If the Promise controller is listed before the standard IDE controller, the kernel parameter ide=reverse is required after updating. With the previous kernel (without direct Promise support), the controller was ignored so the standard IDE controller was detected first. The first disk was then /dev/hda. With the new kernel, the Promise controller is detected immediately and its (up to four) disks are registered as /dev/hda, /dev/hdb, /dev/hdc, and /dev/hdd. The previous /dev/hda disk becomes /dev/hde so is no longer detectable in the boot process.

Updating with YaST2

Following the preparation procedure outlined in *Preparations* on page 42, you can now boot:

1. Boot the system for the installation (see User Guide). In YaST, choose a language, then select 'Update Existing System'. Do *not* select 'New Installation'.

2. YaST will determine whether there are several root partitions. If there is only one, continue with 3. If there are several, select the right partition and confirm with 'Next' (`/dev/hda7` was selected in the example in *Preparations* on page 42).

   YaST reads the "old" `fstab` on this partition to analyze and mount the file systems listed there.

3. Then you have the possibility to make a backup copy of the system files during the update. This option slows down the update process. Use this option if you do not have a recent system backup.

4. In the following dialog, either choose to update only the software that is already installed or to add important new software components to the system ("upgrade mode"). It is advisable to accept the suggested composition (e.g., 'Standard System'). Adjustments can be made later with YaST.

Manual Update

Updating the Base System

Because basic system components, such as libraries, must be exchanged when updating a base system, an update cannot be run from within a currently running Linux system. First, set up the update environment. This is normally done using the CD or DVD or with a custom boot disk. If you are carrying out manual modifications during the update or prefer to perform the entire update with YaST in text mode, follow the steps already described in detail in *Text-Based Installation with YaST2* on page 10. Below is a summary of this procedure.

1. Immediately after booting the kernel from the "boot disk" or from the CD or DVD, linuxrc automatically starts.

2. In linuxrc, specify the language and keyboard settings under 'Settings' and click 'Ok' to confirm each setting.

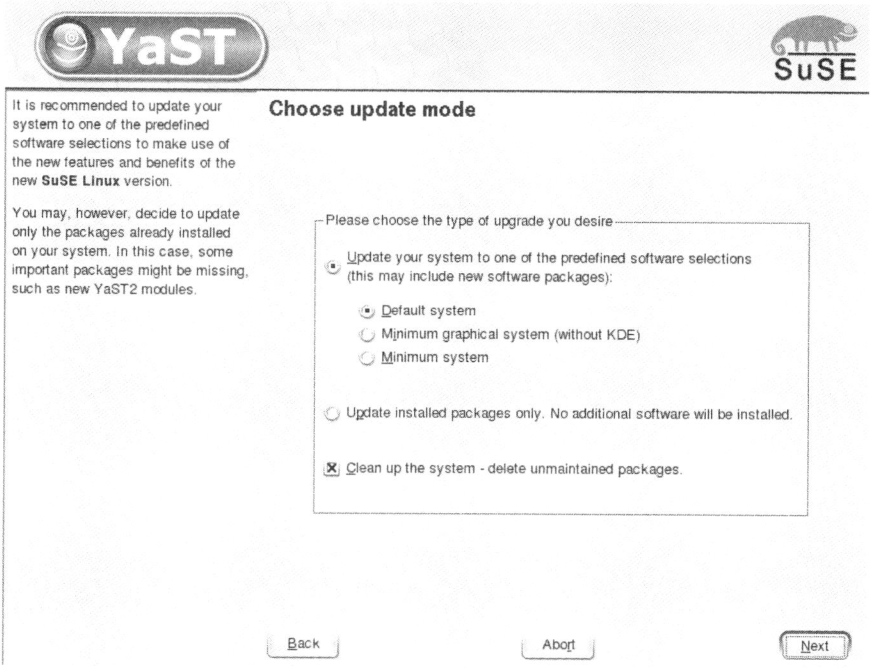

Figure 2.1: Updating the Software

3. You might need to load the required hardware and software drivers via 'Kernel Modules'. See section *The Basis: linuxrc* on page 11 for more details on how to proceed and *Loading Modules* on page 280 for a description of linuxrc.

4. Go to the menu items 'Start Installation / System' → 'Start Installation/Update' to select the source medium (see on page 281).

5. The installation environment is loaded from linuxrc then YaST started.

Following the selection of a language and the hardware detection by YaST, select 'Update existing system' in the YaST opening screen.

Next, YaST attempts to determine the root partition and displays the result for selection or confirmation. Select your root partition from the list (for example, `/dev/sda3`). In this way, prompt YaST to read the "old" `fstab` from this partition. YaST will analyze and mount the file systems listed there.

Then you have the possibility to make a backup copy of the system files during the update. In the following dialog, either choose to update only the software already installed or to add important new software components to the system ("upgrade mode"). It is advisable to accept the suggested composition (e.g., 'Standard system'). Adjustments can be made later with YaST. In the warning dialog, select 'Yes' to start the installation of the new software from the source medium to the system hard disk.

First, the RPM database is checked, then the main system components are updated. YaST automatically creates backups of files modified in the running system since the last installation. In addition, old configuration files are backed up with the endings `.rpmorig` and `.rpmsave` (see *Managing Packages: Install, Update, and Uninstall* on page 54). The installation or update procedure is logged in `/var/adm/inst-log/installation-*` and can be viewed later at any time.

Updating the Rest of the System

After the base system is updated, you will be switched to YaST's update mode. This mode allows you to tailor the rest of the system update to your needs.

Complete the procedure as you would a new installation. Among other things, select a new kernel. The available options are presented by YaST.

Tip

If you boot with loadlin, save the *new* kernel and, possibly, the `initrd` into the `loadlin` directory of your DOS partition.

Tip

Possible Problems

- If certain shell environments no longer behave as expected after the update, check to see if the current "dot" files in the home directory are still compatible with your system. If not, use the current versions in `/etc/skel`. For example:

```
newbie@earth:~ > cp /etc/skel/.profile ~/.profile
```

Updating Individual Packages

Regardless of your overall updated environment, you can always update individual packages. From this point on, however, it is your responsibility to ensure that your system remains consistent. Update advice can be found at `http://www.suse.de/en/support/download/updates/`.

Select components from the YaST package selection list according to your needs. If you select a package essential for the overall operation of the system, YaST issues a warning. Such packages should be updated only in the update mode. For instance, numerous packages contain "shared libraries". If you update these programs and applications in the running system, things might malfunction.

Software Changes from Version to Version

The individual aspects changed from version to version are outlined in the following sections in detail. This summary indicates, for example, whether basic settings have been completely reconfigured, whether configuration files have been moved to other places, or whether common applications have been significantly changed. Only the modifications that would affect the daily use of the system at either the user or the administrator level are mentioned below. The list is by no means complete. The following also makes references to SDB (Support Database) articles. These articles are in the package `sdb_en`, series `doc`.

Problems and bugs for each version have been published on the web server as soon as they were recognized. See the links listed below. Important updates of individual packages can be accessed at `http://www.suse.de/en/support/download/`.

From 7.0 to 7.1

Problems and special issues:
`http://sdb.suse.de/sdb/en/html/bugs71.html`.

- *Kernel:* The "low-level" drivers for special EIDE chip sets are integrated into the standard kernel. `k_eide` or `eide` are no longer necessary as separate images. This means you no longer need to create your own boot disk if you require this driver.

- The runlevels have changed. See Table 12.1 on page 295. The `init` scripts are now located in `/etc/init.d`. If your have already created your own scripts, you should make sure they are backed up before updating.

- The limitation of the package names to eight characters has been removed and many packages may now have more descriptive names.
- The functionality of the package dochost has been integrated into the package susehelp, making dochost obsolete.
- Regarding the former package ypclient: This package is now divided into ypbind and yp-tools and the init-script is called ypbind .

From 7.1 to 7.2

Problems and special issues:
http://sdb.suse.de/sdb/en/html/bugs72.html.

- package nkitb no longer exists. The different programs were moved into several packages: talk, rsh, finger, rwho, telnet, etc.

  A number of programs are already IPv6-ready. For this reason, ensure that DNS is correctly configured — otherwise you might have to wait for the DNS time out for IPv6 queries. Also, in /etc/nsswitch.conf, replace the entry dns with dns6.
- Renaming of several packages (see on the current page); e. g.: package docbook-dsssl-stylesheets, package docbook_3 and package docbook_4.
- You have to install package mod_php4 instead of package mod_php now.
- Changes to follow the current FHS (see section *File System Hierarchy Standard (FHS)* on page 266):
  - ▷ /media (was /cdrom and /floppy)

From 7.2 to 7.3

Problems and special issues:
http://sdb.suse.de/sdb/en/html/bugs73.html.

- Kernel 2.4, which is included in SuSE Linux, has IDE-DMA turned on by default. If you have any problems related to DMA, you can always fall back on the 'Installation — Safe Settings' boot option. Also see on page 10.

- Apart from the DISPLAYMANAGER variable as defined in `rc.config` (as of SuSE Linux 8.0 in `/etc/sysconfig/displaymanager`), the correct runlevel needs to be set in `/etc/inittab`. YaST2 is able to take care of this.

- Samba: The configuration files have been moved to the `/etc/samba` directory to improve clarity.

- MySQL now uses the TCP wrapper library for extended security.

  The new subpackage `mysql-Max` offers all the new and enhanced features, which are automatically available after installation.

- To save space (more than 30 MB), package `allman` is no longer included. The manual pages are, however, still included in the packages.

- DocBook documents, which use certain "features", are accepted by `db2x.sh` (package `docbktls`, now paketdocbook-toys). Users who depend on compatible documents should work with the `--strict` option.

From 7.3 to 8.0

Problems and Special Issues:
`http://sdb.suse.de/sdb/en/html/bugs80.html`.

- Boot disks are shipped only as floppy images (previously `disks` directory, now `boot`). A boot disk is only required if you cannot boot from CD. Depending on your hardware or installation preferences, you can also create floppies from the images `modules1`, `modules2`, etc. Read *Creating a Boot Disk in DOS* on page 21 or *Creating a Boot Disk in a UNIX-Type System* on page 22 for information about creating these disks.

- YaST2 has completely replaced YaST1, even in the text and console mode. When the text says "YaST", it always refers to the new version.

- Some BIOSes require the kernel parameter `realmode-power-off`, which was known as `real-mode-poweroff` up to kernel version 2.4.12.

- The START variables of the `rc.config` for launching services are no longer required. Services are started if the respective links exist in the runlevel directories. These links are created with `insserv`.

- System services are configured by variable lines in the files located under /etc/sysconfig. The settings in /etc/rc.config.d will be applied to the update.
- /etc/init.d/boot is comprised of several scripts and moved to other packages if necessary (see package kbd, package isapnp, package lvm, etc.). See on page 298.
- There have also been some changes made in the network arena. Read *Network Integration* on page 346 for more information about this.
- logrotate is used to manage log files. /etc/logfiles is no longer necessary. See *Log Files — the Package logrotate* on page 268.
- The root login over telnet or rlogin can be permitted by entering specifications in the files under /etc/pam.d. Due to security risks, ROOT_LOGIN_REMOTE can no longer be set to yes.
- PASSWD_USE_CRACKLIB can be activated with YaST.
- If NIS files for autofs will be distributed over NIS, the YaST NIS client module should be used for configuration. There, select 'Start Automounter'. This aspect has made the USE_NIS_FOR_AUTOFS variable obsolete.
- The locate tool for quickly finding files is no longer included in the standard software installation. If desired, install it (package find-locate). If installed, the updatedb process will be started automatically about fifteen minutes after the computer is booted, just as in previous versions.
- The mouse support for pine is activated. This means that pine in an xterm can also be operated with a mouse (or a similar input device) by clicking the menu items. This, however, also means that cut and paste only work by using ⇑ Shift when the mouse support is activated. This is deactivated with a new installation. It is, however, not excluded that the function is still active following an update (when an older ~/.pinerc is present). The option enable-mouse-in-xterm can be deactivated in the configuration for pine.

From 8.0 to 8.1

Problems and Special Issues:
http://sdb.suse.de/sdb/de/html/bugs81.html.

- Changes in the user and group names: To comply with UnitedLinux, some entries in /etc/passwd and /etc/group have been adjusted accordingly.
  - Changed users: ftp is now in group ftp (not in daemon).
  - Renamed groups: www (was wwwadmin); games (was game).
  - New groups: ftp (with GID 50), floppy (with GID 19), cdrom (with GID 20), console (with GID 21), utmp (with GID 22).
- Changes related to FHS (see *File System Hierarchy Standard (FHS)* on page 266):
  - An environment for HTTPD (Apache) is created at /srv/httpd (was /usr/local/httpd).
  - An environment for FTP is created at /srv/ftp (was /usr/local/ftp)
- To ease access to the desired software, the single packages are not stored in a few bulky series any more, but rather in accessible "RPM groups". This also means the CDs do not contain spurious and cryptic directories under suse any more, but only few directories named after architectures, for example, ppc, i586, or noarch.
- The installation status of the following programs has changed for a new installation:
  - The boot loader GRUB, which offers more possibilities than LILO. LILO is preserved when updating the system.
  - The mailer postfix instead of sendmail.
  - The modern mailing list application mailman is installed instead of majordomo.
  - Select harden_suse manually when needed and read the current documentation for it.
- Split packages: rpm to rpm and rpm-devel; popt to popt and popt-devel; libz to zlib and zlib-devel.

  yast2-trans-* is now split by languages: yast2-trans-cs (Czech), yast2-trans-de (German), yast2-trans-es (Spanish), etc. Not all languages are installed to save hard disk space. Install the required packages for the YaST language support as needed.
- Renamed packages: bzip to bzip2.
- Packages no longer supplied: openldap, use openldap2; su1, use sudo.

From 8.1 to 8.2

Problems and Special Issues:
http://sdb.suse.de/sdb/en/html/bugs82.html.

- During a new installation, xinetd is installed instead of inetd and configured with secure values. See directory /etc/xinetd.d. However, during a system update, inetd is retained.
- openjade (package openjade) is the DSSSL engine currently used instead of jade (package jade_dsl) when db2x.sh (package docbook-toys) is run. For compatibility reasons, the individual programs are also available without the prefix 'o'.

  To avoid a conflict with package rzsz, the command-line tool sx continues to be called s2x/sgml2xml or osx.

RPM — the Distribution Package Manager

In SuSE Linux, RPM (rpm), the "Red Hat Package Manager", is used to manage packages. It makes the powerful RPM database available to everyone: users, system administrators, and, of course, package builders. Detailed information about installed software can be queried from the database at any time.

Essentially, rpm has three modes. In one mode, it compiles software applications from "pristine" sources and packages them for installation. In the second, it installs, upgrades, and uninstalls software packaged in the RPM format. Finally, in the third, it supports queries about packages and maintains the RPM database of installed packages.

Installable RPM archives are packed in a special binary format. These archives consist of the program files to install and certain meta information used during the installation by rpm to configure the software package or stored in the RPM database for documentation purposes. RPM archives normally have the extension .rpm.

rpm allows the administration of LSB-compliant packages. Refer to *Linux Standard Base (LSB)* on page 266 for more about LSB.

Tip

For a number of packages, the components needed for software development (libraries, headers, include files, etc.) have been put into separate packages. These development packages are only needed if you want to compile software *yourself*, for example, the most recent GNOME packages. They can be identified by the name extension `-devel` (previously `dev` or `d`), such as the packages package `alsa-devel`, package `gimp-devel`, and package `kdelibs-devel`.

Tip

Verifying Package Authenticity

Since Version 7.1, the SuSE RPM packages have a GnuPG signature:

```
1024D/9C800ACA 2000-10-19 SuSE Package Sign-
ing Key <build@suse.de>
Key fingerprint = 79C1 79B2 E1C8 20C1 890F  9994 A84E DAE8 9C80 0ACA
```

With the command `rpm --checksig apache-1.3.12.rpm`, verify the signature of an RPM package to determine whether it really originates from SuSE or from another trustworthy facility. This is especially recommended for update packages from the Internet. Our public package signature key normally resides in `/root/.gnupg/`. Since version 8.1, the key is additionally located in the directory `/usr/lib/rpm/gnupg/` to enable normal users to verify the signature of RPM packages.

Managing Packages: Install, Update, and Uninstall

Normally, RPM installation can be done simply with `rpm -i ⟨package⟩.rpm`. With this command, the package will be installed — but only if its dependencies are fulfilled and there are no conflicts with other packages. With an error message, `rpm` requests those packages that need to be installed to meet dependency requirements. In the background, the RPM database ensures that no conflicts arise — a specific file can only belong to one package. By choosing different options, you can force `rpm` to ignore these defaults, but this is only for experts. Otherwise, risk compromising the integrity of the system and possibly jeopardize the ability to update the system.

The options `-U` or `--upgrade` and `-F` or `--freshen` can be used to update a package.

```
earth:~ #  rpm -F ⟨package⟩.rpm
```

This option will remove the files of the old version and immediately install the new files. The difference between the two versions is that `-U` installs packages that previously did not exist in the system, but `-F` merely updates previously installed packages. When updating, `rpm` updates configuration files carefully using the following strategy:

- If a configuration file was not changed by the system administrator, `rpm` will install the new version of the appropriate file. No action by the system administrator is required.
- If a configuration file was changed by the system administrator before the update, `rpm` will save the changed file with the extension `.rpmorig` or `.rpmsave` (backup file) and install the version from the new package, but only when the originally installed file and the newer version are different. If this is the case, compare the backup file (`.rpmorig` or `.rpmsave`) with the newly installed file and make your changes again in the new file. Afterwards, be sure to delete all `.rpmorig` and `.rpmsave` files to avoid problems with future updates.
- `.rpmnew` files appear if the configuration file already exists *and* if the `noreplace` label was specified in the `.spec` file.

Following an update, `.rpmsave` and `.rpmnew` files should be removed after comparing them, so they do not obstruct future updates. The `.rpmorig` extension is assigned if the file has not previously been recognized by the RPM database. Otherwise, `.rpmsave` is used. In other words, `.rpmorig` results from updating from a foreign format to RPM. `.rpmsave` results from updating from an older RPM to a newer RPM. `.rpmnew` does not disclose any information as to whether the system administrator has made any changes to the configuration file. A list of these files is available in `/var/adm/rpmconfigcheck`. Some configuration files (like `/etc/httpd/httpd.conf`) purposely are not overwritten to enable a seamless takeover of the running operations using the personal settings.

The `-U` switch is *not* just an equivalent to uninstalling with the (`-e`) option and installing with the (`-i`) option. Use `-U` whenever possible.

To remove a package, enter a command in the format `rpm -e` ⟨*package*⟩. `rpm` will only delete the package if there are no unresolved dependencies. It is theoretically impossible to delete Tcl/Tk, for example, as long as another application requires it. Even in this case, RPM calls for assistance from the database. If such a deletion is — for whatever reason and under unusual circumstances — impossible, even if *no* additional dependencies exist, it may be helpful to rebuild the RPM database using the option `--rebuilddb`. See *RPM Queries* on page 57 for more information about the RPM database.

RPM Queries

With the `-q` option, `rpm` initiates queries, making it possible to inspect an RPM archive (by adding the option `-p`) and also to query the RPM database of installed packages. Several switches are available to specify the type of information required (see Table 2.1).

`-i`	Package information
`-l`	File list
`-f` ⟨*FILE*⟩	Query a package owned by ⟨*FILE*⟩ (the full path must be specified with ⟨*FILE*⟩)
`-s`	File list with status information (implies `-l`)
`-d`	List only documentation files (implies `-l`)
`-c`	List only configuration files (implies `-l`)
`--dump`	File list with complete details (to be used with `-l`, `-c`, or `-d`)
`--provides`	List features of the package that another package can request with `--requires`
`--requires`, `-R`	Capabilities the package requires
`--scripts`	Installation scripts (preinstall, postinstall, uninstall)

Table 2.1: *The Most Important RPM Query Options* (`-q` [`-p`] ... ⟨*package*⟩)

For example, the command `rpm -q -i wget` displays the information shown in Output 3.

```
Name        : wget                    Relocations: (not relocateable)
Version     : 1.8.1                        Vendor: SuSE AG, Nuern-
berg, Germany
Release     : 142                     Build Date: Fri Apr  5 16:08:13 2002
Install date: Mon Apr  8 13:54:08 2002 Build Host: knox.suse.de
Group       : Productivity/Networking/Web/Utilities   Source RPM: wget-
1.8.1-142.src.rpm
```

```
Size        : 2166418                    License: GPL
Packager    : http://www.suse.de/feedback
Summary     : A tool for mirroring FTP and HTTP servers
Description :
Wget enables you to retrieve WWW documents or FTP files from a server.
This might be done in script files or via command line.
[...]
```

Output 3: *rpm -q -i wget*

Option `-f` only works if you specify the complete file name with its full path. You can name as many file names as you want. For example, `rpm -q -f /bin/rpm /usr/bin/wget` results in:

```
rpm-3.0.3-3
wget-1.5.3-55
```

If only part of the file name is known, a shell script must be implemented, shown in File 1. Pass the partial file name to the script shown as a parameter when running it.

```
#! /bin/sh
for i in $(rpm -q -a -l | grep  $1); do
    echo "\"$i\" is in package:"
    rpm -q -f $i
    echo ""
done
```

File 1: *Script to Search for Packages*

The command `rpm -q --changelog rpm`, displays a precise list of information (updates, configuration, modifications, etc.) about a specific package. This example is on the package *rpm*. However, only the last five change entries in the RPM database are listed. All entries (dating back the last two years) are included in the package itself. This query only works if CD 1 is mounted at `/cdrom`:

```
earth:~ #  rpm -qp --changelog /cdrom/suse/i586/rpm-3*.rpm
```

With the help of the installed RPM database, verification checks can be made. These checks are initiated with the option `-V`, `-y`, or `--verify`. With this option, `rpm` will show all files in a package that have been changed since installation. `rpm` uses eight character symbols to give some hints about the following changes:

5	MD5 check sum
S	File size
L	Symbolic link
T	Modification time
D	Major and minor device numbers
U	Owner
G	Group
M	Mode (permissions and file type)

Table 2.2: *RPM Verify Options*

In the case of configuration files, the letter `c` will be printed. For example, if you have changed `/etc/wgetrc` from the package `wget` and have entered `rpm -V wget`, see something like:

```
S.5....T c /etc/wgetrc
```

The files of the RPM database are placed in `/var/lib/rpm`. If the partition `/usr` has a size of 1 GB, this database can occupy nearly 30 MB, especially after a complete update. If the database is much larger than expected, it is useful to rebuild the database with the option `--rebuilddb`. Before doing this, make a backup of the old database. The `cron` script `cron.daily` makes daily copies of the database (packed with gzip) and stores them in `/var/adm/backup/rpmdb`. The number of copies is controlled by the variable ⟨*MAX_RPMDB_BACKUPS*⟩ (default: `5`) in `/etc/sysconfig/backup`. The size of a single backup is approximately 3 MB for 1 GB in `/usr`.

Installing and Compiling Source Packages

All source packages of SuSE Linux carry an `.src.rpm` extension (Source RPM).

Tip

These packages can be handled in the same way as all other packages. The packages, however, will not be found in the RPM database (and are not marked with an `[i]` in YaST), as only "installed" software is listed. This is because the source packages are not incorporated in the RPM database. Only *installed* operating system software is listed in the RPM database.

Tip

The rpm directories in `/usr/src/packages` must exist (if none of your own settings have been made, for example, in `/etc/rpmrc`).

SOURCES this is for the original sources (`.tar.gz` files, etc.) and for distribution-specific adjustments (`.dif` files).

SPECS for the ".spec" files, similar to a meta Makefile, which control the "build" process.

BUILD All the sources are unpacked, patched, and compiled in this directory.

RPMS This is where the completed "binary" packages are stored.

SRPMS here are the "source" RPMs.

When you install a source package with YaST, all the necessary components will be installed in `/usr/src/packages`: the sources and the adjustments in `SOURCES` and the relevant `.spec` file in `SPECS`.

Note

Do not experiment with system components (package `glibc`, package `rpm`, package `sysvinit`, etc.), as this endangers the operability of your system.

Note

The following example uses the `wget.src.rpm` package. After you have installed the package with YaST, you should have the following files:

```
/usr/src/packages/SPECS/wget.spec /usr/src/packages/SOURCES/wget-1.4.5.dif /usr/src/packages/SOURCES/wget-1.4.5.tar.gz
```

`rpm -b ⟨X⟩ /usr/src/packages/SPECS/wget.spec` starts the compilation. Here, ⟨*X*⟩ is a wild card for different stages of the build process (see `rpm --help` or the RPM documentation). The following is only a short explanation:

`-bp` Prepare sources in `/usr/src/packages/BUILD`: unpack and patch.

`-bc` the same as `-bp`, but with additional compilation.

`-bi` the same as `-bp`, but with additional installation of the built software. Caution: if the package does not support the BuildRoot feature, you might overwrite configuration files.

-bb the same as -bi, but with the additional creation of the "binary" package. If the compile was successful, the binary should be in /usr/src/packages/RPMS.

-ba the same as -bb, but with the additional creation of the "source RPM". If the compilation was successful, the binary should be in /usr/src/packages/SRPMS.

--short-circuit lets you skip specific steps.

This binary RPM can now be installed with rpm -i or, preferably, with rpm -U. Installation with rpm makes it appear in the RPM database.

The danger with many packages is that during the build process, unwanted files are added to the running system. To prevent this, use the package build, which creates a defined environment in which the package is built. To establish this "chroot" environment, the build script must be provided with a complete package tree. This tree can be made available on the hard disk, via NFS, or from DVD. The respective position is specified with build --rpms <path>. In contrast to rpm, the build command looks for the SPEC file in the source directory. To build wget anew (like in the above example) and the DVD is mounted in the system under /media/dvd, use the following commands as root:

```
cd /usr/src/packages/SOURCES/
mv ../SPECS/wget.spec .
build --rpms /media/dvd/suse/ wget.spec
```

Subsequently, a minimum environment will be established at /var/tmp/build-root. The package will be built in this environment. Upon completion, the resulting packages are located in /var/tmp/build-root/usr/src/packages/RPMS

The build script offers a number of additional options. For example, you can cause the script to prefer your own RPMs, omit the initialization of the build environment, or limit the rpm command to one of the above-mentioned stages. Additional information can be accessed with the command build --help and in the man page for build (man 1 build).

RPM and Patches

To guarantee the operational security of a system, update packages must be installed in the system from time to time. Previously, a bug in a package could only be eliminated by replacing the entire package. Large packages with small bugs could easily result in large amounts of data. However, since SuSE 8.1, the SuSE RPM offers a new feature enabling the installation of patches in packages.

The most important considerations are demonstrated using pine as an example:

- Is the patch RPM suitable for my system?

  To check this, first query the installed version of the package. For pine, this can be done with the following command:

  ```
  # rpm -q pine
  pine-4.44-188
  ```

  Then check if the patch RPM is suitable for this version of `pine`:

  ```
  # rpm -qp --basedon pine-4.44-224.i586.patch.rpm
  pine = 4.44-188
  pine = 4.44-195
  pine = 4.44-207
  ```

  This patch is suitable for three different versions of `pine`. The installed version in our example is also listed, so the patch can be installed.

- Which files are replaced by the patch?

  The files affected by a patch can easily be seen in the patch RPM. The rpm parameter `-P` serves the selection of special patch features. The list of files is displayed with the following command:

  ```
  # rpm -qpPl pine-4.44-224.i586.patch.rpm
  /etc/pine.conf
  /etc/pine.conf.fixed
  /usr/bin/pine
  ```

  or, if the patch is already installed, with the following command:

  ```
  # rpm -qPl pine
  /etc/pine.conf
  /etc/pine.conf.fixed
  /usr/bin/pine
  ```

- How can a patch RPM be installed in the system?

  Patch RPMs are used just like normal RPMs. The only difference is that a suitable RPM must already be installed.

- Which patches are already installed in the system, and for which package versions?

  A list of all patches installed in the system can be displayed with the command `rpm -qPa`. If only one patch is installed in a new system (like in our example), the list appear as follows:

  ```
  # rpm -qPa
  pine-4.44-224
  ```

  If, at a later date, you want to know which package version was originally installed, this information is also available in the RPM database. For `pine`, this information can be displayed with the following command:

  ```
  # rpm -q --basedon pine
  pine = 4.44-188
  ```

More information, including information on the patch feature of RPM, is available in the man page for `rpm` (`man 1 rpm`).

Tools for RPM Archives and the RPM Database

Midnight Commander (`mc`) can display the contents of RPM archives and copy parts of them. It represents archives as virtual file systems, offering all usual menu options of Midnight Commander: the `HEADER` information can be displayed with F3, the archive structure can be viewed with the cursor keys and Enter, and archive components can be copied with F5.

A front-end for rpm is also available for Emacs. KDE offers the kpackage tool. GNOME offers gnorpm.

Using the Alien (`alien`) Perl script, it is possible to convert or install an "alien" binary package. This tries to convert "old" TGZ archives to RPM before installing. This way, the RPM database can keep track of such a package after it has been installed. Beware: `alien` is still "alpha" software, according to its author — even if it already has a high version number.

Part II

Configuration

YaST2 in Text Mode (ncurses)

This chapter addresses system administrators and experts who do not run an X server on their systems and rely on the text-based installation tool. It provides basic information for starting and operating YaST2 in text mode (ncurses). It also explains how to update your system online automatically to keep it as up-to-date as possible.

Usage

The usage may be unfamiliar, but is very simple. Basically, the entire program can be controlled with Tab, Alt + Tab, Space, the arrow keys (↑ and ↓), Enter, and shortcuts. When Yast2 is started in text mode, the YaST2 Control Center appears first. It is shown in Figure 3.1.

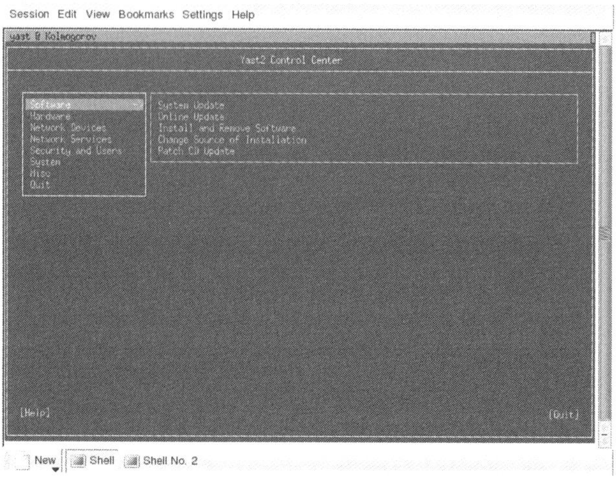

Figure 3.1: The Main Screen of YaST2 in Text-Mode

There are three areas here. The left frame, which is surrounded by a thick white border, features the categories to which the various modules belong. The active category is indicated by a colored background. The right frame, which is surrounded by a thin white border, provides an overview of the modules contained in the active category. The bottom frame contains the buttons for 'Help' and 'Exit'.

When the YaST2 Control Center is started, the category 'Software' is selected automatically. Use the ↓ and ↑ keys to change the category. To start a module from the selected category, press →. The module selection now appears with a thick border. Use the ↓ and ↑ keys to select the desired module. Keep the arrow keys pressed to scroll through the list of available modules. When a module is selected, the module title appears with a colorful background and a brief description is displayed in the bottom frame.

Press Enter to start the desired module. Various buttons or selection fields in the module contain a letter with a different color (yellow by default). Use the combination Alt + letter to select a button directly without navigating there with Tab.

Exit the YaST2 Control Center by pressing the 'Exit' button or by selecting the item 'Exit' in the category overview and pressing Enter.

Restriction of Key Combinations

If your window manager uses Alt key combinations, the Alt combinations in YaST2 might not work. Keys like Alt or ⇑ Shift might be occupied by the settings of the terminal.

Replacing Alt with Esc: Alt shortcuts can be executed with Esc instead of Alt. For example, Esc + H replaces Alt + H.

Replacement of backward and forward navigation by Ctrl+F and Ctrl+B: If the Alt and ⇑ Shift combinations are occupied by the window manager or the terminal, the combinations Ctrl + F (forward) and Ctrl + B (backward) can be used instead.

Restriction of function keys: The F keys are also used for functions. Here, too, certain F key might be occupied by the terminal and may not be available for YaST. However, the Alt key combinations and F keys should always be fully available on a pure text console.

Using the Modules

The following assumes that the Alt key combinations are functional. If necessary, replace the key combinations as described above or switch to a pure text console.

Navigation between buttons and selection lists With Tab and Alt + Tab, switch buttons or the frames containing selection lists.

Navigation in selection lists Use the arrow keys (↑ and ↓) to navigate among the individual elements in an active frame, for example, among the individual modules of a module group in the control center.

Checking of radio buttons and check boxes Select items with empty square brackets (check boxes) with Space or Enter. The buttons at the bottom of the individual modules are selected with Enter when they are selected (green background) or with Alt + yellow key. See Figure 3.2 on the following page.

The function keys The F keys (F1 to F12) enable quick access to the various buttons. Which function keys are actually mapped to buttons depends on which YaST module is active, as the different modules offer different buttons (such as details, info, add, and delete). The various functions mapped to the F keys are explained in the YaST help, which can be accessed with F1.

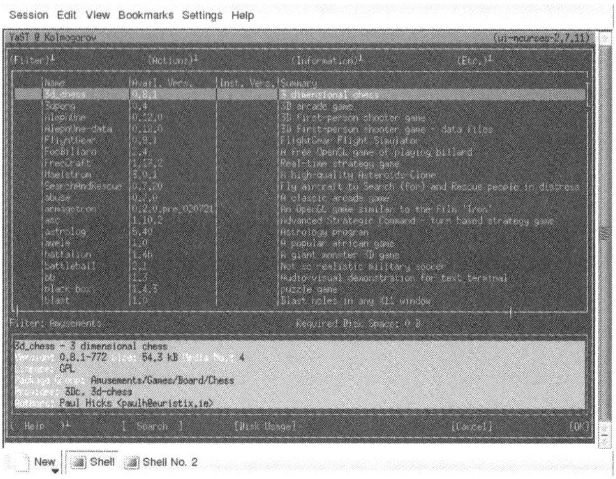

Figure 3.2: The Software Installation Module

Starting the Individual Modules

To save time, the individual YaST2 modules can also be started directly. To start the modules, use `yast` ⟨*modulename*⟩. The network module, for example, is started with `yast lan`. A list of all module names available on your system can be viewed with the command `yast -l` or `yast --list`.

YaST Online Update

The YaST Online Update (YOU) can be controlled and started from the console. As `root`, enter the command

```
earth:/root # yast2 online_update .auto.get
```

to load the latest patch list and all applicable rpms from the first server in the list /etc/suseservers.

To load only specific patches, execute the command with additional options. The possible options are security, recommended, document, YaST2, and optional. security only fetches security-related patches, recommended fetches the updates recommended by SuSE, document provides information on the patches or on the FTP server, YaST2 only fetches YaST2 patches, and optional delivers updates of secondary importance.

Information about the patches is stored in /var/lib/YaST/you/i386/update/8.2_or.X.Y/patches. root permissions are required to read this. X.Y refers to the respective version of SuSE Linux.

Accordingly, the command for downloading security patches is as follows:

```
earth:/root # yast2 online_update .auto.get security
```

Every time you execute .auto.get, the list of FTP servers is loaded to /etc/suseservers. To disable this feature, deactivate the function in the file /etc/sysconfig/onlineupdate by setting the value yes to no in the following line:

```
YAST2_LOADFTPSERVER="yes"
```

You can now install the patches with:

```
earth:/root # yast2 online_update .auto.install
```

This command installs all downloaded patches. If you only want to install a group, use the same options as for .auto.get.

The advantage of this method is that it can be automated. For example, the system administrator can download the packages overnight and install the needed ones in the morning.

The cron Job for YOU

The following are basic instructions for creating a cron job to update the system automatically. Basically, there are two different possibilities for setting up a cron job. The simpler method for this is described here. The following steps are necessary:

1. Become root.

2. Start the crontab editor with `crontab -e`.
3. Press `i` for the insertion mode of vi.
4. Enter the following lines:

```
MAILTO=" "
13 3 * * 0 /sbin/yast2 online_update auto.get
53 3 * * 0 /sbin/yast2 online_update auto.install
```

   The first five elements of the last two lines have the following meaning when read from left to right: minutes, hours, day of the month, month of the year, day of the week (0 is Sunday). `*` disregards that value. In this example, the first entry starts the cron job every Sunday at 3:13 a.m. The second job starts forty minutes later at 3:53 a.m. The line `MAILTO" "` prevents root from receiving the output as an e-mail and can, of course, be omitted.

   Caution

   Enter arbitrary times for the cron jobs and preferably not the times from the example above, because this could overload the FTP server.

   Caution

5. Save the cron job by consecutively pressing (Esc) `:wq` and (↵) or (Esc) `ZZ`.

The cron daemon is automatically restarted and your cron job is added to `/var/spool/cron/tabs/root`.

Booting and Boot Managers

This chapter introduces various methods for booting your installed system. First, some of the technical details of the boot process are explained to improve understanding of the various methods. This is followed by a detailed description of LILO and GRUB.

LILO was the standard boot loader in previous SuSE Linux releases. If you update from an earlier version using LILO, LILO will continue to be used. If you have a new installation, GRUB will be used as default, except if you install the root partition on a raid system or LVM.

Booting a PC

After turning on your computer, the first thing that happens is that the BIOS (Basic Input Output System) takes control, initializes the screen and keyboard, and tests the main memory. Until this task is completed, no external devices or external storage media are known to the system.

Subsequently, the information about the current date, time, and the most important peripheral devices is read from the CMOS setup. After reading the CMOS, the BIOS should recognize the first hard disk, including details such as its geometry. It can then start to load the operating system (OS) from there.

To load the OS, the system loads a 512-byte data segment from the first hard disk into main memory and executes the code stored at the beginning of this segment. The instructions contained there determine the rest of the boot process. This is the reason why the first 512 bytes of the hard disk are often called the *Master Boot Record* (MBR).

Up to this point (loading the MBR), the boot sequence is independent of the installed operating system and is identical on all PCs. Also, all the PC has to access peripheral hardware are those routines (drivers) stored in the BIOS.

Master Boot Record

The layout of the MBR always follows a standard independent of the operating system. The first 446 bytes are reserved for program code. The next 64 bytes offer space for a partition table for up to four partitions. See *Partitioning for Experts* on page 26. Without the partition table, no file systems exist on the hard disk — the disk would be virtually useless without it. The last two bytes must contain a special "magic number" (AA55). Any MBR containing a different number is rejected.

Boot Sectors

Boot sectors are the first sectors on a hard disk partition, except the extended partition that serves as a "container" for other partitions. They offer 512 bytes of space and are designed to contain code able to launch an operating system on this partition. Boot sectors of formatted DOS, Windows, and OS/2 partitions do exactly that. In contrast, Linux boot partitions are empty at the very start. A Linux partition cannot be started directly, although it may contain a kernel and a valid root file system. A boot sector with a valid start code contains the same "magic number" as the MBR in its last two bytes.

Booting DOS or Windows 95/98

The DOS MBR of the first hard disk contains information that determines which partition of a hard disk is "active" — which partition should be searched for the operating system to boot. Therefore, DOS must be installed on the first hard disk. The executable code in the MBR ("first stage boot loader") tests whether the marked partition contains a valid boot sector.

If this is the case, the "second stage boot loader" can be started from there. DOS system programs can now be loaded and you will see the usual DOS prompt. In DOS, only primary partitions can be marked active. Therefore, you cannot use logical partitions inside an extended partition as bootable DOS partitions.

Boot Concepts

The simplest boot concept involves only one machine with one operating system installed. The boot process for this case has already been outlined. The same boot concept can be used for a Linux-only machine. In this case, you could theoretically skip the installation of LILO or GRUB. However, in this case you would not be able to pass additional parameters to the system kernel at boot time. As soon as there is more than one operating system installed, there are several possible boot concepts:

Booting Another OS from a Floppy Disk: One OS can be booted from the hard disk. Other operating systems can be booted using boot disks.

- *Requirements:* the floppy drive must be bootable
- *Example:* install Linux in addition to Windows, but boot Linux from a floppy disk
- *Advantage:* no boot loader needs to be installed
- *Disadvantage:* requires working boot disks and the boot process takes longer
- Depending on the purpose of the computer, it is an advantage or disadvantage that Linux cannot be booted without a disk.

Installing a Boot Manager: Theoretically, this allows you to use an arbitrary number of operating systems on a single machine. The choice of systems is done at boot time. Changing operating systems requires a reboot. The boot manager must work smoothly with all installed operating systems.

Map Files, GRUB, and LILO

The main obstacle for booting an operating system is the fact the kernel usually is a file within a file system on a partition on a disk. These concepts are unknown to the BIOS. To circumvent this, "maps" and "map files" were introduced. These maps simply note the physical block numbers on the disk that comprise the logical files. When such a map is processed, the BIOS loads all the physical blocks in sequence as noted in the map, building the logical file in memory.

The main difference between LILO and GRUB is that LILO relies almost entirely on maps, whereas GRUB tries to get rid of fixed maps during boot as early as possible. This is accomplished by introducing *File System Code* to the boot loader, so files can be found by their path names rather than block numbers. This difference has historical reasons: in the early days of Linux, many file systems were competing for dominance. Werner Almesberger wrote a boot loader that did not need to know in what kind of file system the kernel to boot actually resided. The idea behind the GRUB approach, however, is even older, from the ages of traditional Unix and BSD. These usually had a single file system of choice and often had a reserved space at its beginning in which to embed a boot loader. This boot loader knew the data structures of the file system in which it was embedded and kernels could be found by name in the root directory of that file system.

Another fundamental difference is that the LILO boot code is written in 16-bit assembler while as much of GRUB as possible is written in 32-bit portable C. The impact of this, however, is mostly beyond the scope of this book.

The following section describes the installation and configuration of a boot manager, using the Linux boot manager GRUB as an example. This is followed by a description of the differences when using LILO. A complete description of LILO is available in Almesberger (1994). This description is located in `/usr/share/doc/packages/lilo/user.dvi`. View the text on screen with an application such as `xdvi` or print it with `lpr`.

Boot Loader Configuration with YaST2

The YaST module greatly simplifies the configuration of the boot loader. Nevertheless, you should not use this module without understanding the underlying concept. Refer to *Booting with GRUB* on page 77 for GRUB or *Booting with LILO* on page 80 for LILO before modifying the boot loader configuration. The following explanations mainly refer to the standard boot loader GRUB.

In the YaST2 Control Center, go to 'System' → 'Boot Loader Configuration'. The current boot loader configuration of your system is displayed and can be modified.

The Main Screen

The configuration field with the white background is organized in three columns. The modified options listed in the middle column are marked in the left column under 'Ch.'. The current values are displayed in the right column. To add a new option, click 'Add'. To change the value of an option, select the option then click 'Edit'. To remove an existing option, select it and click 'Delete'.

To the right under the configuration window, find the 'Reset' combo box with the following options:

Propose New Configuration A new configuration suggestion is generated. If an older Linux version or another operating system is found on other partitions, these are integrated in the boot menu. Then decide whether to boot Linux directly or its former boot loader. If you select the second option, you will be taken to a second boot menu when you boot.

Start New Configuration from Scratch Specify the entire configuration yourself without any suggestions.

Edit Configuration Files The existing configuration files are read and can be modified.

Propose a New Configuration and Merge with Other Existing Linux Menus If another operating system and an older Linux version are installed in another partition, the menu will include an entry for the new SuSE Linux, an entry for the other system, and all entries from the old boot loader menu. This process can take some time. This possibility does not exist with LILO.

Use the 'Edit configuration files' button to edit the relevant configuration files in an editor, if desired. Load the file with the help of the selection field and modify it directly. Click 'OK' to save your changes. Click 'Cancel' to exit the boot loader configuration or 'Back' to return to the main screen.

Note

The sequence of the options or commands in GRUB plays an important role. Adhere to the preconfigured sequence, as otherwise the machine might not be able to boot.

Note

Boot Loader Configuration Options

For less experienced users, the configuration with YaST might seem to be somewhat laborious. However, it is easier than directly editing the files. If you select an option with the mouse and click 'Edit', a dialog is dispplayed in which specify individual settings. Click 'OK' to confirm the changes and return to the main dialog. These options differ from boot loader to boot loader. The following section provides a brief introduction to some of the options for GRUB:

Boot Loader Type: Use this option to switch between GRUB and LILO. In the additional dialog, select how the change should be made. You can convert the current GRUB configuration into a similar LILO configuration. Information might be lost during this process if there are no equivalent options. You can also create a new configuration or let YaST generate a new suggestion, which you can modify if necessary. Another possibility is to read the configuration from the hard disk. If you decide to retain the existing boot loader, reload its configuration by means of the last option. However, this is only possible until you exit the boot loader module.

Boot Loader Location: In this dialog, determine where the boot loader is installed: in the Master Boot Record (MBR), in the boot sector of the boot partition, in the boot sector of the root partition, or on a floppy disk. With the option 'Other', freely select the installation target. Refer to the information under *Basics* on page 80.

Disk Order: If you have two or more hard disks in your computer, the sequence according to the BIOS settings can be specified here.

Default: With this option, determine what kernel or operating system to load by default if no selection is made in the boot menu. After expiration of a waiting period, the default system is booted. Click this option then 'Edit' to see an overview of all boot menu entries. Select the desired entry from the list then click 'Set as Default'. You can also edit any entry by clicking 'Edit'. This dialog is identical to the following. You have all possibilities: changing the sequence of the boot menu, adding, editing, or deleting entries, or setting the default entry.

Sections This option in the main screen displays the available menu entries. If you select this option and click 'Edit', you will be taken to the same dialog as with 'Default'.

Activate Boot Loader Partition With this option, activate the partition in whose boot sector the boot loader was installed, regardless of which partition contains the directory `/boot` or / (root) with the boot loader files.

Replace Code in MBR If you change the location of the boot loader, decide whether to overwrite the MBR.

The options in the final section are not explained here. The 'timeout' option, which is used to determine for how long the boot loader waits before it boots the default system, might be of special interest. Here, add a number of additional options by means of the respective buttons.

Depending on which boot loader you use, information about further options is available under *Booting with GRUB* on the current page or under *Structure of lilo.conf* on page 82. A detailed online manual for GRUB is available at `http://www.gnu.org/software/grub/`. Detailed documentation on all LILO options is available in the man page for `lilo.conf` (`man lilo.conf`).

Booting with GRUB

Except the points mentioned earlier, most of the LILO features also apply to GRUB. Some differences will be apparent to the user, however.

Like LILO, GRUB also consists of two stages — a 512-byte first stage to be put into an MBR or a partition boot block and a larger "stage2" found using a map file. From here on, however, things work differently with GRUB. stage2 contains code to read file systems. Currently supported are ext2 (and thus ext3, for GRUB's read-only purposes), reiser FS, jfs, xfs, minix, and the DOS FAT FS as used by Windows. Any file contained in such a file system on a supported BIOS disk device can be displayed, used as a command or menu file, or loaded into memory as a kernel or initrd, just by issuing the appropriate command followed by the BIOS device and a path.

The big difference to LILO is that once GRUB is installed, kernels and menu entries can be added or changed without any further action required. At boot time, GRUB will dynamically locate and reread the files' contents.

The Menu

For the computer user, the most important GRUB file, once GRUB is installed, is the menu file, by default `/boot/grub/menu.lst`. This file contains all information about other partitions or operating systems that may be booted using the menu.

Because of its own code to read file systems, GRUB does a fresh read of the menu file on each boot. There is absolutely no need to update GRUB each time you make changes to the file — just use YaST2 or your favorite editor.

The menu file contains commands. The syntax is quite simple. Each line consists of a command followed by optional parameters separated spaces, as in the shell. Some commands allow an equal sign before their first parameter for historical reasons. Comments are introduced by the hash sign ('#').

To identify the menu entries in the menu overview, give each entry a name or `title`. After the keyword `title`, spaces are skipped and the rest of the line appears as a selectable item when the menu is shown. All commands up to the next `title` will be executed when this menu entry is chosen.

The simplest case is the chain loading of another operating system's boot loader. The command is called `chainloader` and the argument is usually another partition's boot block in GRUB's "block notation", for example:

```
chainloader (hd0,3)+1
```

GRUB's device naming is explained in *Names for BIOS Devices* on the next page. This example means one block from the beginning of a partition.

The command to specify a kernel image is just `kernel`. The first argument is taken as a path to a kernel file on a partition. The remainder is passed to that kernel when it is started.

If the kernel does not have the necessary built-in file system or disk drivers to access the root partition, an `initrd` must be specified. This is a separate GRUB command and takes the path to the initrd file as its only argument. This command must follow the `kernel` command, as the loading address of the initrd will be written into the already-loaded kernel image.

The `root` command simplifies the specification of kernels and initrds. In a strict sense, this command really does not do anything, but is just a shorthand. `root` takes a GRUB device or partition as its only argument and all kernel, initrd, or other file paths that do not explicitly specify a device will have this device prepended, up to the next `root` command.

Implicitly at the end of each menu entry there is a `boot` command, so there is no need to write it into the menu file. If in a situation where you need to interactively type GRUB commands by hand during the boot process, finally issue the `boot` command. `boot` takes no arguments. It just executes the loaded kernel image or chain loader.

Once you have written all your menu entries, specify which entry number to use as `default`. Otherwise, the first one (number `0`) will be used. You can also specify a time-out in seconds after which this should occur. `timeout` and `default` are usually written before the menu entries.

Names for BIOS Devices

The origin of GRUB is revealed by the way it gives names to BIOS devices. A BSD-like scheme is used: the floppy disk devices `0x00, 0x01` are called fd0 and fd1, respectively, and all hard disks recognized by the host BIOS or added by add-on controllers `0x80, 0x81, 0x82` are simply called hd0, hd1, and so on, regardless of their specific type. The problem of linux device name correspondence to BIOS devices is common to both LILO and GRUB. Both use similar heuristics to establish a mapping, but GRUB stores the result in a file that can be corrected.

Partitions on hard disks are identified by appending their number with a separating comma. A complete GRUB path consists of a device name, which is always written in parentheses, and a file path on that device or partition, always with a leading slash. So, for example, on a system with only a single IDE disk and Linux on its first partition, a bootable kernel might be

```
(hd0,0)/boot/vmlinuz
```

Note

Partition numbers in GRUB are zero-based. (hd0,0) corresponds to /dev/hda1.

Note

Installation Using the GRUB Shell

GRUB exists in two versions: a boot loader and a normal Linux program. This program is called the *GRUB shell*. The functionality of installing GRUB as a boot loader on a hard disk or floppy disk is integrated in GRUB and can be used by means of the commands `install` or. Thus, this functionality is available in the GRUB shell when Linux is running and GRUB was loaded when system was booted. This facilitates the recovery of a defective system.

Because GRUB is 32-bit C code, it is quite easy to replace the BIOS calls with Linux system calls to get an identical GRUB program that is able to function within a Linux environment. This program is called the *GRUB shell*. The functionality to install a GRUB onto a disk is present within GRUB itself as the `install` or `setup` command and is thus available via the GRUB shell when Linux is running and when GRUB has just been loaded during the boot process. This greatly eases the repair of a damaged system.

The Linux environment is where the BIOS mapping heuristics come into play: the GRUB shell reads a file `device.map`, which consists of one line specifying the GRUB device and the path name to a Linux device node separated by spaces. Some SCSI adaptor BIOSes allow their disks to be inserted *before* the IDE disks instead of appended after them, some BIOSes are capable of switching first and second hard disk, and others give you full control over the sequence of disks attached to on-board interfaces and all add-on cards. On current PCs, there is no reliable way to detect this. So, in case of trouble, first make sure `device.map` reflects the actual BIOS numbering of your disks. `device.map` is found in the default GRUB directory, `/boot/grub/`.

More Information

The web page `http://www.gnu.org/software/grub/` provides detailed information about GRUB.The online manual is available in English. If texinfo is installed on your machine, view the info pages for GRUB in a shell using the command `info grub`.

Booting with LILO

The Linux boot loader LILO is suitable for installation in the MBR. LILO has access to two real-mode hard disks and is able to find all the data it needs from the *raw* hard drives without any partitioning data. Therefore, operating systems can also be booted from the second hard disk. Unlike with the DOS boot process, the entries in the partition table are ignored when using LILO.

The main difference from the standard DOS boot process is the possibility to load diverse installed operating systems when booting. After loading the `MBR` into memory, LILO is started, allowing the user to select from the list of pre-installed systems. At system start-up, it can load boot sectors from partitions to boot an operating system from the respective partition or load the Linux kernel and boot Linux. It also provides the important possibility of passing a command to the kernel. For security reasons, some or all LILO services can be protected with a password.

Basics

The LILO boot mechanism consists of the following components:

- The *LILO boot sector* with the initial part ("first stage") of the LILO code that activates the actual LILO when the system is booted.
- The LILO machine code, located in `/boot/boot-menu.b`.

- A *map* file (`/boot/map`), where LILO enters the location of Linux kernels and other data during its installation.
- Optional: the *message file* `/boot/message`, which displays the graphical boot menu from which the operating system can be selected
- The different Linux kernels and boot sectors LILO should offer

Caution

Any write access (even through file movements) to any of these files corrupts the map file, requiring you to *update* LILO (see *Updating After Changing the Configuration* on page 85). This is especially important when changing kernels.

Caution

The following locations are suitable for storing the LILO *boot sector*:

On a *floppy disk* This is the simplest, but also the slowest method for booting with LILO. Choose this alternative if you do not want to change the existing boot sector.

In the *boot sector* of a primary Linux partition on the first hard disk This leaves the MBR untouched. Before it can be booted, the partition must be marked active. Start fdisk as `root` with the command `fdisk -s <partition>`. The program will ask for a command. `'m'` gives a list of possible entries and `'a'` marks the selected partition as active.

In the *Master Boot Record* This variation offers the highest flexibility. It is the only alternative possible if all the Linux partitions reside on the second hard disk and there is no extended partition on the first drive. Every setting of the MBR must be edited with extreme care because errors may have severe consequences.

In a boot sector booted by *another boot manager* Try this if you have used another boot manager and want to continue using it. Depending on its flexibility and power, there are several variations. A common case: you have a primary Linux partition on the second hard disk from which you boot Linux. Your boot manager is able to boot this partition via a boot sector. Then activate your Linux partition by installing LILO into this boot sector and telling your boot manager that it is active.

Configuring LILO

LILO is a flexible boot manager that offers many ways of adapting a configuration to your needs. The most important options and meanings are described below. For more detail, look at Almesberger (1994).

LILO is configured in `/etc/lilo.conf`. It is recommended to keep a backup of the previous `lilo.conf` file. Your settings only take effect when you update LILO after changing `/etc/lilo.conf`. See *Installing and Uninstalling LILO* on page 85.

Structure of lilo.conf

`/etc/lilo.conf` starts with a global section followed by one or more system sections for each operating system LILO should start. A new section is started by a line beginning with either image or other.

The order of entries in `/etc/lilo.conf` only matters because the first one in the list is booted by default unless the default option is used or the user selects another entry. This can be set to delay and timeout.

A sample configuration for a computer with both Windows and Linux is shown in File 2. There is a new Linux kernel (`/boot/vmlinuz` and a fallback kernel `/boot/vmlinuz.shipped`) and Windows on `/dev/hda1`. The program MemTest86 is also available.

```
### LILO global section
boot    = /dev/hda              # LILO installation target: MBR
backup  = /boot/MBR.hda.990428   # backup file for the old MBR
                                 # 1999-04-28
vga     = normal                # normal text mode (80x25 chars)
read-only
menu-scheme = Wg:kw:Wg:Wg
lba32                           # Use BIOS to ignore
                                # 1024 cylinder limit
prompt
password = q99iwr4              # LILO password (example)
timeout = 80                    # Wait at prompt for 8 s before
                                # default is booted
message = /boot/message         # LILO's greeting

### LILO Linux section (default)
  image   = /boot/vmlinuz       # Default
  label   = linux
  root    = /dev/hda7           # Root partition for the kernel
```

```
  initrd = /boot/initrd

### LILO Linux section (fallback)
  image   = /boot/vmlinuz.shipped
  label   = Failsafe
  root    = /dev/hda7
  initrd = /boot/initrd.suse
  optional

### LILO other system section (Windows)
  other   = /dev/hda1          # Windows partition
  label   = windows

### LILO memory test section (memtest)
  image   = /boot/memtest.bin
  label   = memtest86
```

File 2: *Sample Configuration of /etc/lilo.conf*

Anything between a `'#'` and the end of a line is regarded as a comment. Spaces and comments are ignored by LILO and can be used to improve readability.

The mandatory entries are explained here. The additional options are described in *Structure of lilo.conf* on the preceding page.

- **Global section** (Parameter part)

  ▷ boot=⟨*bootdevice*⟩

  The device on whose first sector LILO should be installed. ⟨*bootdevice*⟩ may be a floppy disk drive (`/dev/fd0`), a partition (e. g., `/dev/hdb3`), or an entire disk (e. g., `/dev/hda`). The last means installing LILO in the MBR. Default: if this option is missing, LILO is installed on the current root partition.

  ▷ lba32

  With this option, ignore the 1024-cylinder limit of LILO if your BIOS supports this.

  ▷ prompt

  Forces the LILO prompt to be displayed. The default is no prompt (refer to *Structure of lilo.conf* on the facing page, option delay). This is recommended if LILO needs to manage more than one system. timeout should be set to guarantee an automatic reboot if nothing is entered at the prompt.

- ▷ timeout=⟨*tenth-seconds*⟩ Sets a time-out for selecting an operating system to boot. Afterwards, the default system is booted. Specify the time-out in ⟨*tenth-seconds*⟩ (0.1 second increments). Pressing ⇑ Shift or the arrow keys disables the time-out option and LILO waits for orders. Default is set to `80`.

- **Linux section**

  - ▷ image=⟨*kernelimage*⟩

    Enter the name of the kernel image to boot, including its directory location. With a new system, this is most likely `/boot/vmlinuz`.

  - ▷ label=⟨*name*⟩

    This name must be unique in `/etc/lilo.conf`. Otherwise, freely choose a name for the system (e. g., Linux). Maximum length is fifteen characters. Use only letters, numbers, and underscore in names — no blanks or special characters. For more about the specific rules for which characters to use, see Almesberger (1994), Section 3.2.1. The default is the file name of the kernel image (e. g., `/boot/vmlinuz`).

    Select system to boot from the menu by this name. It is recommended, if there are several systems installed, to use a message file displaying the possible selections (see *Structure of lilo.conf* on page 82, option message).

  - ▷ root=⟨*rootdevice*⟩

    This gives the kernel the name of the root partition (e. g., `/dev/hda2`) of your Linux system. This is recommended for security reasons. If this option is omitted, the kernel takes its own root partition ⟨*kernelimage*⟩.

- **Linux part** (Linux — Safe Settings)

  Even if you installed a customized kernel, you are still able to boot the SuSE standard kernel.

  - ▷ optional

    If you decide to delete `/boot/vmlinuz.shipped` (*not recommended*), this section will be skipped without an error message during LILO installation.

- **Other systems**
  - ▷ other=⟨*partition*⟩
    other tells LILO to start the partitions of other systems (e. g., /dev/hda1).
  - ▷ label=⟨*name*⟩
    Select a name for the system. This is recommended, because the default — the raw device name — is not very informative.
- **Memory Test**
  Entry for the memory test program memtest86.

This section merely covers the basic entries required in /etc/lilo.conf. Other useful settings can be found in the man page for lilo.conf (man lilo.conf).

Installing and Uninstalling LILO

As GRUB is installed by default during a new installation, the following section covers a scenario in which LILO is to be integrated with special options in an existing system.

Caution

Before you install LILO, ensure any other existing operating systems can be booted from floppy disk. This is not possible for Windows XP. Especially fdisk must be available. If necessary, SuSE Linux can be booted from the installation CD or DVD.

Caution

Updating After Changing the Configuration

If any of the LILO components have changed or you have modified your configuration in /etc/lilo.conf, update LILO. This is easily done by launching the *Map Installer* as root with /sbin/lilo.

LILO creates a backup of the target boot sector, writes its *first stage* into it, then generates a new map file (see also *Booting with LILO* on page 80). LILO issues a report on each installed system as shown in Output 4.

```
Added linux *
Added suse
Added windows
Added memtest86
```

Output 4: *Output After Launching LILO*

When the installation is completed, the machine can be rebooted with `shutdown -r now`. While rebooting, the BIOS first performs its system test. Immediately afterwards, see LILO and its command prompt, in which to enter parameters and select a boot image from the recently installed configurations. (Tab) shows a list of all systems installed.

Uninstalling LILO

To uninstall LILO, copy the former content of the boot sector over LILO. This requires a valid backup of that former content. See *Structure of lilo.conf* on page 82, option backup.

Caution

A boot sector backup is no longer valid if the partition in question has a new file system. The partition table of an MBR backup becomes invalid if the hard disk in question has been repartitioned since the backup was created. Obsolete "backups" are time bombs. It is best to delete them as soon as possible.

Caution

Restoring a DOS or Windows 95/98 MBR

It is very simple to restore a DOS or Windows MBR. Just enter the MS-DOS command (available since DOS version 5.0):

```
C:\> fdisk /MBR
```

or, on OS/2:

```
C:\> fdisk /newmbr
```

These commands only write the first 446 bytes (the boot code) into the MBR and leave partitions untouched, unless the MBR (see on page 72) is treated as invalid due to an incorrect "magic number". In this case, the partition table is set to zero. Use fdisk to mark the desired start partition as bootable. This is required for the MBR routines of DOS, Windows, and OS/2.

For other restorations, first make a backup of the LILO sector in question — just to be on the safe side. Now check carefully whether your old backup file is the correct one and if it is exactly 512 bytes in size. Finally, write it back with the following commands:

- If LILO resides in partition yyyy (e. g., hda1, hda2):

```
earth:~ # dd if=/dev/yyyy of=New-File bs=512 count=1
earth:~ # dd if=Backup-File of=/dev/yyyy
```

- If LILO resides in the MBR of zzz (e. g., hda, sda):

```
earth:~ # dd if=/dev/zzz of=New-File bs=512 count=1
earth:~ # dd if=Backup-File of=/dev/zzz bs=446 count=1
```

The last command is "cautious" and does not overwrite the partition table. Again, with `fdisk`, mark the desired starting partition as *bootable*.

Restoring the Windows XP MBR

Boot from the Windows XP CD and press the Ⓡ key during the setup to start the Recovery Console. Select your Windows XP installation from the list and enter the administrator password. At the input prompt, enter the command `FIXMBR` and confirm the security query with `y`. Then reboot the computer with `exit`.

Restoring the Windows 2000 MBR

Boot from the Windows 2000 CD. During the setup, press Ⓡ then Ⓒ in the next menu to start the Restore Console. Select your Windows 2000 installation from the list and enter the administrator password. At the input prompt, enter the command `FIXMBR` and confirm the security query with `y`. Then reboot the computer with `exit`.

Creating Boot CDs

This concerns problems arising when attempting to boot a system with the LILO boot manager configured with YaST2. The creation of a system boot disk fails with more recent SuSE Linux versions because the space available on a floppy disk is no longer sufficient for the start-up files.

Procedure

It is possible to create a bootable CD-ROM containing the Linux start-up files if your system has an installed CD writer. This solution is only a workaround. It should normally be possible to configure LILO properly. Refer to the documentation about this subject in `/usr/share/doc/packages/lilo/README`, the man page for `lilo.conf` (`man lilo.conf`), and the man page for `lilo` (`man lilo`).

Boot CD with ISOLINUX

It is easiest to create a bootable CD with the ISOLINUX boot manager. The SuSE installation CDs are also made bootable with isolinux.

- Boot the installed system first using the following alternate procedure:
  - ▷ Boot from the installation CD or DVD as for installation.
  - ▷ Choose the preselected option 'Installation' during the boot sequence.
  - ▷ Choose the language and keyboard map next.
  - ▷ In the following menu, choose 'Boot installed system'.
  - ▷ The root partition is automatically detected and the system is booted from it.
- Install package `syslinux` with YaST2.
- Open a root shell. The following commands create a temporary directory and copy the files required for the booting of the Linux system (the isolinux boot loader as well as the kernel and the initrd) into it:

```
earth:~ # mkdir /tmp/CDroot
earth:~ # cp /usr/share/syslinux/isolinux.bin /tmp/CDroot/
earth:~ # cp /boot/vmlinuz /tmp/CDroot/linux
earth:~ # cp /boot/initrd /tmp/CDroot
```

- Create the boot loader configuration file `/tmp/CDroot/isolinux.cfg` with your preferred editor. Enter the following content:

```
DEFAULT linux
LABEL linux
  KERNEL linux
  APPEND initrd=initrd root=/dev/hdXY [boot parameter]
```

  Enter your root partition for the parameter `root=/dev/hdXY`. It is listed in the file `/etc/fstab`. Enter additional options for the setting `[boot parameter]`, which should be used during booting. The configuration files could, for example, look like this:

```
DEFAULT linux LABEL linux KERNEL linux APPEND initrd=initrd
root=/dev/hda7 hdd=ide-scsi
```

- The following command (entered at a command prompt) then creates an ISO-9660 file system for the CD.

  ```
  mkisofs -o /tmp/bootcd.iso -b isolinux.bin -c boot.cat
    -no-emul-boot -boot-load-size 4
    -boot-info-table /tmp/CDroot
  ```

  The complete command must be entered as one line.

- The file `/tmp/bootcd.iso` can be written to CD after that with either graphical CD writing applications, like KonCD or XCDroast, or simply at a command prompt:

  ```
  cdrecord -v speed=2 dev=0,0,0 /tmp/bootcd.iso -eject
  ```

  The parameter `dev=0,0,0` must be changed according to the SCSI ID of the writer. This can be determined with the command `cdrecord -scanbus`. Also, refer to the man page for `cdrecord` (`man cdrecord`).

- Test the boot CD. Reboot the computer to verify whether the Linux system is started correctly from the CD.

The X Window System

The X Window System is the de facto standard GUI for UNIX. Yet the X Window System is far more than this — X11 is a network-based system. Applications running on the machine earth can display their results on the machine sun, provided the two machines are connected via a network. The network could be a local one (LAN) or a connection between computers thousands of miles away via the Internet.

Among other things, the following sections draw attention to the program xf86config, which can be used instead of SaX2 to configure the monitor, graphics card, keyboard, and mouse. Another focus is the configuration of OpenGL and 3D. See User Guide (2003) for the description of the YaST2 modules.

Historical Background

X11 was first developed as an enterprise of DEC (Digital Equipment Corporation) and the project Athena at MIT (Massachusetts Institute of Technology). The first release of X11R1 was in September 1987. Since release 6, the X Consortium, Inc. has been responsible for the development of the X Window System.

XFree86 ™ is a freely available implementation of X servers for PC systems. It was developed by a handful of ambitious programmers who founded the XFree86 team in 1992. In 1994, this team went on to found The XFree86 Project, whose aim is to continue research and development on X11 and to provide it to the public. The completely revised major release XFree86-4.0 has been available for download from `http://www.XFree86.org` since March 2000. By default, SuSE Linux installs XFree86-4.0. Below, take a closer look at the features of this version.

The following sections cover the configuration of the X server, introducing the two programs SaX2 and xf86config, which can be used to configure the X Window System. To use the available hardware (mouse, graphics card, monitor, keyboard) in the best way possible, the configuration can be optimized manually. Certain aspects of this optimization will be explained. Others are not covered in detail. For more information about configuring the X Window System, refer to the directory `/usr/share/doc/packages/xf86` and to the man page for `XF86Config` (`man XF86Config`).

Caution

Be very careful when configuring your X Window System. Never start the X Window System until the configuration is finished. A wrongly configured system can cause irreparable damage to your hardware (this applies especially to fixed-frequency monitors). The authors of this book and SuSE cannot be held responsible for damage. This information has been carefully researched, but this does not guarantee that all methods presented here are correct and will not damage your hardware.

Caution

Version 4.x of XFree86

This version of SuSE Linux comes with version 4.x of XFree86, which differs from the previously used version 3.3 in a number of ways. Overall, there are hardly any differences for the user when operating the graphical desktop. Applications, such as the graphical desktops KDE or GNOME, behave with the new version in the same way as version 3.3.6 included in earlier distributions.

Advantages

The new X server is no longer a monolithic program, but just a relatively small basic scaffolding to which the necessary program modules can later be added, if and when required. For example, there are no longer many different X servers for different graphics cards as in the previous version, but just one executable program called XFree86, which can be found in the directory `/usr/X11R6/bin`. This is also the actual X server. The graphics driver, which then takes on the task of controlling the graphics card, is a loadable module.

A similar method is used to support the various input devices, fonts, or X protocols. This again consists of individual modules that can be later loaded by the X server. As a rule, you do not need to worry about these modules. The configuration of the modules to operate the graphical desktop on your computer is managed, as far as possible, by SaX2.

Through this module concept, it is easy for a vendor to implement a driver for exotic hardware, such as touch screens or new graphics cards. The developers have even ensured that the necessary modules for various operating systems only need to be made available once, which means that a graphics driver module compiled in FreeBSD, for example, can also be used in Linux and vice versa. This portability, however, is limited to the same hardware platform: a module compiled for Linux on PowerPCs cannot be used on an Intel PC.

Support for the mouse has also been significantly improved. Especially under heavy loads, the reaction of the mouse to mouse movements is considerably faster and more direct than with the previous XFree86 X server. Overall, the output speed has also been improved, so graphics operations are generally performed more quickly than on the old X server due to the completely revised XAA (*XFree86 Acceleration Architecture*).

Compared to XFree86 3.3.x, the configuration file has a slightly different format and is now located in `/etc/X11/XF86Config`. For fine-tuning your X configuration, details on the structure of the configuration file and how it functions can be found in *Optimizing the Installation of the X Window System* on page 103.

Error logging has also been improved. The X server creates a very detailed log file, which you can always find after the X server has started in the file `/var/log/XFree86.0.log`. One of the further features of this version is the support of special options, such as True Type fonts. Other features also include the 3D protocol extension, glx, gamma correction of the screen, and the support of multiple graphics cards for multihead configurations. More information about this can be found in *Optimizing the Installation of the X Window System* on page 103.

Configuration Using xf86config

In most cases, SaX is superior to xf86config for the simple configuration of the X Window System. However, if the configuration does not work with SaX, just use xf86config, which almost always works.

XFree86 4.x includes a similar text-based program, xf86config. At some points, this contains dialogs that have been somewhat modified. It writes the configuration file to `/etc/X11/XF86Config`. Usually XFree86 4.x does not require the use of xf86config, because "problem" graphics cards can also be configured with the framebuffer or with the vga module.

Make sure you have the following information available:

- mouse type, port to which the mouse is connected, and baud rate (the baud rate is normally optional)
- specifications of the graphics card
- monitor data (frequencies, etc.)

If these settings are known or you have your manuals at hand, start the configuration. Only `root` can do this. The configuration is started with:

```
earth:/root # xf86config
```

Mouse

Following the welcome screen, select the mouse type from the following:

```
1. Microsoft compatible (2-button protocol)
2. Mouse Systems (3-button protocol)
3. Bus Mouse
4. PS/2 Mouse
```

```
5. Logitech Mouse (serial, old type, Logitech protocol)
6. Logitech MouseMan (Microsoft compatible)
7. MM Series
8. MM HitTablet
```

Output 5: *Mouse Selection for X*

While selecting the mouse, bear in mind that many of the new Logitech mice are either Microsoft compatible or use the MouseMan protocol. The selection Bus Mouse refers to any bus mouse, including Logitech.

Selection is made by entering the relevant number. There may be a question as to whether to activate "ChordMiddle". This is necessary for some Logitech mice or track balls for activation of the middle mouse button.

```
Please answer the following question with either 'y' or 'n'.
Do you want to enable ChordMiddle?
```

If you have a two-button mouse, emulate the third button by answering 'y' to the next question.

```
Please answer the following question with either 'y' or 'n'.
Do you want to enable Emulate3Buttons?
```

The middle button is emulated by simultaneously pressing the two mouse buttons.

Next, specify the mouse's interface:

```
Now give the full device name that the mouse is connected to, for ex-
ample
/dev/tty00. Just pressing enter will use the default, /dev/mouse.
Mouse device:
```

If you have already entered a port for your mouse during the system installation, just enter /dev/mouse.

Keyboard

Next, determine whether to assign Meta (ESC) to the left Alt key and to assign ModeShift (AltGr) to the right Alt key.

```
Please answer the following question with either 'y' or 'n'.
Do you want to enable these bindings for the Alt keys?
```

If you answer 'y', the left Alt key can serve as the meta key for Emacs and the keys that need ModeShift (AltGr) can be entered.

Monitor

Next, specify your monitor. Be extremely careful with vertical and horizontal frequencies. These values can be found in your monitor manual.

Caution

Setting frequencies incorrectly can lead to irreparable damage to your monitor. The X Window System only addresses video modes that operate the monitor in the given frequency range. Entering frequencies for which the monitor was not designed can cause severe damage to it.

Caution

Some monitors are listed under `/usr/X11R6/lib/X11/doc/Monitors`. However, we cannot be held liable if this information is inaccurate.

To enter the horizontal frequency, the following selection is displayed:

```
hsync in kHz; monitor type with characteristic modes
 1 31.5;                 Standard VGA, 640x480 @ 60 Hz
 2 31.5 - 35.1;          Super VGA, 800x600 @ 56 Hz
 3 31.5, 35.5;           8514 Compatible, 1024x768 @ 87 Hz interl.
                         (no 800x600)
 4 31.5, 35.15, 35.5;    Super VGA, 1024x768 @ 87 Hz il.,
                         800x600 @ 56 Hz
 5 31.5 - 37.9;          Extended Super VGA, 800x600 @ 60 Hz,
                         640x480 @ 72 Hz
 6 31.5 - 48.5;          Non-Interlaced SVGA, 1024x768 @ 60 Hz,
                         800x600 @ 72 Hz
 7 31.5 - 57.0;          High Frequency SVGA, 1024x768 @ 70 Hz
 8 31.5 - 64.3;          Monitor that can do 1280x1024 @ 60 Hz
 9 31.5 - 79.0;          Monitor that can do 1280x1024 @ 74 Hz
10 Enter your own horizontal sync range
Enter your choice (1-10):
```

Output 6: *Input of Horizontal Frequencies of the Monitor*

Only choose one of the predefined modes if you are unsure of the settings for your monitor. Use selection '10' to enter your own frequencies.

The next screen asks you to enter your monitor's vertical frequency. It will also provide a selection:

```
 1 50-70
 2 50-90
 3 50-100
 4 40-150
```

```
5 Enter your own vertical sync range

Enter your choice (1-5):
```

Output 7: *Detailed Vertical Frequencies*

Again, using the known values is preferable to using one of the items '1' to '4'.

Next, enter a name, vendor name, and model for your monitor:

```
Enter an identifier for your monitor definition:
Enter the vendor name of your monitor:
Enter the model name of your monitor:
```

These are just descriptive names used to document your configuration, which do not affect the configuration itself. Merely pressing (↵) will select the default values, which are usually sufficient.

Your monitor configuration is now complete.

Graphics Cards and X server

Next, specify your graphics card:

```
Do you want to look at the card database?
```

If you enter 'y', a selection of predefined cards is presented. Here, select your card by pressing the corresponding number. Do not trust this list blindly, because there can be differences in clock chip and RAMDAC[1] settings.

This is why a menu item appears later for selecting a RAMDAC and a clock chip, although you have entered them already. Then the predefined settings for this card will be presented as an extra option.

The card definitions contain information on clock chips, RAMDAC, and the X server to use. Furthermore, some valuable information concerning the card is written to the device section in `XF86Config`.

If your card is not listed, do not panic. Switch back to the normal configuration by selecting 'q'. Only select one of the defined cards if it matches your card exactly. Selecting a card with a similar name is not recommended. Similar names do not necessarily refer to similar hardware.

More information about how to configure your card is given in *Optimizing the Installation of the X Window System* on page 103.

The X server is configured next.

[1] **R**andom **A**ccess **M**emory **D**igital-to-**A**nalogue **C**onverter

```
1 The XF86_Mono server. This a monochrome server that should work on
  any VGA-compatible card, in 640x480 (more on some SVGA chip sets).
2 The XF86_VGA16 server. This is a 16 color VGA server that should
  work on any VGA-compatible card.
3 The XF86_SVGA server. This is a 256 color SVGA server that supports
  a number of SVGA chip sets. It is accelerated on some Cirrus and WD
  chip sets. It supports 16 and 32-bit color on certain Cirrus
  configurations.
4 The accelerated servers. These include XF86_S3, XF86_Mach32,
  XF86_Mach8, XF86_8514, XF86_P9000, XF86_AGX, XF86_W32, and
  XF86_Mach64.

These four server types correspond to the four different "Screen"
sections in XF86Config (vga2, vga16, svga, accel).

5 Choose the server from the card definition, XF86_S3.

Which one of these four screen types do you intend to run
by default (1-4)?
```

Output 8: *Selecting the X Server*

1 A server for monochrome (black and white) monitors. This should run on any VGA compatible graphics card and at least offer a resolution of 640x480.

2 16 colors server XF86_VGA16. Should run with any VGA compatible card.

3 SVGA server XF86_SVGA. This server supports a wide variety of SVGA cards. Graphic acceleration is used with some Cirrus or WD cards. The 16-bit or 32-bit color mode can be activated with some Cirrus cards.

4 Server for accelerated cards (see below).

5 This item only exists if you have entered a card definition in the previous selection. Here, the server is selected (default) that suits the selected card.

When you have selected a server, you are asked if you want to create a symbolic link to `/usr/X11R6/bin/X`. If you answer with 'y', you are asked whether to put it in `/var/X11R6/bin/X`.

```
Do you want to set it in /var/X11R6/bin?
```

Reply with 'y', because it may not always be possible to write to `/usr` tree.

Afterwards, if you have selected '4' (the accelerated servers) in the previous selection, a menu is presented of all available accelerated X servers.

```
Select an accel server:

1 XF86_S3
2 XF86_Mach32
3 XF86_Mach8
4 XF86_8514
5 XF86_P9000
6 XF86_AGX
7 XF86_W32
8 XF86_MACH64

Which accel server:
```

These servers support each card listed above. To create links, the appropriate server must already be installed. This means you must already have selected the correct server during the installation of your X Window System.

After selecting your X server, configure your graphics. First, specify the amount of memory the video card has.

```
How much memory do you have on your graphics card:

1 256K
2 512K
3 1024K
4 2048K
5 4096K
6 Other

Enter your choice:
```

Output 9: *Specifying the Video Memory*

Next, enter the name, vendor name, and type for your graphics card. If you earlier selected a card from the predefined list, pressing ⏎ will enter this as the default.

```
Enter an identifier for your graphics card definition:

Enter the vendor name of your graphics card:

Enter the model (board) name of your graphics card :
```

If you chose an accelerated X server, you must enter the RAMDAC settings. This only applies to the S3 and AGX servers.

```
1  AT&T 20C490 (S3 server)          att20c490
2  AT&T 20C498/21C498/22C498 (S3)   att20c498
```

```
 3  AT&T 20C505 (S3)                    att20c505
 4  BrookTree BT481 (AGX)               bt481
 5  BrookTree BT482 (AGX)               bt482
 6  BrookTree BT485/9485 (S3)           bt485
 7  Sierra SC15025 (S3, AGX)            sc15025
 8  S3 GenDAC (86C708) (autodetected)   s3gendac
 9  S3 SDAC (86C716) (autodetected)     sdac
10  STG-1700 (S3)                       stg1700
11  TI 3020 (S3)                        ti3020
12  TI 3025 (S3)                        ti3025
13  TI 3020 (S3, autodetected)                      ti3020
14  TI 3025 (S3, autodetected)                      ti3025
15  TI 3026 (S3, autodetected)                      ti3026
16  IBM RGB 514 (S3, autodetected)
ibm_rgb514
17  IBM RGB 524 (S3, autodetected)
ibm_rgb524
18  IBM RGB 525 (S3, autodetected)
ibm_rgb525
19  IBM RGB 526 (S3)
ibm_rgb526
20  IBM RGB 528 (S3, autodetected)
ibm_rgb528
21  ICS5342 (S3, ARK)                               ics5342
22  ICS5341 (W32)                                   ics5341
23  IC Works w30C516 ZoomDac (ARK)                  zoomdac
24  Normal DAC                                      normal
```

Output 10: *Setting RAMDACs*

It is usually best to press ⏎ and not make any custom selections. If you specified a graphics card that supports a given RAMDAC setting, it will be included in the selection list.

After answering these questions, enter a clock chip for accelerated cards, if you have one. Entering a clock chip avoids clock lines, as the clocks needed can be programmed.

```
1  Chrontel 8391                                          ch8391
2  ICD2061A and compatibles (ICS9161A, DCS2824)
icd2061a
3  ICS2595
ics2595
4  ICS5342 (similar to SDAC, but not completely compatible)

ics5342
5  ICS5341
ics5341
6  S3 GenDAC (86C708) and ICS5300 (autodetected)
s3gendac
```

```
 7  S3 SDAC (86C716)
 s3_sdac
 8  STG 1703 (autodetected)
 stg1703
 9  Sierra SC11412
 sc11412
10  TI 3025 (autodetected)                               ti3025
11  TI 3026 (autodetected)                               ti3026
12  IBM RGB 51x/52x (autodetected)
 ibm_rgb5xx
```

Output 11: *Setting the Clock Chip*

If a card without a clock chip is selected, just press ⏎ (thus not selecting a clock chip). If a card has been selected, the clock chip is set as default (if there is one).

If no clock chip has been set, xf86config suggests running X -probeonly to determine the clock timings supported. These are automatically written in `XF86Config` in a separate *clocks* line.

Automatically defined settings can be *very risky*: if the card has a programmable clock chip, the X server, when probing, cannot distinguish between the different clocks and only recognizes clocks 0, 1, and sometimes, 2. All other values are more or less random numbers (normally, clocks 0, 1, and 2 are repeated and are replaced by zeros).

All clocks apart from 0 and 1 are strongly influenced by the preprogrammed clock chip. Thus, clock 2 could have a different setting when probed (and which was written to the file `XF86Config`) than when the X server is later started. Then all the timings would be wrong and the monitor could be severely damaged.

A good indication of a programmable clock chip (and the problems this might entail) is the multiple zeros or repeating timing values. Absolutely, under no circumstances, ever write such values to `XF86Config`.

To configure clock chips, follow these steps:

- The best way is to enter an existing (*programmable*) clock chip if there is one. It will be programmed accordingly and your `XF86Config` will not contain clock lines. Compare chips on the card with the chips offered in the menu. Most newer S3 cards have a programmable clock chip.
- If you *do not have a programmable* clock chip, launch X -probeonly and compare these values with those in the manual. If these values correspond (±2), enter them in `XF86Config`.

Unless the manual offers some pertinent advice, the values can be determined by running X -probeonly (this works best on an unloaded machine). Check whether the values are accurate, as clock values cannot be determined for every card. Many zeros or repeating values are a sign of invalid settings. Enter the correct values into `XF86Config`. Do not omit any values. Do not try to rearrange them or change them in any way. The values must be entered in their exact order.

If the P9000 server is used, the order is irrelevant. Just enter the modes for the desired clock in the *clocks line*.

- In general: if there is a programmable clock chip, there should be *no* clocks line in `XF86Config` (exception, P9000). For cards without a programmable clock chip, there should be a *clocks line* in `XF86Config`. This avoids the tedious (and sometimes even risky) clock probe at each start. Furthermore, for cards with unreadable values, there are no invalid values and there is no risk to your monitor.

After having read the previous section, if you want to let clocks be recognized automatically, just answer 'y' to the following question:

```
Do you want me to run 'X -probeonly' now?
```

Now the screen will turn black before the list of probed clocks appears or a message will appear that no clocks could be found. If you have selected a clock chip, this question will not appear, because the clocks will then be programmed automatically. If this is the case, this section will be skipped.

Caution

If the previous question has been answered with 'y' and the screen remains black for more than thirty seconds, cancel testing immediately with (Ctrl) + (Alt) + (←), or (Ctrl) + (C). If this does not work, switch off the monitor and the computer to prevent damage to your hardware.

Caution

Saving your Configuration

Now write the configuration file. It is recommended to write it to `/etc/XF86Config` to ensure that, even in a networking environment, each machine has its own configuration file — even if they share the `/usr` file system.

Specify `'/etc/XF86Config'` at this point. This concludes xf86config and the configuration of the X Window System.

Optimizing the Installation of the X Window System

This section describes the configuration file, `/etc/X11/XF86Config`. Each *section* starts with the keyword Section <name of section> and ends with EndSection. Below is a rough outline of the most important sections.

Afterwards, learn how to integrate additional fonts, how to configure input devices, and how 3D acceleration is implemented. This is also managed in certain sections of the `XF86Config` file, of course, although integrating an additional font requires the help of external programs, which are included with SuSE Linux. The methods discussed here aim to illustrate the possibilities available and serve as an incentive, but they do not claim to cover all eventualities.

The programs SaX2 and xf86config (for XFree86-4.0) create the file `XF86Config`, by default in `/etc/X11`. This is the primary configuration file for the X Window System. Find all the settings here concerning your graphics card, mouse, and monitor.

`XF86Config` is divided into several sections, each one dealing with a certain aspect of the configuration. A section always has the same form:

```
Section ⟨name of section⟩
  entry 1
  entry 2
  entry n
EndSection
```

The following types of sections exist:

Files	This section describes the paths used for fonts and the RGB color table.
ServerFlags	General switches are set here.
InputDevice	Input devices are configured in this section. Unlike in XFree86-3.3, keyboards, mice, and special input devices (touch pad, joysticks, etc.) are configured via this section. Important terms here are Driver and the options defined by Protocol and Device.

Table 5.1: *continued overleaf...*

Monitor	Describes the monitor used. The individual elements of this are the name, which is referred to later in the Screen definition, the bandwidth, and the allowed sync frequencies (HorizSync and VertRefresh). Settings are given in MHz, kHz, and Hz. Normally, the server refuses any mode line that does not correspond with the specification of the monitor. This is to prevent too high frequencies from being sent to the monitor by accident.
Modes	The mode line parameters are stored here for the specific screen resolutions. These parameters can be calculated by SaX2 on the basis of the values given by the user and normally do not need to be changed. Intervene manually at this point, if, for example, you want to connect a fixed frequency monitor. An exact explanation of the individual parameters would be too much for this book. Find details on the meaning of individual number values in the HOWTO file `/usr/share/doc/howto/en/XFree86-Video-Timings-HOWTO.gz`.
Device	This section defines a specific graphics card. It is referenced by its descriptive name.
Screen	This section puts together a Driver (e. g., vga2), a monitor, and a Device to form all the necessary settings for XFree86. In the Display subsection, specify the size of the virtual screen (Virtual, the ViewPort, and the Modes) used with this virtual screen.
ServerLayout	This section defines the layout of a single or multihead configuration. The input devices InputDevice and the display devices Screen are combined into one section.

Table 5.1: *Sections in* `/etc/X11/XF86Config`

Monitor, Device, and Screen are explained in more detail in the following. Further information about the other sections can be found in the man page for `XFree86` (`man XFree86`) and the man page for `XF86Config` (`man XF86Config`).

There can be several different Monitor sections in `XF86Config`. Even multiple Screen sections are possible. Which one is started depends on the server started.

Screen Section

First, we will take a closer look at the screen section. As mentioned above, this combines a monitor with a device section and determines what resolution and color depth should be used. A screen section might resemble the example in File 3.

```
Section "Screen"
  DefaultDepth  16
  SubSection "Display"
    Depth       16
    Modes       "1152x864" "1024x768" "800x600"
    Virtual     1152x864
  EndSubSection
  SubSection "Display"
    Depth       24
    Modes       "1280x1024"
  EndSubSection
  SubSection "Display"
    Depth       32
    Modes       "640x480"
  EndSubSection
  SubSection "Display"
    Depth       8
    Modes       "1280x1024"
  EndSubSection
  Device        "Device[0]"
  Identifier    "Screen[0]"
  Monitor       "Monitor[0]"
EndSection
```

File 3: *The Screen Section of the File /etc/X11/XF86Config*

The line Identifier (here Screen[0]) gives this section a defined name with which it can be uniquely referenced in the following ServerLayout section. The lines Device and Monitor specify the graphics card and the monitor that belong to this definition. These are just links to the Device and Monitor sections with their corresponding names or "identifiers". These sections are discussed later in more detail.

Using DefaultColorDepth, select which color depth mode the server will use if this is not explicitly stated. There is a Display subsection for each color depth. Depth assigns the color depth valid for this subsection. Possible values for Depth are 8, 16, 24, and 32. Not every X server supports all these modes. For most cards, 24 and 32 are basically the same. Some take 24 for packed pixel 24bpp mode. Others choose 32 for padded pixel mode.

After the color depth, a list of resolutions is set (Modes). This list is checked by the server from left to right. For each resolution, a suitable Modeline is searched, which must correspond to one of the given clock rates or a clock rate to program the card.

The first resolution found is the Default mode. With (Ctrl) + (Alt) + (+) (on the number pad), switch to the next resolution in the list to the right. With (Ctrl) + (Alt) + (-) (on the number pad), switch to the left. This enables you to vary the resolution while X is running.

The last line of the Display subsection with Depth 16 refers to the size of the virtual screen. The maximum possible size of a virtual screen depends on the amount of memory installed on the graphics card and the desired color depth, not on the maximum resolution of the monitor. Because modern graphics cards have a large amount of video memory, you can create very large virtual desktops. However, you may no longer be able to use 3D functionality if you fill most of the video memory with a virtual desktop. If the card has 16 MB video RAM, for example, the virtual screen can be up to 4096x4096 pixels in size at 8-bit color depth. Especially for accelerated cards, however, it is not recommended to use up all your memory for the virtual screen, because this memory on the card is also used for several font and graphics caches.

Device Section

A device section describes a specific graphics card. You can have as many device entries in `XF86Config` as you like, as long as their names are differentiated, using the keyword Identifier. As a rule — if you have more than one graphics card installed — the sections are simply numbered in order the first one is called Device[0], the second one Device[1], and so on. In File 4, see the section from the Device section of a computer in which a Matrox Millennium PCI graphics card is installed.

```
Section "Device"
  BoardName      "MGA2064W"
  BusID          "0:19:0"
  Driver         "mga"
  Identifier     "Device[0]"
  VendorName     "Matrox"
  Option         "sw_cursor"
EndSection
```

File 4: *The Device Section of the File /etc/X11/XF86Config*

If you use SaX2 for configuring, the device section should look something like the above diagram. Both the Driver and BusID are dependent on the hardware installed in your computer and are detected by SaX2 automatically. The BusID defines the PCI or AGP slot in which the graphics card is installed. This matches the ID displayed by the command lspci. The X server wants details in decimal form, but lspci displays these in hexadecimal form.

Via the Driver parameter, specify the driver to use for this graphics card. If the card is a Matrox Millennium, the driver module is called mga. The X server then searches through the ModulePath defined in the Files section in the `drivers` subdirectory. In a standard installation, this is the directory `/usr/X11R6/lib/modules/drivers`. For this purpose, simply `_drv.o` is added to the name, so, in the case of the mga driver, the driver file mga_drv.o is loaded.

The behavior of the X server or of the driver can also be influenced through additional options. An example of this is the option sw_cursor, which is set in the device section. This deactivates the hardware mouse cursor and depicts the mouse cursor using software. Depending on the driver module, there are various options available, which can be found in the description files of the driver modules in the directory `/usr/X11R6/lib/X11/doc`. Generally valid options can also be found in the man page for `XF86Config` (`man XF86Config`) and the man page for `XFree86` (`man XFree86`).

Monitor Section

Monitor sections each describe, in the same way as the device sections, one monitor. The configuration file `/etc/X11/XF86Config` can contain as many Monitor sections as desired. The server layout section specifies which monitor section is relevant.

Monitor definitions should only be set by experienced users. A critical part of the monitor section is the mode lines, which set horizontal and vertical timings for the appropriate resolution. The monitor properties, especially the allowed frequencies, are stored in the monitor section.

Caution

Unless you have an in-depth knowledge of monitor and graphics card functions, nothing should be changed in the mode lines, as this could cause severe damage to your monitor.

Caution

For those who want to develop their own monitor descriptions, the documentation in `/usr/X11/lib/X11/doc` might come in handy. The section Fang

u. a. (1993) deserves a special mention. It describes, in detail, how the hardware functions and how mode lines are created.

A "manual" setting of the mode lines is hardly ever needed nowadays. If you are using a modern multisync monitor, the allowed frequencies and optimal resolutions can, as a rule, be read directly from the monitor by the X server via DDC, as described in the SaX2 configuration section. If this is not possible for some reason, you can also use one of the VESA modes included in the X server. This will function with practically all graphics card and monitor combinations.

Integrating Additional (True Type) Fonts

A standard X11R6 X server installation also includes a large number of fonts. These can be found in the directory `/usr/X11R6/lib/X11/fonts`, each divided into logically connected groups in subdirectories. Make sure only subdirectories of the X server are used that:

- are entered in the files section, Files of the file `/etc/X11/XF86Config` as FontPath
- contain a valid `fonts.dir` file
- were not closed while the X server was running using the command xset −fp or were started while the X server was running using the command xset +fp

Since version 4.0, XFree86 can use not only its own format Type1 (a Postscript format) for scalable fonts and pcf for bitmap ones, but also the ttf (True Type font) fonts. As described in *Version 4.x of XFree86* on page 92, this support is provided via loadable modules of the X server. Thus, you can also use directories containing True Type fonts together with the X server. To do this, hardly any preparation is needed.

A big advantage of most True Type fonts, apart from their very good scalability, is that these fonts almost always contain more than the normal 255 characters of the font for western Europe coded in "iso-8859-1". With these fonts, you can display Cyrillic, Greek, or eastern European languages without any problem and, with special software, even Asian languages.

This description is essentially about the use of fonts as 8-bit character sets. If you want to use characters of Asian languages (Japanese, Chinese, etc.), use special editors, which are also available in SuSE Linux.

An 8-bit character set contains 255 characters and basically consists of the US-ASCII character set, which defines only the first 128 of 255 possible characters, and expands it with further characters. One text character occupies 8-bits in the computer memory. As 127 characters are certainly not enough to record the special characters, for example, of all European languages, the various languages are combined into groups and this group is then given a short name. The relevant character set is named according to the appropriate norm as the "iso-8859-x" character set, where the x stands for a number from 1 to 15. The exact order of characters in the iso-8859-1 character set can be found in the man page for `iso-8859-1` (`man iso-8859-1`).

The more well-known codings are listed in Table 5.2: further ones can be taken from the above-mentioned manual page.

Font	**Supported regions, contains special characters**
iso-8859-1	West European languages: Spanish, German, French, Swedish, Finnish, Danish, and others
iso-8859-2	Central and Eastern Europe: Czech, Rumanian, Polish, German, and others
iso-8859-5	Cyrillic characters for Russian
iso-8859-7	Greek characters for Greek
iso-8859-9	Turkish characters
iso-8859-15	As `iso-8859-1`, but with characters for Turkish and the Euro sign.

Table 5.2: *Important Font Codings*

The user must then, depending on the language used, select the matching encoding. Especially when transferring texts between different computers, the encoding used must also be transferred. The advantage of this procedure is obvious: To receive support for regional special characters, you only need to select the correct encoding and immediately most programs will be able to portray these special characters, since almost all programs use an 8-bit value (one byte) to represent a text character. If the wrong encoding is chosen, the special characters will be wrongly depicted. With most X applications, as well as with the KDE desktop, you can usually select the coding of the character set when you are configuring the font to use. In X applications, the encoding is usually referred to as Encoding.

The disadvantage of this method is that some language combinations are impossible: You cannot, for example, easily write a German text with umlauts in which you mention Russian place names in Cyrillic.

This dilemma can only be solved using a different approach — with the use of Unicode. Unicode codes characters, unlike ASCII, with two or even more bytes, allowing considerably more characters to be represented. Only if you use Unicode can you depict Asian languages with more than 127 characters, such as Chinese, Japanese, or Korean, on the computer. The disadvantage of this method is that most existing software cannot handle these characters and that you can only read or write texts yourself with Unicode characters using special software. For more information about using Unicode fonts in Linux, see `http://www.unicode.org`. It is expected that, in the future, more and more programs will support Unicode characters. SuSE Linux offers the program yudit to enter texts in Unicode. The program yudit can be found in the package `yudit` and, after installation, via the SuSE menu, under Office →Editors.

This background information is followed by a step-by-step description of the installation of additional fonts. In this example, the installation of TrueType fonts is described. Locate the fonts you want to install in your X Window System. If you already have licensed TrueType fonts on your system, you can simply use these. Mount the partition containing the fonts and change to a font directory. In SuSE Linux, you can copy the respective fonts to the directory `/usr/X11R6/lib/X11/fonts/truetype`.

Create symbolic links to the `ttf` files, replacing ⟨*/path/to/the/fonts*⟩ with the respective path under which these fonts are available. Then execute SuSEconfig, which will generate the required entries in the file `fonts.dir`.

```
earth:/usr/X11R6/lib/X11/fonts/truetype #
     ln -s ⟨/path/to/the/fonts⟩/*.ttf .
earth:/usr/X11R6/lib/X11/fonts/truetype #
     SuSEconfig -module fonts
```

If the X server is already running, you can now make the fonts dynamically available. To do this, enter `xset fp rehash`.

Tip

The `xset` command accesses the X server via the X protocol. It must have access permissions for the X server currently running. Find more about this in the man page for `xauth` (`man xauth`).

Tip

Check if the fonts were set up correctly. To do this, use the command `xlsfonts`. If the fonts are correctly installed, the list of all installed fonts,

OpenGL Driver	Supported Hardware
Mesa software rendering (very slow)	for all cards supported by XFree86
nVidia GLX / XFree86 4.x	nVidia Chips: all except for Riva 128(ZX)
DRI / XFree86 4.x	3Dfx Voodoo Banshee 3Dfx Voodoo-3/4/5 Intel i810/i815/i830/i845 Matrox G200/G400/G450/G550 ATI Rage 128(Pro)/Radeon SiS 300/540/630
Mesa/Glide	3Dfx Voodoo Graphics 3Dfx Voodoo II

Table 5.3: Supported 3D Hardware

including the newly installed True Type Fonts, is displayed. You can also use the KDE font manager, which displays the installed fonts with an sample text. This can be started in the KDE Control Center. These newly installed fonts can then be used in all X applications.

OpenGL — 3D Configuration

In Linux, two 3D interfaces are known. One is OpenGL and the other one is GLIDE for 3Dfx Voodoo cards. Almost all modern 3D applications use the OpenGL interface, so 3D hardware acceleration can only be implemented over the OpenGL interface, even in the case of 3Dfx Voodoo cards. Only older applications still use the GLIDE interface directly. The OpenGL driver for 3DfxVoodoo cards also uses the GLIDE interface. Direct3D from Microsoft is not available in Linux.

Hardware Support

SuSE Linux includes several OpenGL drivers for 3D hardware support. Table 5.3 provides an overview.

If you are installing with YaST2 for the first time, activate 3D acceleration during installation, if YaST2 finds hardware for which it is supported. nVidia graphics chips are the only exception. For these, the "dummy" driver included must be replaced by the official nVidia driver. Download it from the nVidia web server (`http://www.nvidia.com`) and install it. Because of licensing restrictions, only the "dummy" nVidia driver package is available in the distribution. For SiS graphics chips, the graphics memory needs to be set to at least 32 MB in the BIOS setup. Additionally, the generic framebuffer support of the kernel must be deactivated.

If an update is carried out instead of a new installation or a 3Dfx add-on graphics adapter (Voodoo Graphics or Voodoo-2) needs to be set up, the procedure for configuring 3D hardware support is different. This depends on which OpenGL driver is used. Further details are described in the following section.

OpenGL Driver

Mesa Software Rendering

This OpenGL driver is used if no 3D support was configured during installation or if no 3D support is available for the particular card in Linux. Mesa software rendering should also be used if the 3D driver causes any problems (representation errors or instability). Make sure the package `mesasoft` is installed then run the script `switch2mesasoft`. If you have an nVidia card, also run the `switch2nv` script so the `nv` driver will be used for XFree86 instead of the `nvidia` driver. With the command `3Ddiag --mesasoft`, check to see if the Mesa software rendering has been properly configured.

nVidia-GLX and DRI

These OpenGL drivers can be quite easily configured using SaX2. In the case of nVidia adapters, the SuSE dummy driver package needs to be replaced with the official driver packages from the nVidia server (`http://www.nvidia.com`). The command `3Ddiag` tests whether nVidia-GLX or DRI have been configured properly.

For security reasons, only users belonging to the group `video` may access the 3D hardware. Verify that all users working locally on the machine are members of this group. Otherwise, the rather slow *Software Rendering Fallback* of the OpenGL driver will be used. Use the command `id` to check whether the current user belongs to the group `video`. If this is not the case, use YaST2 to add the user to the group.

Mesa/Glide

This OpenGL driver must be manually configured with the help of the information provided by the command `3Ddiag --mesaglide`. Details can be found in *The Diagnosis Tool 3Ddiag* on this page. If you have a Mesa/Glide driver, start OpenGL applications as `root`, because only `root` can access the hardware. To allow this, the user currently logged in must enable ⟨*DISPLAY*⟩ for `root`. This can be done with the command `xhost localhost`. The resolution used by the OpenGL application must be supported by GLIDE (resolutions supported are 640×480 and 800×600). Otherwise the very slow "Software Rendering Fallback" of the OpenGL driver will be used.

The Diagnosis Tool 3Ddiag

The diagnosis tool 3Ddiag allows verification of the 3D configuration in SuSE Linux. This is a command line tool that must be started in a terminal.

The application checks, for example, the XFree86 configuration to verify that all packages required for 3D support are installed and the proper OpenGL library is used with the GLX extension. Follow the directions in 3Ddiag if "failed" messages appear. Ideally, you will only see "done" messages on the screen.

Unless 3D support was already activated during installation, the 3D configuration of the Mesa/Glide OpenGL driver using this diagnosis tool is rather complicated. `3Ddiag -h` provides information about options for 3Ddiag.

OpenGL Test Applications

For testing OpenGL, the program `gears` and games like `tuxracer` and `armagetron` (packages have the same names) can be useful. If 3D support has been activated, it should be possible to play these smoothly on a fairly new computer. However, this is not possible or not pleasant with Mesa Software Rendering because of the resulting slide-show effect. Use the `glxinfo` command to verify that 3D is active, in which case the output will contain a line stating "direct rendering: Yes".

Troubleshooting

If the OpenGL 3D test results are negative (the games cannot be smoothly played), use 3Ddiag to make sure no errors exist in the configuration ("failed" messages). If correcting these does not help or if failed messages have not appeared, take a look at the XFree86 log files. Often, you will find the line "DRI is disabled" in the XFree86 4.x file `/var/log/XFree86.0.log`. The exact cause can only be discovered by closely examining the log file — a task requiring some experience.

In such cases, no configuration error exists, as this would have already been detected by 3Ddiag. Consequently, at this point, the only choice is to use the Mesa software rendering OpenGL driver, which does not feature 3D hardware support. Also use Mesa software rendering and forego 3D hardware acceleration if you get OpenGL representation errors or instability.

Installation Support

Apart from Mesa software rendering, all OpenGL drivers in Linux are in developmental phases and are therefore considered experimental. The drivers are included in the distribution because of the high demand for 3D hardware acceleration in Linux. Considering the experimental status of OpenGL drivers, SuSE cannot offer any installation support for configuring 3D hardware acceleration or provide any further assistance with related problems. The basic configuration of the graphical user interface X11 does not include 3D hardware acceleration configuration. If you have problems with 3D hardware support, use Mesa software rendering as already outlined in *Mesa Software Rendering* on page 112.

Additional Online Documentation

- DRI: `/usr/X11R6/lib/X11/doc/README.DRI` (package `XFree86-doc`)
- Mesa/Glide: `/usr/share/doc/packages/mesa3dfx/` (package `mesa3dfx`)
- Mesa general: `/usr/share/doc/packages/mesa/` (package `mesa`)

6

Sound in Linux

While the User Guide merely describes some basic applications for playing audio files, this chapter provides a more extensive overview of the current status of audio software in Linux as well as some supplementary information.

The Basic PCM Types of ALSA

As of version 0.9 of the "Advanced Linux Sound Architecture" (ALSA), the concept for PCM devices was substantially modified and expanded. The user can influence the way ALSA addresses the sound card by selecting a specific PCM type. The main PCM types are called `hw` and `plughw`.

To understand the difference between the two types, consider how a PCM device is opened. It must be opened with specific settings for (at least) the following parameters: sample format, sample frequency, number of channels, number of periods (previously referred to as "fragments"), and size of a period. For example, an application may attempt to play a WAV file with a sample frequency of 44.1 kHz although the sound card does not support this frequency. In this case, ALSA can automatically convert the data in the plug-in layer to a format supported by the sound card. The conversion affects the parameters sample format, sample frequency, and number of channels.

The plug-in layer is activated by selecting the PCM type `plughw`. If the PCM type `hw` is selected, ALSA will try to open the PCM devices directly with the parameters required by the application.

The complete designator for a PCM device consists of the PCM type followed by a colon, the card number, and the device number. Accordingly, the designator could appear as follows:

```
earth:~ # plughw:0,0
```

Mixer Parameters of Soundblaster Live! and Audigy

Apart from the parameters of the AC97 standard as described in the manual, there are many additional options for Soundblaster Live! and Audigy cards. The controls 'AC97', 'Wave', and 'Music' are used for playback. 'AC97' can be used to adjust the level of the 'AC97' mix. This mix also receives input from the 'line', 'mic', and 'CD' signals. 'Wave' adjusts the level of the PCM channels. 'Music' controls the volume of the internal wavetable synthesis of MIDI data.

The 'AC97 Capture' control is used to control the level of the 'AC97' recording sources. Furthermore, 'Wave' and 'Music' can also be selected as recording source. This internal loopback capture can be activated in the 'AC97' standard by selecting the 'Mix' control as recording source.

The Mixer for the Sound Chip Envy24

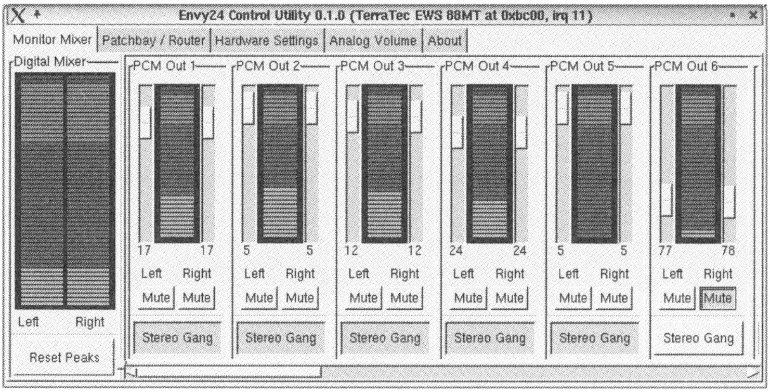

Figure 6.1: Monitor and Digital Mixer in envy24control

envy24control is a mixer application for sound cards using the Envy24 (ice1712) chip. Start this mixer either with 'SuSE' → 'Multimedia' → 'Sound' or from the command line with `envy24control &`.

The following paragraphs describe the most important features of envy24control. The flexibility of the Envy24 results in varying functionalities in different sound cards. The latest details about this sound chip are available in `/usr/share/doc/packages/alsa/alsa-tools/envy24control`.

Monitor and Patchbay in envy24control

The signal levels are displayed in the 'Monitor Mixer' of envy24control. The signals can be mixed digitally within the sound card. The signals with the label 'PCM Out' are generated by applications that send PCM data to the sound card. The signals of the analog inputs are shown under 'H/W In'. The 'S/PDIF' input is displayed to the right. The input and output levels of the analog channels must be set under 'Analog Volume'.

Use the 'Monitor Mixer' sliders for digital mixing. The respective levels are displayed in the 'Digital Mixer'. The output routing of this mix is defined in the 'Patchbay'. For each output channel, the 'Patchbay' contains a row of radio buttons enabling the selection of the desired channel source.

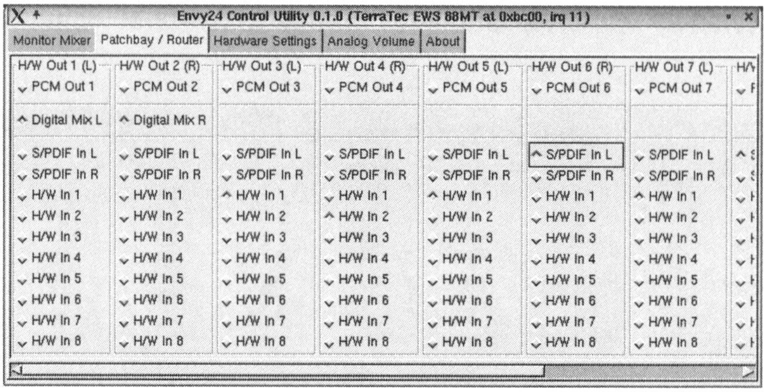

Figure 6.2: The Patchbay

Analog Inputs and Outputs

The amplification for the analog-to-digital and digital-to-analog converters is adjusted under 'Analog Volume'. The 'DAC' sliders are used for the output channels and 'ADC' sliders are used for the input channels. Use the radio buttons to switch the levels between +4 dBu and -10 dBV. The first setting is intended for audio professionals. The -10 dBV setting is used for private purposes.

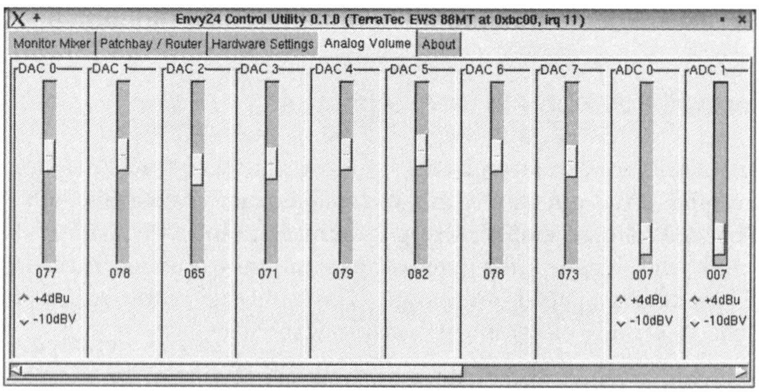

Figure 6.3: The Mixer for Analog Inputs and Outputs

Configuration of the S/PDIF Channels

The S/PDIF channel settings are made under 'Hardware Settings'. The 'Envy24' reacts to volume changes with a delay that can be configured with the 'Volume Change' parameter.

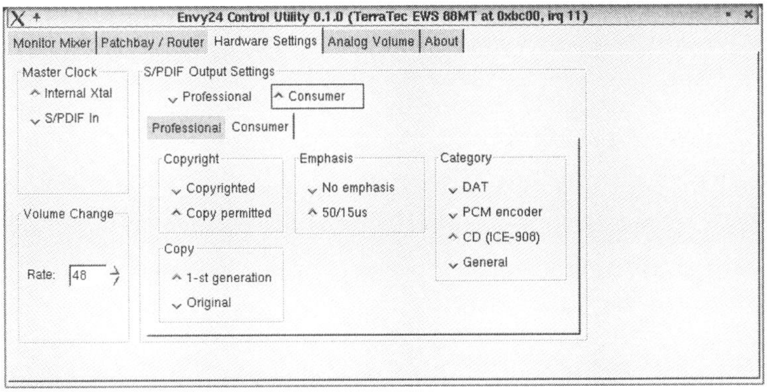

Figure 6.4: Configuring the S/PDIF Parameters with envy24control

Buffering and Latencies

This section explains how uninterrupted audio playback can be ensured. This problem is by no means limited to Linux, but is inherent in all multitasking operating systems. In a multitasking operating system, several processes usually run concurrently. As the processor can only handle one process at a time, each process is assigned a certain amount of time by the operating system's scheduler. The switching action between processes normally happens so quickly that the user does not notice it.

However, during the audio playback even brief interruptions would be noticeable in the form of clicks. Therefore, audio programs use a buffer for the playback, enabling the audio data in the buffer to be emitted continuously by the sound card even when the audio program is interrupted by the scheduler. Accordingly, the playback will be click-free if the buffer is large enough to bridge the longest possible interruption.

The buffer size determines the reaction time (latency) of the program. Therefore, the buffer size is kept as small as possible especially for interactive applications such as real-time synthesizers and DJ mixer consoles. Basically, the length of the interruptions depends on the system load and the priority of the process. Consequently, the size of the buffer required for click-free playback can be reduced by increasing the priority of the audio program. For this reason, many audio programs attempt to switch their processes to real-time priority. However, this is only possible for applications running with `root` privileges.

It is always risky to run a program in `root` mode, as the program is permitted to do anything. If the computer is connected to the Internet, the security risk would be unacceptable. Security bugs in the program could be exploited for the purpose of gaining access to the system.

Caution

The following commands should *never* be executed on machines that can be accessed from the Internet or if a system crash or data loss would have serious consequences.

Caution

The `sudo` mechanism should be used for running a program in `root` mode. We will demonstrate this mechanism by means of the timidity++ application. To enable all users on your system to execute timidity++ with `root` privileges, modify the file `/etc/sudoers`. See the man page for `sudo` (`man sudo`) and the man page for `sudoers` (`man sudoers`) for information on the procedure.

If you are not familiar with the vi editor, select a different editor such as joe:

```
earth:~ #  export EDITOR=joe
```

Then execute `visudo` as `root` and append the following line at the end of the file `/etc/sudoers`:

```
ALL     ALL=(ALL) /usr/bin/timidity
```

Now all users in the system are permitted to execute

```
earth:~ #  sudo timidity
```

to start timidity in `root` mode. The password of the respective user will be queried in case more than five minutes passed since the last `sudo` command.

The JACK Audio Connection Kit

package `jack, qjackconnect`

By means of the JACK Audio Connection Kit, applications can exchange audio data with each other and with the sound card, if they have a JACK interface. Because JACK support has become a common standard, many applications provide the needed interface.

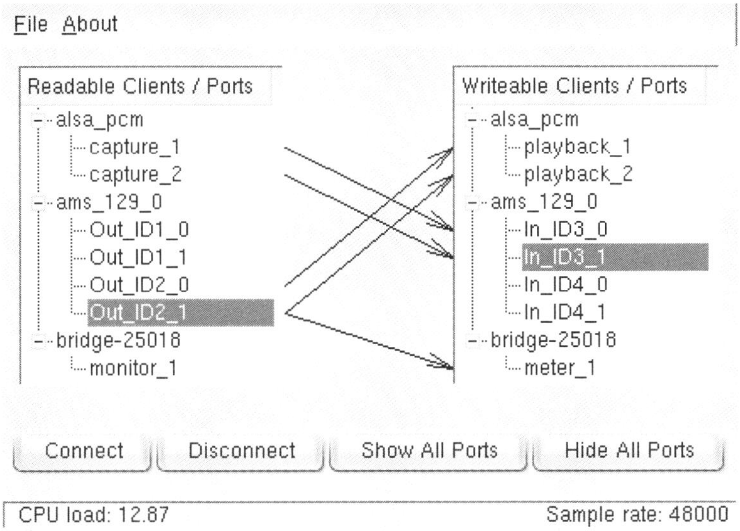

Figure 6.5: QJackConnect *— a Patchbay for* Jack

To use JACK, first start the "engine" with `jackd -d alsa -d hw:0`. JACK was designed to achieve a low latency. Therefore, the engine should run with real-time priority. For more information, read the file `/usr/share/doc/packages/README.SuSE`.

The patchbay QJackConnect helps keep track of the JACK clients running in your system. Following the program launch with `qjackconnect`, the clients with readable ports are listed on the left side and the clients with writeable ports are listed on the right side. If no JACK clients were started, the lists initially only display the inputs and outputs of the sound card. The lists are updated automatically as the port configuration changes. The ports are displayed in a tree view under the client. Connect individual ports by selecting them from the lists and clicking 'Connect'. You can also connect multiple ports simultaneously by selecting clients.

Recording with Audacity

package `audacity`

With Audacity, record and edit audio files. When you start the program for the first time, the first step is the selection of a language. The language setting can also be changed under 'File' → 'Preferences' → 'Interface'. The language change will be effective the next time you start the program.

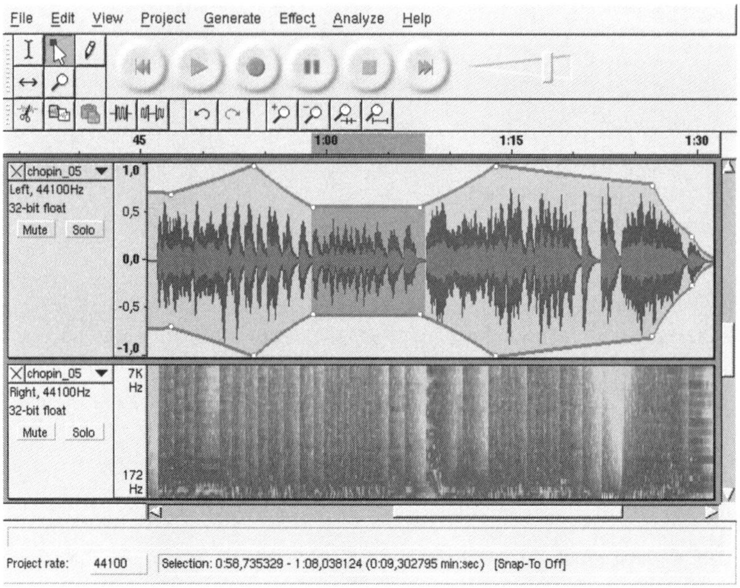

Figure 6.6: Audacity Offers a Spectral View of Audio Data

Recording WAV Files and Importing Files

Click the red recording button to generate an empty stereo track and start the recording. To change the standard parameters, specify the settings under 'File' → 'Preferences'. The items 'Audio I/O' and 'Quality' are important for the recording. If tracks already exist, pressing the recording button creates new tracks. These tracks cannot be seen in the standardly sized program window.

To import audio files, select 'Project' → 'Import Audio'. The program supports the WAV format as well as the compressed MP3 and Ogg Vorbis formats. See *Compressing Audio Data* on page 125 for more information on these formats.

Editing Audio Files

With the 'AudioTrack' menu that can be opened to the left at the beginning of each track, select various views. 'Waveform dB' always sets the data to the maximum amplitude of the track, so is not suitable for checking the signal amplitude.

Depending on the application, various view formats for segment selections are offered under 'Set Selection Format'. With 'Set Snap-To Mode', the segment boundaries are adapted automatically to the selected view format. For example, if you select 'PAL frames' as view format and activate 'Snap-To', the segment boundaries will always be selected in multiples of frames.

The many editing tools are all equipped with tool tips. 'Undo History', which can be actuated with 'View' → 'History', is a useful feature for viewing recent processing steps and undoing them by clicking the respective item in the list. Be cautious when using the 'Discard' button, which deletes processing steps from the list. Subsequently, these steps can no longer be undone.

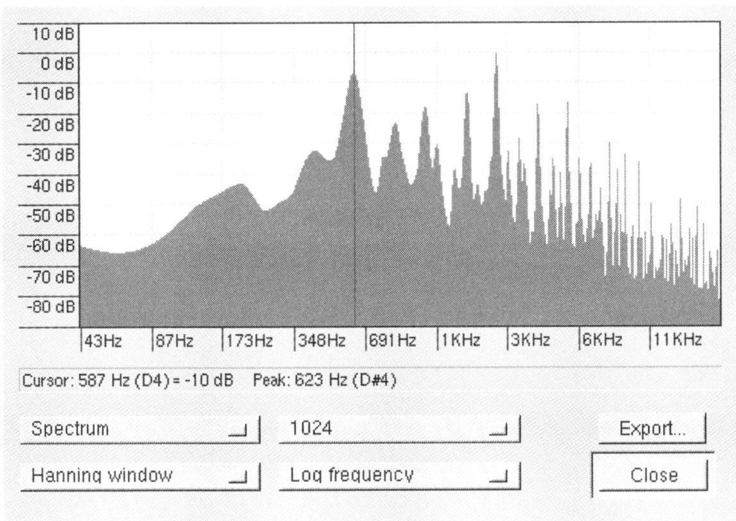

Figure 6.7: *The Spectrum View in Audacity*

The integrated spectrum analysis assists in tracking down any noises. With 'View' → 'Plot Spectrum', view the spectrum of the selected area. You can also select a logarithmic frequency scale in octaves with 'Log frequency'. If you move the mouse pointer within the spectrum, the frequencies of the peaks are automatically be displayed together with the respective notes.

Unwanted frequencies are best removed with the 'FFT Filter' in the 'Effect' menu. In connection with the filtering process, it may be necessary to readjust the signal amplitude with 'Amplify'. Additionally, 'Amplify' can be used to check the amplitude. By default, the 'New Peak Amplitude' is set to 0.0 dB. This value represents the highest possible amplitude in the selected audio format. 'Amplification' shows the value needed to amplify the selected segment to this peak amplitude. A negative value indicates overamplification.

Saving and Export

To save the entire project, select 'File' → 'Save Project' or 'Save Project As'. This generates an XML file with the ending `.aup`, which describes the project. The actual audio data is saved in a directory named for the project with the addition `_data`.

The entire project or the currently selected segment can also be exported as stereo WAV file. Refer to *Compressing Audio Data* on the next page if you want to export in MP3 format.

Direct Recording and Playback of WAV Files

package `kalsatools`

`arecord` and `aplay` are part of the ALSA package and offer a simple and flexible interface for the PCM devices. `arecord` and `aplay` can be used to record and play audio data in formats such as WAV. The command

```
earth:~ #  arecord -d 10 -f cd -t wav mysong.wav
```

records a WAV file of ten seconds in CD quality (16 bit, 44.1 kHz). Display a complete list of options of `arecord` and `aplay` with the command-line option `--help`.

qaRecord is a simple recording program with a graphical user interface and level display. This program uses an internal buffer of about 1 MB (configurable with `--buffersize`). Therefore, it should be able to guarantee uninterrupted recordings even on slow hardware, especially if it is started with real-time priority (see *Buffering and Latencies* on page 119). During the recording process, the currently used buffer size is displayed in the status line under 'Buffer'. The maximum buffer size required so far for this recording is displayed under 'Peak'.

Compressing Audio Data

package vorbis-tools

Uncompressed audio data in CD quality consumes almost ten megabytes per minute. The MP3 procedure was developed by the Fraunhofer IIS for the purpose of drastically compressing these quantities. Unfortunately, this procedure is patented. Therefore, companies that distribute MP3 encoders must pay license fees. The powerful MP3 encoder Lame was developed for Linux. Although the source code of Lame is under the GPL, SuSE is not allowed to include this encoder in the distribution. For more information on the legal situation, refer to the project web page at http://lame.sourceforge.net. The use of Lame is exclusively permitted for research purposes in some countries, including Germany and the USA.

Ogg Vorbis is a free audio compression format, which is now supported by the majority of audio players. The project web page is http://www.xiph.org/ogg/vorbis. The vorbis-tools package includes an encoder and a simple player. The encoder is started from the command line with oggenc. The only parameter needed is the specification of the WAV file to compress. The option -h displays an overview of the other parameters. The latest version of the Ogg encoder even supports encoding with variable bit rate. In this way, an even higher degree of compression can be achieved without sacrificing the quality. Instead of the bit rate, you can now specify the desired quality with the parameter -q. The parameter -b determines the average bit rate. -m and -M can be used to specify the minimum and maximum bit rate, respectively.

ogg123 is a command-line Ogg player. The program requires the specification of a playback device. Start the program with a command like `ogg123 -d alsa09 mysong.ogg`.

ALSA and MIDI

package pmidi, aseqview, vkeybd
package awesfx, snd_sf2, kalsatools

As well as being able to play PCM data, many sound cards also feature MIDI functionality. The ALSA MIDI sequencer implements a powerful architecture for routing MIDI data.

Many sound cards have an external MIDI port for connecting MIDI devices, such as synthesizers, keyboards, and sound modules. If the MIDI port of the card is supported by ALSA, you can use a sequencer application (e.g., jazz) to record and play MIDI files by way of this port. An overview of the MIDI devices provided by your card is available in the KDE Control Center under 'Sound' → 'Midi'. Here, also determine which of these devices to use for playing MIDI files.

On the command line, list the available MIDI devices together with their internal ALSA port numbers with the command `pmidi -l`. For a "Soundblaster Live!" card, the list would appear as follows:

```
Port     Client name                            Port name
 72:0     External MIDI 0                        MIDI 0-0
 73:0     Emu10k1 WaveTable                      Emu10k1 Port 0
 73:1     Emu10k1 WaveTable                      Emu10k1 Port 1
 73:2     Emu10k1 WaveTable                      Emu10k1 Port 2
 73:3     Emu10k1 WaveTable                      Emu10k1 Port 3
```

***File 5:** Soundblaster Live! MIDI Devices*

The first column lists the internal port numbers by which the device is addressed by the ALSA driver. The other columns show the designation and port name of the device. As well as the external MIDI port, several WaveTable ports are listed. Use a command like `pmidi -p 73:0 mysong.mid` to play a MIDI file over one of the listed ports.

Note

Interrupting a MIDI player during playback can leave a continuous sound playing. If this happens, run the `all_notes_off` script or restart ALSA with `rcalsasound restart` as `root`.

Note

Many sound cards (e.g., Soundblaster AWE and Live!) have an internal WaveTable synthesizer that converts MIDI events into audible sounds. These MIDI events can be sent to the WaveTable synthesizer by an external MIDI keyboard or by a program (e.g., MIDI player or sequencer). For Soundblaster AWE and Live! cards, the WaveTable synthesizer must be initialized with a sound font before any sound can be heard.

Loading Sound Fonts (SB Live! and AWE)

The package awesfx contains the sfxload command for loading sound fonts in Soundblaster AWE and Live! cards. Suitable sound font files are available on the driver CD of your sound card. The start-up script of ALSA can automatically load the sound fonts required for the WaveTable synthesis, provided the respective files were installed from the Creative driver CD using YaST2. Currently, the script only works for one sound card. However, ALSA can easily manage up to eight sound cards. In this case, the sound fonts can be loaded with a command like

```
earth:~ #  sfxload -D ⟨n⟩ /usr/share/sfbank/creative/8MBGMSFX.SF2
```

⟨*n*⟩ stands for the number of the sound card (0, 1, etc.). ⟨*n*⟩ does not necessarily have to be to the number under which the sound card was configured, but depends on the sequence according to which the individual sound drivers were loaded. If you do not have your driver CD handy, you can also load one of the sound fonts installed in /usr/share/sounds/sf2.

The sound font Vintage_Dreams_Waves_v2.sf2 by Ian Wilson contains 128 analog synthesizer sounds and 8 drum sets. It is suitable for SB AWE and for SB Live! cards. The ROM sound font gu11-rom.sf2 by Samuel Collins is *only* suitable for SB AWE cards. It provides an extended general MIDI bank for these cards. Review the copyright files and the documentation in /usr/share/doc/packages/snd_sf2. Additional sound fonts can be downloaded from URLs such as http://www.hammersound.net.

vkeybd — Virtual MIDI Keyboard

If you do not have an external MIDI keyboard connected to your sound card, you can use the virtual keyboard vkeybd. The internal port numbers listed with pmidi -l as described above are especially of importance here. To start the program, enter

```
earth:~ #  vkeybd --addr 73:0 &
```

The port address on your system might be different. Specify the first WaveTable port in the list. If an external sound generator is connected, specify the port number of the external MIDI port. vkeybd can be used with a number of additional options. For example, enter

```
earth:~ #  vkeybd --addr 73:0 --octave 5 &
```

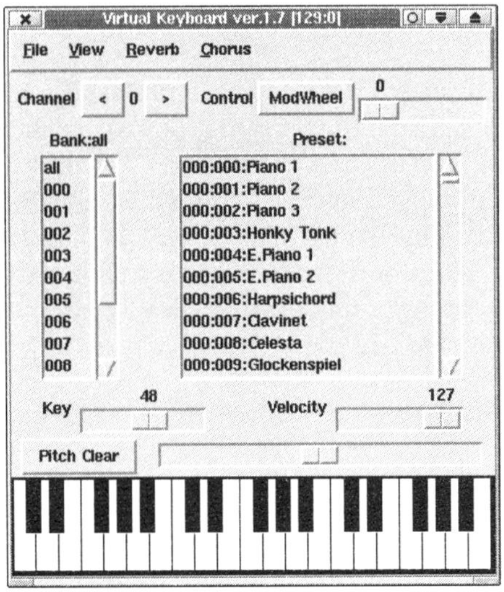

Figure 6.8: vkeybd – a Complete Virtual MIDI Keyboard

to increase the number of displayed octaves to 5. The available command-line options can be viewed with `vkeybd --help` or in the the man page for `vkeybd` (`man vkeybd`).

The instrument designations in the preset list can be configured by specifying a preset file with the option `--preset`. The instrument designations of a sound font file can be extracted with the command `sftovkb`:

```
earth:~ #  cd /usr/share/sounds/sf2

earth:/usr/share/sounds/sf2 #  sftovkb
    Vintage_Dreams_Waves_v2.sf2 >~/vintage.vkb
```

This command saves the name in the file `vintage.vkb` in your home directory. The user interface of vkeybd can be configured by means of the 'view' menu.

The mapping of the keys to the sent MIDI notes is saved in the file `~/.vkeybdrc`. Additional specifications can be made in this file. To perform your own modifications, retrieve the designations of keyboard events using the program xev.

Establishing Connections Between MIDI Ports

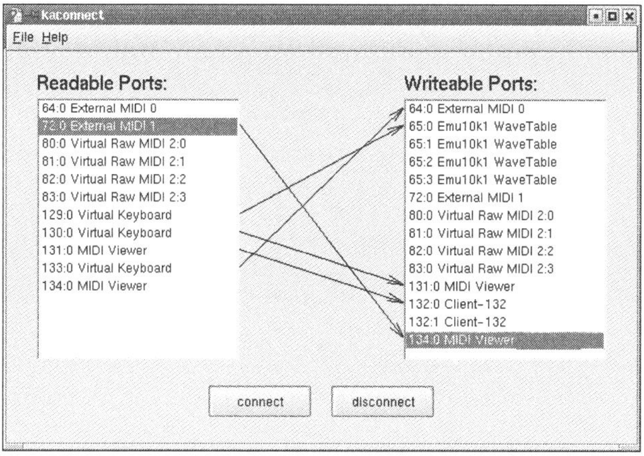

Figure 6.9: Connecting MIDI Ports and Displaying the Status with kaconnect

ALSA provides a sophisticated infrastructure for the connection of several MIDI ports. Sound cards and MIDI programs (provided these support the ALSA sequencer structure) have one or several MIDI ports for communicating with each other. These ports can be connected with the KDE program kaconnect or with the command `aconnect`. On start-up, kaconnect shows the readable and writable MIDI ports available on your system and their connection status.

To demonstrate the procedure, start two MIDI programs with the commands `vkeybd` and `aseqview`.For the connection between MIDI ports, specify the port address of the program after the program name. For example, the first program is assigned the port number `128:0` and the second program `129:0`. The ports of the programs are also displayed by kaconnect.

As vkeybd was started without the parameter `--addr`, the connection between the program port and the WaveTable port (or the external MIDI port) can now be established manually. To do this, select the respective ports and click 'connect'.

To use the command-line tool `aconnect`, enter something like `aconnect 128:0 73:0`.This establishes a unidirectional connection between the sender port `128:0` and the receiver port `73:0`.

You can now establish a connection between the MIDI port of the keyboard and the MIDI port of the ALSA sequencer viewer. If you modify keyboard settings, such as the panning or the pitch wheel (which must first be activated under 'View'), these changes will promptly be reflected in aseqview.

View a list of the ports available for receiving and sending together with their connection status with `aconnect -il` or `aconnect -ol`. Connections established with `aconnect` can be terminated with the option `-d`, as in `aconnect -d 128:0 129:0`. To terminate all connections, use `aconnect -x`. An overview of further command-line options of `aconnect` can be viewed in the man page for `aconnect` (`man aconnect`).

Tip

`aseqnet` allows you to establish MIDI connections with remote network hosts.

Tip

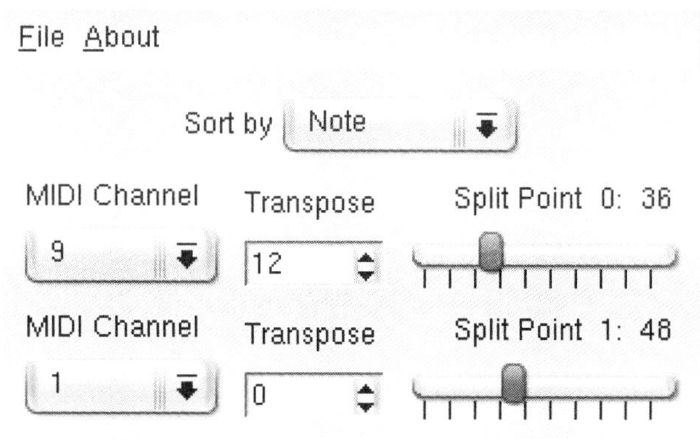

Figure 6.10: *Setting up Split Zones with QMidiRoute*

The program QMidiRoute enables flexible MIDI routing. It sorts the MIDI events received on the writeable MIDI port according to pitch, velocity, or channel and immediately sends them to the readable ports. Using the parameters 'Channel' and 'Transpose', change the channel and the pitch of the lower split zone. For example, if you set channel 9 here, simultaneously play the drums in the lower split zone and another instrument in the upper split zone.

kmid — The KDE MIDI Player

package `kdemultimedia`

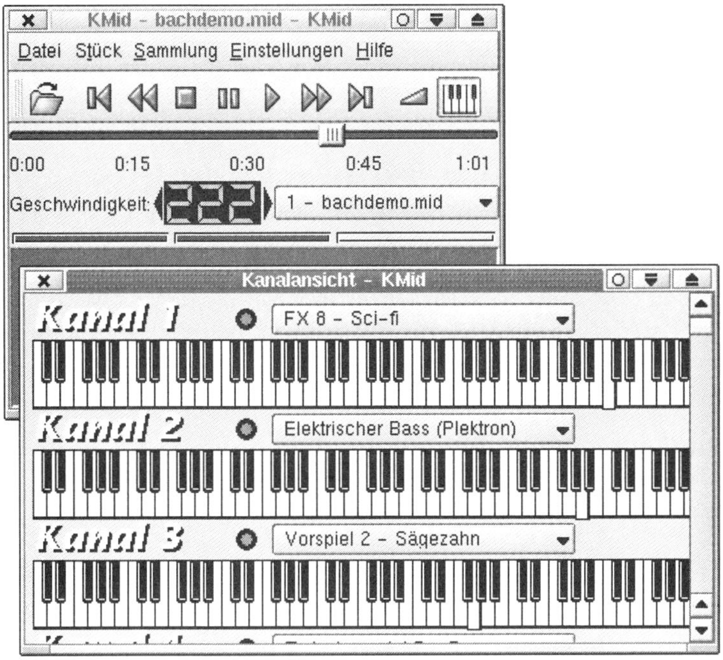

Figure 6.11: Main Window and Channel View of kmid

In the KDE start menu, go to 'Multimedia' → 'Midi/Karaoke Player'. A few demo files for kmid are located in the `/opt/kde2/share/apps/kmid` directory in `.kar` format. These files also contain the lyrics, which are scrolled and highlighted in sync with the playback.

URLs such as `http://www.midi.net` offer an abundance of MIDI files for download. An extensive MIDI archive of classical music is available at `http://www.classicalarchives.com`.

The detailed online help of kmid can be accessed with (F1). In this program, the MIDI ports must be selected correctly in 'Settings' → 'MIDI Settings'.

The channel view presented when you click the keyboard button in the tool bar is especially noteworthy. You may have to enlarge the window to the right to be able to see this item. The channel view — the window size of which might also have to be adjusted — graphically displays the MIDI events on several keyboards. Additionally, the instruments can be changed here.

If kmid is started by clicking on a MIDI file in the KDE file manager

Konqueror, the MIDI settings specified in the KDE Control Center will apply. The configuration specified in the program itself only applies if you start the program separately.

Playing MIDI Files Without a WaveTable Card

package `iiwusynth, timidity`

Not all sound cards have a WaveTable synthesizer for playing MIDI files according to the loaded sound fount (or instrument patch). If this is the case, you can use the software WaveTable synthesizers iiwusynth and timidity++.

The Sound Font Synthesizer iiwusynth

After the program is started with a command like

```
earth:tux #  iiwusynth -a alsa -m alsa_seq gm.sf2
```

iiwusynth will be listed among the writeable MIDI ports and can be used as sound source. In this example, `gm.sf2` is a file in the SoundFont format. Suitable files are available on the Internet. iiwusynth has numerous command-line options that can be displayed with `iiwusynth -h`.

Configuring timidity++

timidity++ is configured by means of the configuration file `/usr/share/timidity/timidity.cfg`. The documentation for the configuration can be viewed with `man timidity.cfg`. Also read the documentation in `/usr/share/doc/packages/timidity`.

Suitable instrument patches are available at `http://www.stardate.bc.ca/eawpatches/html/default.htm`. From this URL you can download the file `eawpats12_full.rar`. The size of this file is 22 MB, but the download is worthwile, as it equips you with a full set of GM/GS/XG instruments. To use the patches with timidity++, proceed as follows. First, switch to user `root`. Then create the directory `/usr/share/timidity/eawpats`, copy `eawpats12_full.rar` there, and change to that directory. The command `unrar x eawpats12_full.rar` decompresses the archive.

Now the file `timidity.cfg` in the directory `/usr/share/timidity/` must be modified to contain only the following two lines:

```
dir /usr/share/timidity/eawpats
source timidity.cfg
```

File 6: timidity.cfg

Aeawpats12_full.rar contains another timidity.cfg, which will show up in the eawpats directory following the decompression. This file is included by means of the source command. Only four lines in this file are of importance:

```
source gravis.cfg
source gsdrums.cfg
source gssfx.cfg
source xgmap2.cfg
```

All other lines can be deleted. The final step is the adjustment of the file permissions. To do this, enter the command chmod -R a+r /usr/share/timidity/eawpats .

If you want to use sound fonts instead of the Gravis instrument patches, modify the file /usr/share/timidity/timidity.cfg. For example, to use the Vintage Dreams sound font with timidity++, you will only need one timidity.cfg consisting of a single line:

```
soundfont /usr/share/sounds/sf2/Vintage_Dreams_Waves_v2.sf2
```

More information on this subject is available in /usr/share/doc/packages/timidity/C/README.sf.

Starting timidity++ with a Graphical Interface

There are few programs that offer as many program interfaces as timidity++. For an overview, enter man timidity. The "Athena Widget Interface" is a mature interface that is started with /usr/bin/timidity -iatv &.

Note

Do not start timidity from the directory /usr/share/timidity.

Note

A recording of the first movement of the first symphony of Brahms, which can be downloaded from http://www.classicalarchives.com/brahms.html, is an impressive example of the rich orchestral sound capacity of MIDI files.

The ALSA Server Mode of timidity++

Enter the following command to start timdity++ in ALSA server mode:

```
earth:~ #  /usr/bin/timidity -iA -B2,8 -Os &
```

A message such as

```
Opening sequencer port: 128:0 128:1
```

will be issued, displaying the MIDI port by which the synthesizer can be addressed (e.g., with `vkeybd --addr 128:0`). To terminate timidity++, enter `killall timidity` to kill all timidity processes.

AlsaModularSynth — Synthesizer and Effect Processor

package `alsamodular`

AlsaModularSynth is a digital copy of an analog modular synthesizer. The program has a JACK interface and can load all kinds of LADSPA effect plug-ins. Therefore, it can also be used as a versatile effect processor.

Enter `ams` to start AlsaModularSynth from the command line. The parameter `-j` activates the JACK mode, provided the JACK engine `jackd` is running (see *The JACK Audio Connection Kit* on page 120). The required port connections can be established with QJackConnect. In the JACK mode, PCM modules are automatically converted to JACK modules (and vice versa). Separate ports are generated for each JACK module. AlsaModularSynth only appears in the list of QJackConnect if at least one JACK module exists.

The directory `/usr/share/doc/packages/alsamodular` contains numerous example patches that demonstrate the various possibilities. Detailed documentation is available under `html` in this directory.

Randomly Playing Patches

A quick overview of some of the sound possibilities is provided by the patches that randomly play sounds without a MIDI keyboard or audio input. `example_ams_demo.ams` generates impressive random music. In `example_ams_demo_scope_spectrum.ams`, this music can even be visualized with the scope and spectrum viewer modules. Open the view of these

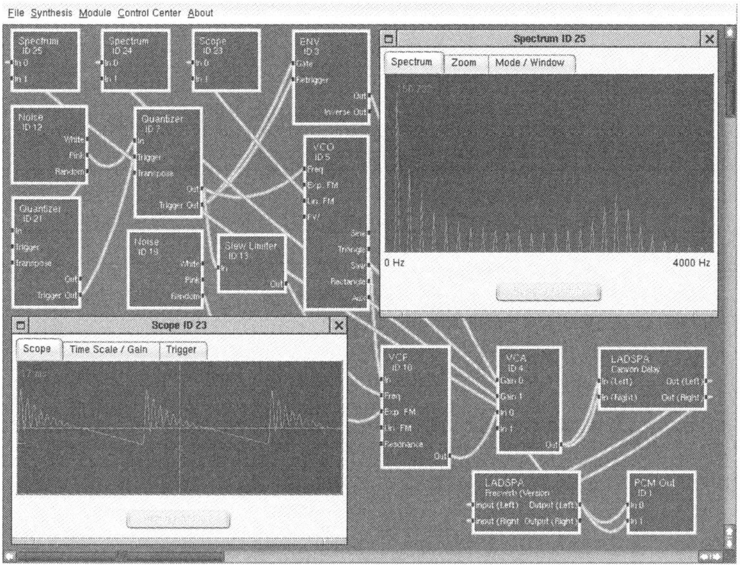

Figure 6.12: AlsaModularSynth with Scope and Spectrum Viewer

modules with the right mouse button. See how the character of the music changes when you change the quantization in the quantizer module (ID 7) from the pentatonic scale to a value such as 1/6 (whole tone scale).

One of the most legendary (and expensive) analog synthesizer modules is the frequency shifter invented by H. Bode and built by R. A. Moog. This module was recently implemented as LADSPA plug-in by S. W. Harris and is therefore available for AlsaModularSynth. In `example_ams_demo_bode.ams`, the effect is applied to the random music. `example_bode.ams` demonstrates the frequency shifter in the spectrum viewer module. One example by the author of the plug-in is `example_bode_wail.ams`. Here, you can realize a feedback by way of the JACK in module in the JACK mode.

`example_wind.ams` shows that even the sound of wind can be generated with AlsaModularSynth. There are also other example patches like `example_random_*` and `sequence0*`

AlsaModularSynth as Effect Processor

Especially in the JACK mode, AlsaModularSynth can be used as a versatile effect processor. One example for this is `example_capture.ams`. If you con-

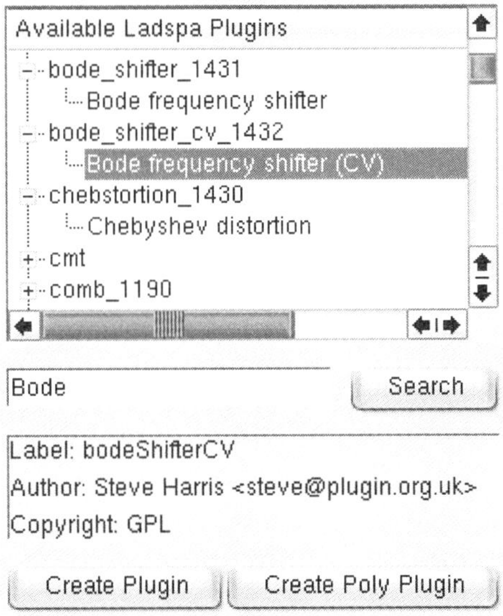

***Figure 6.13:** The Ladspa Browser*

nect an external sound source to your sound card and use alsamixer to specify the correct settings for the capture, the example will work even without JACK. With the 'Ladspa Browser', which is started with 'Module' → 'Show Ladspa Browser', generate modules for LADSPA effects. Plug-ins should always be generated with 'Create Plugin' unless you use AlsaModularSynth as a polyphonic synthesizer. 'Create Poly Plugin' generates a separate plug-in instance for each part.

Synthesizer Patches

After having used the MIDI patchbay kaconnect to connect AlsaModularSynth with a master keyboard (vkeybd or an external keyboard), you can use the program as a synthesizer. If polyphony was not explicitly activated with the parameter `--poly`, AlsaModularSynth is monophonic, just like its classical model. `example_basic.ams` contains the simplest synthesizer patch. In `example_basic_vcf.ams`, the sound is modified by a filter. A filter portamento and resonance were added in `example_basic_vcf_reverb.ams`. In most patches, the pitch bend and modulation wheel are determined by module parameters. To prevent parameter leaps, the movements of these MIDI controllers will only be effective if the current parameter value was accepted once. Just like in many analog synthesizers, the envelope modules are "single triggered" — they are not restarted for legato playback. This enables some interesting phrases.

In `example_full_midi.ams`, the first sixteen MIDI controller events are linked to module parameters. If you do not have a device that can send these events, you can use the software MIDI controller box QMidiControl which is started with `qmidicontrol`. When experimenting with this program, open the 'Control Center' with 'Control Center' → 'Show Control Center'. If the check box 'Follow Midi' is activated here, the most recently moved MIDI controller and the first parameter that was bound to it will automatically be displayed.

Keeping Track with the Control Center

The main purpose of the 'Control Center' is to bind module parameters to MIDI controllers. However, extended parameter control settings, such as the range of sliders, can also be specified here.

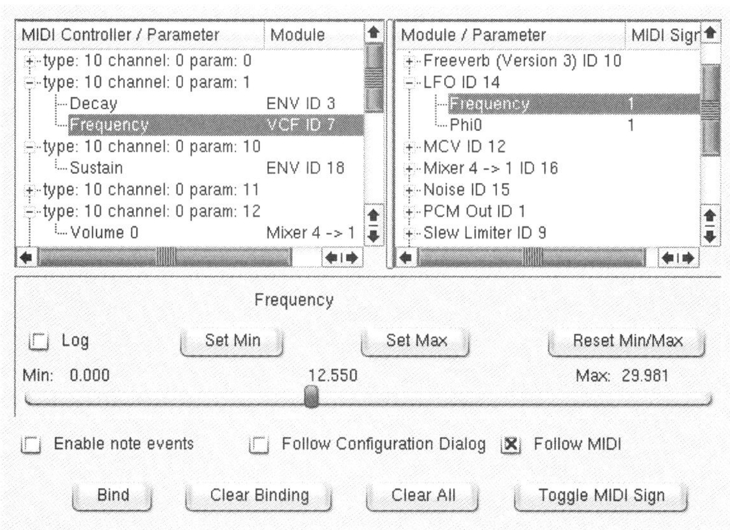

Figure 6.14: MIDI Controllers and Module Parameters in the Control Center

The list to the left displays the MIDI controllers used in a patch. This tree view shows the parameters associated with a controller under the respective controller. As soon as a controller event that does not exist in the list is received via MIDI, it is added to the list.

The list to the right shows the modules and their parameters. When you select a parameter here, the respective control appears, enabling you to modify the parameter and range limits.

To create a MIDI binding, select a controller in the list to the left and a parameter in the list to the right then click 'Bind'. To clear a MIDI binding, simply select the respective parameter in the list to the left under the controller and click 'Clear Binding'. 'Clear All' clears the entire list of MIDI controllers and bindings. With 'Toggle MIDI Sign', you can determine whether a parameter should increase or decrease with rising controller values.

The MIDI Out Module

You might have noticed the two readable ports of AlsaModularSynth in the list to the left in kaconnect. The output of the MIDI events generated by a MIDI Out module is realized by way of these ports. If several MIDI Out modules are used simultaneously, the MIDI events are summed up accordingly. As both notation and controller events can be sent, the module can also be used to control all kinds of parameters via control voltage. To be able to do this, the readable MIDI ports must be connected with the writeable MIDI port. The example `example_midiout_controller.ams` shows the change in an envelope with autogenerated controller events. You can easily follow the movement of the envelope if you open the configuration dialog of the ENV module (ID 5) with the right mouse button. The option 'Follow MIDI' in the 'Control Center' should be deactivated while this patch is running.

If you connect the readable MIDI ports of AlsaModularSynth with a MIDI sound generator, `example_midiout_note.ams` sounds scales controlled by an LFO. `example_midiout_note_velocity.ams` shows that the velocity data can also be autogenerated. `example_midiout_random.ams` generates random music drums.

Writing WAV Files with the WAV Out Module

Using the WAV Out module, you can directly record the signals generated or processed by AlsaModularSynth as a WAV file. In the configuration dialog of the module, select 'New File' to open a file browser. If the file displayed under 'File' is successfully generated, the buttons under 'Record' will be activated and can be used.

NoteEdit and MIDI Sequencers

package `noteedit, jazz, muse, rosegarden` NoteEdit is the most comprehensive Linux software for editing scores with a graphical interface. This program offers the entire range of music symbols for writing scores. With noteedit, you can also play and record MIDI files. The scores can be exported in several formats (including MusixTeX and LilyPond).

Start the program with `noteedit`. `/usr/share/doc/packages/noteedit/examples` contains a number of examples that can be opened with 'File' → 'Open'. To import a MIDI file, go to 'TSE3' → 'TSE3 Midi In'. Select 'TSE3–>Score' to load it to the editor. In 'Filter Dialog', you can specify several settings for the conversion (e.g., quantization).

Under 'Midi' → 'Devices', you can select one of the ALSA MIDI devices configured in your system. The device will subsequently be used for playback and recording. Under 'Staff' → 'Staff Properties', select the instrument, the MIDI channel, and many parameters such as the stereo panorama.

Notes can be entered with the help of the mouse. First, choose the duration of the note and the accidental. Press the middle mouse button to insert a note and the right mouse button to insert a rest. In the 'Insert' menu, find objects such as clefs, meters, and accidentals. These objects can be inserted with the middle mouse button.

Select 'Edit' → 'General properties' → 'allow insertion from keyboard' to configure the keyboard for inserting notes. The pitch is determined with the cursor key and the duration of the notes can be determined with the number pad (if (Num) is active). Press (Enter) to insert a note and (Space) to insert a rest.

More information on noteedit is available in the directory `/usr/share/doc/packages/noteedit`.

In Linux, there are several MIDI sequencers, some of which are very mature. For example, Jazz is a proven, stable program. The development of Rosegarden, the "classic" among sequencer and notation editors for Linux, was resumed recently. Therefore, this is also an interesting program. Furthermore, MusE is a very active project. Meanwhile, the program has become very useful as a sequencer.

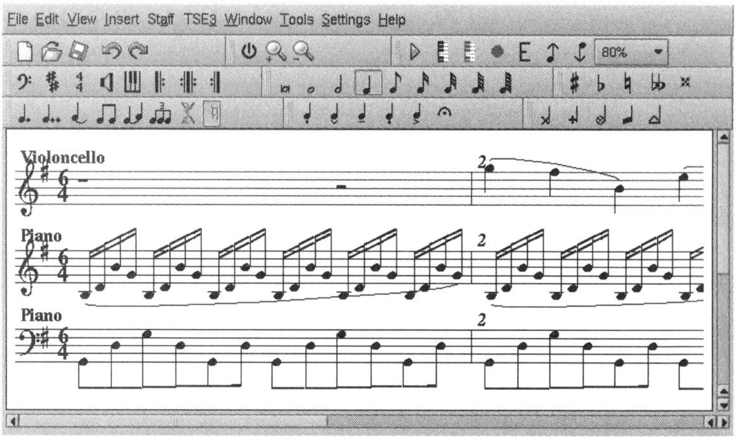

Figure 6.15: *The Composition Editor* noteedit

Printer Operation

This chapter provides some background information about the operation of printers. Numerous examples show how the different parts of the printing system interact. This chapter should help in finding suitable solutions for possible problems and in avoiding unsuitable solution attempts.

Printing Basics

On a Linux system, printers are managed via *print queues*. Before any data is printed, it is sent to the print queue for temporary storage. From there, the print spooler sends the data to the printer.

However, this data is predominantly not available in a form that can be processed by the printer. A graphical image, for example, first needs to be converted into a format the printer can understand. This conversion into a *printer language* is achieved with a *print filter*, a program run by the print spooler to translate data as needed so the printer can process it.

Important Standard Printer Languages

ASCII text Most printers are at least able to print ASCII text. The few devices that cannot print ASCII text directly should be able to understand one of the other standard printer languages mentioned below.

PostScript PostScript is the established printer language under Unix and Linux. PostScript output can be printed directly by PostScript printers. However, these printers are relatively expensive, because PostScript is a powerful yet complex language that requires a lot of computing in the PostScript printer before actually putting something on paper. Adding to the price of PostScript printers are licensing costs.

PCL3, PCL4, PCL5e, PCL6, ESC/P, ESC/P2, and ESC/P raster If a PostScript printer is not available, the print filter uses the program Ghostscript to convert PostScript data into one of these other standard languages. Ghostscript uses different drivers for different printers to make use of specific features offered by the various models, such as color settings.

Processing Print Jobs

1. A print job is started by the user either from the command line or from an application.
2. The corresponding print data is temporarily stored in the print queue. It is retrieved from there by the print spooler, which sends it to the print filter.
3. The print filter performs the following steps:

(a) The filter determines the format of print data.

(b) Print data is converted into PostScript (if not in PostScript format already). ASCII text, for instance, is converted into PostScript using the filter program `a2ps`.

(c) The PostScript data is converted into another printer language, if necessary.

- If the printer is a PostScript model, the data is sent to it with no further processing.
- If the printer is not a PostScript printer, the program Ghostscript is run and uses one of its drivers to convert data into the language of the printer model. This generates the data that is finally sent to the printer.

4. As soon as all the data of the print job has been sent to the printer, the print spooler deletes it from the print queue.

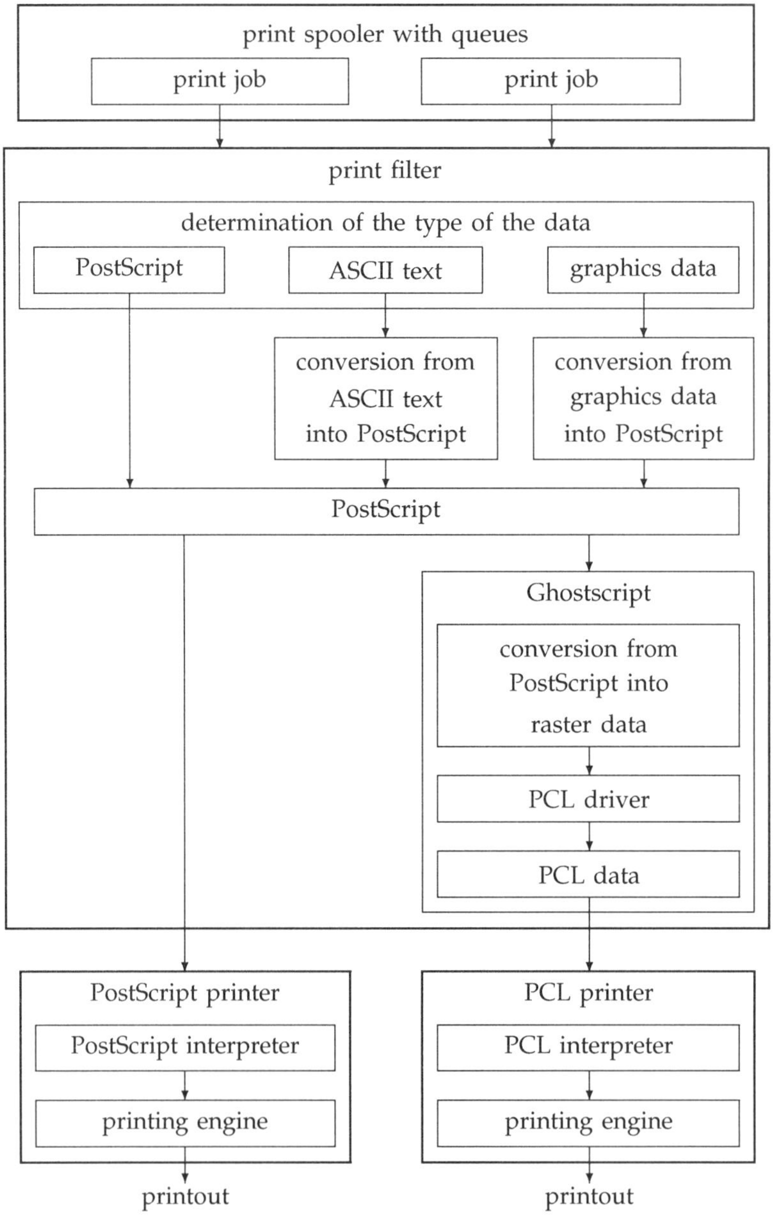
print spooler with queues
print job
print job
print filter
determination of the type of the data
PostScript
ASCII text
graphics data
conversion from
ASCII text
into PostScript
conversion from
graphics data
into PostScript
PostScript
Ghostscript
conversion from
PostScript into
raster data
PCL driver
PCL data
PostScript printer
PostScript interpreter
printing engine
printout
PCL printer
PCL interpreter
printing engine
printout

Various Printing Systems

SuSE Linux supports two different printing systems:

LPRng and lpdfilter — This is a traditional printing system consisting of the print spooler LPRng and the print filter lpdfilter. The configuration of this system must be entirely defined by the system administrator. Normal users can only choose between different print queues that have already been configured. To allow users to choose between different options for a given printer, a number of print queues should be defined beforehand — each for a different printer configuration. For plain black-and-white printers, such as most laser printers, it is sufficient to define just one configuration (the standard queue). For modern color inkjet printers, define several configurations, for example, one for black-and-white printing, one for color printing, and maybe another one for high-resolution photograph printing. Setting up the printer with predefined configurations has the advantage that the system administrator has a lot of control over the way in which the device is used. On the other hand, there is the disadvantage that users cannot set up the printer according to the job at hand, so maybe they will not be able to use the many options offered by modern printers unless the administrator has defined the corresponding print queues beforehand.

CUPS — CUPS allows users to set different options for each print job and does not require the entire configuration of the print queue to be predefined by the system administrator. With CUPS, printer options are stored in a PPD (PostScript printer description) file for each queue. These can be made available to users in printer configuration dialogs. By default, the PPD file gives users control over all printer options, but the system administrator may also limit printer functionality by editing the PPD file.

Under normal conditions, it is not possible to install these two printing systems *concurrently*, as there are conflicts between them. However, YaST2 allows switching between them. See *Configuring a Printer with YaST* on page 150.

General Troubleshooting Hints

The documentation included with SuSE Linux mostly describes general printing problems and ways to solve them. Many of the more specific issues are covered by articles in the Support Database. The Support Database is available in the SuSE Help System and the latest version can be accessed online at `http://sdb.suse.de/en/sdb/html/`.

A good starting point for dealing with printing problems are the Support Database articles *Installing a Printer* and *Printer Configuration with SuSE Linux 8.2*. Find these by entering the keyword "printer" or online at:
`http://sdb.suse.de/en/sdb/html/jsmeix_print-einrichten.html`
`http://sdb.suse.de/en/sdb/html/jsmeix_print-einrichten-82.html`
The latter contains the latest information about configuring a printer in SuSE Linux. You may also want to refer to articles summarizing the most important known problems of each SuSE Linux version:
Known Problems and Special Features in SuSE Linux 8.2 at
`http://sdb.suse.de/en/sdb/html/bugs82.html`
Known Problems and Special Features in SuSE Linux 8.1 at
`http://sdb.suse.de/en/sdb/html/bugs81.html`

If you are not able to find the needed information in the documentation or in the Support Database, feel free to make use of the SuSE Support Services.
For private customers:
`http://www.suse.de/en/private/support/index.html`
For business customers:
`http://www.suse.de/en/business/services/support/index.html`

Preconditions for Printing

General Requirements

- Your printer must be supported by SuSE Linux. To see whether this is the case, consult the following sources:

  SuSE Printer Database — `http://cdb.suse.de` or `http://hardwaredb.suse.de/` (click 'Englisch' to get the English version)

  The linuxprinting.org Printer Database — `http://www.linuxprinting.org/` → 'The Database' (`http://www.linuxprinting.org/database.html`) or `http://www.linuxprinting.org/printer_list.cgi`

  Ghostscript — `http://www.cs.wisc.edu/~ghost/`

  The SuSE Linux Ghostscript Driver List — `/usr/share/doc/packages/ghostscript/catalog.devices` This file lists the Ghostscript drivers included with the current version of SuSE Linux. This is an important detail because sometimes web pages mention a Ghostscript driver not included in SuSE Linux. For license reasons, SuSE Linux comes with GNU Ghostscript. In most cases, GNU Ghostscript offers a suitable driver for your printer.

- The printer has been properly connected to the interface over which it will communicate. For details, read *Manual Configuration of Local Printer Ports* on page 156 and *Manual Configuration* on page 153.
- You should be using one of the standard kernels included on CD, *not* a custom kernel. If you have problems with your printer, install one of the SuSE standard kernels first and reboot before looking further into the problem.
- The 'Default System' is installed to make sure all required packages are available. As long as you have not uninstalled any of the packages of the standard system, things should be ready. Otherwise, install the 'Default System' with YaST2. None of the 'Minimum System' selections are sufficient for printing.

Finding the Right Printer Driver

PostScript printers do not require a special printer driver (see *Processing Print Jobs* on page 142). Other printer types need a Ghostscript driver to produce the data. For non-PostScript devices, choosing the right Ghostscript driver and the right options for it has a big influence on output quality. The Ghostscript drivers available for specific models are listed in the sources mentioned in *General Requirements* on the facing page.

If you cannot find a specific Ghostscript driver for your printer, it may be possible to use another driver already available. Also, some manufacturers support Linux, so your manufacturer might be able to provide specific Ghostscript driver information or drivers. If not, they may be able to provide other information to assist in selection:

- Find out whether your printer is compatible with a model supported by Linux. You may then be able to use the driver for the compatible model. For printers to be *compatible*, they should be able to work correctly using the same binary control sequences. Both printers must understand the same language on the hardware level without relying on additional driver software to emulate it.

  A similar model name does not always mean the hardware is really compatible. Printers that appear very similar on the outside sometimes do not use the same printer language at all.

- Check if your printer supports a standard printing language by asking the manufacturer or checking the technical specifications in the printer manual.

  PCL5e or PCL6 Printers that understand the PCL5e or PCL6 language natively should work with the ljet4 Ghostscript driver and produce output at a resolution of 600x600 dpi. Often, PCL5e is mistaken for PCL5.

  PCL4 or PCL5 Printers that understand the PCL4 or PCL5 language natively should work with one of the following Ghostscript drivers: laserjet, ljetplus, ljet2p, or ljet3. Output resolution is limited to 300x300 dpi, however.

  PCL3 Printers that understand the PCL3 language natively should work with one of these Ghostscript drivers: deskjet, hpdj, pcl3, cdjmono, cdj500, or cdj550.

  ESC/P2, ESC/P, or ESC/P raster Printers that understand ESC/P2, ESC/P, or ESC/P raster natively should work with the stcolor Ghostscript driver or with the uniprint driver in combination with a suitable `*.upp` parameter file (e.g., `stcany.upp`).

The Issue with GDI Printers

Given that most Linux printer drivers are not written by the maker of the hardware, it is crucial that the printer can be driven through one of the generally known languages, such as PostScript, PCL, or ESC/P. Normal printers understand at least one of the common languages. In the case of a GDI printer, the manufacturer has built a device that relies on its own special control sequences. Such a printer only runs under the operating system versions for which the manufacturer has included a driver. Because it cannot be operated through one of the known languages, it must be considered nonstandard and cannot be used with Linux or can only be used with difficulty.

GDI is a programming interface developed by Microsoft for graphical devices. There is not much of a problem with the interface itself, but the fact that GDI printers can *only* be controlled through the proprietary language they use *is* an issue. A better name for them would be "proprietary-language-only printers."

On the other hand, there are printers that can be operated both in GDI mode and in a standard language mode, but they need to be switched accordingly. If you use Linux together with another operating system, it may be possible that the driver set the printer to GDI mode when you last used it. As a result, the printer will not work under Linux. There are two solutions for this: switch the printer back to standard mode under the other operating system before using it under Linux or use only the standard mode, even under the other operating system. In the latter case, it may turn out that printing functionality is limited, such as to a lower resolution.

There are also some very special printers that implement a rudimentary set of a standard printer language, for example, only commands needed for printing raster images. Sometimes these printers can be used in a normal way, as many Ghostscript drivers only use the printer as a raster image device anyway. On the negative side, you may be unable to print ASCII text directly. This should not be too much of a problem, however, as ASCII text is mostly printed through Ghostscript and not directly. The only problem occurs when some of these printers need to be switched explicitlybefore they can print raster images. This requires sending a special control sequence to them — something that can only be achieved with a special driver, but not through Ghostscript.

For some GDI printers, you may be able to obtain Linux drivers directly from the manufacturer. There is no guarantee that such vendor-made drivers will work with other or future Linux versions.

In any case, the above is only true for GDI models. By contrast, printers that understand one of the standard languages do not depend on a particular operating system nor do they require a particular Linux version. However, they often produce the highest quality of output when used with a vendor-made driver.

To sum all this up, SuSE Linux does support the GDI printers listed below. They can be configured using the printer configuration module of YaST2. Be aware that their use will always be rather problematic. Some models might refuse to work at all or their functionality might be limited, for example, to low-resolution black-and-white printing. SuSE does not test GDI printers, so cannot guarantee this list is correct.

- Brother HL 720/730/820/1020/1040, MFC 4650/6550MC/9050, and compatible models.
- HP DeskJet 710/712/720/722/820/1000 and compatible models.
- Lexmark 1000/1020/1100/2030/2050/2070/3200/5000/5700/7000/7200, Z11/42/43/51/52, and compatible models. Lexmark makes its own Linux drivers available at: `http://www.lexmark.com/printers/linuxprinters.html`

- Oki Okipage 4w/4w+/6w/8w/8wLite/8z/400w and compatible models.
- Samsung ML-200/210/1000/1010/1020/1200/1210/1220/4500/5080/6040 and compatible models.

To our knowledge, the following GDI printers are *not supported* by SuSE Linux (this list is not complete by any means):

- Brother DCP-1000, MP-21C, WL-660
- Canon BJC 5000/5100/8000/8500, LBP 460/600/660/800, MultiPASS L6000
- Epson AcuLaser C1000, EPL 5500W/5700L/5800L
- HP LaserJet 1000/3100/3150
- Lexmark Z12/22/23/31/32/33/82, Winwriter 100/150c/200
- Minolta PagePro 6L/1100L/18L, Color PagePro L, Magicolor 6100DeskLaser, Magicolor 2 DeskLaser Plus/Duplex
- Nec SuperScript 610plus/660/660plus
- Oki Okijet 2010
- Samsung ML 85G/5050G, QL 85G
- Sharp AJ 2100, AL 1000/800/840/F880/121

Configuring a Printer with YaST

Print Queues and Configurations

In most cases, you will want to set up more than one print queue for the following reasons:

- If you have more than one printer, you need at least one queue for each of them.

- The print filter can be configured differently for each print queue. By having different queues for one printer, operate it with different configurations. This is not necessary in CUPS, as the user can specify the desired settings. See *Various Printing Systems* on page 145.

If your model is a plain black-and-white printer, such as most laser printers, it will be sufficient to configure just one standard queue. Color inkjets, on the other hand, require at least two different queues (configurations):

- A standard `lp` configuration for quick and inexpensive black-and-white printouts. The traditional name of the default queue is `lp`.
- A `color` configuration or queue used for color printing.

Printer Configuration with YaST2: The Basics

Start the YaST2 printer configuration by selecting it from the YaST2 Control Center or by entering `yast2 printer` in a command line as `root`. Enter `yast2 printer .nodetection` to suppress printer autodetection. For more details about autodetection, see *Parallel Ports* on page 156.

Not all printers are capable of being configured for both print systems. Some options are only supported by either CUPS or LPRng and lpdfilter. YaST2 provides information about this whenever necessary.

Easily switch back and forth between CUPS and LPRng using a submenu of the YaST2 printer configuration. The YaST2 printer configuration module offers the following printing system selections:

CUPS as a Server (default in standard installations) If a printer is connected locally, CUPS must be runningin server mode. If no local queue is configured with YaST2, the CUPS daemon cupsd is not started automatically. If cupsd is already running, the 'cups' service must be activated (for the runlevels 3 and 5). See *Quick Configuration of a Client Machine* on page 207. The following packages are installed for this print system:

- package `cups-libs`
- package `cups-client`
- package `cups`
- package `cups-drivers`
- package `cups-drivers-stp`

CUPS in Client-Only Mode If there is a CUPS network server in the local network (see *Terminology* on page 206) and you exclusively want to print by way of its queues, it is sufficient to run CUPS as client — see *Quick Configuration of a Client Machine* on page 207. The following packages are sufficient for this mode:

- package `cups-libs`
- package `cups-client`

LPRng Select this if you want to use the LPRng and lpdfilter print system or if the network only has an LPD server (see *Terminology* on page 206) whose queues you want to use for printing — see *Quick Configuration of a Client Machine* on page 207. The following packages are required for this setup:

- package `lprng`
- package `lpdfilter`

The package `cups-client` and the package `lprng` are mutually exclusive — they must not be installed at the same time. The package `cups-libs` must always be installed because several programs (such as Ghostscript, KDE, Samba, Wine, and the YaST2 printer configuration) need the CUPS libraries.

The printing system as a whole requires a number of additional packages, although the 'Default system' should include them. The most important ones are:

- package `ghostscript-library`
- package `ghostscript-fonts-std`
- package `ghostscript-x11`
- package `libgimpprint`
- package `a2ps`
- package `file`

The YaST2 printer configuration modules display all configurations that could be created without errors. The YaST2 printer configuration also strictly distinguishes between queues created through YaST2 itself (YaST2 queues) and queues created through other means (non-YaST2 queues). Non-YaST2 queues will never be touched by YaST2. Conflicts only arise if queues have identical names. When editing a queue, you can determine whether it should be managed by YaST2. If you turn a YaST2 queue into a non-YaST2 queue, you can edit the configuration manually (without YaST2) and prevent these changes from being overwritten by YaST2. Likewise, you can turn a non-YaST2 queue into a YaST2 queue to overwrite an existing configuration deliberately with YaST2.

Automatic Configuration

Depending on how much of your hardware can be autodetected and on whether your printer model is included in the printer database, YaST2 will either autoconfigure your printer or offer a reasonable selection of settings that then need to be adjusted manually. If this is not the case, the user must enter the needed information in the dialogs. YaST2 can configure your printer automatically if the following conditions are fulfilled:

- The parallel port or USB interface was set up automatically in the correct way and the printer model connected to it was autodetected.
- Your printer's ID, as supplied to YaST2 during hardware autodetection, is included in the printer database. As this ID may be different from the actual model designation, you may need to select the model manually.

Each configuration should be tested with the print test function of YaST2 to see whether it works as expected. In many cases, configuration data not explicitly supported by the printer manufacturer must be used. For this reason, operability cannot be guaranteed for all settings. Furthermore, the YaST2 test page provides important information about the respective configuration.

Manual Configuration

If one of the conditions for automatic configuration is not fulfilled or if you want your own customized setup, the configuration must be performed manually. The following is an overview of the options to set during manual configuration:

Hardware Port (Interface)

- If YaST2 was able to autodetect the printer model, you may safely assume that the printer connection works as far as the hardware is concerned. You may then leave this part untouched.

- If YaST2 has not autodetected the printer model, there may have been some problem on the hardware level. Some manual intervention is needed to configure the physical connection. Manual configuration requires specification of the port to which the printer is connected. `/dev/lp0` is the first parallel port. `/dev/usb/lp0` is the port for a USB printer. Always test this setting from within YaST2 to see whether the printer is actually responding at the selected interface.

  It is safest to connect a printer to the first parallel port. In this case, the BIOS settings for this port should look like this:

  - IO address: `378` (hexadecimal)
  - Interrupt: (not relevant)
  - Mode: `Normal`, `SPP`, or `Output-Only`.
  - DMA: Disabled

  If the printer does not respond at the first parallel port with these settings, you may need to change the IO address to have the explicit form of `0x378` under the BIOS menu item that lets you configure the advanced settings for parallel ports. If your machine has two parallel ports with IO addresses 378 and 278 (hexadecimal), change them to read `0x378` and `0x278`, respectively. For further details on the topic, see *Parallel Ports* on page 156.

Queue Name The name of the queue is used frequently when issuing print commands. The name should be rather short and consist of lowercase letters (and maybe numbers) only. The following additional options may be defined for the LPRng and lpdfilter printing system:

- Define a queue named `raw` to use for special cases where print data should not be converted by a print filter, but sent to the printer in raw form. Accordingly, when printing through the `raw` queue, print data must already be available in a format (language) your printer model can understand.
- For each queue, define whether an explicit form feed is needed. If enabled, the spooler sends a form feed command at the end of each print job to eject the last page. Normally, the Ghostscript driver takes care of this and you can leave this disabled.

Ghostscript Driver and Printer Language (Printer Model) The Ghostscript driver and the printer language depend on the printer model and are determined by selecting a predefined configuration suitable for the printer model. It can be customized in a separate dialog, if necessary.

In other words, the selection of the manufacturer and the model actually represents the selection of a printer language and a Ghostscript driver with suitable driver settings for your printer.

For non-PostScript models, all printer-specific data is produced by the Ghostscript driver. Therefore, the driver configuration (both choosing the right driver and the correct options for it) is the single most important factor determining the output quality. Your settings affect the printer output on a queue-by-queue basis.

If your printer was autodetected, which means the model is included in the printer database, you will be presented with a choice of possible Ghostscript drivers and with several output options such as:

- black-and-white printing
- color printing at 300 dpi
- color printing at 600 dpi

Each default configuration includes a suitable Ghostscript driver and, if available, a number of driver-specific settings related to the output quality. Any driver-specific settings can be customized in a separate dialog. Click the respective values to view and access any indented submenu entries.

Not all combinations of driver options work with every printer model. This is especially true for higher resolutions. Always check whether your settings work as expected by printing the YaST2 test page. If the output is garbled (for example, with several pages almost empty), you should be able to stop the printer by first removing all sheets then stopping the test print from within YaST2. However, in some cases the printer will refuse to resume work if you do so. It may be better to stop the test print first and wait for the printer to eject all pages itself.

If your model was not found in the printer database, you can select one of the generic Ghostscript drivers for the standard printing languages. These are listed under a generic "manufacturer".

Other Special Settings Unless you are sure about what these options mean, do not change the default settings.

For the CUPS printing system, the following special settings are available:

- Restricting printer use for certain users.
- Queue status: whether the queue is started or stopped and whether it is ready to accept new print jobs.

- Banner page: whether to print out a banner (cover) page at the beginning of each print job and which one. Similarly, whether to add a banner page at the end of each print job and which one.

For the LPRng and lpdfilter printing system, change the following hardware-independent settings:

- The page layout can be changed for ASCII text printouts (but not for graphics or documents created with special application programs).
- You can define an `ascii` print queue for special cases. The `ascii` queue forces the print filter to produce ASCII text output, which may be necessary for some text files that the print filter does not automatically recognize as such, for example, PostScript source code.
- Country-specific settings can be changed to ensure the correct character encoding when sending ASCII text to the printer and when printing plain text in HTML pages from Netscape.

Manual Configuration of Local Printer Ports

Parallel Ports

For the most part, printers are connected to a Linux system through a parallel port. Printers on parallel ports are handled by the `parport` subsystem of the Linux kernel. The basics of parallel port configuration with YaST2 are described in *Manual Configuration* on page 153. The paragraphs below provide more in-depth information on the topic.

The `parport` subsystem manages parallel ports only through the corresponding architecture-specific kernel modules after these are loaded. Among other things, this allows for several devices, such as a parallel port ZIP drive and a printer, to be linked to one parallel port at the *same* time. Device files for parallel printers are counted beginning with `/dev/lp0`. With a SuSE Linux standard kernel, printing over the parallel port requires that the modules `parport`, `parport_pc`, and `lp` are loaded. This is achieved by kmod (the kernel module loader). Normally, these modules are loaded automatically as soon as some process requests access to the device file.

If the kernel module `parport_pc` is loaded without any parameters, it tries to autodetect and autoconfigure all available parallel ports. This may not work in some very rare cases and cause a system lock-up. If that happens, configure it manually by explicitly providing the correct parameters for the `parport_pc` module. This is also the reason why printer autodetection can be disabled for YaST2 as described in *Configuring a Printer with YaST* on page 150.

Manual Configuration of Parallel Ports

The first parallel port (`/dev/lp0`) is configured with an entry in `/etc/modules.conf`, as shown in File 7.

```
alias parport_lowlevel parport_pc
options parport_pc io=0x378 irq=none
```

File 7: */etc/modules.conf: First Parallel Port*

Under `io`, enter the IO address of the parallel port. Under `irq`, keep the default `none` for polling mode. Otherwise, provide the IRQ number for the parallel port. Polling mode is less problematic than interrupt mode as it helps to avoid interrupt conflicts. However, there are combinations of motherboards and printers that only function well if this is set to interrupt mode. Apart from that, interrupt mode ensures a continuous data flow to the printer even when the system is under very high load.

To make the above configuration work, you may still need to change the parallel port settings made available through your machine's BIOS or firmware:

- IO address: `378` (hexadecimal)
- Interrupt: `7` (not relevant for polling mode)
- Mode: `Normal`, `SPP`, or `Output-Only` (other modes will not always work)
- DMA: `Disabled` (should be disabled as long as the mode is set to `Normal`)

If interrupt `7` is still free, enable in `/etc/modules.conf` as shown in File 8.

```
alias parport_lowlevel parport_pc
options parport_pc io=0x378 irq=7
```

File 8: */etc/modules.conf: Interrupt Mode for the First Parallel Port*

However, before enabling interrupt mode, enter the command `cat /proc/interrupts` to see which interrupts are already in use on your system. The output of this command will only list interrupts that are being used at the given moment, something which may change according to the hardware components active. In any case, the interrupt used for a parallel port must not be occupied by any other device. It is probably best to use polling mode if you are not sure about this.

Configuring Additional Parallel Ports

Configure a second parallel port (`/dev/lp1`) by adding the corresponding entries to `/etc/modules.conf`, as shown in File 9. In this case, the default IO address should be set to `278` (hexadecimal). This may be changeable on the hardware level, for example, by setting a jumper on an ISA expansion card.

```
alias parport_lowlevel parport_pc
options parport_pc io=0x378,0x278 irq=none,none
```

File 9: /etc/modules.conf: Two Parallel Ports

Special ISA PnP and PCI Expansion Cards

If you do not know the IO address of an additional parallel port, find it first.

ISA PnP Cards If the card has a means to set the IO address and the interrupt to a fixed value (by setting a jumper, for instance), do so before proceeding with the configuration.

If that is not the case, the values for IO address, interrupt, and mode are set for the card by the system on boot. To find out which values have been set for your ISA PnP card, look for them in the boot messages, as stored in `/var/log/boot.msg`, or with `pnpdump` (included in package `isapnp`).

PCI Cards Find possible IO addresses and interrupts for PCI cards by entering the command `/sbin/lspci -v`. The output should be similar to Output 12.

```
00:0a.0 Parallel controller: ...
        ... IRQ 10
        I/O ports at b400
```

```
I/O ports at b000
I/O ports at a800
I/O ports at a400
```

Output 12: *Partial Output of* `lspci -v` *for a PCI Interface Card*

Each parallel port is assigned a pair of IO addresses 400 (hexadecimal) apart. In our example, one IO port corresponds to `b000` and `b400`. The other one is at `a400` and `a800`. You may need to experiment a bit to see which of the two IO addresses is the right one. The final configuration entry in `/etc/modules.conf` looks like the one shown in File 10.

```
alias parport_lowlevel parport_pc
options parport_pc io=0x378,0xb400,0xa800 \
irq=none,none,none
```

File 10: */etc/modules.conf: PCI Card with Two Parallel Ports*

Enabling and Testing a Parallel Port

After configuration, the parallel port is enabled when you reboot the machine. If you do not want to reboot, run the following commands as `root` to update the module dependency list and to unload all kernel modules related to parallel ports.

```
earth:~ #  depmod -a 2>/dev/null
earth:~ #  rmmod lp
earth:~ #  rmmod parport_pc
earth:~ #  rmmod parport
```

After this, reload the modules with:

```
earth:~ #  modprobe parport
earth:~ #  modprobe parport_pc
earth:~ #  modprobe lp
```

If the printer is capable of direct ASCII text printing, the command

```
earth:~ #  echo -en "\rHello\r\f" >/dev/lp0
```

as `root` should print a single page with the word `Hello` on it.

In the above command, the word `Hello` is enclosed in two `\r` ASCII characters to produce carriage returns. The closing ASCII character `\f` is included to produce a form feed. To test a second or third parallel port in the same way, use `/dev/lp1` or `/dev/lp2`, respectively.

USB Ports

First, make sure the interrupt is enabled for USB in your machine's BIOS. In an Award BIOS, for example, go to the menu 'PNP AND PCI SETUP' and set the entry 'USB IRQ' to `Enabled`. The wording of these menus and entries may vary depending on the BIOS type and version.

Test whether the USB printer is responding by entering the command `echo -en "\rHello\r\f" >/dev/usb/lp0` as `root`. If there is only one USB printer connected to the machine and this printer is able to print ASCII text directly, this should print a single page with the word `Hello` on it.

Some USB printers may need a special control sequence before accepting data over a USB line. The following command, entered as one line without spaces or line breaks, sends a control sequence for an Epson Stylus Color USB printer:

```
echo -en "\x0\x0\x0\x1b\x01\x40\x45\x4a\x4c
\x20\x31\x32\x38\x34\x2e\x34\x0a\x40\x45\x4a\x4c\x20
\x20\x20\x20\x20\x0a" >/dev/usb/lp0
```

In most cases, you should be able to get information about the printer manufacturer and the product name by entering `cat /proc/bus/usb/devices`. If this does not display any information, it will usually be for one of these reasons:

- The USB system has not detected the device (yet), maybe even because it is disconnected from power, so there is no communication between the system and the printer.
- The USB system has detected the device, but neither the manufacturer or the product name are known to it. Accordingly, nothing is displayed, but the system can communicate with the printer.

Sometimes it may happen that the USB printer does not respond anymore, for instance, after unplugging it in the middle of a print job. In such a case, the following commands should be sufficient to restart the USB system:

```
earth:~ # rchotplug stop
earth:~ # rchotplug start
```

If you are not successful with these commands, terminate all processes that use /dev/usb/lp0. Use lsmod to check which USB modules are loaded (usb-uhci, usb-ohci, or uhci) and how they depend on each other. For instance, the entry

```
usbcore  ...  [printer usb-uhci]
```

in the output of lsmod shows that the module usbcore is being used by modules printer and usb-uhci. Accordingly, modules printer and usb-uhci need to be unloaded before unloading usbcore.

As root, enter the following commands (replace usb-uhci with uhci or usb-ohci depending on your USB system):

```
earth:~ # fuser -k /dev/usb/lp0
earth:~ # rchotplug stop
earth:~ # rmmod printer
earth:~ # rmmod usb-uhci
earth:~ # umount usbdevfs
earth:~ # rmmod usbcore
earth:~ # modprobe usbcore
earth:~ # mount usbdevfs
earth:~ # modprobe usb-uhci
earth:~ # modprobe printer
earth:~ # rchotplug start
```

If you have more than one USB printer connected to the system, there is a special issue to consider: All connected devices are autodetected by the USB subsystem with the first USB printer being addressed as device /dev/usb/lp0 and the second one as /dev/usb/lp1. Depending on the model, USB printers can be detected even when they are powerless. Some have the built-in capability to be queried by the system even when powered off. Therefore, to avoid that the system confuses different printers, switch on all printers before booting and try to leave them connected to power all the time.

The IrDA Printer Interface

With IrDA, the system uses an infrared interface to emulate a parallel port. To do so, the Linux drivers provide a simulated parallel port under the device name of `/dev/irlpt0`. A printer connected through infrared is handled in the same way as any other parallel printer except it is made available to the system under the name of `/dev/irlpt0` instead of `/dev/lp0`.

Test the connection to an IrDA printer by entering the command `echo -en "\rHello\r\f" >/dev/irlpt0` as `root`. If the printer is able to print ASCII text directly, this should print a single page with the word `Hello` on it.

Regardless of the outcome of the above test, the printer should appear in the output of `irdadump`. If the irdadump command is not available, install the package `irda`. If irdadump does not display the printer, it is not possible to address the printer. If nothing is displayed, most likely the IrDA system service has not been started, as it is not started automatically when the system is booted. Enter the following commands to start and stop the IrDA systems service:

```
earth:~ #  rcirda start
earth:~ #  rcirda stop
```

Serial Ports

To use a printer connected to a serial port in combination with the LPRng printing system, read the document `/usr/share/doc/packages/lprng/LPRng-HOWTO.html`, in particular, the section `file:/usr/share/doc/packages/lprng/LPRng-HOWTO.html#SECSERIAL`. More information can be obtained from the man page for `printcap` (`man printcap`) as well as in the support database by searching for the keyword "serial".

Manual Configuration of the LPRng and lpdfilter Printing System

Normally, the printing system is configured with YaST2 as described in *Configuring a Printer with YaST* on page 150. SuSE Linux also includes the program lprsetup, which is a bare-bones command-line tool for the configuration of the LPRng and lpdfilter printing system. When setting up a printer with

YaST2, it collects all necessary data then runs lprsetup internally with all the necessary options to write the actual LPRng and lpdfilter configuration.

lprsetup is intended as an expert tool. As such, it will not provide any help to find the correct values for printer options. To see a brief list of the available command line options for `lprsetup`, enter `lprsetup -help` or refer to the man page for `lprsetup` (`man lprsetup`) and the man page for `lpdfilter` (`man lpdfilter`) for further details.

For information regarding Ghostscript drivers and driver-specific options, read *Finding the Right Printer Driver* on page 147 and *Working with Ghostscript* on page 193.

The LPRng Print Spooler

The print spooler used by the LPRng and lpdfilter printing system is LPRng (package `lprng`). The print spooler lpd, or line printer daemon, is usually started automatically on boot. More specifically, the script `/etc/init.d/lpd` is run as part of the boot procedure. After this, the print spooler runs as a daemon in the background. Start and stop it manually with `rclpd start` and `rclpd stop`.

These are the configuration files of LPRng:

/etc/printcap definitions of the system's print queues

/etc/lpd.conf global print spooler configuration

/etc/lpd.perms permission settings

According to the script `/etc/init.d/lpd`, the command `rclpd start` also runs the command `checkpc -f` as a subprocess, which in turn creates spool directories with the appropriate permissions in `/var/spool/lpd` according to the queues defined in `/etc/printcap`. When started, the print spooler first reads the entries in `/etc/printcap` to see which print queues have been defined. The spooler's task is then to manage any jobs queued for printing. In particular, the spooler:

- manages local queues by passing the print data of each job to a print filter (if necessary) then sending it to the printer or to another queue
- handles jobs in the order in which they have been queued

- monitors the status of queues and printers and provides status information when requested
- listens on port 515 to accept or reject print jobs from remote hosts destined for local queues, depending on the configuration
- forwards print jobs to remote print spoolers (listening on port 515 on other hosts) for printing through remote queues.

To learn more about the details of this mechanism, read the *LPRng Howto* (`file:/usr/share/doc/packages/lprng/LPRng-HOWTO.html`) or consult the man page for `printcap` (`man printcap`) and the man page for `lpd` (`man lpd`).

Printing from Applications with LPRng

Applications use the existing queues for printing from the command line. In applications, printer options are not configured directly, but rather through the existing queues.

Applications can use the `lpr` command for printing. To make this work, use the application's printer configuration to select one of the existing queues (e. g., `lp` or `color`) or use the application's print dialog to directly enter the corresponding command (e. g., `lpr -Plp` or `lpr -Pcolor`).

Command-Line Tools for LPRng

This section only provides a short overview of the available tools. For details, consult the *LPRng Howto*, in particular, section `file:/usr/share/doc/packages/lprng/LPRng-HOWTO.html#LPRNGCLIENTS`.

Managing Local Queues

Printing Files

Details on how to use the `lpr` command can be found in the *LPRng Howto* (`file:/usr/share/doc/packages/lprng/LPRng-HOWTO.html#LPR`). The following only covers some basic operations.

To print a file, you normally must enter `lpr -P`⟨*queuename*⟩ ⟨*filename*⟩. If you leave out the `-P`⟨*queuename*⟩ parameter, the printing system defaults to the value of the environment variable `PRINTER`. The same is true for the commands `lpq` and `lprm`. See the man page for `lpr` (`man lpr`), the man page for `lpq` (`man lpq`), and the man page for `lprm` (`man lprm`) for more information. The environment variable `PRINTER` is set automatically on login. Display its current value with `echo $PRINTER`. Change it to expand to another queue by entering `export PRINTER=`⟨*queuename*⟩.

Checking the Status

By entering `lpq -P`⟨*queuename*⟩, check the status of print jobs handled by the specified queue. If you specify `all` as the queue name, `lpq` displays information for all jobs in all queues.

With `lpq -s -P`⟨*queuename*⟩, tell `lpq` to display only a minimum of information. `lpq -l -P`⟨*queuename*⟩ tells `lpq` to be more verbose. With `lpq -L -P`⟨*queuename*⟩, `lpq` displays a detailed status report, which will come in handy when trying to track down errors.

For further information, see the man page for `lpq` (`man lpq`), and section `file:/usr/share/doc/packages/lprng/LPRng-HOWTO.html#LPQ` of the *LPRng Howto*.

Removing Jobs from the Queue

The command

```
newbie@earth:~ > lprm -P⟨queuename⟩ ⟨jobnumber⟩
```

removes the print job with the specified number from the specified queue, if you own the job. A print job is owned by the user who started it. Display the owner and the job number of print jobs with `lpq`.

The command `lprm -Pall all` removes all print jobs from all queues for which you have the required permissions. `root` may remove any jobs in any queues regardless of permissions.

More information can be obtained in the man page for `lprm` (`man lprm`) and in the *LPRng Howto* (`file:/usr/share/doc/packages/lprng/LPRng-HOWTO.html#LPRM`).

Controlling the Queues

The command `lpc option` ⟨*queuename*⟩ displays the status of the specified queue and allows changing it. The most important options are:

`help` Display a short overview of the available options.

`status` ⟨*queuename*⟩ Display status information.

`disable` ⟨*queuename*⟩ Do not accept new jobs for the specified queue.

`enable` ⟨*queuename*⟩ Accept new jobs for the specified queue.

`stop` ⟨*queuename*⟩ Stop printing from the specified queue. If a job is being printed, it will be completed.

`start` ⟨*queuename*⟩ Enable printing from the specified queue.

`down` ⟨*queuename*⟩ Has the effect of `disable` and `stop` combined.

`up` ⟨*queuename*⟩ Has the effect of `enable` and `start` combined.

`abort` ⟨*queuename*⟩ Has the effect of `down`, but aborts all current print jobs immediately. Aborted jobs are preserved, however, and can be resumed after restarting the queue with `up`.

`root` permissions are required to control printer queues with the above commands. Options can be supplied to `lpc` directly on the command line (as in `lpc status all`). You can also run the program without any options, which starts it in dialog mode — it opens the lpc> command prompt. Then enter the options at the prompt. To leave the program, enter either `quit` or `exit`.

If you were to enter `lpc status all`, the output could look like this:

```
Printer          Printing Spooling Jobs Server Subserver
lp@earth          enabled  enabled    2    123       456
color@earth      disabled disabled    0   none      none
laser@earth      disabled  enabled    8   none      none
```

This gives the following information: Queue `lp` is completely enabled and holds two print jobs, one of which is being printed at the moment. Queue `color`, on the other hand, is completely stopped. Finally, the `laser` queue does not print at the moment, but jobs (there are currently eight of them) are still accepted for the queue and are accumulating in the spooler.

Further information can be obtained from the man page for `lpc` (`man lpc`) and the *LPRng Howto* (`file:/usr/share/doc/packages/lprng/LPRng-HOWTO.html#LPC`).

Managing Remote Queues

For each of the commands explained below, replace ⟨*printserver*⟩ with the name or IP address of your print server. ⟨*queuename*⟩ must be a queue on the print server.

Generating Print Jobs

With the LPRng spooler, even remote queues can be addressed directly, using the `lpr` command with the syntax `lpr -P⟨queuename⟩@⟨printserver⟩ ⟨file⟩`. This is only possible if the print server is configured to accept remote print jobs on its queues. This is enabled by default with LPRng.

Checking the Status

Check the status of a queue on a remote host by entering:

```
newbie@earth:~ >  lpq -P⟨queuename⟩@⟨printserver⟩
newbie@earth:~ >  lpq -s -P⟨queuename⟩@⟨printserver⟩
newbie@earth:~ >  lpq -l -P⟨queuename⟩@⟨printserver⟩
newbie@earth:~ >  lpq -L -P⟨queuename⟩@⟨printserver⟩
```

or use

```
newbie@earth:~ >  lpc status ⟨queuename⟩@⟨printserver⟩
newbie@earth:~ >  lpc status all@⟨printserver⟩
```

To list the names of and display status information on all queues of a print server, use either `lpq -s -Pall@⟨printserver⟩` or `lpc status all@⟨printserver⟩`, provided that LPRng is used on the print server.

If printing over a remote queue does not work, querying the status of the queues helps determine the cause of the problem. If LPRng is installed on the print server, enter `lpq -L -P⟨queuename⟩@⟨printserver⟩` to get a detailed status report for remote diagnosis.

Removing Jobs from the Queue

The commands

```
newbie@earth:~ >  lprm -P⟨queuename⟩@⟨printserver⟩ ⟨jobnumber⟩
newbie@earth:~ >  lprm -P⟨queuename⟩@⟨printserver⟩ all
newbie@earth:~ >  lprm -Pall@⟨printserver all⟩
```

delete all print jobs in remote queues that have been issued under your user name. `root` has no special privileges on remote queues. The parameter `all` only works if LPRng is used on the print server host as well.

Using Command-Line Tools for LPRng Troubleshooting

Print jobs are kept in the queue even if you shut down a machine during a printout so are still there after rebooting. To remove a faulty print job, use the commands described above. Rebooting will not remove them.

For example, it sometimes happens that the host-to-printer connection suffers some kind of fault, after which the printer is unable to interpret data correctly. This can cause it to spit out large amounts of paper with meaningless characters on it.

1. In the case of an inkjet model, remove all paper from the trays. Open the paper tray if you have a laser model.
2. In most cases, the print job is still in the queue after that. Print jobs are removed from the queue only after all data has been sent to the printer. Check with `lpq` or `lpc status` to see which queue is printing then delete the job in question with `lprm`.
3. The printer may produce some output even after deleting the job from the queue. To stop this, use the commands `fuser -k /dev/lp0` for a printer on the first parallel port or `fuser -k /dev/usb/lp0` for the first USB printer to terminate all processes still using the printer device.
4. Do a complete reset of the printer by switching it off. Wait a few seconds before putting the paper back into the trays and switching the device back on.

The Print Filter of the LPRng and lpdfilter Printing System

The print filter used in conjunction with LPRng is lpdfilter, which is installed as a package with the same name. The following is a detailed description of the steps involved in processing a print job. If you need to know about the inner workings of the print filter, read the scripts powering it (in particular, `/usr/lib/lpdfilter/bin/if`) and probably also follow the steps described in *Troubleshooting Hints for lpdfilter* on page 177.

1. The print filter (/usr/lib/lpdfilter/bin/if) determines which options to use as passed to it by the print spooler and specified by the print job's control file. Options for the queue to use are also gathered from /etc/printcap and /etc/lpdfilter/⟨*queuename*⟩/conf (where ⟨*queuename*⟩ is the name of the actual queue).

2. If the ascii queue has been specified, the print filter is forced to treat the file as ASCII text. If a queue other than ascii has been specified, the printer filter tries to autodetect the file type. The filter determines the file type using the script /usr/lib/lpdfilter/bin/guess to run file on each file in question. The output of file is used to determine the type according to the entries in the file /etc/lpdfilter/types.

3. The file is converted into a printer-specific data stream according to the file type and the type of queue to use:

   - If the raw queue has been specified, print data is usually sent straight to the printer or forwarded to another queue. However, data may also undergo a simple conversion through recode, if so specified in /etc/lpdfilter/⟨*queuename*⟩/conf. To have an "absolute" raw filter — one that bypasses lpdfilter entirely — remove the line :if=/usr/lib/lpdfilter/bin/if:\ for the corresponding queue in /etc/printcap.
   - If the queue specified is not a raw queue:

     (a) If the data is not in PostScript format, it is first converted into PostScript by running /usr/lib/lpdfilter/filter/type2ps on it (where type is the actual file type determined for the data in question). For example, ASCII text is converted into PostScript with /usr/lib/lpdfilter/filter/ascii2ps, which in turn relies on a2ps to obtain the correct character encoding defined for the queue. This ensures that country-specific special characters are printed correctly in plain text files. For details, see the man page for a2ps (man a2ps).

     (b) If necessary, PostScript data can be converted again if a suitable script is placed in /etc/lpdfilter/⟨*queuename*⟩/pre (where ⟨*queuename*⟩ is the name of the actual queue to use).

     (c) PostScript data is converted into another printer language, as needed.

       ▷ If the printer is PostScript capable, the data is sent directly to the printer (or forwarded to another queue).

However, data can be further processed using the Bash functions "duplex" and "tray", which are defined in `/usr/lib/lpdfilter/global/functions`, to enable duplex printing and paper tray selection through PostScript commands (which requires that the PostScript printer has this functionality).

- ▷ If the printer is not PostScript capable, Ghostscript uses a driver suitable for the native printer language of the model to produce the printer-specific data that is finally sent to the printer (or forwarded to another queue). Ghostscript-relevant parameters are stored either in the `cm` line of `/etc/printcap` or in the file `/etc/lpdfilter/`⟨*queuename*⟩`/upp` (where ⟨*queuename*⟩ is the name of the actual queue to use). If so desired, the Ghostscript output can be reformatted again, if a suitable script is placed in `/etc/lpdfilter/`⟨*queuename*⟩`/post` (where ⟨*queuename*⟩ is the name of the actual queue to use).

(d) The printer-specific data is transferred to the printer (or to another queue). Control sequences for a specific printer can be sent to the printer both before and after the data stream. These must be specified in `/etc/lpdfilter/`⟨*queuename*⟩`/conf`.

Configuration of lpdfilter

Normally, the printing system is configured with YaST2 (as described in *Configuring a Printer with YaST* on page 150), which includes the setup of `lpdfilter`. Some of the more special settings, however, can only be changed by editing the configuration files of the print filter by hand. For each queue, a dedicated configuration file is written to `/etc/lpdfilter/`⟨*queuename*⟩`/conf` (where ⟨*queuename*⟩ is the name of the actual queue to be used).

Customization of lpdfilter

1. By default, files not in PostScript format are converted into that format with `/usr/lib/lpdfilter/filter/type2ps` (where `type` is the actual type of the file in question). If a suitable script is placed in `/etc/lpdfilter/`⟨*queuename*⟩/type2ps, it will be used for the

PostScript conversion of the file. The script must be able to accept data on `stdin` and to output data in PostScript format on `stdout`.

2. If so desired, an additional step can be performed to reformat PostScript data, which requires a suitable script be placed in `/etc/lpdfilter/`⟨*queuename*⟩`/pre`. This may be a script to add custom PostScript preloads, for example. The script must be able to accept data on `stdin` and to output data in PostScript format on `stdout`. Some programs to reformat PostScript are included in the package `psutils`. In particular, the program pstops is capable of performing extensive transformations. See the man page for `pstops` (`man pstops`) for details.

3. Special Ghostscript parameters: When writing the configuration with YaST2, Ghostscript parameters are stored in `/etc/lpdfilter/`⟨*queuename*⟩`/upp` (where ⟨*queuename*⟩ is the name of the actual queue to use), but custom Ghostscript parameters can also be added to this file manually. For details on Ghostscript parameters, read *Working with Ghostscript* on page 193.

4. If so desired, data can be reformatted again after conversion by Ghostscript. This requires a suitable script be placed in `/etc/lpdfilter/`⟨*queuename*⟩`/post` (where ⟨*queuename*⟩ is the name of the actual queue to use). This script must be able to accept data on `stdin` and to output a data stream suitable for the specific printer model on `stdout`.

A Hardware-Independent Example

For the purposes of this example, suppose there is a queue called `testqueue`, which should be configured so ASCII text is printed with line numbers along the left margin. Apart from that, all files should be printed with two pages scaled to fit on one sheet. The scripts `/etc/lpdfilter/testqueue/ascii2ps` and `/etc/lpdfilter/testqueue/pre`, as shown below, would achieve that:

```
#!/bin/bash
cat -n - | a2ps -1 --stdin=' ' -o -
```

File 11: */etc/lpdfilter/testqueue/ascii2ps: ASCII to PostScript Conversion*

```
#!/bin/bash
pstops -q '2:0L@0.6(20cm,2cm)+1L@0.6(20cm,15cm)'
```

File 12: */etc/lpdfilter/test/pre: PostScript Reformatting*

These scripts need to be made executable for all users, which can be achieved with the `chmod` command:

```
earth:~ #  chmod -v a+rx /etc/lpdfilter/testqueue/ascii2ps
earth:~ #  chmod -v a+rx /etc/lpdfilter/testqueue/pre
```

Reformatting files with `pstops` only works with PostScript files created to allow such transformations, as is usually the case.

Using Custom PostScript Preloads

PostScript preloads are small files containing PostScript commands that preceed the print data stream to initialize the printer or the Ghostscript program in the desired way. PostScript preloads are mostly used to enable duplex printing on PostScript printers or to activate a special paper tray. They can also be used for margin and gamma adjustments.

To use preloads, the PostScript printer or Ghostscript must be able to interpret the special commands. Ghostscript, for instance, does not interpret commands related to duplex printing or paper trays.

For this example, the queue `testqueue` is again used:

Duplex Printing To enable or disable duplex printing, create the files `/etc/lpdfilter/testqueue/duplexon.ps` and `/etc/lpdfilter/testqueue/duplexoff.ps` with the following contents:

```
%!PS
statusdict /setduplexmode known
{statusdict begin true setduplexmode end} if {} pop
```

File 13: /etc/lpdfilter/testqueue/duplexon.ps: Enabling Duplex Printing

```
%!PS
statusdict /setduplexmode known
{statusdict begin false setduplexmode end} if {} pop
```

File 14: /etc/lpdfilter/testqueue/duplexoff.ps: Disabling Duplex Printing

Paper Tray Selection To enable the default paper tray 0 or tray number 2, create the files `/etc/lpdfilter/testqueue/tray0.ps` and `/etc/lpdfilter/testqueue/tray2.ps`:

```
%!PS
statusdict /setpapertray known
{statusdict begin 0 setpapertray end} if {} pop
```

File 15: */etc/lpdfilter/testqueue/tray0.ps: Enabling Tray 0*

```
%!PS
statusdict /setpapertray known
{statusdict begin 2 setpapertray end} if {} pop
```

File 16: */etc/lpdfilter/testqueue/tray2.ps: Enabling Tray 2*

Margin Settings To adjust margin settings, create a file like `/etc/lpdfilter/testqueue/margin.ps`.

```
%!PS
<<
/.HWMargins [left bottom right top]
/PageSize [width height]
/Margins [left-offset top-offset]
>>
setpagedevice
```

File 17: */etc/lpdfilter/testqueue/margin.ps: Margin Adjustments*

The margin settings `left`, `bottom`, `right`, and `top` and the paper size measures `width` and `height` are specified in points (with one point equaling 1/72 inches or about 0.35 mm). The margin offsets `left-offset` and `top-offset` are specified in pixels, so depend on the resolution of the output device.

To change only the position of the printed area, it is sufficient to create a file like `/etc/lpdfilter/testqueue/offset.ps`.

```
%!PS
<< /Margins [left-offset top-offset] >> setpagedevice
```

File 18: */etc/lpdfilter/testqueue/offset.ps: Changing the Position of the Printed Area*

Gamma Correction To adjust the gamma distribution between colors, use a file like /etc/lpdfilter/testqueue/cmyk.ps or /etc/lpdfilter/testqueue/rgb.ps:

```
%!PS
{cyan exp} {magenta exp} {yellow exp} {black exp}
setcolortransfer
```

File 19: /etc/lpdfilter/testqueue/cmyk.ps: CMYK Gamma Correction

```
%!PS
{red exp} {green exp} {blue exp} currenttransfer \
setcolortransfer
```

File 20: /etc/lpdfilter/testqueue/rgb.ps: RGB Gamma Correction

You need to know which color model is used by your printer (either CMYK or RGB) to make this work. The values to use for cyan, magenta, yellow, and black or for red, green, and blue should be determined through testing. Normally, these should be in the range between 0.001 and 9.999.

To get a rough idea of the effect of the above filtering actions on the output, display them on screen. To see how a sample file looks without gamma correction, enter:

```
earth:~ # gs -r60 \
    /usr/share/doc/packages/ghostscript/examples/colorcir.ps
```

To see how it looks with gamma correction according to the above sample filters:

```
earth:~ # gs -r60 /etc/lpdfilter/testqueue/cmyk.ps \
    /usr/share/doc/packages/ghostscript/examples/colorcir.ps
earth:~ # gs -r60 /etc/lpdfilter/testqueue/rgb.ps \
    /usr/share/doc/packages/ghostscript/examples/colorcir.ps
```

The above commands must be entered as a single line without the backslash ('\').

End the test by pressing Ctrl + C.

Resetting the Printer To reset the printer to its original state each time, use a file like /etc/lpdfilter/testqueue/reset.ps:

```
%!PS
serverdict begin 0 exitserver
```

File 21: /etc/lpdfilter/testqueue/reset.ps: Printer Reset

To activate one of the above PostScript preloads, create a file similar to /etc/lpdfilter/testqueue/pre:

```
#!/bin/bash
cat /etc/lpdfilter/testqueue/preload.ps -
```

File 22: /etc/lpdfilter/testqueue/pre: Activating a PostScript Preload

In this file, replace preload.ps with the name of your custom preload file. In addition, make this script executable and readable for all users, which can be achieved with chmod in the following way:

```
earth:~ # chmod -v a+rx /etc/lpdfilter/testqueue/pre
earth:~ # chmod -v a+r /etc/lpdfilter/testqueue/preload.ps
```

Use the mechanism described above to insert PostScript commands not only before the print data, but also after it. For instance, with a script like /etc/lpdfilter/testqueue/pre, reset the printer to its original state after each print job is finished:

```
#!/bin/bash
cat /etc/lpdfilter/testqueue/preload.ps -
/etc/lpdfilter/testqueue/reset.ps
```

File 23: /etc/lpdfilter/testqueue/pre: Inserting a PostScript Preload and a PostScript Reset

A Sample GDI Printer Configuration

This section provides an example for the customized configuration of a `gdi` print queue. As explained in *The Issue with GDI Printers* on page 148, it is often nearly impossible to make such printers run under Linux. However, special driver programs are available for some GDI models. In most cases, they are designed to run as Ghostscript add-ons with the driver reformatting the Ghostscript output into the printer's own language. Often these drivers make limited use of the printer's functionality, however, allowing only black-and-white printing, for example. If such a driver is available, Ghostscript can be used with it in the following way (also see *Working with Ghostscript* on page 193):

1. Ghostscript converts the PostScript data into a raster of pixel dots then uses one of its drivers to convert the rasterized image into a format appropriate for the GDI driver at a suitable resolution. Data is then passed to the GDI driver.

2. The rasterized image is converted by the GDI driver into a data format suitable for the printer model.

For the steps described below, it is assumed that a GDI printer driver suitable for SuSE Linux 8.2 is already installed or can be downloaded from the Internet. It is also assumed that the driver works in the way described above. In some cases, you may need some familiarity with the way source code is handled under Unix or how to handle these installations (from `.zip` or `.tar.gz` archives or maybe from `.rpm` packages).

After unpacking such an archive, you will often find the latest installation instructions included in some of the files, typically in `README` or `INSTALL`, or even in a `doc` subdirectory. If you have downloaded a `.tar.gz` archive, you usually need to compile and install the driver yourself.

For the purposes of the example explained below, the following setup is assumed:

- The driver program has been installed as `/usr/local/bin/printerdriver`.

- The required Ghostscript driver is `pbmraw` with an output resolution of 600 dpi.

- The printer is connected to the first parallel port — `/dev/lp0`.

The Ghostscript driver and the resolution may be different for your printer. Read the documentation included with the driver to find out about these.

First, create the gdi queue. To do so, log in as root and run lprsetup, as follows:

```
earth:~ #  lprsetup -add gdi -lprng -device /dev/lp0 \
     -driver pbmraw -dpi 600 -size a4dj -auto -sf
```

This command must be entered as a single line without the backslash ('\').

Now, create the script /etc/lpdfilter/gdi/post:

```
#!/bin/bash
/usr/local/bin/printerdriver ⟨gdi_driver_parameters⟩
```

File 24: /etc/lpdfilter/gdi/post: Running the GDI Printer Driver

Read the documentation of the driver program to find out what options exist for it. Specify them under ⟨*gdi_driver_parameters*⟩ as needed. Make the script executable for all users and restart the print spooler:

```
earth:~ #  chmod -v a+rx /etc/lpdfilter/gdi/post
earth:~ #  rclpd stop
earth:~ #  rclpd start
```

From now on, users should be able to print with this command:

```
newbie@earth:~ >  lpr -Pgdi ⟨filename⟩
```

Troubleshooting Hints for lpdfilter

Enable different debug levels for lpdfilter by uncommenting (removing the '#' sign in front of) the corresponding line of the main filter script /usr/lib/lpdfilter/bin/if.

```
# DEBUG="off"
# DEBUG="low"
DEBUG="medium"
# DEBUG="high"
```

File 25: /usr/lib/lpdfilter/bin/if: Debug Levels

With DEBUG="low" enabled, the program logs its stderr output to the file /tmp/lpdfilter.if-$$.XXXXXX (where $$ is the process ID and XXXXXX a unique random string).

With DEBUG="medium" enabled, the program logs, in addition to its own error output, the stderr output of the scripts in /usr/lib/lpdfilter/filter if these scripts are run by /usr/lib/lpdfilter/bin/if. The debugging output is written to /tmp/lpdfilter.name-$$.XXXXXX (where name is the name of the script run and $$.XXXXXX a string composed in the way described above).

With DEBUG="high" enabled, all error output is logged as above. Additionally, all output normally destined to the printer is redirected to a log file named /tmp/lpdfilter.out-$$.XXXXXX (where $$.XXXXXX is a string composed in the way described above).

To avoid losing control over the logging activity, you may want to remove the log files with rm -v /tmp/lpdfilter* before each new test run.

Custom Print Filters for the LPRng Spooler

The aim of this section is not to show you how to build an alternative to lpdfilter, but rather to lay out the inner workings of the Linux printing engine. We do this by demonstrating how to write a custom printer filter. The example explained below has been kept simple to show just the basic mechanism. This is also the reason why no provisions are made in the filter scripts to do any error checking. The following example is based on the assumption that the printer is connected to the first parallel port (/dev/lp0).

Any print filter must accept data from the print spooler on standard input. The filter must then convert the data into the printer-specific format and issue it on standard output. Now the print spooler takes care of the data again and makes sure it is transferred from the filter's standard output to the /dev/lp0 printer device. This is where the Linux kernel comes in: it transfers all data arriving at the printer device to the corresponding IO address (e.g., 0x378). The printer receives this data over the parallel line and interprets it to print accordingly.

On most systems, normal users do not have direct access to the printer device, therefore root permissions are needed for the commands below. Also, in any commands like cat ascii-file >/dev/lp0, replace ascii-file with the name of an existing ASCII file.

Basic Filtering Operations

You can print with the simple command `echo -en "\rHello\r\f" >/dev/lp0`. This, however, does not activate the print spooler nor does it use any filter. It writes to the printer device `/dev/lp0` directly. The command sends the ASCII signs `'\r'`, `'H'`, `'e'`, `'l'`, `'l'`, `'o'`, `'\r'`, and `'\f'` directly to the printer device. The ASCII character for carriage return, `'\r'`, causes the carriage (printer head) to return to its start position. The ASCII form feed character, `'\f'`, causes the printer to eject the page.

The commands `cat ascii-file >/dev/lp0` and `echo -en "\f" >/dev/lp0` still do not activate the spooler or a print filter, but again send characters directly to the printer device `/dev/lp0`. The first command sends the characters of the ASCII file to the printer. The second one adds a form feed character to eject the page.

Under Linux, ASCII text lines are separated only by a line feed character. By contrast, line breaks under DOS and Windows consist of a line feed ASCII character and a carriage return ASCII character. If you enter the commands

```
earth:~ #  cat /etc/hosts >/dev/lp0
earth:~ #  echo -en "\f" >/dev/lp0
```

to send the ASCII file `/etc/hosts` directly to the printer, the output will probably appear as follows:

```
first line
          second line
                            ...
```

The reason is that the printer only performs a line feed but no carriage return (since there is actually no carriage return character between the two lines).

However, it is possible to tell printers to perform both a line feed and a carriage return whenever a line feed character is sent. With the escape sequence `\033&k2G`, all printers that understand the PCL3 language can be reconfigured to perform both a line feed and a carriage return upon receiving an ASCII line feed character. Send the escape sequence to the printer with `echo -en "\033&k2G" >/dev/lp0` after which it should interpret line breaks in the expected way when printing an ASCII file.

Another problem may arise when trying to print country-specific characters, such as umlauts. DOS and Windows use an encoding for these that is different from that used by Linux. Printers are mostly preconfigured for the DOS and Windows environment. As a remedy, enter

```
earth:~ # cp ascii-file ascii-file.ibmpc
earth:~ # recode lat1..ibmpc ascii-file.ibmpc
```

to copy `ascii-file` to `ascii-file.ibmpc` then recode `ascii-file.ibmpc` according to the DOS and Windows standard. After that, the commands

```
earth:~ # cat ascii-file.ibmpc >/dev/lp0
earth:~ # echo -en "\f" >/dev/lp0
```

should print both the umlauts and the line breaks in the correct way. The special escape sequence to correct the line break behavior is no longer needed, because `ascii-file.ibmpc` has been recoded to have DOS and Windows line breaks and umlauts.

To sum this up, the sequence of commands

```
earth:~ # cp ascii-file ascii-file.ibmpc
earth:~ # recode lat1..ibmpc ascii-file.ibmpc
earth:~ # cat ascii-file.ibmpc >/dev/lp0
earth:~ # echo -en "\f" >/dev/lp0
```

should correctly print an ASCII file on any printer that accepts ASCII directly and is preconfigured for the DOS and Windows character encoding. Automate this by creating a print filter that reformats ASCII text for your printer according to the above steps.

A Sample Custom Print Filter

First, become `root` and create a subdirectory for the custom filter then change into that subdirectory:

```
earth:~ # mkdir /usr/local/myprinterfilter
earth:~ # cd /usr/local/myprinterfilter
```

Create a Bash script (basically a text file) named `asciifilter` with the contents shown in File 26.

```
#!/bin/bash

# make a temporary file
INPUT="$(mktemp /tmp/asciifilter.$$.XXXXXX)"
```

```
# first store everything from stdin in $INPUT
# to have the input as a regular file
cat >$INPUT

# recode the INPUT
recode lat1..ibmpc $INPUT

# add a form feed at the end of $INPUT
# to get the last page out of the printer
echo -en "\f" >>$INPUT

# send $INPUT to stdout
cat $INPUT

# remove the INPUT file
rm $INPUT
```

File 26: */usr/local/myprinterfilter/asciifilter*

Make this script executable for all users by entering

```
earth:~ #  chmod -v a+x /usr/local/myprinterfilter/
earth:~ #  chmod -v a+rx /usr/local/myprinterfilter/asciifilter
```

Now use `lprsetup` to create a new print queue (enter `lprsetup --help` to see what the options do). The queue name used in our example is `af`, for "ascii filter."

```
earth:~ #  lprsetup -add af -lprng -device /dev/lp0 -raw -sf
```

In the `af` entry of `/etc/printcap`, look for the `if` line and replace `/usr/lib/lpdfilter/bin/if` with `/usr/local/myprinterfilter/asciifilter` such that the complete `af` entry looks similar to File 27.

```
af:\
        :cm=lpdfilter drv= method=raw color=no:\
        :lp=/dev/lp0:\
        :sd=/var/spool/lpd/af:\
        :lf=/var/spool/lpd/af/log:\
        :af=/var/spool/lpd/af/acct:\
        :if=/usr/local/myprinterfilter/asciifilter:\
        :la@:mx#0:\
        :tr=:cl:sh:
```

File 27: */etc/printcap: Custom Filter Entry*

Finally, stop then restart the print spooler with `rclpd stop` and `rclpd start`. From now on, every user should be able to print through the new `af` queue with the command `lpr -Paf ascii-file`.

The CUPS Printing System

Naming Conventions

Client or *client program* refers to a program that sends print jobs to a CUPS daemon. A *print daemon* is a local service that accepts print jobs either to forward them or to process them locally. *Server* refers to a daemon able to deliver print data to one or more printers. Each server functions as a daemon at the same time. In most cases, however, there is no special distinction to make between a server and a daemon, neither from the developer or from the user standpoint.

IPP and Server

Print jobs are sent to servers by CUPS-based programs, such as `lpr`, `kprinter`, or `xpp`, and with the help of the *Internet Printing Protocol*, IPP. IPP is defined in RFC-2910 and RFC-2911 (see `http://www.rfc-editor.org/rfc.html`). IPP is somewhat similar to HTTP with identical headers but different content data. It also uses its own dedicated communication port 631, which has been registered with IANA (the Internet Authority for Number Allocation).

Print data is transferred to a CUPS daemon, which is also acting as a local server in most cases. Other daemons can be addressed using the environment variable `CUPS_SERVER`.

With the help of the broadcast function of the CUPS daemon, locally managed printers can be made available elsewhere in the network (using UDP port 631). They then appear as print queues on all other daemons configured to accept and use these broadcast packets. This makes it possible to "see" printers on other hosts after booting without configuring them locally, something that may be quite useful in corporate networks. On the other hand, this feature may pose a security risk if the host is connected to the Internet. When enabling printer broadcasting, make sure the daemon broadcasts into the local network only, access is limited to clients on the LAN, and the public IP address (the one used for the Internet connection) is not within the local IP range. Otherwise, remote users relying on the same ISP would be able to "see" and use the broadcast printers as well. In addition to that, such broadcasts mean more network traffic so may increase connection costs. Prevent a local printer from broadcasting IPP packets into the Internet by configuring the SuSEfirewall accordingly. No extra configuration is needed to receive broadcast IPP packets. A broadcast address must only be specified for outgoing print jobs. This may be configured with YaST2, for example.

IPP is used for the communication between a local and a remote CUPS daemon or server. More recent network printers also have built-in support for this protocol (there are a number of models from different makers). Find more information about this on the web pages of manufacturers or in your printer's manual. IPP is also supported by Windows 2000 and newer Microsoft systems, although originally the implementation was somewhat flawed. These problems may have disappeared or it may be necessary to install a Service Pack to repair them.

Configuration of a CUPS Server

There are many ways to set up a printer with CUPS and to configure the daemon: with command-line tools, with YaST2, with the KDE Control Center, or even through a web browser interface. The following sections are limited to the command-line tools and YaST2.

Caution

When using the web browser interface for CUPS configuration, be aware that there is a risk of compromising the `root` password. The password will be transmitted as plain text if the URL specified includes the real host name. Therefore, you should always use `http://localhost:631/` as the host address.

Caution

For the above reason, the CUPS daemon can only be accessed for administration if addressed as `localhost` (which is identical to the IP address `127.0.0.1`) by default. Entering a different address returns an error message, even if it is valid.

To configure a locally connected printer, first set up a CUPS daemon on the local host. To do so, install package `cups` together with the PPD files provided by SuSE as included in package `cups-drivers` and package `cups-drivers-stp`. After that, start the server as `root` with the command `/etc/rc.d/cups restart`. If you configure it with YaST2, the above steps are already covered by selecting CUPS as the printing system and installing a printer.

PPD (PostScript Printer Description) files contain options for printer models in the form of a standard set of PostScript commands. They are required for printer installation under CUPS. SuSE Linux comes with precompiled PPD files for many printers from a number of manufacturers. Manufacturers may also offer PPD files for their PostScript printers on web sites and installation CDs (often in an area called something like "Windows NT Installation").

The local daemon can also b started so printers of all broadcasting servers are available locally, although there is no local printer. This facilitates the use of these printers from within KDE applications and OpenOffice.org, for example.

Broadcasting can be enabled either with YaST2. Alternatively, enable it by setting the `Browsing` directive to `On` (the default) and the `BrowseAddress` directive to a sensible value, like `192.168.255.255`, in the file `/etc/cups/cupsd.conf`. After that, tell the CUPS daemon explicitly to grant access to incoming packets, either under `<Location /printers>` or, preferably, under `<Location />`, where you would have to include a line like `Allow From some-host.mydomain` (see `file:/usr/share/doc/packages/cups/sam.html`). When finished editing the file, tell the daemon to reread its configuration by entering the command `/etc/rc.d/cups reload` as `root`.

Network Printers

Network printers are printers that have a built-in print server interface (such as the JetDirect interface in some HP printers) or printers connected to a print server box or a router box enabled as a print server. Windows machines offering printer shares are not print servers in the strict sense (although CUPS can handle them easily in a way similar to print servers).

In most cases, a network printer supports the LPD protocol, which uses port 515 for communication. Check lpd availability with the command:

```
netcat -z hostname.domain 515 && echo ok || echo failed
```

If such a server is available, CUPS can be configured to access it under a *device URI*, an address in the form `lpd://server/queue`. Read about the concept of device URIs in `file:/usr/share/doc/packages/cups/sam.html`.

However, you should probably not use the LPD protocol for a network printer, but rather the printer's built-in port 9100 if available (HP, Kyocera, and many others) or port 35 (QMS). In this case, the device URI must have the form `socket://server:port/`.

To use printers made available through Windows, install package `samba-client` first and configure this package — enable the correct work group and make other settings. A device URI for Windows printers may be specified in several ways, but the most frequent one has the syntax `smb://user:password@host/printer`. For other configurations, see `file:/usr/share/doc/packages/cups/sam.html` and the man page for `smbspool` (`man smbspool`).

If you have a small network consisting of several (Linux) machines and have set up a print server for it, avoid configuring the printer for each and every client host by enabling the broadcast function of the daemon (see above). Thus, when you modify the configuration (for instance, to use the new standard paper size `Letter`), it is sufficient to do this once on the server side (also see *Specifying Options for Queues* on page 190). Although the configuration is saved locally on the server side, it is propagated to all clients in the network with the help of the CUPS tools and the IPP protocol.

Internal CUPS Print Job Processing

Conversion into PostScript

Basically the CUPS daemon should be able to handle any file type, although PostScript is always the safest bet. CUPS processes non-PostScript files by identifying the file type according to `/etc/cups/mime.types` first then converting the file into PostScript by calling the appropriate conversion tool for it as defined in `/etc/cups/mime.convs`. With CUPS, files are converted into PostScript on the server side rather than on the client side. This feature was introduced to ensure that special conversion operations necessary for a particular printer model are only performed on the corresponding server machine.

Accounting

After conversion into PostScript, CUPS calculates the number of pages for each print job. This is done with the help of pstops (an internal version of the program located at `/usr/lib/cups/filter/pstops`). The accounting data for print jobs are written to `/var/log/cups/page_log`. Each line in this file contains the following information:

- printer name (for example, `lp`)
- user name (for example, `root`)
- job number
- date and time (in square brackets)

- current page number
- number of copies

Other Filtering Programs

CUPS can also use other, special filters, if the corresponding printing options have been enabled. These are the most important ones:

psselect: Allows limiting the printout to certain pages of a document.

ps-n-up: Allows printing several pages on one sheet.

Read `file:/usr/share/doc/packages/cups/sum.html` for information about how to enable the various options.

Conversion into the Printer-Specific Language

The next step is the launch of the filter needed for generating printer-specific data. These filters are located in `/usr/lib/cups/filter/`. The suitable filter is determined in the PPD file in the `*cupsFilter` entry. If this entry does not exist, the print system assumes that the printer is a PostScript model. All device-specific printing options, such as the resolution and paper size, are processed in this filter.

Writing a custom printer-specific filter script is not a trivial task. It is therefore best left to a specialist.

Transferring Data to the Printer

As the final step, CUPS calls one of its back-ends. A back-end is a special filter that transfers print data to a device or to a network printer (see `file:/usr/share/doc/packages/cups/overview.html`). The back-end maintains the communication with the device or network printer (as specified through a device URI during configuration). If the back-end is `usb`, for example, CUPS runs `/usr/lib/cups/backend/usb`, which in turn opens (and locks) the corresponding USB device file, initializes it, and passes the data coming from the print filter. When the job is finished, the back-end closes the device and unlocks it.

The following back-ends are currently available: `parallel`, `serial`, `usb`, `ipp`, `lpd`, `http`, `socket` (included in package `cups`). Also available are `canon` and `epson`, included in `cups-drivers-stp`, and `smb`, included in `samba-client`.

Filterless Printing

To print files without any filtering, use the `lpr` command with `-l` or use the `lp` command with the `-oraw` option. Usually, the printout will not work, as no printer-specific conversion is performed or other important filters are omitted. The options are similar for other CUPS tools.

Tips and Tricks

OpenOffice.org

When printing from OpenOffice.org applications, CUPS is supported such that a running CUPS daemon is autodetected and queried for available printers and options (this is different from StarOffice 5.2, where it was still necessary to perform a setup for each printer). An extra CUPS setup from within OpenOffice.org should not be necessary.

Printing to or from Windows

Printers connected to a Windows machine can be addressed through a device URI, such as `smb://server/printer`. To print from a Windows machine to a CUPS server, set the entries `printing = CUPS` and `printcap name = CUPS` in the Samba configuration file `/etc/samba/smb.conf` (this is preset in SuSE Linux). Following modifications in `/etc/samba/smb.conf`, the Samba server must be restarted. See `file:/usr/share/doc/packages/cups/sam.html` for details.

Setting up a Raw Printer

A raw printer can be set up by leaving out the PPD file during configuration, which effectively removes all filtering and accounting features from CUPS. For this purpose, the data must be sent in the printer-specific data format.

Custom Printer Options

The configuration options, such as a different default resolution, can be modified and saved for each user. The configuration is saved in the file `~/.lpoptions`. If such a reconfigured printer is removed on the server side, it will still be visible in various tools, such as `kprinter` and `xpp`. You can still select it even if it no longer exists, which causes problems. Experienced users can easily remove the superfluous lines from `~/.lpoptions` with an editor. Refer to the Support Database article *Print Settings with CUPS*.

Compatibility with LPR

CUPS can be configured to accept print jobs from LPR-type printing systems. Either use YaST2 to make the necessary changes to /etc/inetd.conf or use some other means to remove the comment signs from the beginning of the printer line in /etc/inetd.conf. To switch back to LPRng, reinsert the comment sign.

Troubleshooting in CUPS

By default, the configuration file /etc/cups/cupsd.conf contains the following section:

```
# LogLevel: controls the number of messages logged to the ErrorLog
# file and can be one of the following:
#
#     debug2    Log everything.
#     debug     Log almost everything.
#     info      Log all requests and state changes.
#     warn      Log errors and warnings.
#     error     Log only errors.
#     none      Log nothing.
#

LogLevel info
```

To detect errors in CUPS, set LogLevel debug and use rccups reload to have cupsd use the modified configuration file. Subsequently, /var/log/cups/error_log will contain detailed messages that assist in detecting the cause of problems.

Before starting a test, use

```
earth:~ #  echo "LABEL $(date)" | tee -a /var/log/cups/error_log
```

to insert a mark that will be entered in /var/log/cups/error_log. This makes it easier to find the messages after the test.

Printing from Applications

Applications use the existing queues for printing from the command line. In applications, printer options are not configured directly, but rather through the existing queues.

In the printer dialog, select the desired queue. Because package cups-client includes some command-line tools to print with CUPS, such as lpr command, applications can use the lpr command for printing (e.g., lpr -Plp or lpr -Pcolor). However, to be able to enter print commands, the print dialog in KDE has to be set to 'Print through an external program'. See *Quick Configuration of a Client Machine* on page 207.

In addition, there are several graphical tools for CUPS, such as xpp or the KDE program kprinter, which allow you to choose among queues and to change both CUPS standard options and printer-specific options as made available through the PPD file. To use kprinter as the uniform print dialog for various applications, enter the print command kprinter or kprinter -stdin in the print dialog of the applications. The selection of the print command depends on the application. By doing this, the kprinter dialog will be displayed after the print dialog of the application, allowing you to specify the queue and other options. When using this approach, make sure there is no conflict between the settings in the print dialog of the application and those in kprinter. If possible, the settings should only be specified in kprinter.

Command-Line Tools for the CUPS Printing System

The command-line tools of the CUPS printing system and their manual pages are included in package cups-client. Further documentation is provided by the package cups and installed in /usr/share/doc/packages/cups, in particular the *CUPS Software Users Manual*, found at /usr/share/doc/packages/cups/sum.html and the *CUPS Software Administrators Manual* at /usr/share/doc/packages/cups/sam.html. If a CUPS daemon runs locally on your host, you should also be able to access the documentation at http://localhost:631/documentation.html.

As a general rule, it is useful to remember that CUPS command-line tools sometimes require options be supplied in a certain order. Consult the corresponding manual pages if you are unsure about specific options.

Managing Local Queues

Printing Files

To print a file, enter the "System V style" print command lp -d ⟨*queuename*⟩ ⟨*file*⟩ or a "Berkeley style" command like lpr -P⟨*queuename*⟩ ⟨*file*⟩. Additional information can be obtained with the man page for lpr (man lpr) and the man page for lp (man lp), as well as in the section "Using the Printing System" of the *CUPS Software Users Manual* (`file:/usr/share/doc/packages/cups/sum.html#USING_SYSTEM`).

The `-o` parameter allows specification of a number of important options, some of which directly influence the type of printout. More information is available in the man page for `lpr` (`man lpr`) and the man page for `lp` (`man lp`) as well as in the section "Standard Printer Options" of the *CUPS Software Users Manual* (`file:/usr/share/doc/packages/cups/sum.html#STANDARD_OPTIONS`).

Checking the Status

To check the status of a queue, enter the "System V style" command `lpstat -o` ⟨*queuename*⟩ `-p` ⟨*queuename*⟩ or the "Berkeley style" command `lpq -P`⟨*queuename*⟩. If you do not specify a queue name, the commands will display information on all queues. With `lpstat -o`, the output will show all active print jobs in the form of a ⟨*queuename*⟩-⟨*jobnumber*⟩ listing.

With `lpstat -l -o` ⟨*queuename*⟩ `-p` ⟨*queuename*⟩, the output is more verbose. `lpstat -t` or `lpstat -l -t` displays the maximum amount of available information.

For additional information, consult the man page for `lpq` (`man lpq`), the man page for `lpstat` (`man lpstat`), and the section "Using the Printing System" of the *CUPS Software Users Manual* (`file:/usr/share/doc/packages/cups/sum.html#USING_SYSTEM`).

Removing Jobs from the Queue

Enter the "System V style" command `cancel` ⟨*queuename*⟩-⟨*queuename*⟩ or the "Berkeley style" command `lprm -P`⟨*queuename*⟩ ⟨*queuename*⟩ to remove the job with the specified number from the specified queue. For additional information, consult the man page for `lprm` (`man lprm`), the man page for `cancel` (`man cancel`), and the section "Using the Printing System" of the *CUPS Software Users Manual* (`file:/usr/share/doc/packages/cups/sum.html#USING_SYSTEM`).

Specifying Options for Queues

To see how to specify hardware-independent options that affect the type of printout, read the section "Standard Printer Options" in the *CUPS Software Users Manual* (`file:/usr/share/doc/packages/cups/sum.html#STANDARD_OPTIONS`). The section "Saving Printer Options and Defaults", which is found at `file:/usr/share/doc/packages/cups/sum.html#SAVING_OPTIONS`, explains how to save option settings.

Printer-specific options affecting the type of printout are stored in the PPD file for the queue in question. They can be listed with the command `lpoptions -p` ⟨*queuename*⟩ `-l`. The output has the following form:

```
option/text: value value value ...
```

The currently active setting is marked with an asterisk (`'*'`) to the left, for example:

```
PageSize/Page Size: A3 *A4 A5 Legal Letter
Resolution/Resolution: 150 *300 600
```

According to the above output, the `PageSize` is set to `A4` and the `Resolution` to `300` dpi.

The command `lpoptions -p` ⟨*queuename*⟩ `-o option=value` changes the value for the given option. With the above sample settings in mind, use the command `lpoptions -p` ⟨*queuename*⟩ `-o PageSize=Letter` to set the paper size for the specified queue to `Letter`.

If the above `lpoptions` command is entered by a normal user, the new settings are stored for that user only in the file `~/.lpoptions`. By contrast, if the `lpoptions` command is entered by `root`, the settings specified are stored in `/etc/cups/lpoptions` and become the default for all local users of the queue. The PPD file is not touched by this, however.

If (and only if) you change the contents of a PPD file for a given queue, the new settings apply to all users in the local network who print through this queue. The system administrator can change the defaults of a PPD file with a command like:

```
earth:~ #  lpadmin -p ⟨queuename⟩ -o option=value
```

Accordingly, to change the default paper size of the sample queue to `Letter` for all users in the local network, enter the command:

```
earth:~ #  lpadmin -p ⟨queuename⟩ -o PageSize=Letter
```

For more information, refer to the Support Database article *Print Settings with CUPS* available at `http://sdb.suse.de/en/sdb/html/jsmeix_print-cups-options.html`.

Managing Remote Queues

For each of the commands explained below, replace ⟨*printserver*⟩ with the name or IP address of your print server. ⟨*queuename*⟩ must be a queue on the print server.

This section merely covers the basic commands. Additional options and information sources are referred to in *Managing Local Queues* on page 189.

Generating Print Jobs

You can use the "System V style" command `lp -d` ⟨*queuename*⟩ `-h` ⟨*printserver*⟩ ⟨*file*⟩ to generate a print job for the specified queue on the specified print server This is only possible if the print server was configured to accept remote print jobs on its queues. This is not enabled by default in CUPS, but can easily be configured in the CUPS server settings in a submenu of the YaST2 printer configuration module.

Checking the Status

Check the status of a queue on the print server with the "System V style" command `lpstat -h` ⟨*printserver*⟩ `-o` ⟨*queuename*⟩ `-p` ⟨*queuename*⟩.

Removing Jobs from the Queue

The "System V style" command `cancel -h` ⟨*printserver*⟩ ⟨*queuename*⟩-⟨*jobnumber*⟩ removes the print job with the specified job number from the specified queue on the print server.

Using Command-Line Tools for CUPS Troubleshooting

In the case of a broken print job, the troubleshooting procedure is basically the same as the one described in *Using Command-Line Tools for LPRng Troubleshooting* on page 168, with the difference that CUPS requires different commands for the second step:

1. Remove all paper from the printer so the printer stops working.
2. Check which queue is currently printing by entering `lpstat -o` (or `lpstat -h` ⟨*printserver*⟩ `-o`) then remove the problematic print job with `cancel` ⟨*queuename*⟩-⟨*jobnumber*⟩ (or with `cancel -h` ⟨*printserver*⟩ ⟨*queuename*⟩-⟨*jobnumber*⟩).

3. If necessary, use the `fuser` command to kill leftover programs.
4. Do a complete reset of the printer.

Working with Ghostscript

Ghostscript is a program that accepts PostScript and PDF files as input then converts them into several other formats. Ghostscript includes a number of drivers to achieve this. These are sometimes also referred to as "devices."

Ghostscript converts files in two steps:

1. PostScript data is rasterized — the graphical image is broken into a fine-grained raster of pixel dots. This step is performed independently from the Ghostscript driver used later. The finer the raster (the higher the resolution), the higher the output quality. On the other hand, doubling the resolution both horizontally and vertically (for example) means that the number of pixels must quadruple. Accordingly, the computer needs four times the CPU time and amount of memory to double the resolution.
2. The dot matrix that makes up the image is converted into the desired format (a printer language, for example) with the help of a Ghostscript driver.

Ghostscript can also process PostScript files to display them on screen or convert them into PDF documents. To display PostScript files on screen, you should probably use the program gv (rather than relying on bare Ghostscript commands), which gives a more convenient graphical interface.

Ghostscript is a very big program package and has a number of command-line options. Apart from the information available with the the man page for `gs` (`man gs`), the most important part of the documentation is the list of Ghostscript drivers, which is found in `/usr/share/doc/packages/ghostscript/catalog.devices` and the files `/usr/share/doc/packages/ghostscript/doc/index.html`, `/usr/share/doc/packages/ghostscript/doc/Use.htm`, `/usr/share/doc/packages/ghostscript/doc/Devices.htm`, `/usr/share/doc/packages/ghostscript/doc/hpdj/gs-hpdj.txt`, `/usr/share/doc/packages/ghostscript/doc/hpijs/hpijs_readme.html`, and `/usr/share/doc/packages/ghostscript/doc/stp/README`.

When executed from the command line, Ghostscript processes any options then presents its own `GS>` prompt. Exit from this dialog mode by entering `quit`.

If you enter `gs -h`, Ghostscript displays its most important options and lists the available drivers. This listing, however, only includes generic driver names, even for drivers that support many different models, such as `uniprint` or `stp`. The parameter files for `uniprint` and the models supported by `stp` are explicitly named in `/usr/share/doc/packages/ghostscript/catalog.devices`.

Sample Operations with Ghostscript

Find a number of PostScript examples in the directory `/usr/share/doc/packages/ghostscript/examples`. The color circle in `/usr/share/doc/packages/ghostscript/examples/colorcir.ps` is well suited for test printouts.

Displaying PostScript under X

Under X, the graphical environment, use `gs` to view a PostScript file on screen. To do so, enter the following command as a single line, omitting the backslash ('\'):

```
newbie@earth:~ >  gs -r60 \
     /usr/share/doc/packages/ghostscript/examples/colorcir.ps
```

In the above command, the `-r` option specifies the resolution, which must be appropriate for the output device (printer or screen). Test the effect of this option by specifying a different value, for example, `-r30`. To close the PostScript window, press Ctrl + C in the terminal window from which `gs` was started.

Conversion into PCL5e

The conversion of a PostScript file into the printer-specific format of a PCL5e or PCL6 printer can be achieved with a command like

```
newbie@earth:~ >  gs -q -dNOPAUSE -dSAFER -
     sOutputFile=/tmp/out.prn \
     -sDEVICE=ljet4 -r300x300 \
     /usr/share/doc/packages/ghostscript/examples/colorcir.ps \
     quit.ps
```

Again, the command must be entered as a single line and without any backslash ('\'). With this command, it is assumed that the file /tmp/out.prn does not exist yet.

Conversion into PCL3

To convert a PostScript file into the printer-specific format of a PCL3 printer, enter one of the following commands:

```
newbie@earth:~ >  gs -q -dNOPAUSE -dSAFER -
     sOutputFile=/tmp/out.prn \
     -sDEVICE=deskjet -r300x300 \
     /usr/share/doc/packages/ghostscript/examples/colorcir.ps \
     quit.ps
```

```
newbie@earth:~ >  gs -q -dNOPAUSE -dSAFER -
     sOutputFile=/tmp/out.prn \
     -sDEVICE=hpdj -r300x300 \
     -sModel=500 -sColorMode=mono -dCompressionMethod=0 \
     /usr/share/doc/packages/ghostscript/examples/colorcir.ps \
     quit.ps
```

```
newbie@earth:~ >  gs -q -dNOPAUSE -dSAFER -
     sOutputFile=/tmp/out.prn \
     -sDEVICE=cdjmono -r300x300 \
     /usr/share/doc/packages/ghostscript/examples/colorcir.ps \
     quit.ps
```

```
newbie@earth:~ >  gs -q -dNOPAUSE -dSAFER -
     sOutputFile=/tmp/out.prn \
     -sDEVICE=cdj500 -r300x300 \
     /usr/share/doc/packages/ghostscript/examples/colorcir.ps \
     quit.ps
```

```
newbie@earth:~ >  gs -q -dNOPAUSE -dSAFER -
     sOutputFile=/tmp/out.prn \
     -sDEVICE=cdj550 -r300x300 \
     /usr/share/doc/packages/ghostscript/examples/colorcir.ps \
     quit.ps
```

Again, each of the above commands must be entered as a single line, without the backslashes.

Conversion into ESC/P, ESC/P2, or ESC/P Raster

These are some sample commands to convert a PostScript file into the printer-specific format of an ESC/P2, ESC/P, or ESC/P raster printer.

```
newbie@earth:~ >  gs -q -dNOPAUSE -dSAFER -
     sOutputFile=/tmp/out.prn \
     @stcany.upp \
     /usr/share/doc/packages/ghostscript/examples/colorcir.ps \
     quit.ps
```

```
newbie@earth:~ >  gs -q -dNOPAUSE -dSAFER -
     sOutputFile=/tmp/out.prn \
     -sDEVICE=stcolor -r360x360 \
     -dBitsPerPixel=1 -sDithering=gsmono -dnoWeave \
     -sOutputCode=plain \
     /usr/share/doc/packages/ghostscript/examples/colorcir.ps \
     quit.ps
```

The above commands also show that the `uniprint` Ghostscript driver, which is called through a parameter file (`stcany.upp` in our example), requires a different command syntax than "regular" Ghostscript drivers. Because all driver options are stored in the `uniprint` parameter file, they do not have to be specified on the Ghostscript command line itself.

Sending the Output Directly to the Printer

With each of the above commands, the output is written in the corresponding printer language and stored in the file `/temp/out.prn`. This file can be sent directly to the printer by `root` without the use of a print spooler or any filtering. For a printer connected to the first parallel port, this can be achieved with the command `cat /tmp/out.prn >/dev/lp0`.

Processing PostScript and PDF Files

Ghostscript can generate PostScript and PDF files, convert both formats to each other, and even merge PostScript and PDF files in mixed order.

Conversion from PostScript to PDF:

```
newbie@earth:~ >  gs -q -dNOPAUSE -dSAFER -
     sOutputFile=/tmp/colorcir.pdf \
     -sDEVICE=pdfwrite \
     /usr/share/doc/packages/ghostscript/examples/colorcir.ps \
     quit.ps
```

Conversion of the generated PDF file /tmp/colorcir.pdf to PostScript:

```
newbie@earth:~ >  gs -q -dNOPAUSE -dSAFER -
     sOutputFile=/tmp/colorcir.ps \
     -sDEVICE=pswrite /tmp/colorcir.pdf quit.ps
```

Following the reconversion from PDF to PostScript, the file /tmp/colorcir.ps does not match the original file /usr/share/doc/packages/ghostscript/examples/colorcir.ps. However, there should be no visible difference in the printout.

Merging PostScript and PDF files into a PostScript file:

```
newbie@earth:~ >  gs -q -dNOPAUSE -dSAFER -
     sOutputFile=/tmp/out.ps \
     -sDEVICE=pswrite \
     /usr/share/doc/packages/ghostscript/examples/escher.ps \
     /tmp/colorcir.pdf quit.ps
```

Merging PostScript and PDF files into a PDF file:

```
newbie@earth:~ >  gs -q -dNOPAUSE -dSAFER -
     sOutputFile=/tmp/out.pdf \
     -sDEVICE=pdfwrite /tmp/out.ps \
     /usr/share/doc/packages/ghostscript/examples/golfer.ps \
     /tmp/colorcir.pdf quit.ps
```

Depending on the files you use, it may not be possible to merge some PostScript and PDF files.

Working with a2ps

Before an ASCII file can be printed through Ghostscript, it needs to be converted into PostScript, because this is the input format that Ghostscript expects. This conversion can be achieved with a2ps (package a2ps package). As package a2ps is not installed by default, you will normally have to install it yourself.

The a2ps program is a powerful, versatile tool that lets you convert simple text files into high-quality PostScript output. It has a large number of command-line options. Learn about these in the man page for a2ps (man a2ps) or read the full documentation of a2ps as an info page.

Sample Operations with a2ps

Using a2ps to Prepare a Text File for Printing

As a first example, a2ps can be used to convert a text file into PostScript, with two pages scaled down so they fit on one sheet. This can be achieved with the command:

```
newbie@earth:~ >  a2ps -2 --medium=A4dj \
     --output=/tmp/out.ps textfile
```

The output of a2ps can then be displayed under X with `gs -r60 /tmp/out.ps` to get a preview of the printout. If the printout is more than one sheet, hit (↵) in the terminal window from which `gs` was started to scroll down to the next page. To exit `gs`, enter (Ctrl) + (C).

Take the output of a2ps and convert it into your printer's language by entering:

```
newbie@earth:~ >  gs -q -dNOPAUSE -dSAFER -
     sOutputFile=/tmp/out.prn \
     ⟨driverparameters⟩ /tmp/out.ps quit.ps
```

In the above command, specify your own driver parameters under ⟨*driverparameters*⟩ as described in the previous section.

As `root`, you can send the output of Ghostscript directly to the printer without relying on a spooler or any further filtering with the command `cat /tmp/out.prn >/dev/lp0`. It is assumed here that the printer is connected to the first parallel port (`/dev/lp0`).

Printing Business Cards

To demonstrate the possibilities of a2ps, this section shows how to use the program to make and print a stack of simple business cards. First, create a plain text file called `card` that contains the necessary data as shown in File 28.

```
Title FirstName LastName
Street
PostalCode City
E-mail: user@domain
Phone: AreaCode-Number-Extension
```

File 28: *card: Business Card Data File*

Append a form feed character (\f) to this to ensure that a2ps treats each card as an individual page.

```
newbie@earth:~ >  echo -en "\f" >>card
```

Now, multiply the contents of the file to have a set of ten cards in one cards file:

```
newbie@earth:~ >  for i in $(seq 1 10) ; do cat card >>cards ;
     done
```

Use `cat cards | wc -L` to find out how many characters the longest line of cards contains.

Now do the actual PostScript conversion. We want ten cards per sheet printed in two columns with five cards each with a box or frame around them. We also want to use the maximum font size as allowed by the longest line and no additional header or footer lines. All this can be done with the command:

```
newbie@earth:~ >  a2ps -i -j -R --medium=a4dj --columns=2 --
     rows=5 \
     --no-header --chars-per-line=number --output=cards.ps cards
```

This command must be entered on a single line without the backslash ('\'). For number, fill in the number of characters in the longest line as determined above, increased by one.

Finally, preview the printout with `gs -r60 cards.ps` then send the output to the printer as described in the previous section. Alternatively, print the file in the normal way with `lpr card.ps`.

Reformatting PostScript with psutils

To use one of the reformatting programs described below, generate a PostScript input file by printing to a file, such as /tmp/in.ps, from within an application. Check with `file /tmp/in.ps` to see whether the generated file is really in PostScript format.

The package psutils includes a number of programs to reformat PostScript documents. The program pstops, in particular, allows you to perform extensive transformations. Details can be obtained in the man page for pstops (`man pstops`). The package psutils is not included in the standard setup of SuSE Linux, so you may need to install it.

The following commands only work if the application program has created a PostScript file appropriate for such reformatting operations. This should mostly be the case, but there are some applications that cannot generate PostScript files in the required way.

psnup

The command `psnup -2 /tmp/in.ps /tmp/out.ps` takes `/tmp/in.ps` as its input and transforms it into the output file `/tmp/out.ps` in such a way that two pages are printed side by side on one sheet. However, with the contents of two pages being included on one, the complexity of the resulting document is much higher and some PostScript printers may fail to print it, especially if they are equipped with only a small amount of standard memory.

pstops

The program `pstops` allows you to change the size and positioning of PostScript documents. For example, the command `pstops '1:0@0.8(2cm,3cm)' /tmp/in.ps /tmp/out.ps` scales the document by a factor of 0.8, which effectively scales down an A4 page from about 21x30 cm to about 17x24 cm. This, in turn, leaves an additional margin of about 4 cm on the right and 6 cm on the top. Therefore, the document is also shifted by 2 cm towards the right and 3 cm towards the top to get roughly the same margins everywhere.

This `pstops` command shrinks the page by quite an amount and also provides for relatively wide margins, so it should generate a page that is almost always printable — even with those applications that are far too optimistic about the limits set by your printer. You can use a command like the above for those cases where the application's printer output in `/etc/in.ps` is too large for the printable area.

As another example, the commands

```
newbie@earth:~ >  pstops '1:0@0.8(2cm,3cm)' /tmp/in.ps
     /tmp/out1.ps
newbie@earth:~ >  psnup -2 /tmp/out1.ps /tmp/out.ps
```

place two heavily scaled-down pages on one sheet, leaving quite a lot of space between them. To improve this, include instructions to position each of the pages individually:

```
newbie@earth:~ >  pstops '2:0L@0.6(20cm,2cm)+1L@0.6(20cm,15cm)' \
     /tmp/in.ps /tmp/out.ps
```

The above command must be entered as a single line without the `'\'`.

The following is a step-by-step explanation of the page specifications as expressed by `pstops '2:0L@0.6(20cm,2cm)+1L@0.6(20cm,15cm)'`:

2:0 ... +1 Two pages are merged into one and pages are counted modulo 2, which means that the pages modulo 2 are alternately counted as page 0 (modulo 2) and page 1 (modulo 2).

0L@0.6(20cm,2cm) Pages with the logical number 0 are turned to the left by 90 degrees and scaled down by a factor of 0.6. They are then shifted to the right by 20 cm and to the top by 2 cm.

1L@0.6(20cm,15cm) To match the above reformatting, pages with the logical number 1 are turned to the left by 90 degrees, and scaled down by a factor of 0.6. They are then shifted to the right by 20 cm and to the top by 15 cm.

Visualization of the pstops Example

In the case of PostScript files, the origin of coordinates is located in the bottom left corner of a page in normal position, as indicated by the `+'. This is a page with the logical number 0, which has three lines of text:

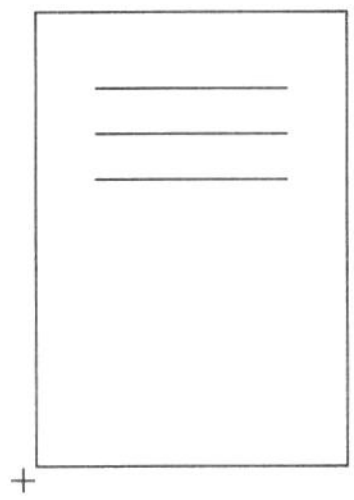

After turning it to the left by 90 degrees, it looks like this:

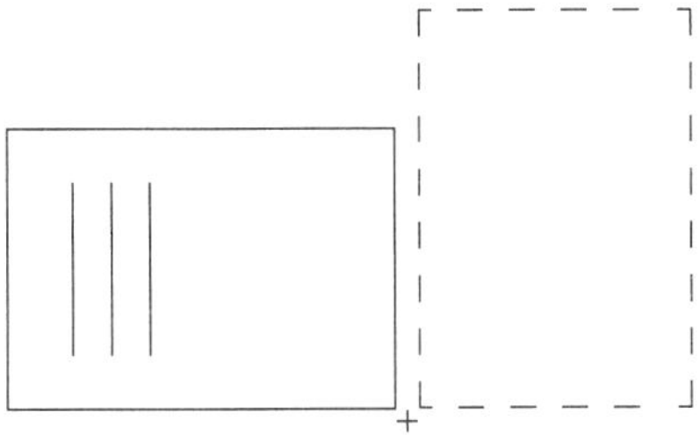

Now, scale it by a factor of 0.6:

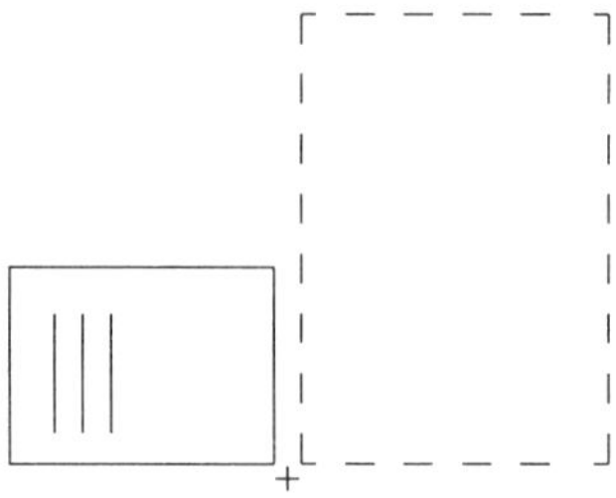

Finally, move it to the right by 20 cm and up by 2 cm:

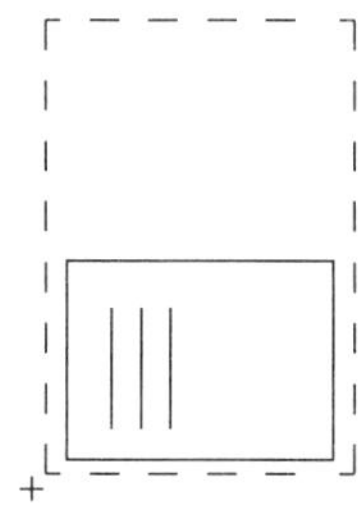

This is merged with the page that has the logical number 1, with two lines of text on it:

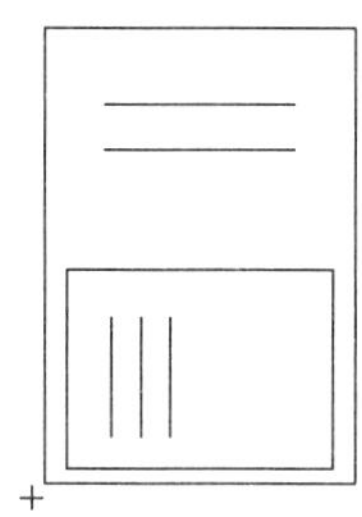

Now page 1 is turned by 90 degrees to the left:

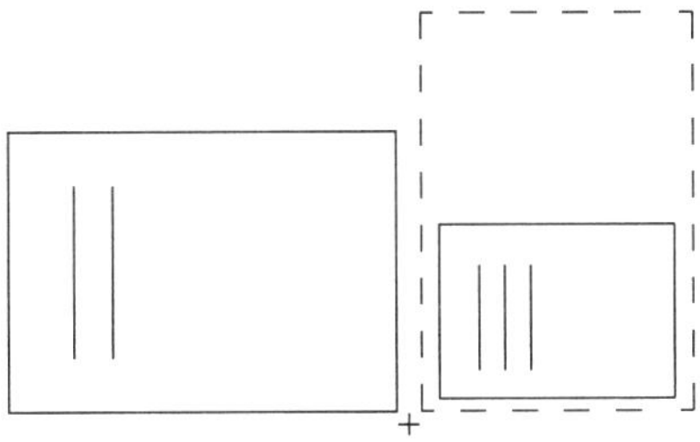

After scaling by factor 0.6, it looks like this:

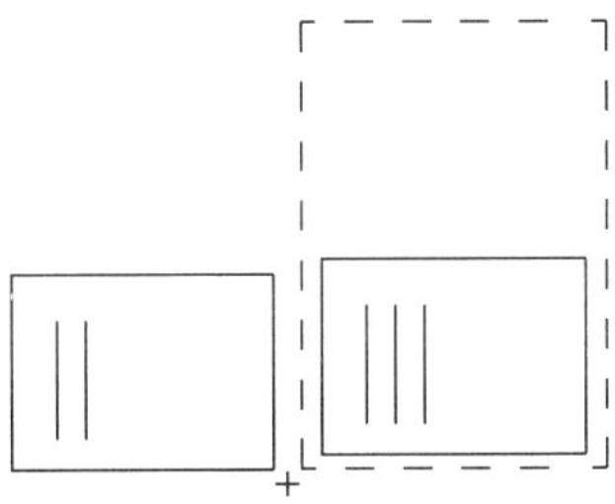

To finish up, page 1 is moved 20 cm to the right and 15 cm to the top:

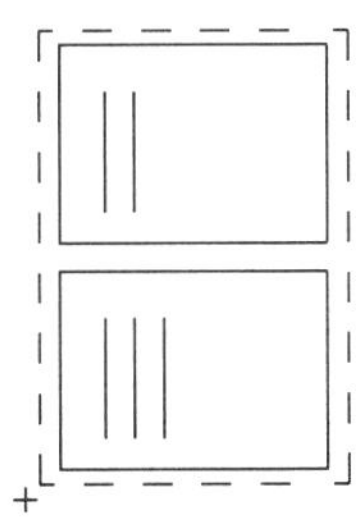

psselect

psselect enables the selection of individual pages. With `psselect -p2-5 /tmp/in.ps /tmp/out.ps`, pages 2, 3, 4, and 5 are selected from `/tmp/in.ps` and written to `/tmp/out.ps`. The command `psselect -p-3 /tmp/in.ps /tmp/out.ps` selects all pages up to page 3. The command `psselect -r -p4- /tmp/in.ps /tmp/out.ps` selects the pages from page 4 to the last page and prints them in reverse order.

Using Ghostscript to View the Output

On a graphical display, the PostScript file `/tmp/out.ps` can be viewed with `gs -r60 /tmp/out.ps`. Scroll through the pages by pressing ↵ in the terminal window from which you started Ghostscript. Terminate with Ctrl + C.

As a graphical front-end for Ghostscript, use `gv`. To view the above-mentioned output file, for example, enter `gv /tmp/out.ps`. The program is especially useful whenever there is a need to zoom in or out on a document or to view it in landscape orientation (although this has no effect on the file contents). It can also be used to select individual pages, which can then be printed directly from within `gv`.

ASCII Text Encoding

In plain text files, each character is represented as a certain numeric code. Characters and their matching codes are defined in code tables. Depending on the code tables used by an application and by the print filter, the same code may be represented as one character on the screen and as another one when printed.

Standard character sets only comprise the range from code 0 to code 255. Of these, codes 0 through 127 represent the pure ASCII set, which is identical for every encoding. It comprises all "normal" letters as well as digits and some special characters, but none of the country-specific special characters. Codes 128 through 255 of the ASCII set are reserved for country-specific special characters, such as umlauts.

However, the number of special characters in different languages is much larger than 128. Therefore, codes 128 to 255 are not the same for each country. Rather, the same code may represent different country-specific characters, depending on the language used.

The codes for Western European languages are defined by ISO-8859-1 (also called Latin 1). The ISO-8859-2 encoding (Latin 2) defines the character sets for Central and Eastern European languages. Code 241 (octal), for example, is defined as the (Spanish) inverted exclamation mark in ISO-8859-1, but the same code 241 is defined as an uppercase A with an ogonek in ISO-8859-2. The ISO-8859-15 encoding is basically the same as ISO-8859-1, but, among other things, it includes the Euro currency sign, defined as code 244 (octal).

A Sample Text

The commands below must be entered as a single line without any of the backslashes ('\') at the end of displayed lines.

Create a sample text file with:

```
newbie@earth:~ >  echo -en "\rCode 241(octal):  \
     \241\r\nCode 244(octal):  \244\r\f" >example
```

Visualizing the Sample with Different Encodings

Under X, enter these commands to open three terminals:

```
xterm -fn -*-*-*-*-*-*-14-*-*-*-*-*-iso8859-1 -title iso8859-1 &
xterm -fn -*-*-*-*-*-*-14-*-*-*-*-*-iso8859-15 -title iso8859-15 &
xterm -fn -*-*-*-*-*-*-14-*-*-*-*-*-iso8859-2 -title iso8859-2 &
```

Use the terminals to display the sample file in each of them with `cat example`. The "iso8859-1" terminal should display code 241 as the inverted (Spanish) exclamation mark and code 244 as the general currency symbol. The "iso8859-15" terminal should display code 241 as the inverted (Spanish) exclamation mark and code 244 as the Euro symbol. The "iso8859-2" terminal should display code 241 as an uppercase A with an ogonek and code 244 as the general currency symbol.

Due to the fact that character encodings are defined as fixed sets, it is not possible to combine all the different country-specific characters with each other in an arbitrary way. For example, the A with an ogonek cannot be used together with the Euro symbol in the same text file.

To obtain more information (including a correct representation of each character), consult the corresponding man page in each terminal — the man page for `iso_8859-1` (`man iso_8859-1`) in the "iso8859-1" terminal, the man page for `iso_8859-15` (`man iso_8859-15`) in the "iso8859-15" terminal, and the man page for `iso_8859-2` (`man iso_8859-2`) in the "iso8859-2" terminal.

Printing the Sample with Different Encodings

When printed, ASCII text files, such as the `example` file, are treated in a similar way according to the encoding set for the print queue used. However, word processor documents should not be affected by this, because their print output is in PostScript format (not ASCII).

Consequently, when printing the above `example` file, characters are represented according to the encoding set for ASCII files in your printing system. You can also convert the text file into PostScript beforehand to change the character encoding as needed. The following `a2ps` commands achieve this for the `example` file:

```
newbie@earth:~ >  a2ps -1 -X ISO-8859-1 \
     -o example-ISO-8859-1.ps example
newbie@earth:~ >  a2ps -1 -X ISO-8859-15 \
     -o example-ISO-8859-15.ps example
newbie@earth:~ >  a2ps -1 -X ISO-8859-2 \
     -o example-ISO-8859-2.ps example
```

When printing the files `example-ISO-8859-1.ps`, `example-ISO-8859-15.ps`, and `example-ISO-8859-2.ps`, the files are printed with the encoding determined with `a2ps`.

Printing in a TCP/IP Network

Find extensive documentation about the LPRng printing system in the *LPRng-Howto* in `/usr/share/doc/packages/lprng/LPRng-HOWTO.html` and on the CUPS printing system in the *CUPS Software Administrators Manual* in `/usr/share/doc/packages/cups/sam.html`.

Terminology

Print server

Print server refers to a complete, dedicated printing host with the required CPU power, memory, and hard disk space.

Print server box or network printer

- *Print server box* refers to a computer with relatively limited resources, which is equipped with both a TCP/IP network link and a local printer port. This includes "router boxes" with a built-in printer port.
- A *network printer* is a printer device with its own TCP/IP port. Basically, it is a printer with an integrated print server box. Network printers and print server boxes are handled in essentially the same way.

There is an important distinction to be made between a network printer or a print server box on the one hand and a true print server on the other. As a somewhat special case, there are large printer devices that have a complete print server included with them to make them network-capable. These are treated like print servers because clients will talk to the printer only through the server and not directly.

LPD server An *LPD server* is a print server that is addressed with the LPD protocol. This is the case if the print server runs the LPRng and lpdfilter print system (lpd, to be precise) or the CUPS print system configured in a way that the machine can be addressed with the LPD protocol.

IPP server or CUPS server An "IPP server" or *CUPS server* is a print server that is addressed with the IPP protocol. This is the case if the print server runs the CUPS print system (cupsd, to be precise).

CUPS network server The term "CUPS network server" refers to a CUPS server that was specifically configured to share its queues with other network hosts via UDP broadcast (using UDP port 631).

Quick Configuration of a Client Machine

Usually, client machines in a network do not have any locally connected printers. Rather, the client sends print jobs to a print server. If you have a print server and an additional local printer is connected to the client, you need a client configuration as well as a configuration for the local printer. The print system on the client machine should be selected in accordance with the print system on the print server.

Configuration for an LPD Server

If there is no CUPS network server in the network, but only an LPD server, use the LPRng and lpdfilter print system on the client. In this case, the client machine does not require any further configuration, as even remote queues can be addressed directly when using the LPRng spooler. See *Command-Line Tools for LPRng* on page 164.

However, this is only possible if the LPD server was configured to allow the client to print to its queues. To print from applications, enter
`lpr -P⟨queuename⟩@⟨printserver⟩`
in the application. This corresponds to the procedure described in *Managing Remote Queues* on page 167. However, no file name is specified.

Some applications are preconfigured to use CUPS and must be switched to LPRng. Especially KDE and the KDE printing program kprinter must be set to 'Print through an external program'. If this is not done, it will not be possible to enter the print command.

Configuration for a CUPS Network Server

If the print server is a CUPS network server, start the YaST2 printer configuration module, click 'Change' then 'Advanced' and select one of the following options:

CUPS as a server (default in standard installations) If no printer is connected locally, no local queue was configured with YaST2. In this case, cupsd is not started automatically, Activate the 'cups' service to start cupsd (normally for the runlevels 3 and 5).

The client machine does not require any further configuration, as a CUPS network server broadcasts its queues to all network hosts at regular intervals. Therefore, the queues of the network server will automatically be available on the client machine after a short time.

However, this is only possible if the broadcasting function is enabled on the CUPS network server, the broadcast address used is suitable for the client machine, and the client machine is permitted to print to the queues of the CUPS network server.

CUPS in client-only mode If you merely want to print via the queues of the CUPS network server, CUPS can be run in client-only mode. In the YaST2 *client-only* printer configuration, specify the name of the CUPS network server.

In this mode, the client machine does not run cupsd and the file `/etc/printcap` does not exist. However, applications that cannot be configured to use CUPS will only offer the queues listed in the local `/etc/printcap`. In this case, it is advisable to run CUPS in server mode, as the local cupsd will automatically generate an `/etc/printcap` containing the queue names of the CUPS network server.

TCP/IP Network Printing Protocols

The following lists the different methods that can be used to implement printing on a TCP/IP network. The decision of which one to use does not so much depend on the hardware, but more on the possibilities offered by each protocol. Accordingly, the YaST2 printer configuration asks you to select a protocol and not a hardware device when setting up network printing.

Printing over the LPD protocol
Print jobs are forwarded to a remote queue over the LPD protocol. To allow this, the protocol must be supported both on the client and the server side.

Client side

LPRng
The `lpd` of LPRng supports the LPD protocol. For remote printing, a local queue must be set up through which the local `lpd` can forward the print job to a remote queue, using the LPD protocol.
LPRng also allows network printing without a local `lpd` running. With this method, the `lpr` included in package `lprng` uses the protocol to directly forward a print job to the remote queue.

CUPS
CUPS has support for the LPD protocol, but only through the CUPS daemon `cupsd`. To enable this, a local queue must be set up through which the print job can be relayed by the local `cupsd` to the remote queue using the LPD protocol.

Server side

Print server
The printer must be connected locally to the print server and the print server itself must support the LPD protocol.

Network printer or print server box
The print server box or network printer must support the LPD protocol, which should normally be the case.

Printing over the IPP protocol
Print jobs are forwarded to a remote queue over the IPP protocol. To allow this, the protocol must be supported both on the client and the server side.

Client side

LPRng
LPRng does not yet support the IPP protocol.

CUPS

CUPS supports the IPP protocol through `cupsd`. For this method, a local queue must be set up, which can be used by the local cupsd to forward print jobs to a remote queue using the IPP protocol.
CUPS also allows network printing without a local `cupsd` running. With this method, the program `lp` included in package `cups-client` or the programs `xpp` or `kprinter` use the IPP protocol to directly forward a print job to a remote queue.

Server side

Print server

The printer must be connected locally to the print server and the print server itself must support the IPP protocol.

Network printer or print server box

The print server box or network printer must support the IPP protocol, which is only the case with some recent devices.

Direct remote printing through TCP sockets

With this method, there is no print job that gets relayed to a remote queue. No protocol capable of handling print jobs and queues is involved in the process (neither LPD nor IPP). Rather, printer-specific data is transferred to a remote TCP port via TCP sockets, which must be supported both on the client and on the server side.

Client side

LPRng and lpdfilter

The `lpd` of the LPRng printing system supports streaming data directly via TCP sockets. To enable this, there must be a local queue that can be used by the local `lpd` to convert the data of each print job into the printer-specific format (with the help of lpdfilter) and to transfer them to the remote TCP port via TCP sockets after conversion.
With LPRng, it is also possible to implement this method without a local `lpd`. This requires that `lpr` (included in package `lprng`) is called with the `-Y` option to transfer data directly to the remote TCP port via TCP sockets. For details on this, see the man page for `lpr` (`man lpr`). However, there is no print filter involved at all, which means print data must be in the printer-specific format from the beginning.

CUPS

CUPS supports the direct transfer of print data via TCP sockets, but only if `cupsd` is running. To enable this method, there must be a local queue that can be used by the local `cupsd` to convert the data of each print job into the printer-specific format and to stream data to the remote TCP port via TCP sockets after conversion.

Server side

Network printer or print server box

Print server boxes and network printers normally keep a TCP port open to transfer a data stream in the printer-specific format directly to the printer.

HP network printers, in particular, HP JetDirect print server boxes, use port 9100 as the default for this kind of data stream. JetDirect print server boxes with two or three local printer ports listen on TCP ports 9100, 9101, and 9102. The same ports are used by many other print server boxes. If you are not sure about this, ask the manufacturer or consult the printer manual to find out which port is used by your device for raw socket printing. Additional information about this can be found in the *LPRng-Howto* (`file:/usr/share/doc/packages/lprng/LPRng-HOWTO.html`), especially `file:/usr/share/doc/packages/lprng/LPRng-HOWTO.html#SECNETWORK`, `file:/usr/share/doc/packages/lprng/LPRng-HOWTO.html#SOCKETAPI`, and `file:/usr/share/doc/packages/lprng/LPRng-HOWTO.html#AEN4858`.

Printing over the SMB protocol

With this method, print jobs are converted into the printer-specific format first then transferred via the SMB protocol to a remote share that represents a remote printer. Both the client and the server side must support the SMB protocol. Although neither LPRng and lpdfilter or CUPS have direct support for the SMB protocol, they can support it indirectly with the help of `smbclient` and `smbspool`, respectively. Both programs are included in package `samba-client`.

Client side

LPRng and lpdfilter

LPRng needs lpdfilter to support the SMB protocol. There must be a local queue through which the local `lpd` can convert the print job into the printer-specific format with the help of lpdfilter. The latter then forwards the data with the help of `smbclient` to the remote share, using the SMB protocol.

CUPS

There must be a local queue that can be used by the local `cupsd` to convert data into the printer-specific format. After that, data is transferred to the remote share by `smbspool` using the SMB protocol.

Server side

SMB print server

The printer must be connected to an SMB print server. The latter is usually a DOS or Windows machine, although it could also be a Samba server powered by Linux.

The SMB print server must support the SMB protocol and access to the printer (to the corresponding share) must have been enabled on the server side.

Filtering for Network Printers

This section describes the possible ways to implement filtering for network printers. Independent of the filtering method used, there should be exactly one point in the entire process chain where the input file is converted into the final format — the one your printer requires to put the data on paper (PostScript, PCL, ESC/P).

The conversion must be accomplished somehow somewhere by a print filter. It should run on a machine with sufficient CPU power and disk space to handle the task. This is especially true when using Ghostscript to convert data for high-resolution color and photo printouts on non-PostScript devices. Network printers and print server boxes usually do not have any built-in filtering capabilities, so they mostly require a print server.

If your printer is a PostScript model, you may be able to do without a print server. Also, PostScript printers are often able to autodetect whether their input is in ASCII or PostScript format and switch accordingly. To print ASCII texts containing country-specific characters, it may be necessary to set the printer to the respective character encoding or to use `a2ps` to convert the ASCII text into a PostScript file with the respective encoding. See *ASCII Text Encoding* on page 204. However, as long as the printing volume is not too high, a PostScript printer does not usually require a dedicated print server as most applications are able to produce ASCII or PostScript output.

Network printers and print server boxes, on the other hand, often do not have the resources to handle higher printing volumes on their own. You will then need a dedicated print server with sufficient disk space to store all the print jobs queued temporarily.

Prerequisites

The printer model must be supported by SuSE Linux, because print data must be converted into the printer-specific language by a filter, as described for local printers (see *Manual Configuration of Local Printer Ports* on page 156 and the subsequent sections).

Terminology

- A *client* is the host on which the print job is issued.
- *Print server box* also refers to network printers (and not only print server boxes in the narrower sense), because both are treated the same way.
- *Print server* refers to a central, dedicated host that handles all print jobs from all the network's clients. A print server can either send data to a locally connected printer or transfer it to print server boxes through a TCP/IP network.
- *Forwarding (queue)* refers to a queue that forwards or relays print jobs to remote queues, but does not do any filtering.
- *Filter (queue)* refers to a queue that filters (converts) print jobs.
- A *prefilter (queue)* is a queue that filters print jobs then transfers the resulting data to a forwarding queue on the same host.
- A *forwarding filter (queue)* is a queue that filters print jobs and forwards the resulting data to a remote queue.
- *Streaming filter (queue)* refers to a queue that filters print jobs then streams the resulting data to a remote TCP port.
- The above terms may be combined with *LPD(-based)*, *IPP(-based)*, or *SMB(-based)* to indicate the protocol used in conjunction with the method.

Possible Filtering Methods for Network Printing

Print server box with filtering by client
The filtering is performed on the client side. A complete printing system must run on the client — either the LPRng and lpdfilter system or the complete CUPS printing system.

Client using the LPD protocol (LPRng or CUPS)

Prefilter followed by forwarding (LPRng only)
This is the classic remote printing solution involving two queues on the client side, one for filtering and one for forwarding.

1. Client: The prefilter queue converts the print job into the printer format then transfers the data to the forwarding queue as a new print job.
2. Client: The forwarding queue relays the print data to the print server box (LPD-based forwarding).
3. LPD print server box: The print data is transferred to the printer.

Forwarding filter (LPRng or CUPS) With this method, filtering and forwarding is performed by one queue. If used with the LPRng printing system, the method is also called "lpr bounce" or "lpd bounce."

1. Client: The print job is converted into the printer format and forwarded to the print server box (LPD-based forwarding filter).
2. LPD print server box: The print data is transferred to the printer.

Client using the IPP protocol (CUPS only)

Forwarding filter (CUPS only)

1. Client: The print job is converted into the printer format and forwarded to the print server box (IPP-based forwarding filter).
2. IPP print server box: The print data is transferred to the printer.

Client using TCP socket (LPRng or CUPS)

Streaming filter (LPRng or CUPS)

1. Client: The print job is converted into the printer format and streamed to the print server box (streaming filter).
2. Print server box: The print data is transferred to the printer.

Print server box with filtering by print server
Because the filtering is performed on the print server, the latter must run a complete printing system (including the corresponding daemon),

either LPRng and lpdfilter or CUPS. On the other hand, running a complete printing system on the client side is not strictly required (because the server does all the filtering), provided the client issues print jobs with the `lpr` command (in the case of LPRng) or with `lp`, `xpp`, or `kprinter` (in the case of CUPS) and jobs are directly sent to the print server. In either case, the print server must support the protocol used by the client (either LPD or IPP).

When the print server receives a print job, it processes it in the same way as described above for a client. The client may use one protocol to send print jobs to the print server and the latter another protocol to send data to the print server box.

Client using the LPD protocol (LPRng only)

Direct print command (LPRng only)

1. Client: Sends the print job directly to the print server with the `lpr` command.
2. LPD print server: Converts the print job into the printer format and sends the data to the print server box.

Forwarding (LPRng only)

1. Client: Forwards the print job to the print server (LPD-based forwarding).
2. LPD print server: Converts the print job into the printer format and sends the data to the print server box.

Client using the IPP protocol (CUPS only)

Direct print command (CUPS only)

1. Client: Sends the print job directly to the print server using the `lp` command or the programs `xpp` or `kprinter`.
2. IPP print server: Converts the print job into the printer format and sends the data to the print server box.

Printer connected to a print server with filtering by the print server

If the print server has a local printer connected to it, the procedure is the same as described under *Print server box with filtering by print server*, with the difference that it sends the data to the printer.

Printer connected to a print server with filtering by the client

This is probably not such a good idea, regardless of whether you have an LPD or an IPP print server. To implement this, you would need to install and configure a complete printing system on each client host. As a better solution, consider a printer connected to a print server with filtering by the print server.

SMB print server with filtering by client

Filtering cannot be easily implemented on an SMB print server. In that sense, an SMB print server is treated in the same way as a print server box.

Client using the SMB protocol (LPRng or CUPS)

SMB-based forwarding filter (LPRng or CUPS)

1. Client: Converts the print job into the printer format and forwards the data to the SMB print server (SMB-based forwarding filter).
2. SMB print server: Sends the data to the printer.

Remote Printer Troubleshooting

Checking the TCP/IP network

First, make sure everything is in order with the TCP/IP network in general, including name resolution (see *Linux in the Network* on page 333).

Checking the filter configuration

Connect the printer to the first parallel port of your computer. To test the connection, initially set it up as a local printer to exclude any network-related problems. If the printer works locally, you have found the correct Ghostscript driver and other configuration options.

Testing a remote lpd

The command `netcat -z host 515 && echo ok || echo failed` tests whether `lpd` can be reached via TCP on port 515 of `host`. If `lpd` cannot be reached in this way, it is either not running at all or there is some basic network problem.

As `root`, enter the command
`echo -e "\004queue" | netcat -w 2 -p 722 host 515`
to get a (possibly very long) status report about the `queue` on the `host`, if `lpd` is running and the host is reachable. If the daemon does not respond, it is either not running at all or there is a basic network problem. If `lpd` does respond, the output should give an idea why printing through the `queue` on `host` does not work. These are some examples:

```
lpd: your host does not have line printer access
```

```
lpd: queue does not exist
printer: spooling disabled
printer: printing disabled
```

Output 13: lpd Status Messages

If you get messages like the ones above, the problem lies with the remote `lpd`.

Testing a remote cupsd
The command `netcat -u -l -p 631 & PID=$!  ; sleep 40 ; kill $PID` can be used to check if there is a CUPS network server in the network. By default, CUPS network servers broadcasts its queues via port 631 at thirty-second intervals. After waiting for forty seconds, the output should appear as follows if a broadcasting CUPS network server exists:

```
... ipp://ServerName.Domain:631/printers/queuename
```

Output 14: CUPS Network Server Broadcast

The command `netcat -z host 631 && echo ok || echo failed` tests whether `cupsd` can be reached via TCP on port 631 of `host`. If `cupsd` cannot be reached in this way, it is either not running at all or there is some basic network problem.

With the command `lpstat -h host -l -t`, get a (possibly very long) status report about all queues on `host`, provided `cupsd` is running and the host is reachable.

With the command `echo -en "\r" | lp -d queue -h host`, send a print job consisting of a single carriage return character to test if the `queue` on `host` accepts any print jobs. This test command should not print out anything or only cause the printer to eject an empty page.

Testing a remote SMB server
To test the basic operability of an SMB server, enter:

```
earth:~ #  echo -en "\r" \
    | smbclient '//HOST/SHARE' 'PASSWORD' \
    -c 'print -' -N -U 'USER' \
    && echo ok || echo failed
```

This command must be entered as a single line without the backslash ('\'). For HOST, enter the host name of the Samba server. For SHARE, enter the name of the remote queue. For PASSWORD, enter the password string. Replace USER with the user name. This test command should not print out anything or only cause the printer to eject an empty page.

The command `smbclient -N -L host` displays any shares on the `host` that are currently available. Details on this can be obtained from the man page for `smbclient` (`man smbclient`).

Troubleshooting an unreliable network printer or print server box

Spoolers on print server boxes often become unreliable when having to deal with relatively high printing volumes. As the cause of this lies with the server side spooler, there is mostly no way to fix this.

As a workaround, however, circumvent the spooler on the print server box by using TCP sockets to directly stream data to the printer connected to the host. This turns the print server box into a mere data converter between the two different data streams (TCP/IP network and local printer line), which effectively makes the printer behave like a local printer although it is connected to the print server box. Without the spooler acting as an intermediary, this method also gives much more direct control over the printer device in general.

To use this method, you need to know the corresponding TCP port on the print server box. If the printer is switched on and properly connected, you should be able to determine the TCP port a minute or so after booting the print server box with the program `nmap`. Running `nmap` on the print server box may return an output similar to this:

```
Port        State       Service
23/tcp      open        telnet
80/tcp      open        http
515/tcp     open        printer
631/tcp     open        cups
9100/tcp    open        jetdirect
```

This output means:

- You can log in on the above print server box with `telnet` to look for important information or to change basic configuration options.

- The above print server runs an HTTP daemon, which can provide detailed server information or allow you to set specific printing options.
- The print spooler running on the print server box can be reached over the LPD protocol on port 515.
- The print spooler running on the print server box can also be reached over the IPP protocol on port 631.
- The printer connected to the print server box can be accessed directly via TCP sockets on port 9100.

Print Servers Supporting Both LPD and IPP

Supporting Both Protocols through CUPS

By default, the CUPS daemon only supports the IPP protocol. However, the program `/usr/lib/cups/daemon/cups-lpd` from the package `cups` makes it possible for a CUPS daemon to accept print jobs arriving via the LPD protocol on port 515. This requires that the corresponding service is enabled for `inetd` — either with YaST2 or by enabling the corresponding line in `/etc/inetd.conf` manually.

Supporting Both Protocols by Using LPRng and lpdfilter with CUPS

There may be situations where you want to run both LPRng and lpdfilter and CUPS on one system, maybe because you want to enhance the functionality of LPD with some CUPS features or because you need the LPRng and lpdfilter system as an add-on for certain special cases.

Running the two systems together on the same system will lead to a number of problems, however. Below, we list the most important of these and briefly explain the limitations resulting from them. The topic is too complex to describe them in any greater detail here. There are several ways to solve these issues, depending on the individual case.

- You should not rely on YaST2 for configuration if you install both printing systems. The printer configuration module of YaST2 has not been written with this case in mind.
- There is a conflict between package `lprng` and package `cups-client`, because they contain a number of files with identical names, such as `/usr/bin/lpr` and `/usr/bin/lp`. You should, therefore, not install package `cups-client`. This, however, means that no CUPS-based

command-line tools are available, but only those included with LPRng. You are still able to print through CUPS print queues from the X Window System with `xpp` or `kprinter`, however, as well as from all application programs with built-in support for CUPS.

- By default, `cupsd` creates the `/etc/printcap` file when started and writes the names of CUPS queues to it. This is done to maintain compatibility with applications that expect queue names in `/etc/printcap` to offer them in their print dialogs. With both printing systems installed, disable this `cupsd` feature to reserve `/etc/printcap` for exclusive use by the LPRng and lpdfilter printing system. As a result, applications that get queue names only from `/etc/printcap` can use only these local queues, but not the remote queues made available by CUPS through the network.

Hotplugging Services

Hardware components that can be connected and disconnected from the system while it is running are growing more common. As well as USB, the most prominent example for this kind of component, there are PCI, PCMCIA, Firewire, SCSI, and other interfaces.

Hotplug systems are responsible for recognizing newly-connected or installed hardware and automatically making it available for use. Components that will be removed again need, furthermore, to be prepared for this event. If removed without prior warning, resources must be freed again.

Hotplugging in Linux

Little programs called daemons watch parts of a system for external events. The inetd daemon, for example, watches incoming network requests. The daemon for hotplugging is the kernel itself. The driver for an interface must be able to recognize new devices and report them to the system in a standardized way. USB, PCMCIA, Firewire, the network subsystem, and, to some extent, PCI are able to do this in the 2.4 kernel. This part of hotplugging is firmly built into the corresponding modules and cannot be influenced without changing the kernel.

Note

PCMCIA devices are only being handled by the hotplugging service if they are CardBus cards and the PCMCIA system kernel was selected. They then appear as PCI devices. More detailed information about this can be found in the section on PCMCIA.

Note

The second part of the hotplugging service initiates the necessary steps for the respective registration and release of devices and is a collection of scripts in the directory `/etc/hotplug` with the main script `/sbin/hotplug`. This script is the interface between the kernel and the collection of hotplugging scripts. These scripts are referred to as the "hotplug system" for the course of this chapter.

When a hot-pluggable device is connected or removed, the kernel calls the `/sbin/hotplug/` script and passes additional information to the corresponding hardware component. This script directs the tasks — depending on the type of hardware — to additional scripts. These insert or remove the modules respectively and call other programs for the configuration of the components. These programs are located in `/etc/hotplug` and always end with `.agent`.

Hotplugging and Coldplugging

Although the kernel always passes hotplug events to `/sbin/hotplug`, the hotplug system needs to be started initially with the command `rchotplug start`. All hotplug events are discarded if hotplug has not been started.

Aside from this, there are components recognized by the kernel even before the file system can be accessed. These events are simply lost. This is why the scripts /etc/hotplug/*.rc attempt to create these events artificially for already existing hardware. The term "coldplugging" is used in this respect. If the USB base modules have not been loaded until then, they are loaded and the USB device file system usbdefs is mounted.

After hotplug has been stopped by calling rchotplug stop, no more events can be evaluated. Hot-plugging can be completely deactivated if the hardware configuration is never changed during operation. This, however,requires other methods of installing USB or PCMCIA devices.

The path /etc/sysconfig/hotplug contains a few variables that control the behavior of hotplug. For instance, the variable ⟨*HOTPLUG_DEBUG*⟩ influences the verbosity of hotplug. The variables ⟨*HOTPLUG_START_USB*⟩, ⟨*HOTPLUG_START_PCI*⟩, and ⟨*HOTPLUG_START_NET*⟩ determine that only events of a certain type are evaluated. All the other variables are explained in detail in the corresponding subsections. All the hotplug messages are logged in the file /var/log/messages — the system log.

USB

When a new USB device is connected, the script /etc/hotplug/usb.agent determines an appropriate driver and ensures that it is loaded. This driver is not necessarily a kernel module. Many USB cameras, for instance, are directly accessed by applications.

The assignment of drivers to hardware is multistaged: First, the file /etc/hotplug/usb.usermap is checked for an entry that specifies whether this hardware should be handled by an application or by a dedicated initialization script. If neither is the case, an individual assignment to a kernel module is searched for in /etc/hotplug/usb.handmap. If nothing is found there (which is most often the case), the assignment table of the kernel, /lib/modules/⟨*kernelversion*⟩/modules.usbmap, is queried. An additional USB hardware scan is run at this point, which triggers further actions if KDE is used. An appropriate YaST configuration module is presented, for instance, for devices connected for the first time or applications are run for using the new device. This mechanism runs in parallel to the other actions triggered by /etc/hotplug/usb.agent.

USB devices are differently by the usb.agent, according to type:

storage devices hard disks, for example, are handled by the script /usr/sbin/checkhotmounts as soon as the required drivers are loaded.

network devices create their own hotplug event in the kernel as soon as these are registered. The `usb.agent` merely records hardware information which is later used by the network event. This is only a transient solution for the 2.4 kernel and fails whenever more than one USB network devices are employed. This however happens only very rarely.

cameras are accessed by way of the hardware-scanning KDE mechanism. The access permissions of the device file are additionally set by `/etc/hotplug/usb/usbcam` to those of the logged-in user so he can access the device when using KDE.

mice only require a loaded module that, in this case, is loaded for immediate use.

keyboards needed during booting so are not handled by hotplug.

ISDN modem not installed automatically yet.

There are some USB-specific variables in `/etc/sysconfig/hotplug`. ⟨*HOTPLUG_USB_HOSTCONTROLLER_LIST*⟩ contains the driver for the USB controller in the order in which loading is attempted. When a driver is loaded successfully, those modules that need to be unloaded on removal of the component are listed in ⟨*HOTPLUG_USB_MODULES_TO_UNLOAD*⟩. All remaining USB modules are not unloaded, because it cannot be determined with certainty whether they are still required by a device. The variable ⟨*HOTPLUG_USB_NET_MODULES*⟩ contains the names of those modules that provide a network interface. A hardware descriptor for later reference on network events is stored when one of these modules is loaded. This process is logged in the system log.

PCI and PCMCIA

PCMCIA cards require a careful scrutiny because hotplug only handles CardBus cards. This handling is furthermore only done if the PCMCIA system of the kernel is activated. This condition is explained in more detail in the software section of the PCMCIA chapter.

CardBus cards are, technically-speaking, almost PCI devices. This is why both are handled by the same hotplug script — `/etc/hotplug/pci.agent`. It essentially determines a driver for the card and loads it. In addition to this, a record of where the new card has been connected (PCI bus or PCMCIA slots and the slot designator) is stored, so a later hotplug network event can read this information and select the correct configuration.

The determination of the drive is two-staged in this case: the file /etc/hotplug/pci.handmap is searched for individual settings and, if nothing was found, the PCI driver table of the kernel /lib/modules⟨*kernelversion*⟩/modules.pcimap is subsequently searched. To change the driver assignment, the file /etc/hotplug/pci.handmap should be altered, as the other list is overwritten on a kernel update.

Unlike with USB, no special actions are executed depending on the type of PCI or CardBus card. The kernel creates a hotplug network event for network cards, which induces the installation of the interface. Further action must ensue manually for all other cards. The hotplug system is, however, still being expanded in this respect.

As soon as the card is removed, the employed modules are unloaded again. Should this lead to problems with certain modules, this can be prevented by writing the names of those modules into ⟨*HOTPLUG_PCI_MODULES_NOT_TO_UNLOAD*⟩.

Network

When a new network interface is registered or unregistered in the kernel, the kernel creates a hotplug network event. This is evaluated by /etc/hotplug/net.agent. Only ethernet, token ring, and wireless LAN interfaces are currently taken into account. Other mechanisms exist for all other kinds of networks, like modems or ISDN. Network interfaces which are provided by PCMCIA cards and are handled by cardmanager instead of hotplug are likewise not handled here. A message then appears in the system log.

First, which hardware provides the interface is determined. Because the 2.4 kernel cannot provide such information, a record created following the USB or PCI event is used. Although this works well in most cases, it is regarded as a temporary quick fix only. For this reason, two network cards cannot be connected simultaneously. To use multiple hotplug-enabled network cards, connect them subsequently with the computer. A latency of a few seconds between connections is sufficient. This transmission of information is logged in /var/log/messages.

Insert additional individual actions to execute following the installation of a new network device in /sbin/ifup. Details about this can be found in the man page for ifup (man ifup). It is also possible to apply different default routing depending on the connected hardware. Refer to the man page for route (man route) for details.

If the probing of the hardware behind the interface fails and only one hotplug network device is used, the description of the network hardware in `/etc/sysconfig/hotplug` can be written to the variable ⟨*HOTPLUG_NET_DEFAULT_HARDWARE*⟩. This string must correspond to what should be used by `/sbin/ifup` for the allocation of the correct configuration. The variable ⟨*HOTPLUG_NET_TIMEOUT*⟩ determines for how long `net.agent` waits for a dynamically-created hardware desciption.

Other Devices and Further Development

All the kinds of hotplugging-enabled devices not described above are currently not handled. Hotplugging, however, is undergoing massive development that depends heavily on the abilities of the kernel. It is expected that better possibilities will be offered with the kernel 2.6.

Configuring and Using Laptop Computers

Laptop computers have unique needs. These include Power Management (APM and ACPI), infrared interfaces (IrDA), and PC cards (PCMCIA). Occasionally, such components can also be found in desktop computers. These are essentially no different than those used in laptops. For this reason, their use and configuration is summarized in this chapter.

PCMCIA

PCMCIA stands for "Personal Computer Memory Card International Association." It is used as a general term for all hardware and software involved.

The Hardware

The essential component is the PCMCIA card. There are two distinct types:

PC cards These are currently the most used cards. They use a 16-bit bus for data transmission, are usually relatively cheap, are generally stable, and are fully supported.

CardBus Cards This is a more recent standard. It uses a 32-bit bus, which makes them faster, but also more expensive. Because the data transfer rate is frequently restricted at another point, it is often not worth the extra cost. There are now many drivers for these cards, although some are still unstable. This also depends on the available PCMCIA controller.

If the PCMCIA service is active, determine the type of the inserted card with the command `cardctl ident`. A list of supported cards can be found in `SUPPORTED.CARDS` in `/usr/share/doc/packages/pcmcia`. The current version of the PCMCIA-HOWTO is also located there.

The second necessary component is the PCMCIA controller or the PC card or CardBus bridge. This establishes the connection between the card and the PCI bus and, in older devices, the connection to the ISA bus as well. These controllers are almost always compatible with the Intel chip i82365. All common models are supported. The type of controller is shown with the command `probe`. If this is a PCI device, the command `lspci -vt` also shows some interesting information.

The Software

Differences Between PCMCIA Systems

There are currently two PCMCIA systems — external PCMCIA and kernel PCMCIA. The external PCMCIA system by David Hinds is the older system, which makes it better tested. It is still being developed. The sources of the modules used are not integrated in the kernel sources, which is why it is called an "external" system. From kernel 2.4, there are alternative modules in the kernel sources. These form the kernel PCMCIA system. The basic modules were written by Linus Torvalds. They support the more recent CardBus bridges better.

Unfortunately, these two systems are not compatible. There are various sets of card drivers in both systems. For this reason, only one system can be used, depending on the hardware involved. The default in SuSE Linux is the more recent kernel PCMCIA. It is possible to change the system, however. To do this, the variable ⟨*PCMCIA_SYSTEM*⟩ in the file `/etc/sysconfig/pcmcia` must be given either the value `external` or `kernel`. Then PCMCIA must be restarted with `rcpcmcia restart`. For temporary changes, use the commands `rcpcmcia restart external` or `rcpcmcia restart kernel`. If pcmcia is not running, use the option start instead of restart. Detailed information about this can be found in `/usr/share/doc/packages/pcmcia/README.SuSE`

The Base Module

The kernel modules for both systems are located in the kernel packages. In addition, the packages `pcmcia` and `hotplug` are required. When PCMCIA is started, the modules `pcmcia_core`, `i82365` (external PCMCIA) or `yenta_socket` (kernel PCMCIA), and `ds` are loaded. In some very rare cases, the module `tcic` is required instead of `i82365` or `yenta_socket`. They initialize the existing PCMCIA controller and provide basic functionality.

The Card Manager

Because PCMCIA cards can be changed while the system is running, a daemon to monitor the activity in the slots is required. Depending on the PCMCIA system chosen and the hardware used, this task is performed by the card manager or the hotplug system of the kernel. With external PCMCIA, only the card manager is used. For kernel PCMCIA, the card manager only handles PC Card cards. CardBus cards are handled by hotplug. The card manager is started by the PCMCIA start script after the base modules have been loaded. Because hotplug manages other subsystems apart from PCMCIA, it has its own start script. See also *Hotplugging Services* on page 221.

If a card is inserted, card manager or hotplug determines the type and function of the card then loads the corresponding modules. If this is successful, card manager or hotplug starts certain initialization scripts, depending on the function of the card, which in turn establish a network connection, mount partitions from external SCSI hard drives, or carry out other hardware-specific actions. The scripts for the card manager are located in

/etc/pcmcia. The scripts for hotplug can be found in /etc/hotplug. If the card is removed, card manager or hotplug terminates the various card activities using the same scripts. Finally, those modules that are no longer required are unloaded.

Both the start process of PCMCIA and card events are recorded in the system log (/var/log/messages). Here, it is specified which PCMCIA system is currently used and which daemons have been used by which scripts to set up things. In theory, a PCMCIA card can simply be removed. This works very well for network, modem, or ISDN cards as long as there are no open network connections. It does not work in connection with partitions mounted to an external hard drive or with NFS directories. Here, ensure that these units are synchronized and cleanly unmounted. This is no longer possible, of course, if the card has already been removed. In case of doubt, the command cardctl eject may be of help. This command deactivates all cards still in the laptop. To deactivate one card, also specify the slot number, for example, cardctl eject 0.

Configuration

Whether PCMCIA or hotplug is started when booting can be specified with the YaST2 runlevel editor or on the command line using chkconfig. In /etc/sysconfig/pcmcia, there are four variables:

⟨***PCMCIA_SYSTEM***⟩ Specifies which PCMCIA system to use.

⟨***PCMCIA_PCIC***⟩ Contains the name of the module that addresses the PCMCIA controller. Normally, the start script detects this name on its own. The module is only entered here if this goes wrong. Otherwise, this variable should be left empty.

⟨***PCMCIA_CORE_OPTS***⟩ Intended for parameters for the module pcmcia_core. They are only rarely required, however. These options are described in the man page for pcmcia_core (man pcmcia_core).

⟨***PCMCIA_PCIC_OPTS***⟩ Parameters for the module i82365. Refer to the man page for i82365 (man i82365). If yenta_socket is used, these options are ignored, because yenta_socket has no options.

The assignment of drivers to PCMCIA cards for the card manager can be found in the files /etc/pcmcia/config and /etc/pcmcia/*.conf. First, config is read then the *.conf in alphabetical order. The last entry found for a card is decisive. Details on the syntax of these files can be found in the man page for pcmcia (man pcmcia). The assignment of drivers to PCMCIA cards for hotplug is described in *Hotplugging Services* on page 221).

Network Cards (Ethernet, Wireless LAN, and Token Ring)

These can be set up with YaST2 like normal network cards. Select 'PCMCIA' as the card type. All other details about setting up the network can be found in the network chapter. Read the notes there about hotpluggable cards.

ISDN

Even for ISDN PC cards, configuration is done to a large extent using YaST2, as with other ISDN cards. It is not important which PCMCIA card offered there is chosen, but only that it is a PCMCIA card. When setting up hardware and provider, make sure the operating mode is set to `hotplug` and not to `onboot`.

ISDN modems also exist for PCMCIA cards. These are modem cards or multifunction cards with an additional ISDN connection kit. They are treated like an ordinary modem.

Modem

For modem PC cards, there are normally no PCMCIA-specific settings. As soon as a modem is inserted, it is available under `/dev/modem`.

There are also "soft modems" for PCMCIA cards. As a rule, these are not supported. If there are some drivers, they must be integrated individually into the system.

SCSI and IDE

The corresponding driver module is loaded by the card manager or hotplug. When a SCSI or IDE card is inserted, the devices connected to it are available. The device names are detected dynamically. Information about existing SCSI or IDE devices can be found in `/proc/scsi` or `/proc/ide`.

External hard drives, CD-ROM drives, and similar devices must be switched on before the PCMCIA card is inserted into the slot. SCSI devices must be actively terminated.

> **Note**
>
> Before a SCSI or IDE card is removed, all partitions on the devices connected must be unmounted. If you have forgotten to do this, you can only access these devices again after rebooting the system, even if the rest of the system continues to run in a stable manner.
>
> **Note**

You can also install Linux entirely on these external hard drives. However, the boot process is then somewhat more complicated. A boot disk is required in all cases — containing the kernel and an initial ramdisk (initrd). More information about this can be found in *Booting with the Initial Ramdisk* on page 273. The initrd contains a virtual file system that includes all required PCMCIA modules and programs. The boot disk and boot disk images are constructed in the same way. With these, you could always boot your external installation. It is, however, tiresome to load the PCMCIA support every time by hand. More advanced users might create their own boot floppy disk, customized to their own particular system. Hints for doing this can be found in the PCMCIA-HOWTO in the section *Booting from a PCMCIA Device*.

Switching Configurations — SCPM

Often with mobile computers, various configuration profiles are required. With PCMCIA devices, this was never a problem, thanks to the PCMCIA schemes. Because the users of the built-in network cards or USB and firewire devices would also like to use different profiles for system configuration, there is, from SuSE Linux 8.0, the package SCPM (System Configuration Profile Management). For this reason, SuSE no longer supports the PCMCIA schemes. To continue to use these, the configuration must be modified by hand under `/etc/pcmcia`. We recommend using SCPM instead, because any part of the system configuration can be administered here — not just the PCMCIA parts.

Troubleshooting

Occasionally, there are problems with certain laptops and certain cards when using PCMCIA. Most difficulties can be solved with little trouble, if you approach the problem systematically.

Caution

Because both external PCMCIA and kernel PCMCIA are available in parallel in SuSE Linux, consider one special feature when loading modules manually. The two PCMCIA systems use modules of the same name and are located in different subdirectories under `/lib/modules/`⟨*kernelversion*⟩. The subdirectories are named `pcmcia` for kernel PCMCIA and `pcmcia-external` for external PCMCIA. For this reason, the subdirectory must be specified when loading modules manually, either with `insmod /lib/modules/`⟨*kernel version*⟩`/`⟨*subdirectory*⟩`/`⟨*file name of module*⟩ or with `modprobe -t` ⟨*subdirectory*⟩ ⟨*module name*⟩.

Caution

First, find out if the problem is with the card or with the PCMCIA-based system. For this reason, always start the computer first without the card inserted. Only insert the card when the base system appears to function correctly. All meaningful messages are recorded in `/var/log/messages`. The file should therefore be viewed, with `tail -f /var/log/messages` while the necessary tests are made. In this way, the error can be narrowed down to one of the two following cases.

Nonfunctional PCMCIA Base System

If the system hangs when booting with the message PCMCIA: "Starting services" or other strange things happen, starting PCMCIA the next time the system is booted can be prevented by entering `NOPCMCIA=yes` at the boot prompt. To isolate the error further, the base modules of the PCMCIA system used are manually loaded.

These commands are used to do this:

`earth:~ #` **`modprobe -t ⟨dir⟩ pcmcia_core`**

`earth:~ #` **`modprobe -t pcmcia-external i82365`** (for external PCMCIA) or

`earth:~ #` **`modprobe -t pcmcia yenta_socket`** (for kernel PCMCIA)

or, in very rare cases,

`earth:~ #` **`modprobe -t ⟨dir⟩ tcic`**

and

`earth:~ #` **`modprobe -t ⟨dir⟩ ds`**

The critical modules are the first two.

If the error occurs when pcmcia_core is loaded, the manual pages for pcmcia_core can help. The options described there can first be tested using modprobe. As an example, switch off the APM support for the PCMCIA module. In a few cases, there could be problems with this. Use the setting do_apm=0 to deactivate power management:

```
modprobe -t ⟨dir⟩ pcmciacore do_apm=0
```

If the chosen option is successful, it can be written to the variable ⟨*PCMCIA_CORE_OPTS*⟩ in the file /etc/sysconfig/pcmcia:

```
PCMCIA_CORE_OPTS="do_apm=0"
```

Checking free IO areas can lead to problems in isolated cases if other hardware components are disturbed by this. Get around this with probe_io=0. If several options should be used, they must be separated by spaces:

```
PCMCIA_CORE_OPTS="do_apm=0 probe_io=0"
```

If errors occur when loading the module i82365, refer to the man page for i82365 (man i82365).

A problem in this context is a resource conflict — if an interrupt, IO port, or memory area is occupied twice. Although the module i82365 checks these resources before they are made available to a card, sometimes just this check will lead to problems. Thus, checking the interrupt 12 (PS/2 devices) on some computers leads to the mouse or keyboard hanging. In this case, the parameter irq_list=⟨*List of IRQs*⟩ can help. The list should contain all IRQs to use. For example, enter the command modprobe i82365 irq_list=5,7,9,10 or permanently add the list of IRQs to /etc/sysconfig/pcmcia:

```
PCMCIA_PCIC_OPTS="irq_list=5,7,9,10"
```

In addition, there are /etc/pcmcia/config and /etc/pcmcia/config.opts. These files are evaluated by card manager. The settings made in them are only relevant when loading the driver modules for the PCMCIA cards. In /etc/pcmcia/config.opts, IRQs, IO ports, and memory areas can be included or excluded. The difference from the option irqlist is that the resources excluded in config.opts are not used for a PCMCIA card, but are still checked by the base module i82365.

Improperly Functioning or Nonfunctional PCMCIA Card

Here, there are basically three variations: the card is not detected, the driver cannot be loaded, or the interface made available by the driver is set up incorrectly.

Determine whether the card is managed by the card manager or hotplug. For external PCMCIA, card manager always takes control, for kernel PCMCIA, card manager manages PC card cards and hotplug manages CardBUS cards. Here, only card manager is discussed. Hotplug problems are discussed in *Hotplugging Services* on page 221.

- **Unrecognized Card**
  If the card is not recognized, the message "Unsupported Card in Slot x" appears in `/var/log/messages`. This message means card manager cannot assign a driver to the card. To do this, `/etc/pcmcia/config` or `/etc/pcmcia/*.conf` are required. These files function as the driver database. This driver database can be easily extended if you take existing entries as a template. Find out, with the command `cardctl ident`, how the card identifies itself. More information about this can be found in the PCMCIA-HOWTO Section 6 and in the man page for `pcmcia` (`man pcmcia`). After modifying `/etc/pcmcia/config` or `/etc/pcmcia/*.conf`, the driver assignment must be reloaded with the command `rcpcmcia reload`.

- **Driver Not Loaded**
  One reason for this occurring is that a wrong assignment has been made in the driver database. This can happen, for example, if a vendor uses a different chip in an apparently unchanged card model. Sometimes there are also alternative drivers that work better for certain models than the default driver. In these cases, precise information about the card is required. It can also be useful here to ask a mailing list or the Advanced Support Service.

  Another cause is a resource conflict. For most PCMCIA cards, it is irrelevant with which IRQ, IO port, or memory area they are operated, but there are exceptions. First test only one card and, if necessary, switch off other system components, such as the sound card, IrDA, modem, or printer. The allocation of system resources can be viewed with the command `lsdev` (it is quite normal that several PCI devices share the same IRQ).

  One possible solution would be to use a suitable option for the module `i82365` (see PCMCIA_PCIC_OPTS). Many card driver modules also have options. Find these using the command `modinfo`

/lib/modules/⟨*the correct pcmcia directory*⟩/⟨*driver*⟩.o (the complete path is needed to locate the correct driver). There is also a manual page for most modules. `rpm -ql pcmcia | grep man` lists all manual pages contained in package `pcmcia`. To test the options, the card drivers can also be unloaded by hand. Again, ensure that the module is using the correct PCMCIA system.

When a solution has been found, the use of a specific resource can, in general, be allowed or forbidden in the file `/etc/pcmcia/config.opts`. There is even room here for options for card drivers. If the module `pcnet_cs` should be operated exclusively with IRQ 5, for example, the following entry is required:

```
module pcnet_cs opts irq_list=5
```

One problem that sometimes occurs with 10/100-Mbit network cards is incorrect automatic identification of the transmission method. Use the command `ifport` or `mii_tool` to view and modify the transmission method. To have these commands run automatically, the script `/etc/pcmcia/network` must be individually adjusted.

- **Incorrectly Configured Interface**
  In this case, it is recommended to check the configuration of the interface to eliminate rare configuration errors. For network cards, the dialog rate of the network scripts can be increased by assigning the value `DEBUG=yes` to the variable in `/etc/sysconfig/network/config`. For other cards or if this is of no help, there is still the possibility of inserting the line `set -x` into the script run by card manager (see `/var/log/messages`). With this, each individual command of the script is recorded in the system log. If you have found the critical part in a script, the corresponding commands can be entered in a terminal and tested.

Installation via PCMCIA

PCMCIA is already required for installation if you want to install via network or if the CD-ROM is operated via PCMCIA. To do this, start with a boot floppy disk. In addition, one of the module floppy disks is required.

After booting from floppy disk (or after selecting 'Manual Installation' booting from CD), the program `linuxrc` is started. Select 'Kernel Modules (Hardware Drivers)' → 'Load PCMCIA Module'. Two entry fields appear in which to enter options for the modules pcmcia_core and i82365. Normally, these fields can be left blank. The manual pages for pcmcia_core and i82365 are available as text files on the first CD in the directory docu.

SuSE Linux 8.2 is then installed with the external PCMCIA system. During the installation, system messages are sent to various virtual consoles. Switch to them using (Alt) + (function key).

During the installation, there are terminals on which commands can be run. As long as linuxrc is running, use console 9 (a very spartan shell). After YaST2 starts, there is a bash shell and many standard system tools on console 2.

If the wrong driver module for a PCMCIA card is loaded during installation, the boot floppy disk must be modified manually. This requires a detailed knowledge of Linux, however. When the first part of the installation is finished, the system is partially or completely rebooted. In rare cases, it is possible that the system will hang when the PCMCIA is started. At this point the installation is already at an advanced stage, so Linux can be started without PCMCIA using the boot option NOPCMCIA=yes, at least in text mode. See also *Troubleshooting* on page 232. It is possible that you can change some settings for the system on console 2 before the first part of the installation is completed, so the reboot will run successfully.

Other Utilities

cardctl is an essential tool for obtaining information from PCMCIA and carrying out certain actions. In cardctl, find many details. Enter just cardctl to obtain a list of the valid commands.

There is also a graphical front-end for this program — cardinfo, shown in Figure 9.1 on the next page) — with which the most important things can be controlled. For this to work, the package pcmcia-cardinfo must be installed.

Additional helpful programs from the pcmcia package are ifport, ifuser, probe, and rcpcmcia. These are not always required. To find out about everything contained in the package pcmcia, use the command rpm -ql pcmcia.

Updating the Kernel or PCMCIA Package

If you want to update the kernel, you should use the kernel packages provided by SuSE. If it is necessary to compile your own kernel, the PCMCIA

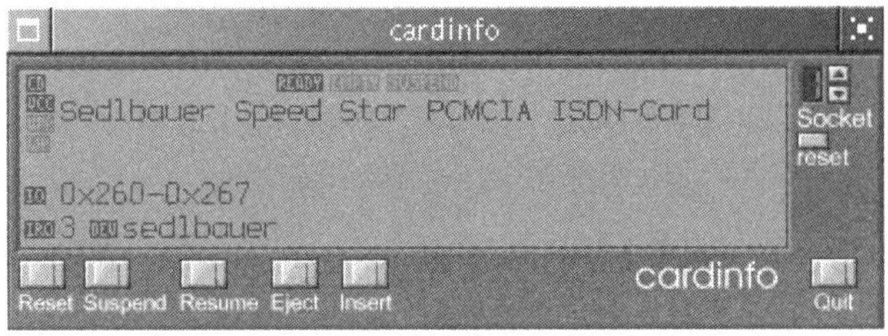

Figure 9.1: The cardinfo Program

modules must also be recompiled. It is important that the new kernel is already running when these modules are recompiled, because various information is extracted from it. The `pcmcia` package should already be installed, but not started. In case of doubt, run the command `rcpcmcia stop`. Install the PCMCIA source package and enter

```
rpm -ba /usr/src/packages/SPECS/pcmcia.spec
```

The new packages will be stored in `/usr/src/packages/RPMS`. The package `pcmcia-modules` contains the PCMCIA modules for external PCMCIA. This package must be installed with the command `rpm --force`, because the module files belong officially to the kernel package.

For More Information

For more information about specific laptops, visit the Linux Laptop home page at `http://linux-laptop.net`. Another good source of information is the Moblix home page at`http://tuxmobil.org/`. As well as a lot of interesting information, also find a Laptop-Howto and an IrDA-Howto. In addition, there is also the article Laptops and Notebooks (PCMCIA) in the SuSE Support Database at `http://sdb.suse.de/en/sdb/html/laptop.html` (or locally at `file:/usr/share/doc/sdb/en/html/laptop.html`).

APM and ACPI — Power Management

Power management requires correspondingly designed hardware and existing BIOS routines. Most notebooks and many modern desktop computers meet these requirements. The APM (Advanced Power Management) standard has generally been used so far for this. These are basically functions implemented in the BIOS of the computer. This is why power management does not work equally well on all devices. It is currently advisable to use APM on laptops with a functioning implementation of it. This is because there are manufacturers that dropped APM in favor of completely relying on the more recent ACPI (Advanced Configuration and Power Interface) standard. ACPI is, however, based on a more complex concept and requires a good cooperation of hardware manufacturers, BIOS programmers, and operating system experts. The Linux implementation of ACPI is still incomplete and therefore only partially usable. A substantial improvement in this matter can only be expected for the 2.6 kernel.

Power Saving Functions

While many of these functions are of general interest, they become really important in mobile environments. These functions are described below along with the systems on which they can be used.

Standby This operating mode only turns the display off and in some systems throttles the processor load. Not every APM offers this function. This corresponds to the ACPI state S1.

Suspend (to memory) The complete state of the system is written to random access memory (RAM) and the entire system is subsequently put to sleep. The computer consumes only very little power in this state, allowing battery power to span stretches of time between twelve hours up to several days. The advantage of this state is the ability to resume work at the same point within a few seconds without having to boot and load necessary applications first. It is sufficient with most modern devices to close the lid to suspend and to simply open to resume work. This corresponds to the ACPI state S3.

Hibernation (suspend to disk) The computer can last for longer than a winter in this operating state (the term hibernation alludes to this), because the state of the system is completely written to hard disk and the system is subsequently turned off. Resuming from hibernation takes between half a minute and one and a half minutes and the state upon suspension is likewise completely restored. Some manufacturers offer sensible hybrid variations of this mode (for instance, RediSafe in IBM Thinkpads). Hibernation corresponds to the ACPI state S4. Linux also offers a pure software solution, which, however, is not included in SuSE Linux. Information is available at `http://falcon.sch.bme.hu/~seasons/linux/swsusp.html`.

Monitoring the state of the battery Apart from monitoring the charge status, it is equally important to take appropriate action when the power reserves run out. This is also handled by the BIOS APM routines in most cases. The `apmdacpid` or `klaptopdaemon` can be alternatively used for this.

Automatic power-off The computer is completely turned off following a shutdown. This is especially of importance when an automatic shutdown is executed shortly before the battery runs out.

Shutdown of system components The substantial component for conserving power is the hard disk, which can be spun down for a shorter or longer amount of time depending on the reliability of the whole system. However, the risk of a loss of data rises with the duration of the rest periods. Other components can be deactivated via ACPI (at least theoretically) or permanently in the BIOS setup. The infrared port should, where applicable, be deactivated for as long as its services are not required (see *IrDA — Infrared Data Association* on page 252).

Processor speed control APM generally only offers the possibility to select from various settings in the BIOS setup. Special tools are available for controlling hardware-specific settings on some devices, such as `tpctl` and `apmiser` from the package `tpctl` for IBM Thinkpads. The processor speed can be controlled with the procspeed application from the package `apmd`. The processor speed can only be influenced directly with ACPI. Therefore, these possibilities are covered in the ACPI section.

APM

Some of the power saving functions are executed by the APM itself. Standby and suspend can be activated with key combinations or by closing the lid on many laptops. There is, at first, basically no need for contribution to this on part of the operating system. Corresponding packages and a suitable kernel must be installed if it is desired to invoke these functions by command, if it is necessary to execute certain actions before suspension, or to simply check the battery level.

APM support is integrated in the precompiled kernels of SuSE Linux. However, it is only activated if ACPI is not implemented in the kernel and an APM BIOS is detected. The APM support can be activated at the boot prompt with `acpi=off`. The command `cat /proc/apm` can be used to check if APM was activated. Everything is in order if a line containing various numbers is returned. Now, the command `shutdown -h` should shut down the computer.

Spurious behavior can occasionally arise from some incompletely compliant BIOS implementations. Some problems can be circumvented with special boot parameters, which previously were kernel configuration options. All parameters are entered at the boot prompt in the form apm=⟨*parameter*⟩:

on or off activate or deactivate APM support

(no-)allow-ints Allow interrupts during the execution of BIOS functions

(no-)broken-psr The BIOS has a broken "GetPowerStatus" function

(no-)realmode-power-off Reset the processor to "real mode" before shutdown

(no-)debug Log APM events in the system log.

(no-)power-off Power off the system after shutting down.

bounce-interval=⟨*n*⟩ Blackout time in 1/100ths of a second following a suspend event during which additional suspend events are ignored.

idle-threshold=⟨*n*⟩ Percentage of system activity under which the BIOS function idle is called (0=always, 100=never)

idle-period=⟨*n*⟩ Period of time in hundredths of a second during which the system activity is evaluated

The APM Daemon (apmd)

The apmd daemon monitors the battery and can invoke certain actions when a standby or a suspend event occurs. It is located in the package `apmd`. It is not indispensable for operation, yet can be helpful for some problems.

apmd is not started automatically on boot. The settings for the system services, however, can be modified with the YaST2 runlevel module if necessary. The `chkconfig` utility can alternatively be used. The service can be called manually with the command `rcapmd start`.

A few configuration variable are present in `/etc/sysconfig/powermanagement`. Only a few hints are provided here because the file is commented.

APMD_ADJUST_DISK_PERF This determines that the behavior of the hard disk follows the state of power supply. There is a also series of other variables that either begin with APMD_BATTERY or APMD_AC. The former contain settings for the operation with battery power, the latter for the operation with external power supply.

APMD_BATTERY/AC_DISK_TIMEOUT After how long a period of disk inactivity should it be spun down. The values are described in *Rest for the Hard Disk* on page 251 or in the man page of hdparm, option -S.

APMD_BATTERY/AC_KUPDATED_INTERVAL The time between runs of the kernel update daemon.

APMD_BATTERY/AC_DATA_TIMEOUT The maximum age of buffered data.

APMD_BATTERY/AC_FILL_LEVEL The maximum fill level of the hard disk buffer.

APMD_PCMCIA_EJECT_ON_SUSPEND Problems sometimes occur despite PCMCIA being compiled into kernels with APM support. Some of the card drivers do not resume correctly from a suspend (xirc2ps_cs). This is why apmd can deactivate the PCMCIA system prior to a suspend and can reactivate it afterwards. The variable APMD_PCMCIA_EJECT_ON_SUSPEND is set to yes for this.

APMD_INTERFACES_TO_STOP Network interfaces that should be stopped prior to a suspend and started afterwards can be entered here.

APMD_INTERFACES_TO_UNLOAD This variable should be used if the driver modules of the interfaces mentioned before should equally be unloaded.

APMD_TURN_OFF_IDEDMA_BEFORE_SUSPEND It is also sometimes the case that resuming from a suspend does not work if an IDE device (hard disk) remained in DMA mode.

Furthermore, there are additional options, like for adjusting the key repeat rate or the system clock after a suspend or for shutting down the laptop properly when the APM BIOS sends a "battery critical" event. The script /usr/sbin/apmd_proxy, which performs the jobs described above, can be adjusted to any requirements for even more specialized actions.

Further Commands

package apmd contains a few additional handy utilities. The utility apm checks and returns the current battery charge level or puts the system into standby (apm -S) or suspend (apm -s) mode. Refer to the man page for apm (man apm).

The command apmsleep suspends the system for a given time.

tailf can be used instead of tail -f to watch a log file without preventing the hard disk from spinning down.

There are of course also tools for the X Window System. The package apmd also contains the xapm utility for displaying the charge level of the battery. The kbatmon applet displays the charge level of the rechargeable battery to users of the KDE desktop and can also suspend the system. The xosview monitoring utility is likewise interesting as an alternative.

ACPI

ACPI is the abbreviation for Advanced Configuration and Power Interface. ACPI is designed to enable the operating system to configure and control the individual hardware components. Accordingly, ACPI supersedes both PnP as well as APM. The part of ACPI responsible for initializing the hardware is not covered in this chapter. Additionally, there is little to do for the user in this regard.

The BIOS provides tables containing information about the individual components and methods for the access to the hardware. This information is used by the operating system for tasks such as assigning interrupts or activating or deactivating components as needed. However, as operations performed by the operating system perform operations integrated in the BIOS, the functionality depends on the BIOS implementation. The boot messages are logged to /var/log/boot.msg. Here ACPI reports which tables it was able to find and read.

DSDT Differentiated System Description Table: Contains information about the components of the computer and how these can be configured.

FADT Fixed ACPI Description Table: Contains information about the implementation of the ACPI hardware register block and the physical address of the DSDT.

MADT Multiple APIC Description Table: Describes the implementation and configuration of the APIC.

RSDT Root System Description Table: Table containing pointers to the other tables. The pointer to the RSDT (RSDP) must be located in the low memory range.

SSDT Secondary System Description Table: This table is a continuation of the DSDT. There can be several SSDTs. The distribution to several tables increases the flexibility especially for OEM.

XSDT Extended Root System Description Table: Contains the same information as RSDT, but can also accommodate pointers to description headers larger than 32 bits. Alternatively, the RSDP can also point to the XSDT.

The ACPI standard defines a variety of system states. The main states are as follows:

G0 System working

G1 System sleeping, change to G0 without booting the OS (suspend)

G2 Soft-off, OS must boot when switched on

G3 Mechanical off, system is without power (mechanical main switch is off)

Furthermore, there are six sleep states that further distinguish G0, G1, and G2:

S0 System working

S1 Standby (less power consumption, rapid wake-up)

S2 Another type of standby that is rarely implemented in devices.

S3 Suspend (very low power consumption, rapid wake-up).

S4 Hibernation or suspend to disk (no power consumption, wake-up takes a little longer — twenty to one hundred seconds, depending on the hardware).

S5 Soft-off (G2)

Furthermore, the states D0–D3 are available for all hardware components. In these states, the individual components are active, suspended, or off. There are special states for specific operational situations only known to the processor. The C states are introduced by CPU commands and cannot be influenced directly:

C0 Processor working

C1 Processor issues special low power instructions that consume less energy but allow rapid return to working state.

C2 Like C1, with even less power consumption but longer wake-up time.

C3 Like C2, even more savings, but the first-level cache is rendered inconsistent (only implemented in few devices and rarely used).

The performance states are associated with special processor technologies, such as Speedstep (Intel) or PowerNow (AMD), and involve changes in the clock frequency and the CPU core voltage:

P0 Maximum clock frequency and core voltage

P1 First saving stage, reduced frequency and voltage

P2 Next saving stage (if available)

P3 ...

The third possibility to give the processor some rest is throttling. In this approach, the clock signal of the CPU is interrupted temporarily.

T0 0% clock throttling

T1 12% clock throttling

T2 25% clock throttling

T4 ...

The P and T states can be set directly by the user (or a daemon). The main difference is the level of energy saving. Throttling merely yields linear savings, e.g., 25% clock throttling corresponds to 25% less performance and 25% less energy consumption (only for the processor). In contrast, the energy savings due to a performance change resulting from the reduced core voltage exceed the performance loss. The performance cutback is also used for "passive cooling", unlike the active cooling by means of the fan. It is also meaningful if you want to charge the battery quicker while you are using the computer.

In addition, ACPI provides information about the battery, AC adapter, temperature, and fan. It also reports system events such as "close lid" or "low battery".

ACPI in Action

If the kernel detects an ACPI BIOS when the system is booted, ACPI is activated automatically (and APM is deactivated). The boot parameter `acpi=on` might be necessary for some older machines. The computer must support ACPI 2.0 or later. Check the boot messages of the kernel in `/var/log/boot.msg` to see if ACPI was activated. In this case, there is also a directory `/proc/acpi`, which will be described later.

Then a number of modules must be loaded for OSPM ("Operating System Power Management"). These are loaded by the start script of the ACPI daemon. If any of these modules causes problems, it can be excluded from the loading or unloading process in `/etc/sysconfig/powermanagement`. The system log (`/var/log/messages`) contains the messages of the modules. Here, see which components were detected.

In `/proc/acpi`, you will now find a number of files that provide information on the system state or which can be used to actively change some states. However, many features do not work yet, either because they are still under development or because they are not implemented by the manufacturer.

Caution

To date, neither suspend to RAM or suspend to disk (hibernation) work with ACPI. Due to kernel-specific reasons, these features will only be available starting with kernel 2.6 (or kernel 2.5). If you think you can do it, you can integrate the sw-susp patch in your kernel.

Caution

All files (except dsdt and fadt) can be read with `cat`. In some of the files, settings can be modified by using `echo X > file` to specify suitable values for X (all objects in `/proc` are not real files on the hard disk but an interface for the kernel). Here is a description of the most important files:

/proc/acpi/info General information about ACPI

/proc/acpi/alarm Here, specify when the system should wake from sleep. The time is set with `echo year-month-day hour:minute:second > /proc/acpi/alarm`. However, as the sleep states do not work yet, it is folly to set an alarm.

/proc/acpi/sleep Provides information about the possible sleep states. In the future, it will be possible to actuate a suspend here. Currently, the only states that might work are S1 (standby) and S5 (off, off immediately, no clean shutdown): `echo 1 > /proc/acpi/sleep`.

/proc/acpi/event All events are reported here. These are processed by a daemon, such as 'acpid' or 'ospmd'. If no daemon accesses this file, the events can be read with `cat /proc/acpi/event` (terminate with Ctrl + C). A brief click on the power button or closing the lid are some of these events.

/proc/acpi/dsdt and /proc/acpi/fadt These files contain the ACPI tables DSDT and FADT. These files can be read with `acpidmp`, `acpidisasm`, and `dmdecode`. These programs and their documentation are located in the package `pmtools`. Example: `acpidmp DSDT | acpidisasm`.

/proc/acpi/ac_adapter/AC/state Is the AC adapter connected?

/proc/acpi/battery/BAT*/{alarm,info,state} Detailed information about the battery state. To read the battery charge level, last full capacity from info is compared with remaining capacity from state. This can be done more conveniently with special programs. The charge level at which a battery event is triggered can be specified in alarm.

/proc/acpi/button This directory contains information about various switches.

/proc/acpi/fan/FAN/state Shows if the fan is currently active. It can also be switched on and off manually by writing 0 (on) or 3 (off) into this file. However, both the ACPI code in the kernel and the hardware (or the BIOS) overwrite this setting when it gets too warm.

/proc/acpi/processor/CPU0/info Information about the energy saving possibilities of the processor.

/proc/acpi/processor/CPU0/power Information about the current processor state. An asterisk next to C2 indicates that the processor is idle. This is the prevailing state, as you can see from the figure for usage.

/proc/acpi/processor/CPU0/performance Here you can read or set the performance — use the Speedstep or PowerNow capabilities of the CPU.

/proc/acpi/processor/CPU0/throttling This file enables further linear throttling of the processor.

/proc/acpi/processor/CPU0/limit If performance and throttling are automatically controlled by a daemon, the limits that should not be exceeded can be specified here. There are limits defined by the system and a user-definable limit. With `echo 1:5 > /proc/acpi/processor/CPU0/limit`, prevent the states P0 or T0–T4 from being used.

/proc/acpi/thermal_zone/ There is a subdirectory for each thermal zone. A thermal zone is an area with similar thermal properties whose number and names are selected by the hardware manufacturer. However, many of the possibilities offered by ACPI are rarely implemented. Rather, the temperature control is handled in the conventional way directly by the BIOS. The operating system is not given much opportunity to intervene, as the life span of the hardware is at stake. Therefore, the some of the following descriptions only have a theoretical value.

/proc/acpi/thermal_zone/*/temperature The current temperature of the thermal zone.

/proc/acpi/thermal_zone/*/state The states indicates if everything is "ok" or if ACPI uses "active" or "passive" cooling. Everything is "ok" in the case of ACPI-independent fan control.

/proc/acpi/thermal_zone/*/cooling_mode Here, select the preferred cooling method under full ACPI control, either passive (less performance, but very economical) or active (always full performance and uninterrupted fan noise).

/proc/acpi/thermal_zone/*/trip_points Here, determine the temperature at which something like passive or active cooling, a suspend ("hot"), or a shutdown ("critical") should be actuated.

/proc/acpi/thermal_zone/*/polling_frequency If the value in "temperature" is not updated automatically as soon as the temperature changes, switch to "polling mode" here. The command `echo X > /proc/acpi/thermal_zone/*/polling_frequency` causes the temperature to be queried every X seconds. Set X=0 to deactivate the "polling".

The ACPI Daemon (acpid)

The ACPI daemon processes events similarly to the APM daemon. These are currently merely some switching events, like the operation of the power button or the closing of the lid. All events are logged in the system log. The variables `ACPI_BUTTON_POWER` and `ACPI_BUTTON_LID` contain instructions for these events. The script `/usr/sbin/acpid\_proxy` can be modified as well as the configuration of the acpid utility in `/etc/acpi/` for more control options.

Unlike `apmd`, little is preconfigured here, as ACPI in Linux is still in a very dynamic development stage. If necessary, configure `acpid` yourself. If you have any suggestions on preparatory actions, please send an e-mail to `feedback@suse.de`.

ospmd

The ospmd (Operating System Power Management Daemon) is an alternative to the acpid. Unfortunately, it is not very highly developed as yet. Currently, it is more like a feasibility study.

There is a number of more or less comprehensive ACPI tools. Some are pure info tools that display the battery state, the temperature, and so forth (acpi, klaptopdaemon, wmacpimon, etc.). Some facilitate the access to the structures under /proc/acpi (akpi, kacpi, gtkacpiw). Others are daemons that control the CPU performance depending on the configuration, temperature, and system load (speedstep and heatload).

To see which of these tools are available, start the YaST software module and search for "acpi". The enclosed programs include online documentation.

Troubleshooting

There are two different types of problems. On one hand, there might be error in the ACPI cord of the kernel that was not detected in time. In this case, a solution will be made available for download. On the other hand, there might be problems in the BIOS of a computer. This happens more often and is more annoying. Unfortunately, deviations from the ACPI specifications are sometimes purposely integrated in the BIOS to circumvent errors of the ACPI implementation in other widespread operating systems. Hardware components that have serious mistakes in the ACPI implementation are recorded in a blacklist to prevent the Linux kernel from using ACPI for these components.

If you encounter a problem, the first thing you should do is update the BIOS. This will solve many problems. If the computer does not boot properly, one of the following boot parameters may be helpful:

pci=noacpi Do not use ACPI for configuring the PCI devices.

acpi=oldboot Only perform a simple resource configuration. Do not use ACPI for other purposes.

acpi=off Disable ACPI.

Another important step is to take a closer look at the boot messages. To do this, use the command `dmesg | grep -2i acpi` (or all other messages, since the problem may be due to something else than ACPI) the computer has booted. If an error occurs with the parsing of an ACPI table, at least the most important table — the DSDT — can be replaced by integrating an improved table in an individual kernel. This will cause the faulty DSDT of the

BIOS to be ignored. However, this is not a simple task and requires some assistance by an expert. Bug-fixed DSDTs are available on the Internet for some computers.

For the kernel configuration, there is a switch that activates ACPI debug messages. If you compiled and installed a kernel with ACPI debugging, experts looking for an error can be supported with detailed information.

If you experience BIOS or hardware problems, it is always advisable to contact the manufacturer of the device. Although the manufacturers may not always be able to provide assistance for Linux, it is still important that they hear the word "Linux" as often as possible. The manufacturers will only take it seriously if they realize that an adequate number of their customers utilize Linux. Of course you can also contact the manufacturer to tell him that you use Linux on the hardware without any difficulties.

Additional documentation and help is available in the following sources:

- `http://www.columbia.edu/~ariel/acpi/acpi_howto.txt` (slightly outdated ACPI HowTo, incomplete)
- `http://www.cpqlinux.com/acpi-howto.html` (more detailed ACPI HowTo, contains patches of DSDT)
- `http://www.intel.com/technology/iapc/acpi/faq.htm` (ACPI FAQ @Intel)
- `http://www.brodo.de/english/pub/acpi/proc/processor.html` (description of the subdirectory `/proc/acpi/processor`)
- `http://acpi.sourceforge.net/` (the ACPI4Linux project at Sourceforge)
- `http://www.brodo.de/english/pub/acpi/index.html` (ACPI patches)
- `http://codecs.home.sapo.pt/acpi/index.html` (ACPI patches)
- `http://www.poupinou.org/acpi/` (DSDT patches by Bruno Ducrot)
- `http://www.brodo.de/cpufreq/` (the Linux CPUFreq project)
- `http://falcon.sch.bme.hu/~seasons/linux/swsusp.html` (kernel hibernation: swsusp project)

Rest for the Hard Disk

An idling hard disk can be spun down in Linux. The hdparm utility serves the purpose of modifying various settings of a hard disk. The `-y` option puts the hard disk instantly into standby mode and the `-Y` option turns it off completely. The command `hdparm -S` ⟨x⟩ results in the hard disk spinning down after a certain time of inactivity. The ⟨x⟩ variable has a nonlinear scale: `0` turns the mechanism off and the hard disk runs continuously. Values between `1` and `240` are multiplied by five seconds. Values between `241` and `251` correspond to one to eleven times thirty minutes.

One problem is the number of processes in Linux that write to the hard disk, continuously waking it up. It is hence important to understand how Linux handles data that is supposed to be written to the hard disk.

All data is first written into a buffer in random access memory. This buffer is watched by the kernel update daemon kupdated.The buffer is flushed to the hard disk every time the data reaches a certain age or the buffer becomes filled to a certain degree. The size of the buffer is dynamic and depends on the size of the memory and the system load. kupdated is set by default to small time intervals because the preservation of data integrity is a primary goal. It checks the buffer every five seconds and informs the bdflush daemon when data is older than thirty seconds or the buffer is filled by more than thirty percent. The bdflush daemon then writes the data to the hard disk. It also writes independently of kupdated, for instance, when the buffer is full. Operators of a stable system can modify these settings. They must, however, be aware that this is done by risking data corruption.

The settings can be read with `cat /proc/sys/vm/bdflush`. The first value is the the flushing threshold of the buffer. The sixth value is the maximum age limit for buffered data in hundredths of a second. The fifth value is the checking interval for kupdated and is likewise given in hundredths of a second. For instance, to increase the kupdated interval to one minute, the new values are entered into this file with

```
echo 30 500 0 0 6000 > /proc/sys/vm/bdflush
```

The unchanged values are simply copied from the output and the trailing values can be omitted. Thus, entering

```
echo 60 > /proc/sys/vm/bdflush
```

changes the flushing threshold of the buffer to sixty percent. The remaining values are described in the file `Documentation/filesystems/proc.txt` of the kernel sources.

Note

Changes to the settings of the kernel update daemon influence data intergrity. If in doubt, leave them be.

Note

The settings for the hard disk time-out, the kupdated interval, the buffer threshold, and the maximum age of data can be duplicated in `/etc/sysconfig/powermanagement`: one set for battery operation and one set for external power supply. The variables are described in the section about apmd and within the file itself. "Journaling file systems", like reiserfs or ext3, write their metadata independently of bdflush, which prevents the hard disk from spinning down. At the time of writing, ext3 and jbd respect the fifth value of `/proc/sys/vm/bdflush` and also write their metadata less often if this value were raised. This is not yet the case for reiserfs. It is best to rely on the ext2 file system in cases of doubt.

It is necessary to observe how any used applications behave. Good text editors, for instance, regularly keep hidden backups of the currently changed file on disk. This will repeatedly wake up the hard disk. Such program features can also be turned off, but this endangers data integrity.

IrDA — Infrared Data Association

IrDA ("Infrared Data Association") is an industry standard for wireless communication with infrared light. Many laptops sold nowadays are equipped with an IrDA compatible transceiver that enables communication with other devices, such as printers, modems, LANs, or other laptops. The transfer speed ranges from 2400 bps up to 4 Mbps.

There are two IrDA operation modes. The standard mode SIR accesses the infrared port through a serial interface. This mode works on almost all systems and is sufficient for most requirements. The faster mode FIR requires a special driver for the IrDA chip. There are not, however, such drivers for all chips. The desired mode additionally must be set in the BIOS setup of the computer. This is also where it can be determined which serial interface is used for the SIR mode.

Information about IrDA can be found in the IrDA how-to by Werner Heuser at `http://tuxmobil.org/Infrared-HOWTO/Infrared-HOWTO.html` and on the web site of the Linux IrDA Project `http://irda.sourceforge.net/`.

Software

The necessary kernel modules are included in the kernel package. The package `irda` provides the necessary helper applications for supporting the infrared interface. The documentation can be found at `/usr/share/doc/packages/irda/README` after the installation of the package.

Configuration

The IrDA system service is not started automatically by the booting process. Use the YaST2 runlevel module to change the settings of the system services. The application `chkconfig` can be used alternatively. IrDA unfortunately consumes noticeably more battery power, because a "discovery packet" is sent every few seconds to detect other peripheral devices automatically. This is why IrDA should only be started when needed. The interface can always be activated manually with the command `rcirda start` or deactivated with the `stop` parameter. All necessary kernel modules are automatically loaded when the interface is activated.

The file `/etc/sysconfig/irda` contains only the one variable ⟨*IRDA_PORT*⟩. This is where the interface used in SIR mode is set. The script `/etc/irda/drivers` of the infrared support package sets this variable.

Usage

Data can be sent to the device file `/dev/irlpt0` for printing. The device file `/dev/irlpt0` acts just like the normal `/dev/lp0` cabled interface except the printing data is sent wireless with infrared light.

Printers used with the infrared interface are installed just like printers connected to the parallel or serial ports. Make sure the printer is in visible range of the infrared interface and the infrared support is started.

Communication with other hosts and with mobile phones or other similar devices is conducted through the device file `/dev/ircomm0`. The Siemens S25 and Nokia 6210 mobile phones, for instance, can dial and connect to the Internet with the wvdial application using the infrared interface. A data synchronization with a Palm Pilot is equally possible in this way when the device setting of the corresponding application has been set to `/dev/ircomm0`.

Only those devices can be accessed without any other adjustments that support the printer or IrCOMM protocols. Devices that support the IROBEX protocol, such as the 3Com Palm Pilot, can be accessed with special applications like irobexpalm and irobexreceive. Refer to the IR-HOWTO on this subject. The protocols supported by the device are stated in brackets behind the name of the device in the output of irdadump. IrLAN protocol support is still a "work in progress" — it is unfortunately not stable yet but will surely also be available for Linux in the near future.

Troubleshooting

The superuser `root` can check with the command `irdadump` whether the other device has been recognized by the system in case devices do not work at the infrared interface.

Something similar to Output 15 appears regularly when a Canon BJC-80 printer is in visible range of the computer:

```
21:41:38.435239 xid:cmd 5b62bed5 > ffffffff S=6 s=0 (14)
21:41:38.525167 xid:cmd 5b62bed5 > ffffffff S=6 s=1 (14)
21:41:38.615159 xid:cmd 5b62bed5 > ffffffff S=6 s=2 (14)
21:41:38.705178 xid:cmd 5b62bed5 > ffffffff S=6 s=3 (14)
21:41:38.795198 xid:cmd 5b62bed5 > ffffffff S=6 s=4 (14)
21:41:38.885163 xid:cmd 5b62bed5 > ffffffff S=6 s=5 (14)
21:41:38.965133 xid:rsp 5b62bed5 < 6cac38dc S=6 s=5 BJC-80
                        hint=8804 [ Printer IrCOMM ] (23)
21:41:38.975176 xid:cmd 5b62bed5 > ffffffff S=6 s=* erde
                        hint=0500 [ PnP Computer ] (21)
```

Output 15: *IrDA: irdadump*

Check the configuration of the interface in case there is no output or the other device does not reply. Verify that the correct interface is used. The infrared interface is sometimes located at `/dev/ttyS2` or at `/dev/ttyS3` and another interrupt than IRQ 3 is used sometimes. These settings can be checked and modified in the BIOS setup menu of almost every laptop.

A simple CCD video camera can also help in determining whether the infrared LED lights up at all. Most video cameras can see infrared light, whereas the human eye cannot.

Part III

System

The Linux Kernel

The kernel is the heart of a Linux system. Although the following sections will not teach you how to be a kernel "hacker", they will tell you how to install a SuSE update kernel and introduce the basics of compiling a customized kernel. If you proceed as outlined in this chapter, you can keep your current functional kernel. Later, if your new kernel works as desired, change it to the default.

The standard SuSE kernel, located in the directory /boot, is configured to support as wide a range of hardware as possible. There is no need to compile your own kernel, unless you want to test experimental features and drivers. Several Makefiles are provided with the kernel to automate the process. All you need to do is select the hardware settings and other kernel features. As you need to know your computer system pretty well to make the right selections, we recommend modifying an existing and working configuration file for your first attempt.

Kernel Update

To install an official SuSE update kernel, download the update rpm from the SuSE FTP server or a mirror like ftp://ftp.gwdg.de/pub/linux/suse/. Before installing this package, it is recommended to save the current kernel and initrd under a different name. As root, enter the following two commands:

```
cp /boot/vmlinuz /boot/vmlinuz.old
cp /boot/initrd /boot/initrd.old
```

Now, install the new kernel with the command `rpm -Uvh ⟨packagename⟩`. Replace ⟨*packagename*⟩ with the exact name of the kernel rpm to install.

Since SuSE Linux 7.3, reiserfs is the standard file system. It requires the use of an "initial ramdisk". Therefore, use the command mk_initrd to write the new initial ramdisk.

To be able to boot the old kernel, configure the boot loader accordingly (for more information refer to *Booting and Boot Managers* on page 71). Finally, reboot to load the new kernel.

To reinstall the original kernel from the SuSE Linux CDs, the procedure is almost the same, except you copy the kernel rpm from the directory boot on CD 1 or the DVD. Now, install as described above. If you receive an error message saying that a newer kernel rpm is already installed, add the option --force to the above rpm command.

Kernel Sources

To build a kernel, the package kernel-source must be installed. Additional packages, like the C compiler (package gcc), the GNU binutils (package `binutils`), and the include files for the C compiler (package `glibc-devel`), are selected for installation automatically by YaST2.

After installation, the kernel sources are located in `/usr/src/linux-`⟨*kernel-version*⟩`.SuSE`. If you plan to experiment with different kernels, unpack them in different subdirectories and create a symbolic link to the current kernel source. As there are software packages that rely on the sources being in `/usr/src/linux`, maintain this directory as a symbolic link to your current kernel source. YaST2 does this automatically.

Kernel Configuration

The most recently compiled configuration is stored in the file `/boot/vmlinuz.config`. To modify the configuration of the currently-used kernel, go to the directory `/usr/src/linux` as user `root` and enter `make oldconfig` to generate the file `.config`. Alternatively, copy the configuration file with the command `cp /boot/vmlinuz.config .config`.

The kernel configuration tools will read the file `.config` and offer all settings for modification. The kernel can be configured at the command line, in a menu in text-mode, or in a menu in the X Window System. The following is a short overview of these three methods.

Configuration on the Command Line

To configure the kernel, make sure your working directory is `/usr/src/linux` and enter `make config`. Choose the options you want supported by the kernel. There are two or three possibilities: (Y), (N), or (M). `'m'` means that this device is not compiled directly into the kernel, but loaded as a module instead. Any driver needed to boot the system should be integrated into the kernel, not loaded as a module. With (↵), confirm the default settings read from the file `.config`. Pressing any other key accesses a short help text about the current option.

Configuration in Text Mode

A much more convenient way of configuring the kernel is to use `make menuconfig`. With `menuconfig`, you do not have to go through all the questions. Instead, select the areas of interest from the menu. The default settings are read from the file `.config`. To load another configuration, select 'Load an Alternate Configuration File' and enter the file name.

Configuration in the X Window System

If you have installed and configured the X Window System (package `xf86`) and Tcl/Tk (package `tcl` and package `tk`), you can use `make xconfig`. It uses a GUI (Graphical User Interface) that makes kernel configuration very user-friendly. If you have not logged in to the X Window System as `root`, enter the command `xhost +localhost` (replacing `localhost` with the name of the local host) to allow `root` to take over the display. The default settings are taken from the file `/usr/src/linux/.config`.

Kernel Modules

There is a wide variety of PC hardware components. To use this hardware properly, you need a "driver" with which the operating system (in Linux, the "kernel"), can access this hardware. There are basically two ways of integrating drivers into your system:

- The drivers can be compiled directly into the kernel. Such a kernel ("in one piece") is referred to as a *monolithic* kernel. Some drivers are only available in this form.
- Drivers can be loaded into the kernel on demand. In this case, the kernel is referred to as a *modularized* kernel. This has the advantage that only those drivers really needed are loaded and the kernel thus contains nothing unnecessary.

Which drivers to compile into the kernel and which to load as run-time modules is defined in the kernel configuration. Basically, components not required for booting the system should be built as modules. This makes sure the kernel does not get too big to be loaded by the BIOS or a boot loader. Drivers for `ext2`, the SCSI drivers on a SCSI-based system, and similar drivers should be compiled into the kernel. In contrast, items such as `isofs`, `msdos`, or `sound`, which are not needed for starting your computer system, should definitely be built as modules. Kernel modules are located in `/lib/modules/`⟨*Version*⟩, where ⟨*Version*⟩ is the current kernel version.

Handling Modules

The following commands are available:

- `insmod`
  insmod loads the requested module after searching for it in a subdirectory of `/lib/modules/⟨Version⟩`. It is better, however, to use `modprobe` (see below) rather than `insmod`.

- `rmmod`
  Unloads the requested module. This is only possible if this module is no longer needed. For example, the isofs module cannot be unloaded while a CD is still mounted.

- `depmod`
  Creates the file `modules.dep` in `/lib/modules/⟨Version⟩` that defines the dependencies of all the modules. This is necessary to ensure that all dependent modules are loaded with the selected ones. If START_KERNELD is set in `/etc/rc.config`, this file will be rebuilt each time the system is started.

- `modprobe`
  Loads or unloads a given module while taking into account dependencies of this module. This command is extremely powerful and can be used for a lot of things (e. g., probing all modules of a given type until one is successfully loaded). In contrast to insmod, modprobe checks `/etc/modules.conf` and therefore is the preferred method of loading modules. For detailed information on this topic, refer to the corresponding man page.

- `lsmod`
  Shows which modules are currently loaded as well as how many other modules are using them. Modules started by the kernel daemon are tagged with `autoclean`. This label denotes that these modules will automatically be removed once they reach their idle time limit.

- `modinfo`
  Shows module information.

/etc/modules.conf

`/etc/modules.conf` affects how modules are loaded. Refer to the man page for depmod (`man depmod`).

Enter the parameters for modules that access hardware directly in this file. Such modules may need system-specific options (e. g., CD-ROM driver or network driver). The parameters entered here are, for the most part, identical to those given to the boot prompt of the kernel. However, in many cases the names used at the boot prompt are different. If a module failed to load, try specifying the hardware in this file and use modprobe instead of insmod to load the module.

Kmod — the Kernel Module Loader

The kernel module loader is the most elegant way to use modules. Kmod performs background monitoring and makes sure the required modules are loaded by modprobe as soon as the respective functionality is needed in the kernel.

To use Kmod, set the corresponding variable in the kernel configuration 'Kernel module loader' (`CONFIG_KMOD`). Kmod is not designed to automatically unload modules. The potential saving in memory is only marginal for the RAM capacity of computers today. See also `/usr/src/linux/Documentation/kmod.txt`. For reasons of performance, it is better for server machines, which have special tasks to perform and need only a few drivers, to have a "monolithic" kernel.

Settings in the Kernel Configuration

All the kernel's configuration options cannot be covered here in detail. Make use of the numerous help texts available on kernel configuration. The latest kernel documentation is always in `/usr/src/linux/Documentation`.

Compiling the Kernel

We recommend compiling a "bzImage". As a rule, this avoids the problem of the kernel getting too large, as can easily happen if you select too many features and create a "zImage". You will then get error messages like "kernel too big" or "System is too big".

After customizing the kernel configuration, start compilation by entering:

```
earth:/usr/src/linux # make dep
earth:/usr/src/linux # make clean
earth:/usr/src/linux # make bzImage
```

These three commands can be entered on one line as well:

```
earth:/usr/src/linux #  make dep clean bzImage
```

After a successful compilation, you will find the compressed kernel in /usr/src/linux/arch/\suselxarch{}/boot. The kernel image — the file that contains the kernel — is called bzImage. If you cannot find this file, an error probably occurred during the kernel compilation. In the Bash shell, enter the following command to launch the kernel compilation again and write the output to a file kernel.out:

```
earth:/usr/src/linux #  make bzImage 2>&1 | tee kernel.out
```

If you have configured parts of your kernel to load as modules, launch the module compilation. Do this with make modules.

Installing the Kernel

After the kernel is compiled, it must be installed so it can be booted. If you use LILO, LILO must be updated as well. To prevent unpleasant surprises, it is recommended that you keep the old kernel (e.g., as /boot/vmlinuz.old), so you can still boot it if the new kernel does not function as expected:

```
earth:/usr/src/linux #  cp /boot/vmlinuz /boot/vmlinuz.old
earth:/usr/src/linux #  cp arch/i386/boot/bzImage /boot/vmlinuz
earth:/usr/src/linux #  lilo
```

The Makefile target make bzlilo performs these three steps in one go.

Note

If you are using GRUB as the boot loader, it does not need to be reinstalled. Therefore only carry out the first two steps to copy the kernel to the right place in the system.

Note

Now the compiled modules need to be installed. By entering:

```
earth:/usr/src/linux #  make modules_install
```

copy these to the correct directories in /lib/modules/⟨*Version*⟩. This overwrites the old modules with the same kernel version. However, the original modules can be reinstalled together with the kernel from the CDs.

Tip

You should make sure that modules whose functionality may now have been directly compiled into the kernel are removed from /lib/modules/⟨*Version*⟩. Otherwise, unexpected effects could occur. This is one reason why the inexperienced user is *strongly* advised against compiling the kernel.

Tip

To enable GRUB or LILO to boot the old kernel (now /boot/vmlinuz.old), add an image entry with label Linux.old in your /boot/grub/menu.lst or /etc/lilo.conf respectively. This procedure is described in detail in *Booting and Boot Managers* on page 71. When you have adapted /etc/lilo.conf to your needs, enter lilo. If you are using LILO as the boot loader, LILO must be reinstalled after modifications to /etc/lilo.conf with the command lilo. GRUB does not need to be reinstalled.

The file /System.map contains kernel symbols required by the modules to ensure successful launching of kernel functions. This file depends on the current kernel. Therefore, once you have compiled and installed the kernel, copy /usr/src/linux/System.map to the directory (/boot). This file is regenerated each time the kernel is recompiled. If you create your kernel using make bzlilo or make zlilo, this is done for you automatically. If you get an error message like "System.map does not match current kernel", System.map probably has not been copied.

Cleaning Your Hard Disk After Compilation

If you are low on hard disk space, delete the object files generated during kernel compilation using make clean in the /usr/src/linux directory. If you have plenty of disk space and plan to reconfigure the kernel on a regular basis, you might want to skip this. Recompiling the kernel is considerably faster then, because only the parts affected by changes will actually be recompiled.

11

Special Features of SuSE Linux

This chapter provides information about the *Filesystem Hierarchy Standard* (FHS) and *Linux Standard Base* (LSB). Various software packages and special features, such as booting with "initrd", linuxrc, and the rescue system, are described in detail.

Linux Standards

File System Hierarchy Standard (FHS)

SuSE Linux strives, as far as possible, to conform to the *File system Hierarchy Standard* (FHS, package `fhs`). See also `http://www.pathname.com/fhs/`. For this reason, it is sometimes necessary to move files or directories to their "correct" places in the file system.

Linux Standard Base (LSB)

SuSE supports the *Linux Standard Base* project. Current information on this can be found at `http://www.linuxbase.org`.

The LSB specification version for 8.1 is 1.2. From now on, the Filesystem Hierarchy Standard (FHS) is included in the specification and defines settings, such as the package format and the initialization of the system. See Chapter *The SuSE Linux Boot Concept* on page 293.

teTeX — TeX in SuSE Linux

TeX is a complete typesetting system which runs on various platforms. It is expandable with macro packages like LaTeX. It consists of very many single files that have to be assembled according to the *TeX Directory Structure* (TDS) (ref. `ftp://ftp.dante.de/tex-archive/tds/` teTeX is a compilation of current TeXapplications.

teTeX is employed in SuSE Linux with a configuration that complies with the requirements of both the TDS and the FHS.

Example Environments for FTP and HTTP

About FTP

To make it easier to set up an FTP server, the package `ftpdir` includes an example environment. This is installed in `/srv/ftp`.

About HTTP

Apache is the standard web server in SuSE Linux. Together with the installation of Apache, some example documents are made available in /srv/www. To set up your own web server, include your own DocumentRoot in /etc/httpd/httpd.conf and store your files (documents, picture files) accordingly.

Hints on Special Software Packages

Package bash and /etc/profile

1. /etc/profile
2. ~/.profile
3. /etc/bash.bashrc
4. ~/.bashrc

Users can make personal entries in ~/.profile or in ~/.bashrc respectively. To ensure the correct processing of these files, it is necessary to copy the basic settings from /etc/skel/.profile or /etc/skel/.bashrc respectively into the home directory of the user. It is recommended to copy the settings from /etc/skel following an update. Execute the following shell commands to prevent the loss of personal adjustments:

```
mv ~/.bashrc ~/.bashrc.old
cp /etc/skel/.bashrc ~/.bashrc
mv ~/.profile ~/.profile.old
cp /etc/skel/.profile ~/.profile
```

The personal adjustments then need to be copied back from the files *.old.

cron Package

The cron tables are now located in /var/cron/tabs. /etc/crontab serves as a system-wide cron table. Enter the name of the user who should run the command directly after the time table (see File 29, here root is entered). Package-specific tables, located in /etc/cron.d, have the same format. See the man page for cron (man 8 cron).

```
1-59/5 * * * * root test -x /usr/sbin/atrun && /usr/sbin/atrun
```

File 29: *Example of an Entry in /etc/crontab*

/etc/crontab cannot be processed with crontab -e. It must be loaded directly into an editor, modified, then saved.

A number of packages install shell scripts to the directories /etc/cron.hourly, /etc/cron.daily, /etc/cron.weekly, and /etc/cron.monthly, whose instructions are controlled by /usr/lib/cron/run-crons. /usr/lib/cron/run-crons is run every fifteen minutes from the main table (/etc/crontab). This guarantees that processes that may have been neglected can be run at the proper time. Do not be surprised if, shortly after booting, the user nobody turns up in the process tables and is highly active. This probably means that nobody is just updating the locate (see Section *Settings for the Files in /etc/sysconfig* on page 316).

The daily system maintenance jobs have been distributed to various scripts for reasons of clarity (package aaa_base). Apart from aaa_base, /etc/cron.daily thus contains for instance the components backup-rpmdb, clean-tmp or clean-vi.

Log Files — the Package logrotate

There are a number of system services ("daemons"), which, along with the kernel itself, regularly record the system status and specific events to log files. This way, the administrator can regularly check the status of the system at a certain point in time, recognize errors or faulty functions, and troubleshoot them with pinpoint precision. These log files are normally stored in /var/log as specified by FHS and grow on a daily basis. The package logrotate package helps control the growth of these files.

Changing to logrotate

The old settings listed below will be adopted when updating from a version older than SuSE Linux 8.0:

- Entries from /etc/logfile not associated with a particular package are moved to /etc/logrotate.d/aaa_base.
- The variable MAX_DAYS_FOR_LOG_FILES from the former rc.config file is mapped as dateext and maxage in the configuration file. Refer to the man page for logrotate (man 8 logrotate).

Configuration

Configure logrotate with the file /etc/logrotate.conf. In particular, the include specification primarily configures the additional files to read. SuSE Linux ensures that individual packages install files in /etc/logrotate.d (e.g., syslog or yast).

```
# see "man logrotate" for details
# rotate log files weekly
weekly

# keep 4 weeks worth of backlogs
rotate 4

# create new (empty) log files after rotating old ones
create

# uncomment this if you want your log files compressed
#compress

# RPM packages drop log rotation information into this directory
include /etc/logrotate.d

# no packages own lastlog or wtmp - we'll rotate them here
#/var/log/wtmp {
#    monthly
#    create 0664 root utmp
#    rotate 1
#}

# system-specific logs may be also be configured here.
```

File 30: Example for /etc/logrotate.conf

logrotate is controlled through cron and it is called daily by /etc/cron.daily/logrotate.

Note

The create option reads all settings made by the administrator in /etc/permissions*. Ensure that no conflicts arise from any personal modifications.

Note

Man Pages

For some GNU applications (e. g., tar) the man pages are no longer maintained. They have been replaced by info files. info is GNU's hypertext system. Typing `info info` gives a starting help for using `info`. `info` can be launched via `emacs -f info` or on its own with `info`. The programs `tkinfo` and `xinfo` are easy to use or you can access the SuSE help system.

The Command ulimit

With the `ulimit` (*user limits*) command, it is possible to set limits for the use of system resources and to have these displayed. `ulimit` is especially useful for limiting the memory available for applications. With this, an application can be prevented from using too much memory on its own, which could bring the system to a standstill.

`ulimit` can be used with various options. To limit memory usage, use the options listed in Table 11.1.

`-m`	maximum size of physical memory
`-v`	maximum size of virtual memory (swap)
`-s`	maximum size of the stack
`-c`	maximum size of the core files
`-a`	display of limits set

Table 11.1: `ulimit`*: Setting Resources for the User*

System-wide settings can be made in `/etc/profile`. There, creating core files must be enabled, needed by programmers for "debugging". A normal user cannot increase the values specified in `/etc/profile` by the system administrator, but he can make special entries in his own `~/.bashrc`.

```
# Limits of physical memory:
ulimit -m 98304

# Limits of virtual memory:
ulimit -v 98304
```

File 31: *ulimit: Settings in ~/.bashrc*

Details of memory must be specified in KB. For more detailed information, see the man page for bash (man bash).

Note

Not all shells support ulimit directives. PAM (for instance, pam_limits) offers comprehensive adjustment possibilities should you depend on encompassing settings for these restrictions.

Note

The free Command

The free command is somewhat misleading if your goal is to find out how much RAM is currently being used. The relevant information can be found in /proc/meminfo. These days, users, who have access to a modern operating system such as Linux, should not really have to worry much about memory. The concept of "available RAM" dates back to before the days of unified memory management. The slogan *free memory is bad memory* applies well to Linux. As a result, Linux has always made the effort to balance out caches without actually allowing free or unused memory.

Basically, the kernel does not have direct knowledge of any applications or user data. Instead, it manages applications and user data in a "page cache". If memory runs short, parts of it will be either written to the swap partition or to files, from which they can initially be read with the help of the mmap command (see the man page for mmap (man 2 mmap)).

Furthermore, the kernel also contains other caches, such as the "slab cache" where the caches used for network access are stored. This may explain differences between the counters in /proc/meminfo. Most, but not all of them, can be accessed via /proc/slabinfo.

The File /etc/resolv.conf

Domain name resolution is handled through the file /etc/resolv.conf. Refer to *DNS — Domain Name Service* on page 358 on this.

This file is updated by the script /sbin/modify_resolvconf exclusively, with no other program having permission to modify /etc/resolv.conf directly. Enforcing this rule is the only way to guarantee that the system's network configuration and the relevant files are kept in a consistent state.

Settings for GNU Emacs

GNU Emacs is a complex work environment. More information is available at `http://www.gnu.org/software/emacs/`. The following sections cover the configuration files processed when GNU Emacs is started.

On start-up, Emacs reads several files containing the specifications of the user, system administrator, and distributor for customization or preconfiguration. The initialization file `~/.emacs` is installed to the home directories of the individual users from `/etc/skel`. `.emacs`, in turn, reads the file `/etc/skel/.gnu-emacs`. If a user wants to customize the program, the `.gnu-emacs` should be copied to the home directory and the desired settings should be specified there:

```
cp /etc/skel/.gnu-emacs  /.gnu-emacs
```

`.gnu-emacs` defines the file `~/.gnu-emacs-custom` as `custom-file`. If users specify settings with the customize options, these will be saved to `~/.gnu-emacs-custom`.

When the package `emacs` is installed in SuSE Linux, the file `site-start.el` is installed in the directory `/usr/share/emacs/site-lisp`. The file `site-start.el` is loaded *before* the initialization file `~/.emacs`. Among other things, `site-start.el` makes sure that special configuration files distributed with Emacs add-on packages are loaded automatically (e.g., the package `psgml`). Configuration files of this type are also located in `/usr/share/emacs/site-lisp` and always begin with `suse-start-`. The local system administrator can specify system-wide settings in `default.el`.

More information about these files is available in the Emacs info file under *Init File*: `info:/emacs/InitFile`. Information about how to prevent these files from loading is also provided at this location.

The components of Emacs are split in several packages:

- The base package `emacs`.
- Usually, the package `emacs-x11` should be installed. This package contains the program *with* X11 support.
- The package `emacs-nox` contains the program *without* X11 support.
- The package `emacs-info`: online documentation in info format.
- The package `emacs-el` contains the uncompiled library files in Emacs Lisp. These are not required at run-time.

- Numerous add-on packages that can be installed if needed: the package emacs-auctex (for LaTeX), the package psgml (for SGML and XML), the package gnuserv (for client/server operation), and others.

Booting with the Initial Ramdisk

As soon as the Linux kernel has been booted and the root file system (/) mounted, programs can be run and further kernel modules can be integrated to provide additional functions. To mount the root file system, certain conditions must be met. The kernel needs the corresponding drivers to access the device on which the root file system is located (especially SCSI drivers). The kernel must also contain the code needed to read the file system (ext2, reiserfs, romfs, etc.). It is also conceivable that the root file system is already encrypted. In this case, a password is needed to mount the file system.

For the problem of SCSI drivers, a number of different solutions are possible: the kernel could contain all imaginable drivers. This might be a problem because different drivers could conflict with each other. Also, the kernel will become very large because of this. Another possibility is to provide different kernels, each one containing just one or a few SCSI drivers. This method also has the problem that a large number of different kernels are required, a problem then increased by the differently optimized kernels (Pentium optimization, SMP). The idea of loading the SCSI driver as a module leads to the general question answered by the concept of an *initial ramdisk*: creating a way of being able to run user space programs even before the root file system is mounted.

Concept of the Initial Ramdisk

The *initial ramdisk* (also called "initdisk" or "initrd") solves precisely the problems described above. The Linux kernel provides an option of having a small file system loaded to a RAM disk and running programs there before the actual root file system is mounted. The loading of initrd is handled by the boot loader (GRUB, LILO, etc.). Boot loaders only need BIOS routines to load data from the boot medium. If the boot loader is able to load the kernel, it can also load the initial ramdisk. Special drivers are not required.

The Order of the Booting Process with initrd

The boot loader loads the kernel and the `initrd` to memory and starts the kernel. The boot loader informs the kernel that an `initrd` exists and where it is located in memory.

If the `initrd` was compressed (which is typically the case), the kernel decompresses the `initrd` and mounts it as a temporary root file system. A program called linuxrc is then started. This program can now do all the things necessary to mount the proper root file system. As soon as linuxrc finishes, the temporary `initrd` is unmounted and the boot process continues as normal with the mounting of the proper root file system. Mounting the `initrd` and running linuxrc can be seen as a short interlude during a normal boot process.

The kernel tries to remount `initrd` to the `/initrd` directly after the actual root partition is booted. If this fails because the mount point `/initrd` does not exist, for example, the kernel will attempt to unmount `initrd`. If this does not work, the system is fully functional, but the memory taken up by `initrd` can no longer be unlocked and thus will no longer be available.

linuxrc

These are the only requirements for the program linuxrc in the `initrd`. It must have the special name `linuxrc` and it must be located in the root directory of the `initrd`. Apart from this, it only needs to be executable by the kernel. This means that linuxrc may be dynamically linked. In this case, the "shared libraries" in `/lib` must be completely available in `initrd`. linuxrc can also be a shell script. For this to work, a shell must exist in `/bin`. In short, `initrd` must contain a minimal Linux system that allows the program linuxrc to be run. When SuSE Linux is installed, a statically-linked linuxrc is used to keep `initrd` as small as possible (space on boot disks is very limited). linuxrc is run with `root` permissions.

The Real Root File System

As soon as linuxrc terminates, `initrd` is unmounted and discarded, the boot process carries on as normal, and the kernel mounts the real file system. What is mounted as the root file system can be influenced by linuxrc. It just needs to mount the `/proc` file system and write the value of the real root file system in numerical form to `/proc/sys/kernel/real-root-dev`.

Boot Loaders

Most boot loaders (above all, GRUB, LILO, and syslinux) can handle `initrd`. Individual boot loaders are given instructions for how to use `initrd` as follows:

GRUB Enter the following line in `/boot/grub/menu.lst`:

```
initrd (hd0,0)/initrd
```

Because the loading address of the initrd is written to the loaded kernel image, the `initrd` command must follow the `kernel` command.

LILO

Enter the following line in `/etc/lilo.conf`:

```
initrd=/boot/initrd
```

The file `/boot/initrd` is the *initial ramdisk*. It can be, but does not have to be, compressed.

syslinux

Enter the following line in `syslinux.cfg`:

```
append initrd=initrd ⟨further parameters⟩
```

Using initrd in SuSE

Installing the System

The `initrd` has already been used for some time for the installation: the user can load modules and make the entries necessary for an installation (above all, for the source medium). linuxrc then starts YaST, which carries out the installation. When YaST has finished, it tells linuxrc where the root file system of the freshly installed system is located. linuxrc writes this value to `/proc`, terminates, and informs the kernel to continue booting into the newly installed system.

For an installation of SuSE Linux, you are, from the very beginning, booting the system being installed. A real reboot after installation only takes place if the kernel does not match the modules installed in the system. Because SuSE Linux uses a kernel for uniprocessor systems during installation, a reboot is only necessary if an SMP kernel was installed in the system with the corresponding modules.

Booting the Installed System

In the past, YaST has provided more than forty kernels for installing in the system, with the only basic difference a specific SCSI driver. This was necessary to be able to mount the root file system after booting. Further drivers could then be loaded afterwards as modules. Because optimized kernels are now available, this concept is no longer feasible — by now, over one hundred kernel images would be needed.

This is why an `initrd` is used now, even to start the system normally. The way it is used is similar to that for an installation. The linuxrc used here, however, is simply a shell script with the task of loading a given module. Typically, this is just one single module — the very SCSI driver needed to access the root file system.

Creating an initrd

An `initrd` is created by means of the script `mkinitrd` (previously `mk_initrd`). In SuSE Linux, the modules to load are specified by the variable INITRD_MODULES in `/etc/sysconfig/kernel`. After installation, this variable is automatically occupied by the correct values (the installation linuxrc knows which modules were loaded). The modules were loaded in exactly the order in which they appear in INITRD_MODULES. This is especially important if a number of SCSI drivers are used, because otherwise the names of the hard disks would change. Strictly speaking, it would be sufficient just to load those drivers needed to access the root file system, because the automatic loading of additional SCSI drivers may cause problems (how should it be "triggered" if hard disks hang on the second SCSI adapter). All SCSI drivers needed at the installation are loaded by means of `initrd`.

The current `mkinitrd` checks if a SCSI driver is needed for the root file system. If you run `mkinitrd` on a system where / is found on EIDE hard disks, an `initrd` is not needed as the kernel used for SuSE Linux already contains the EIDE driver. As there are more and more special EIDE controllers coming onto the market, in the future it will probably be necessary, in such cases, to use an `initrd` to boot the installed system.

Note

Because the loading of the `initrd` with the boot loader runs in the same way as loading the kernel itself (LILO notices, in its `map` file, the location of the files), LILO must be updated after every change in `initrd`. After every run of `mkinitrd`, run `lilo`.

Note

Possible Difficulties — Self-Compiled Kernels

A self-compiled kernel can often lead to the following problem: out of habit, the SCSI driver is hard-linked to the kernel, but the existing `initrd` remains unchanged. When you boot, the following occurs. The kernel already contains the SCSI driver, so the hardware is detected. `initrd`, however, now tries to load the driver again as a module. With some SCSI drivers, especially with `aic7xxx`, this leads to the system blocking. Strictly speaking, this is a kernel error. An already existing driver should not be allowed to be loaded again as a module. The problem is already known from another context, however (serial drivers).

There are several solutions to the problem: either configure the driver as a module (then it will be correctly loaded in the `initrd`) or remove the entry for `initrd` from the file `/etc/lilo.conf`. An equivalent to the latter solution is to remove the variable INITRD_MODULES then run `mkinitrd`, which then realizes that no `initrd` is needed.

Prospects

It is quite possible in the future that an `initrd` will be used for many more and much more sophisticated things than loading modules needed to access `/`.

- High-end EIDE drivers
- Root file system on RAID software (linuxrc sets up the `md` devices)
- Root file system on the LVM
- Root file system is encrypted (linuxrc asks for the password)
- Root file system on a SCSI hard disk on a PCMCIA adapter

For More Information

`/usr/src/linux/Documentation/ramdisk.txt`
`/usr/src/linux/Documentation/initrd.txt`
the man page for `initrd` (`man 4 initrd`)

linuxrc

linuxrc is started during the boot of the kernel, usually as a prelude to a Linux system installation, before the "actual" booting commences (the kernel must first be properly configured, of course). This allows you to boot a small, modularized kernel and to load the few drivers needed as modules from a floppy disk.

If needed, linuxrc assists in loading the related drivers.

You can also use linuxrc as a boot tool for an already installed system. You can even start a totally independent RAM disk–based rescue system, for example, if something serious should happen to your hard disk or you have simply forgotten your `root` password. More about this below, in Section *The SuSE Rescue System* on page 282.

Main Menu

After you have selected the language and keyboard, find yourself in linuxrc's main menu (see Figure 1.2 on page 12). Normally, linuxrc is used to start Linux. Go to the start menu to start an installation ('Start installation / system').

Settings / Preferences

Specify your settings in respect to 'Language', 'Screen' (Color/monochrome), 'Keyboard Layout', and 'Debug (Experts)'.

System Information

In 'System Information' (Figure 11.1 on the next page), check a number of other things, besides kernel messages, such as the I/O addresses of PCI cards or the size of the main memory recognized by Linux.

You can check some system information in 'System information'. Here, check the used interrupts, I/O ports used, main memory, and recognized PCI devices as detected by Linux.

The next lines show how a hard disk and a CD-ROM connected to an (E)IDE controller announce their start. In this case, you do not need to load additional modules:

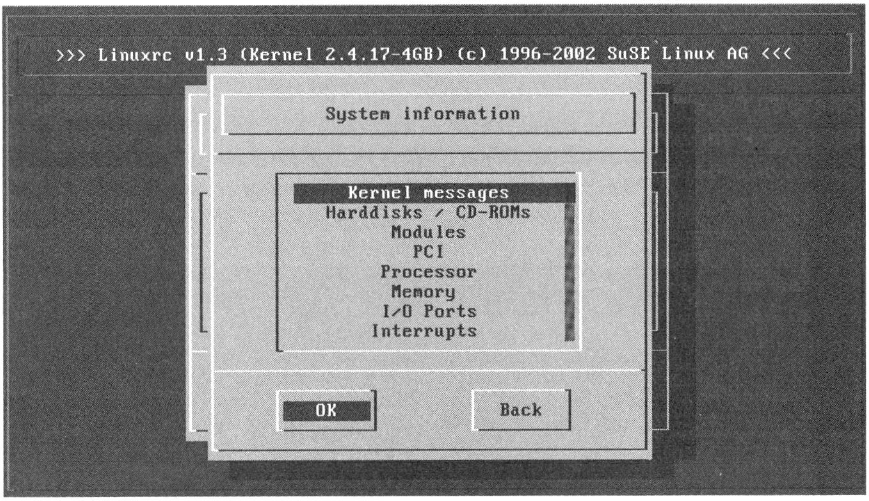

Figure 11.1: System Information

```
hda: ST32140A, 2015MB w/128kB Cache, LBA, CHS=1023/64/63
hdb: CD-ROM CDR-S1G, ATAPI CD-ROM drive
Partition check:
 hda: hda1 hda2 hda3 < hda5 >
```

If you booted a kernel that already had a SCSI driver compiled, you do not need this SCSI driver as a module as well. Quite typical announcements when loading SCSI adapters and connected devices might look like this:

```
scsi : 1 host.
Started kswapd v 1.4.2.2
scsi0 : target 0 accepting period 100ns offset 8 10.00MHz FAST SCSI-II
scsi0 : setting target 0 to period 100ns offset 8 10.00MHz FAST SCSI-II
  Vendor: QUANTUM   Model: VP32210          Rev: 81H8
  Type:   Direct-Access                     ANSI SCSI revision: 02
Detected scsi disk sda at scsi0, channel 0, id 0, lun 0
scsi0 : target 2 accepting period 236ns offset 8 4.23MHz synchronous SCSI
scsi0 : setting target 2 to period 248ns offset 8 4.03MHz synchronous SCSI
  Vendor: TOSHIBA   Model: CD-ROM XM-3401TA  Rev: 0283
  Type:   CD-ROM                            ANSI SCSI revision: 02
scsi : detected 1 SCSI disk total.
SCSI device sda: hdwr sector= 512 bytes. Sectors= 4308352 [2103 MB] [2.1 GB]
Partition check:
 sda: sda1 sda2 sda3 sda4 < sda5 sda6 sda7 sda8 >
```

Loading Modules

Select which kinds of modules you need. If you booted via disk, the corresponding data must be read by linuxrc and displayed in a list.

If you have booted from CD or from DOS (via loadlin), these modules are already set in linuxrc. This saves tedious loading, but requires additional memory.

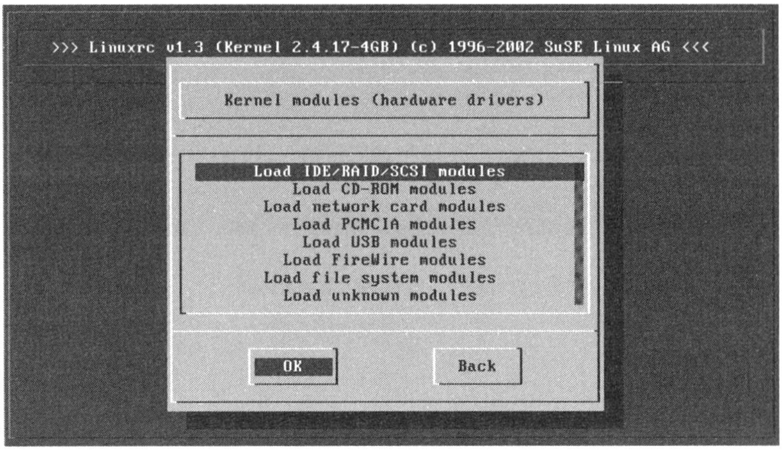

Figure 11.2: Load Modules

linuxrc offers a list of available drivers. On the left is the name of the module and, on the right, a short description of its usage. For some components, there are a variety of drivers from which to choose (even newer alpha drivers).

Passing Parameters

When you have found a suitable driver, move to it with the cursor and press ⏎. This opens a dialog box in which to add additional parameters for this module.

Beware that — in contrast to entering the parameters at the kernel prompt (as in MILO, LILO, or SYSLINUX) — multiple parameters for the same module must be separated here by a blank space.

In most cases, it is not necessary to specify the hardware in detail. Most drivers find their components automatically. Specifying parameters is only

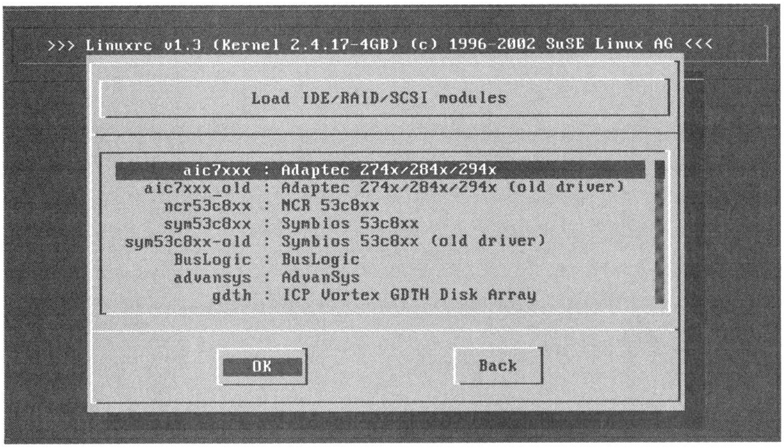

Figure 11.3: *Selection of SCSI Drivers*

necessary if you have a network card or an older CD-ROM drive with a proprietary controller card. If in doubt, just try pressing ↵.

Recognizing and initializing certain hardware can take some time. Switching to virtual console 4 (Alt + F4) lets you watch the kernel messages while loading. SCSI drivers need a while, as they have to wait for each device to load.

The messages are displayed by linuxrc so you can verify that everything ran smoothly. If it fails, the messages might give a hint as to why.

Start Installation / System

Once you have set up hardware support via modules, proceed to the 'Start installation / system' menu.

From here, a number of procedures can be started: 'Start installation' (an update is also started from this item), 'Boot installed system' (the root partition must be known), 'Start rescue system' (refer to Section *The SuSE Rescue System* on the following page), and 'Eject CD'.

'Start Live-CD' is only available if you booted a "LiveEval CD". Download ISO images from the FTP server (`live-eval-\variable{VERSION}`):

```
ftp://ftp.suse.com/pub/suse/i386/
```

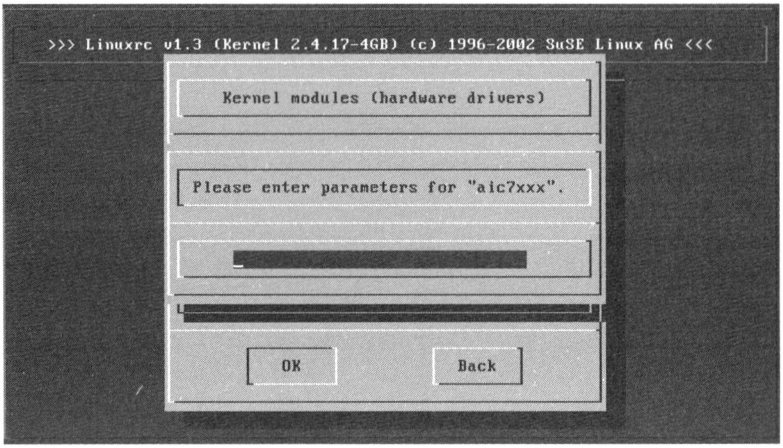

Figure 11.4: Entering Parameters for a Module to Load

Tip

The item 'Start Live-CD' can be of great use if, for example, you want to test, without actually installing, if the computer in question or the laptop you might want to buy is at all compatible with SuSE Linux — such a test ought to be possible in every modern PC shop, without any trouble.

Tip

For the installation (Figure 11.5 on the next page), choose various sources for the installation and similarly for the rescue system (see Figure 11.5 on the facing page).

The SuSE Rescue System

SuSE Linux contains several Linux rescue systems so that, in emergencies, your Linux partitions on the hard disks are reachable "from the outside": via a boot disk or the "Rescue" System, loaded from disk, CD, the network, or the SuSE FTP server. There is also a bootable SuSE Linux CD (the *"LiveEval CD"*) that can be used as a rescue system. The rescue system includes several help programs with which you can remedy large problems with inaccessible hard disks, misconfigured configuration files, or other similar problems.

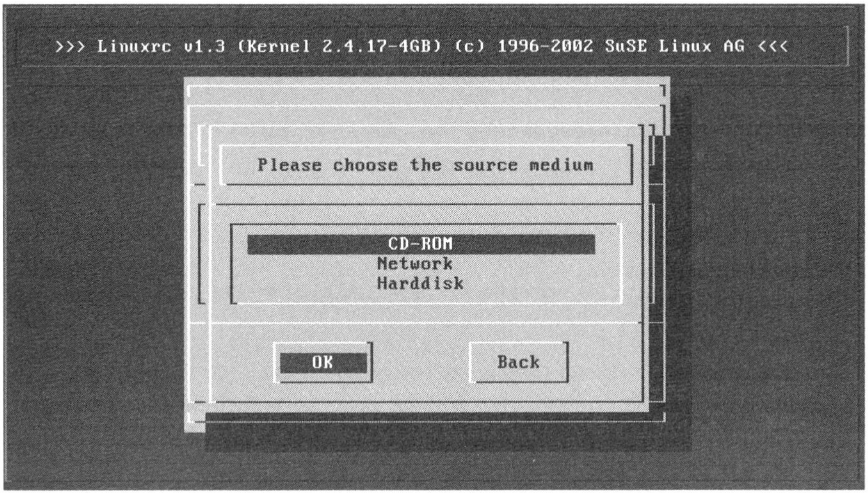

Figure 11.5: Selection of Source Media in linuxrc

Another aspect of the rescue system is Parted, which is used for modifying the partition size. This program can be launched from inside the rescue system itself, if you do not want to take advantage of the resizer integrated in YaST2. Information on Parted can be found at:

`http://www.gnu.org/software/parted/`

Tip

Always have a boot and rescue disk at hand, because the slight effort for creating and maintaining the disk is negligible in comparison to the time wasted and work involved when, in the case of emergency, you cannot access your system or your CD-ROM drive.

Tip

Preparations

For setting up your rescue system, you need two disks free of errors: one as a future boot disk and the other for the compressed image of a small root file system. The image file `bootdisk` for booting the system and the file `rescue` for the root file system can be found on the first CD in the `boot` directory.

There are three ways to set up the root file system on the disk:

- with YaST
- in a console using the Linux commands

```
earth:~ #  /sbin/badblocks -v /dev/fd0 1440
earth:~ #  dd if=/media/cdrom/boot/rescue of=/dev/fd0 bs=18k
```

- at the DOS prompt (where the CD-ROM drive is `Q:`)

```
Q:\> cd \dosutils\rawrite Q:\dosutils\rawrite> rawrite.exe
```

As of Version 8.0, the rescue disk is currently based on libc5 (SuSE Linux 5.3), since it is possible in this to save some programs, such as an editor, fdisk, or e2fsck to a disk.

Note

The rescue disk cannot be mounted, because it is not a file system. It only contains the compressed images of one. Directions for reading the file system are in the following paragraph.

Note

To read the image, you will need to decompress the image file then mount the decompressed image as user `root`. If your Linux kernel support the *loop device*, the procedure is as follows:

```
earth:~ #  cp /media/cdrom/boot/rescue /root/rescue.gz
earth:~ #  gunzip /root/rescue.gz
earth:~ #  mount -t ext2 -o loop /root/rescue /mnt
```

Starting the Rescue System

The rescue system is launched by the SuSE boot disk you created or by your bootable CD or DVD. It is required that the disk and CD-ROM or DVD drives are bootable. If necessary, change the boot series in the CMOS setup. Following are the steps for starting the rescue system:

1. Start your system with the SuSE boot disk created yourself or with the first SuSE Linux CD or DVD inserted into the corresponding drive.
2. Launch the entire system or choose 'Manual Installation' so that 'boot options' can be entered and kernel modules to load can be defined.

3. Make the respective settings for language and keyboard.
4. Select the item 'Installation/Start system' in the main menu.
5. If you started with the boot disk, now insert the installation CD or the `rescue` disk with the compressed image of the rescue system.

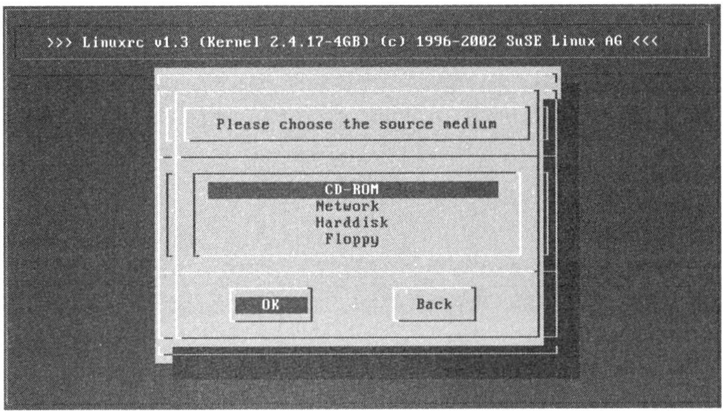

Figure 11.6: Source Medium for the Rescue System

6. In the menu 'Start installation/system' select the item 'Start rescue system' (see Figure 1.3 on page 14) then specify the desired source medium (Figure 11.6).

   Subsequently, we will introduce a few tips on selection options:

   'CD-ROM': When loading the rescue system, the path `/cdrom` is exported. This makes the installation from *this* CD possible.

   'Network': For starting the `rescue` system over a network connection, the network card's driver must be loaded first. See the general information on this in Section *Installation from a Network Source* on page 18. Several protocols exist for this purpose (see Figure 11.7 on the following page), such as NFS, FTP, or SMB.

   'Hard disk': Load the `rescue` system from the hard disk.

   'Floppy Disk': The `rescue` system can also be started from the floppy disk, especially if the computer only has a small amount of working memory.

Regardless of the medium chosen, the rescue system will be decompressed, loaded onto a RAM floppy disk as a new root file system, mounted, and started. Now it is ready for use.

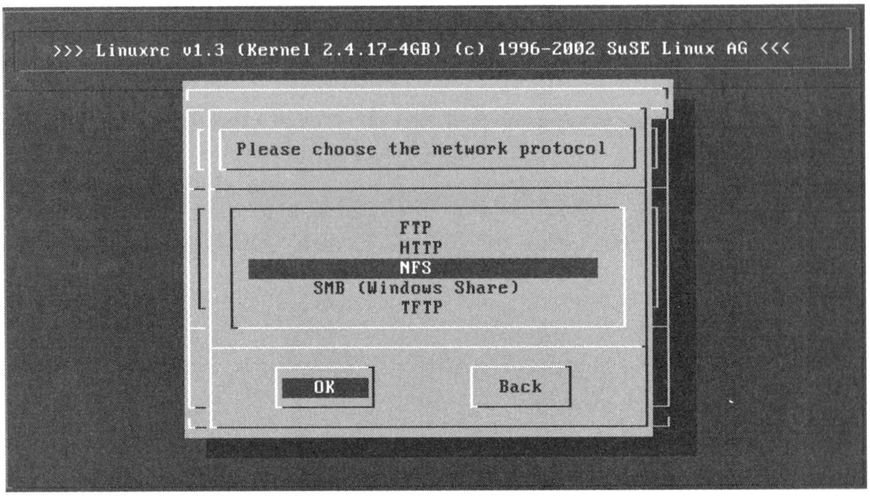

Figure 11.7: Network Protocols

Working with the Rescue System

The rescue system provides three virtual consoles on keys Alt + F1 to Alt + F3. Here, `root` may log in without a password. Alt + F4 accesses the system console, where you can view the kernel and syslog messages.

A shell and lots of other useful utilities (net tools), such as the mount program, can be found in the `/bin` directory. In `sbin`, find important file and network utilities for reviewing and repairing the file system (e.g., e2fsck).

Furthermore, this directory contains the most important binaries for system maintenance, such as fdisk, mkfs, mkswap, mount, mount, init, and shutdown, as well as ifconfig, route, and netstat for maintaining the network.

An editor, vi, is located in `/usr/bin`. Also, tools like grep, find, and less, along with telnet are available.

Accessing Your Normal System

To mount your SuSE Linux system using the rescue system, use the mount point `/mnt`. You can also use or create another directory.

As an example, assume your normal system is put together according to the `/etc/fstab` shown in the example File 32.

```
/dev/sdb5     swap     swap     defaults   0   0
/dev/sdb3     /        ext2     defaults   1   1
/dev/sdb6     /usr     ext2     defaults   1   2
```

File 32: Sample /etc/fstab

Caution

Pay attention to the order of steps outlined in the following section for mounting the various devices.

Caution

To access your entire system, mount it step-by-step in the `/mnt` directory using the following commands:

```
earth:/ # mount /dev/sdb3 /mnt
earth:/ # mount /dev/sdb6 /mnt/usr
```

Now, you can access your entire system and, for example, correct mistakes in configuration files such as `/etc/fstab`, `/etc/passwd`, and `/etc/inittab`. The configuration files are now located in the `/mnt/etc` directory instead of in `/etc`.

To recover even completely lost partitions with the fdisk program by simply setting it up again, determine where on the hard disk the partitions were previously located and make a printout of the `/etc/fstab` directory as well as the output of the command

```
earth:~ # fdisk -l /dev/⟨disk⟩
```

Instead of the ⟨*disk*⟩ variable, insert, in order, the device names of your hard disks, such as `hda`.

Repairing File Systems Damaged file systems are tricky problems for the rescue system. This could happen after an unscheduled shutdown caused by power failure or a system crash. Generally, file systems cannot be repaired on a running system. If you encounter really severe problems, you may not even be able to mount your root file system so the system boot ends in a "kernel panic". Here, the only chance is to repair the system from the "outside" using a rescue system.

The SuSE Linux rescue system contains the utilities e2fsck and dumpe2fs (for diagnosis). These should remedy most problems.

In an emergency, man pages often are not available. That is why we have included them in this manual in Appendix C on page 519.

Example: If mounting a file system fails due to an *invalid* superblock, the e2fsck program would probably fail, too. If this were the case, your superblock may be corrupted, too. There are copies of the superblock located every 8192 blocks (8193, 16385, etc.). If your superblock is corrupted, try one of the copies instead. This is accomplished by entering the command:

```
earth:~ # e2fsck -f -b 8193 /dev/damaged_partition
```

The `-f` option forces the file system check and overrides e2fsck's error so that — since the superblock copy is intact — everything is fine.

Virtual Consoles

Linux is a multiuser and multitasking system. The advantages of these features can be appreciated, even on a stand-alone PC system.

In text mode, there are six virtual consoles available. Switch between them using (Alt) + (F1) to (Alt) + (F6). The seventh console is reserved for X11. More or fewer consoles can be assigned by modifying the file `/etc/inittab`.

To switch to a console from X11 without leaving X11, use (Ctrl) + (Alt) + (F1) to (Ctrl) + (Alt) + (F6). (Alt) + (F7) then returns to X11.

Keyboard Mapping

To standardize the keyboard mapping of programs, changes were made to the following files:

```
/etc/inputrc
/usr/X11R6/lib/X11/Xmodmap
/etc/skel/.Xmodmap
/etc/skel/.exrc
/etc/skel/.less
/etc/skel/.lesskey
/etc/csh.cshrc
/etc/termcap
/usr/lib/terminfo/x/xterm
/usr/X11R6/lib/X11/app-defaults/XTerm
/usr/share/emacs/⟨VERSION⟩/site-lisp/term/*.el
/usr/lib/joerc
```

These changes only affect applications that make use of `terminfo` entries or whose configuration files are changed directly (`vi`, `less`, etc.). Other non-SuSE applications should be adjusted to these defaults.

Under X, the compose key ("multikey") can be accessed using the key combination Ctrl + ⇑ Shift (right). Also see the corresponding entry in `/usr/X11R6/lib/X11/Xmodmap`.

Local Adjustments — I18N/L10N

SuSE Linux is, to a very large extent, internationalized and can be modified for local needs in a flexible manner. In other words, internationalization ("I18N") allows specific localizations ("L10N"). The abbreviations I18N and L10N are derived from the first and last letters of the words and, in between, the number of letters omitted.

Settings are made via LC_* variables defined in the file `/etc/sysconfig/language`. This refers not only to "native language support", but also to the categories *Messages* (Language), *Character Set*, *Sort Order*, *Time and Date*, *Numbers*, and *Money*. Each of these categories can be defined directly via its own variable or indirectly via a variable in the file `language` (see the man page for `locale` (`man 5 locale`)).

1. RC_LC_MESSAGES, RC_LC_CTYPE, RC_LC_COLLATE, RC_LC_TIME, RC_LC_NUMERIC, RC_LC_MONETARY: These variables are passed to the shell without the RC_ prefix and determine the above categories. The files concerned are listed below.

   The current setting can be shown with the command `locale`.

2. RC_LC_ALL: This variable (if set) overwrites the values of the variables mentioned in item 1.

3. RC_LANG: If none of the above variables are set, this is the "fallback". By default, SuSE Linux only sets RC_LANG. This makes it easier for users to enter their own values.

4. ROOT_USES_LANG: A `yes` or `no` variable. If it is set to `no`, `root` always works in the POSIX environment.

The other variables can be set via the `sysconfig` editor.

The value of such a variable contains the language code, country code, encoding, and modifier. The individual components are connected by special characters:

`LANG=⟨language⟩[[_⟨COUNTRY⟩].Encoding[@Modifier]]`

Some Examples

You should always set the language and country codes together. Language settings follow the standard ISO 639 (`http://www.evertype.com/standards/iso639/iso639-en.html` and `http://www.loc.`

gov/standards/iso639-2/). Country codes are listed in ISO 3166, see (http://www.din.de/gremien/nas/nabd/iso3166ma/codlstp1/en_listp1.html). It only makes sense to set values for which usable description files can be found in /usr/lib/locale. Additional description files can be created from the files in /usr/share/i18n using the command localedef. A description file for en_US.UTF-8 (for English and United States) can be created with:

```
earth:~ # localedef -i en_US -f UTF-8 en_US.UTF-8
```

LANG=en_US.ISO-8859-1

This sets the variable to English language, country to United States, and the character set to ISO-8859-1. This character set does not support the Euro sign, but it will be useful sometimes for programs that have not been updated to support ISO-8859-15. The string defining the charset (ISO-8859-1 in our case) will then be evaluated by programs like Emacs.

LANG=en_US.UTF-8

If you use a Unicode xterm, it is necessary to specify UTF-8 as well. To achieve this, make a small shell script called uxterm to start xterm with UTF-8 loaded each time. See File 33.

```
#!/bin/bash
export LANG=en_US.UTF-8
xterm -fn \
'-Misc-Fixed-Medium-R-Normal--18-120-100-100-C-90-ISO10646-1' \
-T 'xterm UTF-8' $*
```

File 33: uxterm to Start a Unicode xterm

SuSEconfig reads the variables in /etc/sysconfig/language and writes the necessary changes to /etc/SuSEconfig/profile and /etc/SuSEconfig/csh.cshrc. /etc/SuSEconfig/profile is read or "sourced" by /etc/profile. /etc/SuSEconfig/csh.cshrc is sourced by /etc/csh.cshrc. This makes the settings available system-wide.

Settings for Language Support

Files in the category *Messages* are, as a rule, only stored in the language directory (e. g., en) to have a fallback. If you set LANG to en,_US and the "message" file in /usr/share/locale/en_US/LC_MESSAGES does not exist, it will fall back to /usr/share/locale/en/LC_MESSAGES.

A fallback chain can also be defined, for example, for Breton → French or for Galician → Spanish → Portuguese:

```
LANGUAGE="br_FR:fr_FR"
LANGUAGE="gl_ES:es_ES:pt_PT"
```

If desired, use the Norwegian variants "nynorsk" and "bokmål" instead (with additional fallback to no):

```
LANG="nn_NO"
LANGUAGE="nn_NO:nb_NO:no"
```

or

```
LANG="nb_NO"
LANGUAGE="nb_NO:nn_NO:no"
```

Note that in Norwegian, LC_TIME is also treated differently.

Possible Problems

- The thousand comma is not recognized. LANG is probably set to en, but the description the glibc uses is located in /usr/share/locale/en_US/LC_NUMERIC. LC_NUMERIC, for example, must be set to en_US.

For More Information

- *The GNU C Library Reference Manual*, Chap. "Locales and Internationalization"; included in package glibc-info.
- Markus Kuhn, *UTF-8 and Unicode FAQ for Unix/Linux*, currently at http://www.cl.cam.ac.uk/~mgk25/unicode.html.
- *Unicode-Howto*, by Bruno Haible file:/usr/share/doc/howto/en/html/Unicode-HOWTO.html.

The SuSE Linux Boot Concept

Booting and initializing a UNIX system can challenge even an experienced system administrator. This chapter gives a short overview of the SuSE Linux boot concept. The new implementation is compatible with the *System Initialization* section of the LSB specification (Version 1.3). Refer to *Linux Standard Base (LSB)* on page 266 for more information about LSB.

The simple words "Uncompressing Linux..." signal that the kernel is taking control of your hardware. It checks and sets your console — more precisely: the BIOS registers of graphics cards and output format — to read BIOS settings and to initialize basic hardware interfaces. Next, your drivers "probe" existing hardware and initialize it accordingly. After checking the partitions and mounting the root file system, the kernel starts init, which "boots" (Unix jargon) the main system with all its programs and configurations. The kernel controls the entire system, including hardware access and the CPU time programs use.

The init Program

The program init is responsible for correctly initializing all system processes. Thus, it is the father of all processes in the entire system.

init takes a special role. It is started directly by the kernel and resists *signal 9*, which normally kills processes. All other programs are either started directly by init or by one of its "child" processes.

init is centrally configured via the `/etc/inittab` file. Here, the "runlevels" are defined (see *Runlevels* on the current page). It also specifies which services and daemons are available in each of the levels.

Depending on the entries in `/etc/inittab`, several scripts are run by init. For reasons of clarity, these scripts all reside in the directory `/etc/init.d`.

The entire process of starting the system and shutting it down is maintained by init. From this point of view, the kernel can be considered a background process whose task it is to maintain all other processes and to adjust CPU time and hardware access according to requests from other programs.

Runlevels

In Linux, *runlevels* define how the system is started. After booting, the system starts as defined in `/etc/inittab` in the line `initdefault`. Usually this is `3` or `5` (see Table 12.1 on the facing page). An alternative to this is assigning a special runlevel at boot time (e. g., at the boot prompt). The kernel passes any parameters it does not need directly to init.

To change runlevels while the system is running, enter init with the appropriate number. Only the superuser is allowed to do this. `init 1` starts *single*

Runlevel	Meaning
0	System halt
S	Single user mode; from boot prompt with US keyboard layout
1	Single user mode
2	Local multiuser without remote network (standard)
3	Full multiuser with network
4	Unused
5	Full multiuser mode with network and xdm
6	System reboot

Table 12.1: *Valid Runlevels in Linux*

user mode, which is used for the maintenance and administration of your system. After finishing work in *S* mode, the system administrator can change the runlevel to 3 again by typing `init 3`. Now all essential programs are started and users can log in and work with the system.

Table 12.1 below gives an overview of available runlevels. Runlevel 2 should not be used on a system with a `/usr` partition mounted via NFS.

Halt the system using `init 0` or reboot it with `init 6`.

Runlevel `5` is the default runlevel in all SuSE Linux standard installations. It allows users to log in directly to a graphical user interface.

If you have already installed and configured the X Window System properly as described in *The X Window System* on page 91) and want users to log in via a graphical user interface, change the runlevel to `5`. Try it first by typing `init 5` to see whether the system works as expected. Afterwards, set the default runlevel to 5 in YaST.

Caution

Modifying `/etc/inittab`

If `/etc/inittab` is damaged, the system might not boot properly. Therefore, be extremely careful while editing `/etc/inittab` and always keep a backup of an intact version. To repair damage, try entering `init=/bin/sh` after the kernel name at the LILO boot prompt to boot directly into a shell. After that, replace `/etc/inittab` with your backup version using the `cp` command.

Caution

Changing Runlevels

Generally, two things happen when you change runlevels. First, *stop scripts* of the current runlevel are launched, closing down some programs essential for the current runlevel. Then *start scripts* of the new runlevel are started. Here, in most cases, a number of programs will be started.

For example, the following occurs when changing from runlevel 3 to 5:

- The administrator (`root`) tells init to change runlevels:

  ```
  root@earth:/ >  init 5
  ```

- init now consults its configuration file (`/etc/inittab`) and realizes it should start `/etc/init.d/rc` with the new runlevel as a parameter.

- Now rc calls all the stop scripts of the current runlevel, but only for those where there is no start script in the selected new runlevel. In our example, these are all the scripts that reside in `/etc/init.d/rc3.d` (old runlevel was 3) and start with a `'K'`. The number following `'K'` guarantees a certain order to start, as there are some dependencies to consider.

  Note

  The names of the stop scripts always begin with `'K'` for kill. Start scripts begin with `'S'` for start.

  Note

- The last things to start are the start scripts of the new runlevel. These are (in our example) in `/etc/init.d/rc5.d` and begin with an `'S'`. The same procedure regarding the order in which they are started is applied here.

When changing into the same runlevel as the current runlevel, init only checks `/etc/inittab` for changes and starts the appropriate steps (e.g., for starting a getty on another interface).

Option	Meaning
start	Starts service.
stop	Stops service.
restart	Stops service and restarts if service is already running. If it is not running, it starts the service.
reload	Load configuration of service again without stopping and restarting it.
force-reload	Load configuration of the service again if the service supports this. If not, a restart is carried out.
status	Show current status.

Table 12.2: Summary of init Script Options

Init Scripts

Scripts in /etc/init.d are divided into two sections:

- scripts executed directly by init. This only applies while booting and shutting down the system immediately (power failure or a user pressing Ctrl + Alt + Del).
- scripts started indirectly by init. These are run when changing the runlevel and always call the master script /etc/init.d/rc, which guarantees the correct order of the relevant scripts.

All scripts are located in /etc/init.d. Scripts for changing the runlevel are also found there, but are called via symbolic links from one of the subdirectories (/etc/init.d/rc0.d to /etc/init.d/rc6.d). This is just for clarity reasons and avoids duplicate scripts (e. g., if they are used in several runlevels). Because every script can be executed as both a start and a stop script, these scripts have to understand the parameters "start" and "stop". The scripts understand, in addition, the "restart", "reload", "force-reload", and "status" options. These different options are explained in Table 12.2.

After leaving runlevel 3, /etc/init.d/rc3.d/K40network is run. /etc/init.d/rc runs the /etc/init.d/network script with the stop parameter. After entering runlevel 5, the same script is started. This time, however, with the start parameter.

Links in these runlevel-specific subdirectories simply serve to assign the scripts to a certain runlevel. Adding and removing the required links is done by the program insserv (or by the link /usr/lib/lsb/install_initd) when installing and uninstalling packages. Refer to the man page for insserv (man 8 insserv).

Below is a short introduction to the boot and stop scripts launched first (or last, respectively) as well as an explanation of the maintaining script.

boot Executed while starting the system directly using init. It is independent of the chosen runlevel and is only executed once. Here, the proc and pts file systems are mounted and the blogd (Boot Logging Daemon) is activated. If the system is booted for the first time after an update or an installation, the initial system configuration is started.

The script boot is also responsible for starting all the scripts in /etc/init.d/boot.d with a name that starts with 'S'. There, the file systems are checked and loop devices are configured if needed. The system time is also set. If an error occurs while automatically checking and repairing the file system, the system administrator can intervene after first entering the root password.

Last to be executed is the script boot.local.

boot.local Here, enter additional commands to execute at boot before changing into a runlevel. It can be compared to AUTOEXEC.BAT on DOS systems.

boot.setup General settings to make while changing from *single user mode* to another runlevel. Here, keyboard maps are loaded and the kernel daemon is started, which loads modules automatically.

halt This script is only executed while changing into runlevel 0 or 6. Here, it is executed either as halt or as reboot. Whether the system shuts down or reboots depends on how halt is called.

rc This script calls the appropriate stop scripts of the current runlevel and the start scripts of the newly selected runlevel.

With this concept in mind, you can create your own scripts. A skeleton has been prepared in /etc/init.d/skeleton. The exact format is described in the LSB outline. This defines specifically the order of steps and in which levels the script should be processed.

Now, create the links in the corresponding rc?.d to your script to make sure it is launched when you change runlevels (see *Changing Runlevels* on page 296 for script names). Refer to the man page for init.d (man 7 init.d) and the man page for insserv (man 8 insserv) for the necessary technical background. Use the YaST Runlevel Editor to create these links with a graphical front-end. See *The YaST Runlevel Editor* on the current page.

Caution

Creating your own init scripts
Faulty init scripts may freeze your machine. Handle them with utmost care and, if possible, subject them to heavy testing in the multiuser environment. Some useful information about init scripts can be found in *Runlevels* on page 294.

Caution

The YaST Runlevel Editor

After this expert module starts, it is initialized. The current default runlevel is shown in the next dialog. This "operation mode" starts after your system boots. In SuSE Linux, this is usually runlevel 5 (full multiuser operation with network and KDM, the graphical login). Runlevel 3 also works well (full multiuser operation with network). With the help of YaST, a different default runlevel can be set. See Table 12.1 on page 295.

'Runlevel properties' continues to an overview of all the services and daemons, supplemented with information as to whether they have been activated on your system and for which runlevels. Highlight a line with the mouse and activate the check boxes for runlevels '0', '1', '2', '3', '5', '6', and 'S' and, with that, state which service or daemon should be activated for which runlevel. Runlevel 4 is undefined — this is always reserved for custom settings.

With 'Start' and 'Stop', decide whether a server should be implemented. The current status is checked via 'Update', if this has not already been done automatically. 'Reset to Default Value' allows you to restore the default settings to their initial state following installation. 'Activate Service' only appears if the service is currently disabled. 'Reset All Services to Default Value' restores all services to their original state following installation. 'Finish' saves the system configuration.

Caution

Changing runlevel settings
Faulty runlevel settings may render a system unusable. Before applying your changes, make absolutely sure you know about their consequences.

Caution

SuSEconfig and /etc/sysconfig

The main configuration of SuSE Linux can be done via the configuration files in `/etc/sysconfig`. Former versions of SuSE Linux relied on `/etc/rc.config` for system configuration. This configuration file has become obsolete with the current version of SuSE Linux. `/etc/rc.config` will not be created at installation time any more as all system configuration will be done via `/etc/sysconfig`. If an update is issued, an existing `/etc/rc.config` will remain intact.

The configuration files in `/etc/sysconfig` are interpreted by single scripts. For example, the network configuration files are only read by the network scripts.

Moreover, a large number of configuration files are generated from the settings in `/etc/sysconfig`. This is the task of `/sbin/SuSEconfig`. If you change the network configuration, for example, the file `/etc/host.conf` is regenerated, as it depends on the configuration made.

If you change anything in those files manually, you need to run `/sbin/SuSEconfig` afterwards to make sure all changes to the appropriate configuration files are made at the correct places. If you change the configuration with YaST, it automatically executes `/sbin/SuSEconfig` and updates your configuration files.

This concept enables you to make basic changes to your configuration without having to reboot the system. Since some changes are rather complex, some programs must be restarted for the changes to take effect. If the network configuration has changed, the network programs can be restarted using the commands: `rcnetwork stop` and `rcnetwork start`. As you can see, you can easily start and stop init scripts by hand.

Generally, we recommend the following steps for configuring your system:

- Bring the system into *single user mode* (Runlevel 1) with `init 1`.

- Change the configuration files as needed. This can be done using an editor of your choice or using the *sysconfig Editor* of YaST.
- Execute `/sbin/SuSEconfig` to make the changes take effect. If you have changed the configuration files with YaST, this is done automatically.
- Bring your system back to the previous runlevel with something like `init 3`.

This procedure is mainly relevant if you have changed system-wide settings (such as network configuration). It is not necessary to go into *single user mode* for small changes, but it ensures all relevant programs are correctly restarted.

Tip

To disable the automatic configuration of SuSEconfig, set the variable ⟨*ENABLE_SUSECONFIG*⟩ in `/etc/sysconfig/suseconfig` to `no`. Do not disable SuSEconfig if you want to use the SuSE installation support. It is also possible to disable the autoconfiguration partially.

Tip

Using the YaST /etc/sysconfig Editor

The files where the most important SuSE Linux settings are stored are located in the `/etc/sysconfig` directory. The sysconfig editor presents the settings options in an easy-to-read manner. The values can be modified and subsequently added to the individual configuration files in this directory. In general, it is not necessary to edit them manually, however, because these files are automatically adjusted when installing a package or configuring a service.

Caution

Modifications of `/etc/sysconfig/` files
Do not modify the `/etc/sysconfig` files if you lack previous experience and knowledge. It could do considerable damage to your system.

Caution

The YaST sysconfig dialog is split into three parts. The left part of the dialog window shows a tree view of all configurable variables. As soon as you have selected a variable, the right part of the will display both the current selection

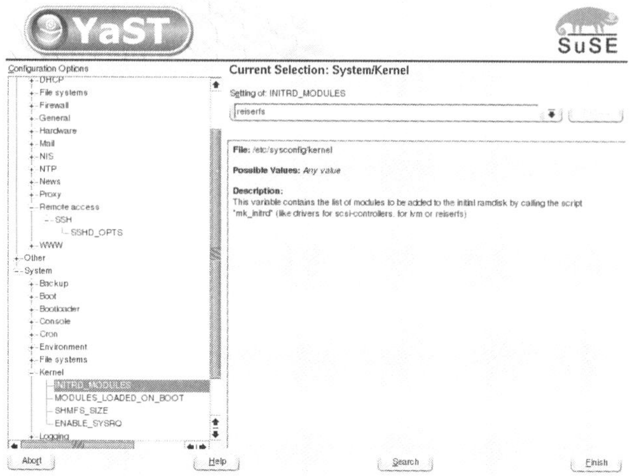

Figure 12.1: *YaST: Configuring with the Sysconfig Editor*

and the current setting of this variable. Below, a third window will display a short description of the variable's purpose, possible values, the default value, and the actual configuration file from which this variable originates. Make your choice, change the values as appropriate, and accomplish the configuration by leaving this dialog with 'Finish'.

System Configuration: Scripts and Variables

This section describes a selection of system parameters, including their default settings. If you do not use YaST to change the configuration files in `/etc/sysconfig`, make sure you set empty parameters as two quotation marks (e. g., ⟨*KEYTABLE=""*⟩) and surround parameters that contain a blank with quotation marks. Parameters consisting of only one word do not need to be quoted. The following section features some of the most important configuration files. For configuration files and variables not mentioned here, refer to the documentation given in the `/etc/sysconfig` files.

Settings for the Files in /etc/sysconfig

`apache` Configuration of the HTTP daemon Apache. This overview only covers the most important variables that need to be set by default or are vital for a basic understanding of Apache. Refer to the Apache documentation, which you can install as package apache-doc for further information or browse http://httpd.apache.org/docs/ and http://modules.apache.org.

HTTPD_PERFORMANCE="slim"
Specify the performance class of your Apache. Choose from slim, mid, thick, and enterprise for the number of clients to serve. SuSEconfig will set MinSpareServers, MaxSpareServers, StartServers, and MaxClients accordingly (see /sbin/conf.d/SuSEconfig.apache)

HTTPD_START_TIMEOUT="2"
Time-out during server start-up (in seconds). After this time, the start script decides whether the httpd process has started without an error. Increase this value if you use mod_ssl and your certificate is passphrase protected.

HTTPD_SEC_ACCESS_SERVERINFO="no"
Enable or disable the status module to provide server status and server info.

HTTPD_SEC_SAY_FULLNAME="yes"
Which information should be provided at the bottom of server-generated documents (e.g., error messages)? yes provides version number and server name. email adds a mailto: instruction to the version number and server name. This option correlates with the ServerSignature directive of Apache. If no information should be revealed, set the parameter to no.

HTTPD_SEC_SERVERADMIN=""
Set the e-mail address of the server administrator (ServerAdmin directive) This address is added to the server's responses if ⟨*HTTPD_SEC_SAY_FULLNAME*⟩ is set to email. If empty, it defaults to webmaster@$HOSTNAME. HOSTNAME is set in /etc/HOSTNAME. Note that the ServerAdmin directives inside the VirtualHost statements are not changed, including the one for the SSL virtual host.

HTTPD_SEC_PUBLIC_HTML="yes"
Allow access to UserDirs (like /home/*/public_html)? If yes, this is defined in /etc/httpd/suse_public_html.conf.

HTTPD_CONF_INCLUDE_FILES=""
Here, name files, separated by spaces, that should be included by httpd.conf. This allows you to add, for example, VirtualHost statements without touching /etc/httpd/httpd.conf itself, which means that SuSEconfig will continue doing its job (since it would not

touch `httpd.conf` when it detects changes made by the admin via the md5sum mechanism).

HTTPD_AWSTATS_COMBINED_LOG="yes"
Should Apache write an extra combined log file? This is necessary for the awstats program (`yes` or `no`).

HTTPD_DDT="yes"
Should the DDT admin CGI be enabled? It is used to create and manage accounts on a local DDT (Dynamic DNS Tools) server.

MAILMAN_APACHE="yes"
Enable the web front-end for Mailman?

HTTPD_SEC_MOD_MIDGARD="yes"
Enable the `midgard` module. Midgard is an Open Source content management system.

HTTPD_SEC_MOD_PERL="yes"
Enable the Perl module.

HTTPD_SEC_MOD_PHP="yes"
Enable the PHP module.

HTTPD_SEC_MOD_PYTHON="yes"
Enable the Python module.

HTTPD_SEC_NAGIOS="yes"
Allow access to Nagios's web interface (configured in `/etc/httpd/nagios.conf`).

HTTPD_SEC_MOD_SSL="no"
Enable the SSL module. Before you can enable this module, you need a server certificate. A test certificate can be created by entering

```
cd /usr/share/doc/packages/mod_ssl
./certificate.sh
```

as `root`. Also, you need to set the ServerName inside the `<VirtualHost _default_:443>` block to the fully qualified domain name (see `$HOSTNAME` in `/etc/HOSTNAME`). If your server certificate is protected by a passphrase, increase the value of ⟨*HTTPD_START_TIMEOUT*⟩.

ZOPE_PCGI="no"
If unset, Zope runs as a stand-alone server. Remember Apache must be installed to use PCGI.

ZOPE_KEEP_HOMES="yes"
If Zope is handled by apache-pcgi and user home directories should be handled by Apache, set the variable to `yes`.

apache2 Configuring Apache version 2.0.

ENABLE_SUSECONFIG_APACHE_MPM="yes"
Because Apache uses different multiprocessing modules (MPMs) that can be installed in parallel, SuSEconfig can maintain symbolic links to the actual httpd binary and modules.
Switching this variable to no implies ENABLE_SUSECONFIG_APACHE=no. Some values out of this configuration file will still be used by the start script.

ENABLE_SUSECONFIG_APACHE="yes"
Should SuSEconfig.apache change the configuration?

APACHE_MPM=""
MPMs (multiprocessing modules) to use.

HTTPD_START_TIMEOUT="2"
Time-out during server start-up (in seconds). After this time, the start script decides whether the httpd process has started without an error. Increase this value if you use mod_ssl and your certificate is passphrase protected.

APACHE_SERVERSIGNATURE="on"
Which information should be provided at the bottom of server-generated documents (e.g., error messages)? yes provides version number and server name. email adds a mailto: instruction to the version number and server name. This option correlates with the ServerSignature directive of Apache. If no information should be revealed, set the parameter to no.

APACHE_SERVERADMIN=""
Set the e-mail address of the server administrator (ServerAdmin directive) This address is added to the server's responses if ⟨*HTTPD_SEC_SAY_FULLNAME*⟩ is set to email. If empty, it defaults to webmaster@$HOSTNAME. HOSTNAME is set in /etc/HOSTNAME. Note that the ServerAdmin directives inside the VirtualHost statements are not changed, including the one for the SSL virtual host.

APACHE_SERVERTOKENS="OS"
This variable determines the type and amount of information revealed about the server in the server response header field (installed modules, versions, etc.). For further details refer to: http://httpd.apache.org/docs-2.0/mod/core.html#servertokens

APACHE_EXTENDED_STATUS="off"
If mod_status is used, extended information about the server (e.g., CPU usage) is included in the status report.

APACHE_CONF_INCLUDE_FILES=""
Here, name files, separated by spaces, that should be included by `httpd.conf`. This allows you to add, for example, `VirtualHost` statements without touching `/etc/httpd/httpd.conf` itself, which means that SuSEconfig will continue doing its job (since it would not touch `httpd.conf` when it detects changes made by the admin via the md5sum mechanism).

APACHE_CONF_INCLUDE_DIRS=""
Name the directories, separated by spaces, that should be included by `httpd.conf`. Apache will recursively include all the files contained in these directories.

LOADMODULES="access actions alias auth auth_dbm autoindex cgi dir env expires include log_config mime negotiation setenvif status suexec userdir"
Specify the modules subsequently loaded by SuSEconfig without the need of touching `httpd.conf`.

APACHE_SERVER_FLAGS=""
Determine which server flags are handed over to `httpd` at start time. You may also specify some other command line flags here.

APACHE_HTTPD_CONF=""
Which `httpd.conf` should be used. If not specified otherwise here, `/etc/apache2/httpd.conf` is used.

HTTPD_AWSTATS_COMBINED_LOG="yes"
Should Apache write an extra combined log file? This is necessary for the awstats program (`yes` or `no`).

autoinstall AutoYast2 the autoinstaller of YaST.

REPOSITORY="/var/lib/autoinstall/repository"
Repository with all profiles holding the configuration details of the hosts to install.

CLASS_DIR="/var/lib/autoinstall/classes"
Use classes to simplify the creation of profiles for complex installation scenarios. They will be stored in `/var/lib/autoinstall/classes`.

PACKAGE_REPOSITORY=""
Location in which to store the installation data and packages for SuSE Linux.

backup Backup of the RPM database

RPMDB_BACKUP_DIR="/var/adm/backup/rpmdb"
Where should cron.daily backups of the RPM database be stored? If you do not want backups, set the variable to `""` .

MAX_RPMDB_BACKUPS="5"
Number of backups of the RPM database.

RCCONFIG_BACKUP_DIR="/var/adm/backup/rpmdb"
If you want cron.daily to backup `/etc/rc.config` and the files in `/etc/sysconfig`, specify a directory where the backups will be stored. The backups will be made every time cron.daily is called and the the content of those files has changed. Setting the variable to `""` disables this feature.

MAX_RCCONFIG_BACKUPS="5"
Here, set the maximum number of backup files for the `/etc/rc.config` and `/etc/sysconfig` files.

boot Important setting for the boot process.

PROMPT_FOR_CONFIRM="no"
Use this variable for interactive debugging of the start-up process. If set to `yes`, the system will ask whether to confirm every step of the boot process.

CONFIRM_PROMPT_TIMEOUT="5"
Set how long (in seconds) the system should wait for a user confirm during the boot process before the default answer is assumed.

FLOW_CONTROL="no"
If set to `yes`, the boot process can be stopped by pressing Ctrl + S and continued by pressing Ctrl + Q (xon/xoff flow control).

FSCK_MAX_INST="10"
This variable limits the maximum number of file system checkers that can be run in parallel. A large number of file system checkers running in parallel can cause CPU overloads in configurations with a large number of disk being used.

bootsplash Configuring the boot splash screen.

THEME=""
Choose the boot splash theme from the those residing under `/usr/share/splash/themes/`.

SPLASH="yes"
Enable or disable the splash screen on the first console at boot time.

clock time settings

HWCLOCK=""
If your hardware clock is set to GMT (*Greenwich Mean Time*), set this to `-u`. Otherwise, set it to `--localtime`. This setting is important for the automatic change from and to daylight savings time.

TIMEZONE=""
The time zone is also important for the change from and to daylight savings time. This sets `/usr/lib/zoneinfo/localtime`.

console Settings for the console.

FB_MODULES=""
You may want to load a framebuffer display driver into your kernel to change graphics modes and other things with fbset in console mode. Most people will not enter anything here, as it will not work with vesafb already active. It is advantageous to have framebuffer support compiled into your kernel. Some XFree86 drivers (especially in XFree86-4.x) do not work well if you enable framebuffer text mode.

FBSET_PARAMS=""
If your kernel has framebuffer support or loads it as a module, you might want to change the resolution or other parameters. These can be set with ⟨*FBSET_PARAMS*⟩. To get a list of possible parameters and their meanings, refer to the man page for `fbset` (`man fbset`) or enter `fbset -h` in the console.

Caution

Setting framebuffer parameters
Framebuffer modes are extremely hardware-dependent. A wrong decision here might damage your monitor. Consider the following things before setting framebuffer modes:

vesafb does not (currently) support changing the display mode.

Do not set modes your monitor cannot handle. Watch out for the maximum horizontal frequency. Old monitors might even be damaged if you exceed their capabilities.

Caution

CONSOLE_FONT=""
Font for the console loaded at boot. Additional settings are: ⟨*CONSOLE_SCREENMAP*⟩, ⟨*CONSOLE_UNICODEMAP*⟩, and ⟨*CONSOLE_MAGIC*⟩.

CONSOLE_UNICODEMAP=""
Some fonts come without a unicode map. You can then specify the unicode mapping of your font explicitly. Find these maps under `/usr/share/kbd/unimaps/`. Normally, this variable is not needed.

CONSOLE_SCREENMAP=""
Does your console font need to be translated to unicode? Choose a screenmap from `/usr/share/kbd/consoletrans/`.

CONSOLE_MAGIC=""
For some fonts, the console has to be initialized with ⟨*CONSOLE_MAGIC*⟩. This option is normally not needed.

SVGATEXTMODE="80x25"
⟨*SVGATEXTMODE*⟩ comes from the package `svgatext`, which allows higher text resolutions (up to 160x60) on SVGA cards. The variable contains a valid mode from `/etc/TextConfig`. Configure this file to suit the needs of your graphics card. The procedure is explained in `/usr/share/doc/packages/svgatext`. The default is `80x25`. SVGATextMode resolutions are used in runlevels 1, 2, 3, and 5.

cron Daily administration work on the system. The cron daemon automatically starts certain programs at specified times. It is recommended to activate it on computers that run all the time. An alternative or supplement is the AT daemon.

Note

A number of system settings require regular execution of certain programs. Therefore, the cron daemon should be active on every system.

Note

MAX_DAYS_IN_TMP="0"
cron.daily can check for old files in `tmp` directories. It will delete all files not accessed for more than the days specified here. Leave it empty or set it to `0` to disable this feature. Enable this feature if your system is used by several users to avoid an overflow of your `/tmp` directory.

TMP_DIRS_TO_CLEAR="/tmp /var/tmp"
Specify the directories from which old files should be deleted.

OWNER_TO_KEEP_IN_TMP="root"
Specify whose files should not be deleted even after the time set.

CLEAR_TMP_DIRS_AT_BOOTUP="no"
Set this to `yes` to entirely remove (`rm -rf`) all files and subdirectories from the temporary directories defined in ⟨*TMP_DIRS_TO_CLEAR*⟩ on boot. This feature ignores ⟨*OWNER_TO_KEEP_IN_TMP*⟩ — all files will be removed without exception.

DELETE_OLD_CORE="no"
Should old core files be deleted? If set to `no`, cron.daily will tell you if it finds old core files. This feature requires ⟨*RUN_UPDATEDB*⟩ be set to `yes` and package `findutils-locate` needs to be installed.

MAX_DAYS_FOR_CORE="7"
Maximum age of core files in days.

REINIT_MANDB="yes"
Should the manual page database (mandb and whatis) be recreated by cron.daily?

DELETE_OLD_CATMAN="yes"
Should old preformatted man pages (in `/var/catman`) be deleted?

CATMAN_ATIME="7"
How long (in days) should old preformatted man pages be kept before deleting them?

dhcpd Configure the DHCP server.

DHCPD_INTERFACE="eth0"
Enter a space-separated list of interfaces on which the DCHP server should be listening.

DHCPD_RUN_CHROOTED="yes"
Should dhcpd run in a "chroot jail"? Refer to dhcpd's README.SuSE (`/usr/share/doc/packages/dhcp/README.SuSE`) for further details.

DHCPD_CONF_INCLUDE_FILES=""
`dhcpd.conf` can contain `include` statements. If you enter the names of any include files here, *all* conf files will be copied to `\$chroot/etc/` when dhcpd is started in the chroot jail. `/etc/dhcpd.conf` is always copied.

DHCPD_RUN_AS="nobody"
Leave empty or enter `root` to let dhcpd run as `root`. Enter `nobody` to run dhcpd as user `nobody` and group `nogroup`.

DHCPD_OTHER_ARGS=""
Other arguments with which dhcpd should be started. See `man dhcpd` for details.

dhcrelay DHCP Relay Agent. A DHCP relay agent allows you to relay DHCP (and Bootp) requests from one subnet without a DHCP server to one with a DHCP server.

DHCRELAY_INTERFACES=""
Interfaces on which the DHCP relay agent should listen (separated by spaces).

DHCRELAY_SERVERS=""
Specify a space-separated list of DHCP servers to be used by the DHCP relay agent.

displaymanager Display manager configuration.

DISPLAYMANAGER=""
Set the display manager for login. Possible values: `console`, `xdm` (traditional display manager of X Window System), `kdm` (display manager of KDE), `gdm` (display manager of GNOME), or `wdm` ("WINGs display manager").

DISPLAYMANAGER_REMOTE_ACCESS="no"
Allow remote access to your display manager. Default is `no`.

DISPLAYMANAGER_ROOT_LOGIN_REMOTE="no"
Allow remote access to your display manager for user `root`.

DISPLAYMANAGER_STARTS_XSERVER="yes"
Display manager starts a local X server. Set to `no` for remote access only.

KDM_SHUTDOWN="auto"
⟨*KDM_SHUTDOWN*⟩ determines who will be able to shutdown the system in kdm. Valid values are `root`, `all`, `none`, `local`, and `auto`.

KDM_USERS=""
Enter a space-separated list of users for whom icons should be displayed. If empty, the system defaults will be taken.

KDM_BACKGROUND=""
Specify a special background for KDM.

KDM_GREETSTRING=""
To be greeted by the system in a special way, enter the greeting words here.

gconf2 Configuring the gconf daemon.

GCONF2_CONF_SOURCE="distribution"
Choose the default configuration source for the gconf daemon. Determine from where new users get their GNOME desktop configuration. If set to `source`, the default settings from the GNOME2 sources will be used. As an alternative, choose `distribution` for the default settings of the distributions. You may specify other sources here as well.

hardware Hardware settings.

DEVICES_FORCE_IDE_DMA_ON=""
Switch on DMA for the listed IDE devices.

DEVICES_FORCE_IDE_DMA_OFF=""
Switch off DMA for the listed IDE devices.

hotplug Configuring the hotplug service.

HOTPLUG_DEBUG="default"
This variable controls the amount of output of the hotplug service. With `default`, "", or `no`, it prints only few messages and errors to `syslog`. Set it to `off` and it will be absolutely quiet. With `verbose` (or `yes`), it prints some extra debug output. With `max`, it will fill `syslog` with every single detail.

HOTPLUG_START_USB="yes"
Enable or disable USB hotplug event handling.

> **Note**
>
> **Disabling USB hotplug**
> Disabling USB hotplug while having USB input devices loaded as modules will render your keyboard unusable.
>
> **Note**

HOTPLUG_USB_USE_USBMODULES="no"
Enable or disable the use of `/sbin/usbmodules`. The default is not to use this function.

HOTPLUG_USB_HOSTCONTROLLER_LIST="usb-uhci uhci usb-ohci ehci-hcd"
The host controller drivers will be probed in this order.

HOTPLUG_USB_STATIC_MODULES="evdev joydev"
Specify the modules to load when usb hotplug starts. Mainly, these are modules for which no hotplug events are created, such as input devices. If you are using the old XFree86 3.x, add `mousedev` and `input`.

HOTPLUG_USB_MODULES_TO_UNLOAD="scanner"
These modules should be unloaded on an USB "remove" event. For some devices, it is useful to reinitialize the hardware.

HOTPLUG_USB_NET_MODULES="pegasus usbnet catc kaweth CDCEther"
If one of these modules is loaded or unloaded, it is treated like a network device and the system creates a hardware description for the following "net event".

HOTPLUG_USB_DELAY="3"
The USB stack will load some drivers in the background. Other runlevel scripts may be run before a needed driver is loaded.

HOTPLUG_START_NET="yes"
Enable or disable NET hotplug event handling.

HOTPLUG_NET_DEFAULT_HARDWARE=""
One day in the future, there will be ways to obtain information on which type of hardware is behind a given network interface. Currently, there is no easy way to get this information. At the moment, we use the following work-around: hardware descriptions are written at the USB or PCI hotplug events then read by the NET event. If you plug several devices at a time, this might cause race conditions. If the work-around fails, the string in ⟨*HOTPLUG_NET_DEFAULT_HARDWARE*⟩ is used when if{up,down} is called. Set it to what you use as hotplug NIC: `pcmcia`, `usb`, or `firewire`.

HOTPLUG_NET_TIMEOUT="8"
Specify how long to wait for a hardware description from a USB or PCI event (in seconds). If this value equals `0`, the hotplug service will not wait for a hardware description and always use the value of ⟨*HOTPLUG_NET_DEFAULT_HARDWARE*⟩. The default value here is `8`, because some PCMCIA NICs need a long time for some negotiation jobs.

HOTPLUG_START_PCI="yes"
Enable or disable PCI hotplug event handling.

HOTPLUG_PCI_MODULES_NOT_TO_UNLOAD=""
These modules should not be unloaded on a PCI "remove" event, because they cause too much trouble.

HOTPLUG_START_IEEE1394="yes"
Enable or disable IEEE1394 (Firewire) hotplug event handling.

HOTPLUG_IEEE1394_NET_MODULES="eth1394"
If one of these modules is loaded or unloaded, the device is assumed to be a network device and a hardware description for the following net event is created.

HOTPLUG_IEEE1394_MODULES_NOT_TO_UNLOAD=""
These modules should not be unloaded on an IEEE1394 "remove" event.

irda IrDA is the infrared interface used, for example, by notebooks. To activate it permanently, run `insserv /etc/init.d/irda`.

IRDA_PORT="/dev/ttyS1"
Currently, the UART (SIR) mode is supported in the normal configuration. The variable ⟨*IRDA_PORT*⟩ sets the used serial port. Check your BIOS setup to find out which is correct. If you have a supported FIR chipset, specify the name of the corresponding kernel module in ⟨*IRDA_PORT*⟩, for example, `IRDA_PORT="toshoboe"`. FIR

must be enabled in the BIOS setup first. Sometimes, you additionally have to disable the serial port, which would be used in SIR mode via `setserial /dev/ttyS<x> uart none`

`isdn/` Here, find all the scripts needed for ISDN.

`ispell` Configuring the ispell spell checker.

ENGLISH_DICTIONARY="system american british"
SuSEconfig.ispell maintains a symbolic link from the `english` (default) dictionary to either `american` or `british`. If only one is installed, the link will point to this one. If both are installed, the space-separated value of ⟨*ENGLISH_DICTIONARY*⟩ takes effect. The magic word `system` expands to the system's default language (as defined in `/etc/sysconfig/language`'s ⟨*RC_LANG*⟩), if it is one of the English languages, and expands to the empty string otherwise. The symlink will point to the first installed dictionary in the list.

`java` Configuring Java.

CREATE_JAVALINK="yes"
SuSEconfig can automatically create the links `/usr/lib/java` and `/usr/lib/jre` that point to a suitable JDK or JRE respectively if you set ⟨*CREATE_JAVALINK*⟩ to `yes`. If you are not satisfied with the choice it makes, set ⟨*CREATE_JAVALINK*⟩ to `no` and set the link manually.

JAVA_JRE_THREADS_TYPE="green"
Configuration for the package `java-jre`. Set this to `native` if you want *real* multithreading, for example, in combination with SMP systems.

JAVA_THREADS_TYPE="green"
Configuration for the package `java`. Set this to `native` if you want *real* multithreading, for example, in combination with SMP systems.

`joystick` Joystick configuration

GAMEPORT_MODULE_0=""
Gameport module names, for example, `ns558` for legacy gameport support.

JOYSTICK_MODULE_0=""
Joystick module names, usually `analog`.

JOYSTICK_MODULE_OPTION_0=""
Joystick module options, such as `js=gameport` for analog.

JOYSTICK_CONTROL_0=""
Control name of sound driver to activate (via alsactl).

JOYSTICK_CONTROL_PORT_0=""
Port to use (via alsactl). Some sound cards, like ens1371, need the port address (typically 0x200).

kernel Kernel.

INITRD_MODULES=""
This variable contains the list of modules to add to the initial ramdisk with the script `mk_initrd` (like drivers for SCSI controllers, LVM, or reiserfs).

MODULES_LOADED_ON_BOOT=""
This variable contains the list of modules to load once the main file system is active.

SHMFS_SIZE=""
Size parameter for mounting the shmfs file system. The kernel defaults to half the available RAM size, but this might not be enough for some special setups.

keyboard Keyboard layout.

KEYTABLE="de-latin1-nodeadkeys"
Defines the key layout. If you use a US keyboard, this variable can remain empty.

KBD_RATE="24.0"
Rate of automatic keyboard repetition. Set this to a value between 2 and 30 times per second. The variable for the delay also needs to be set: ⟨*KBD_DELAY*⟩.

KBD_DELAY="500"
Set the delay after which the automatic key repetition starts. Possible values: `250`, `500`, `750`, and `1000` in milliseconds. Also set the variable ⟨*KBD_RATE*⟩.

KBD_NUMLOCK="bios"
Set this to `no` and NumLock will not be enabled at boot. Other options are `yes`, `""` , or `bios` for BIOS setting.

KBD_SCRLOCK="no"
Enable or disable ScrollLock.

KBD_CAPSLOCK="no"
Do not enable CapsLock at boot time.

KBD_DISABLE_CAPS_LOCK="no"
Disable CapsLock and make it a normal Shift key?

KBD_TTY="tty1 tty2 tty3 tty4 tty5 tty6 tty7 tty8 tty9 tty10 tty12 tty13 tty14 tty15 tty16 tty17 tty18 tty19 tty20"
Limit (NumLock), (CapsLock), and (ScrollLock) to certain TTYs. "" means all.

COMPOSETABLE="clear winkeys shiftctrl latin1.add"
Compose tables to load. See `/usr/share/doc/packages/kbd/README.SuSE` for further details on key tables.

language Settings for language and locale.

RC_LANG="en_US"
Sets variable `LANG` for locale. This is the default for local users, as long as no ⟨*RC_LC_**⟩ variables are used. The respective `sysconfig` variables are ⟨*RC_LC_ALL*⟩ (overwrites `LC_*` and `LANG`), ⟨*RC_LC_MESSAGES*⟩, ⟨*RC_LC_CTYPE*⟩, ⟨*RC_LC_MONETARY*⟩, ⟨*RC_LC_NUMERIC*⟩, ⟨*RC_LC_TIME*⟩, and ⟨*RC_LC_COLLATE*⟩. See *Local Adjustments — I18N/L10N* on page 290.

ROOT_USES_LANG="ctype"
Should locale settings be used for `root`? `ctype` means that root uses just ⟨*LC_CTYPE*⟩.

locate The locate database allows files on the system to be found quickly. It is usually updated shortly after booting the system in case your machine does not run nonstop (see *cron Package* on page 267).

RUN_UPDATEDB="no"
Should the database for locate (`locate`) get updated once a day? More detailed configuration of updatedb is possible with the following variables.

RUN_UPDATEDB_AS="nobody"
Specify the user executing updatedb. Default, for security reasons, is `nobody`.

UPDATEDB_NETPATHS=""
Normally, uptdatedb only scans local hard disks, but can include net paths in the database as well. If you specify directories here, they will be scanned.

UPDATEDB_PRUNEPATHS="/mnt /media/cdrom /tmp /usr/tmp /var/tmp /var/spool /proc /media"
Specify the directories to skip for the daily updatedb runs.

UPDATEDB_NETUSER=""
User, such as `nobody`, to search net paths.

UPDATEDB_PRUNEFS=""
Specify the type of file systems to exclude from the updatedb runs.

mail Settings for e-mail.

FROM_HEADER=""
`From:` line defined for the whole system. If "", the FQDN is used. See *Domain Name System* on page 340.

MAIL_CREATE_CONFIG="yes"
Set this to `no` if SuSEconfig should not generate the configuration files (e.g., you want to generate `/etc/sendmail.cf` yourself). If you want to generate a sendmail configuration `/etc/sendmail.cf` from parameters given in `/etc/sysconfig/sendmail`, use `yes`.

SMTPD_LISTEN_REMOTE="no"
Set this to `yes` if external e-mails should be accepted. This is necessary for any mail server. If set to `no` or empty, only mails from the local host are accepted.

mouse Mouse settings.

MOUSEDEVICE=""
Specify the mouse device which is used on the console by gpm. The default value is generated by YaST.

MOUSETYPE=""
This variable determines the mouse type which defines the mouse protocol used by gpm for the mouse device specified in ⟨*MOUSEDEVICE*⟩. The default value is generated by YaST.

GPM_PARAM=""
Define your own option for gpm here. If left empty, gpm will be started with the option `-m $MOUSEDEVICE -t $MOUSETYPE`.

network Directory for network configuration.

network/config Some general settings for network configuration.

DEFAULT_BROADCAST="+"
⟨*DEFAULT_BROADCAST*⟩ is read when a ⟨*BROADCAST*⟩ is not set elsewhere. Choose from the following values: `""` for no broadcast address, - for ⟨*IPADDR*⟩ without host bits, or + for ⟨*IPADDR*⟩ with all host bits set.

GLOBAL_POST_UP_EXEC="yes"
Should certain scripts be executed after an interface has been brought up? Set this variable to `yes` and save those scripts under `/etc/sysconfig/network/if-up.d`.

GLOBAL_PRE_DOWN_EXEC="yes"
Should certain scripts be executed before an interface is brought down? Set this variable to `yes` and store those scripts under `/etc/sysconfig/network/if-down.d`.

CHECK_FOR_MASTER="yes"
To require an interface (master) to be up before an alias (labeled address) can be set up, set ⟨*CHECK_FOR_MASTER*⟩ to `yes`. Technically, this is not necessary, because labeled and unlabeled addresses are equivalent. This setting serves just for the convenience of ifconfig users.

CHECK_DUPLICATE_IP="yes"
If ifup should check if an IP address is already in use, set this to `yes`. Make sure packet sockets (⟨*CONFIG_PACKET*⟩) are supported in the kernel, since this feature uses arping, which depends on that. Also be aware that this takes one second per interface. Consider that when setting up a lot of interfaces.

DEBUG="no"
Switch on and off debug messages for all network configuration scripts. If set to `no`, most scripts still can enable it locally with `-o debug`.

USE_SYSLOG="yes"
Should error messages from network configuration scripts go to `syslog`? If no, `stderr` is used.

MODIFY_RESOLV_CONF_DYNAMICALLY="yes"
There are some services (`ppp`, `ippp`, `dhcp-client`, `pcmcia`, and `hotplug`) that have to change `/etc/resolv.conf` dynamically at certain times. To prevent these services from changing `/etc/resolv.conf` at all, set this variable to `no`. If unsure, leave it at the default, which is `yes`.

MODIFY_NAMED_CONF_DYNAMICALLY="no"
Like ⟨*MODIFY_RESOLV_CONF_DYNAMICALLY*⟩, except it modifies `/etc/named.conf`. If unsure, leave it at the default, which is `no`.

network/dhcp Setting up DHCP (Dynamic Host Configuration Protocol).

Note

To configure one or more interfaces for DHCP configuration, change the ⟨*BOOTPROTO*⟩ variable in `/etc/sysconfig/network/ifcfg-<interface>` to `dhcp` (and possibly set ⟨*STARTMODE*⟩ to `onboot`).

Note

Most of these options are used only by dhcpcd, not by the ISC dhclient, which uses a configuration file. Most of the options can be overridden by setting them in the ifcfg-* files, too.

DHCLIENT_BIN=""
Which DHCP client should be used? If empty, dhcpcd is tried then dhclient. Other possible values are dhcpcd for the DHCP client daemon or dhclient for the ISC dhclient.

DHCLIENT_DEBUG="no"
Start in debug mode? Debug info will be logged to /var/log/messages for dhcpcd or to /var/log/dhclient-script for ISC dhclient.

DHCLIENT_SET_HOSTNAME="no"
Should the DHCP client set the host name? If yes, take care that the host name is not changed during a running X session or the ⟨*DISPLAY*⟩ variable cannot be read anymore. As a consequence, no new windows could be opened.

DHCLIENT_MODIFY_RESOLV_CONF="yes"
Should the DHCP client modify /etc/resolv.conf at all? If not, set this to no. The default is yes. resolv.conf will also stay untouched when ⟨*MODIFY_RESOLV_CONF_DYNAMICALLY*⟩ in /etc/sysconfig/network/config is set to no.

DHCLIENT_SET_DEFAULT_ROUTE="yes"
Should the DHCP client set a default route (default gateway)? When multiple copies of dhcpcd run, it would make sense that only one of them does it.

DHCLIENT_MODIFY_NTP_CONF="no"
Should the DHCP client modify the NTP configuration? If set to yes, /etc/ntp.conf is rewritten (and restored upon exit). If this is unwanted, set this variable to no. The default is no.

DHCLIENT_MODIFY_NIS_CONF="no"
Should the DHCP client modify the NIS configuration? If set to yes, /etc/yp.conf is rewritten (and restored upon exit). If this is unwanted, set this variable to no. The default is no.

DHCLIENT_SET_DOMAINNAME="yes"
Should the DHCP client set the NIS domain name? (Only valid if the server supplies the NIS domain option).

DHCLIENT_KEEP_SEARCHLIST="no"
When writing a new /etc/resolv.conf, should the DHCP client take an existing search list and add it to the one derived from the DHCP server?

DHCLIENT_LEASE_TIME=""
Specifies (in seconds) the lease time suggested to the server. The default is infinite. For a mobile computer, you probably want to set this to a lower value.

DHCLIENT_TIMEOUT="999999"
This setting is only valid for dhcpcd. Specify a time-out in seconds after which dhcpcd terminates if it does not get a reply from the DHCP server.

DHCLIENT_REBOOT_TIMEOUT=""
This setting is only valid for dhcpcd. This time-out controls how long dhcpcd tries to reacquire a previous lease (init-reboot state), before it starts getting a new one.

DHCLIENT_HOSTNAME_OPTION="AUTO"
Specify a string used for the host name option field when dhcpcd sends DHCP messages. By default, the current host name is sent (`AUTO`), if one is defined in `/etc/HOSTNAME`. Use this variable to override this with another host name or leave empty not to send a host name.

DHCLIENT_CLIENT_ID=""
Specifies a client identifier string. By default, the hardware address of the network interface is sent as client identifier string, if none is specified here.

DHCLIENT_VENDOR_CLASS_ID=""
Specifies the vendor class identifier string. `dhcpcd` uses the default vendor class identifier string (system name, system release, and machine type) if it is not specified.

DHCLIENT_RELEASE_BEFORE_QUIT="no"
Send a ⟨*DHCPRELEASE*⟩ to the server (sign off the address)? This may lead to getting a different address and host name next time an address is requested. However, some servers require it.

DHCLIENT_SLEEP="0"
Some interfaces need time to initialize. Add the latency time in seconds so these can be handled properly. This setting should be made on a per interface basis, rather than here.

network/ifcfg-eth0 Configure the first network card. These settings can be done with YaST.

STARTMODE=""
⟨*STARTMODE*⟩ tells ifup when a interface should be set up. Possible values are `onboot` for an automatic start at boot time, `manual` when

ifup is called manually, and hotplug when ifup is called by hotplug or pcmcia.

BOOTPROTO=""
With ⟨*BOOTPROTO*⟩, choose between a static configuration with fixed IP addresses or dhcp.

IPADDR=""
Set the IP address if static configuration is desired.

NETMASK=""
Specify the netmask of your net or subnet.

BROADCAST=""
Enter the broadcast address of your network.

PREFIXLEN=""
Alternatively, specify the prefix length.

NETWORK=""
Specify the address of your network.

network/ifcfg-lo The loopback device.

network/wireless Configuring wireless LANs. Use the YaST network modules.

news Settings for access to NNTP servers.

ORGANIZATION=""
The text entered here will appear in every news posting sent from this machine.

NNTPSERVER="news"
Address of the news server. If you receive news via UUCP and they are locally stored, set this variable to localhost.

onlineupdate Settings for YaST Online Update.

YAST2_LOADFTPSERVER="yes"
When starting YOU (YaST Online Update), should the default FTP server list be updated via a call from wget to www.suse.de? This list is stored under /etc/suseservers. Set the variable to no if you do not want to reload the FTP server list.

pcmcia PCMCIA System and PC Cards.

PCMCIA_SYSTEM="kernel"
Set the variable to external or kernel. If only one of these systems is installed, this variable will be ignored.

PCMCIA_PCIC=""
Specify socket driver for the selected pcmcia system. Possible values are i82365 or tcic for external pcmcia system or yenta_socket, i82365, or tcic for kernel pcmcia. If it is left empty, the start script will try to determine the correct driver or use a reasonable default.

PCMCIA_PCIC_OPTS=""
Socket driver timing parameters. These parameters are described in man page i82365 (or man tcic).

PCMCIA_CORE_OPTS=""
pcmcia_core options as described in man pcmcia_core. For more information, look for "CORE_OPTS" in the PCMCIA-HOWTO under /usr/doc/packages/pcmcia.

postfix Configuring postfix. Use the YaST mail module for this.

powermanagement apmd.

APMD_DEBUG="no"
Make apmd and the apmd_proxy-script more verbose. Set this variable to yes to see when and how apmd_proxy is called. To see everything printed to stdout and stderr within apmd_proxy, set it to error. If you are interested in every single command within apmd_proxy, set it to all. Anything but no makes apmd itself verbose. Default value is no.

ACPI_MODULES_NOT_TO_LOAD=""
The acpid will all modules required for acpi. If some of those modules are known to cause trouble, add them to this variable and they will be skipped.

ACPI_BUTTON_POWER="shutdown"
What action should be executed if the power button is pressed?

ACPI_BUTTON_LID="ignore"
What action should be executed if the lid is closed?

APMD_WARN_LEVEL="10"
If you like to be warned when battery capacity goes below a certain level, you can set this level here in percent of maximum battery capacity. Set it to 0 to switch this and the following three options off. Default value is 10.

APMD_WARN_ALL="no"
For apmd warnings to be sent to all terminals, set this to yes. Otherwise the warnings will be logged in your syslog file. Default is no.

APMD_WARN_STEP="0"
This warning can be repeated every time the capacity has decreased by ⟨*WARN_STEP*⟩% of the maximum battery capacity. `0` means off. Default is `0`.

APMD_CHECK_TIME="0"
By default apmd checks the battery status every time it receives an event from the BIOS. For it to be checked more often, set it to a value greater than 0 seconds. Note that this will wake up your disk at every check. Default value is `0`.

APMD_ADJUST_DISK_PERF="no"
For saving power, you should let your hard disk spin down after an idle time. That is not needed when on wall power. Set ⟨*ADJUST_DISK_PERF*⟩ to `yes` if apmd should check this. Note that this does not help much if any process (like an text editor) writes frequently to your disk. Default value is `no`.

APMD_BATTERY_DISK_TIMEOUT="12"
Specify the time-out for your disk to be spun down when on battery. As this time-out is not just a matter of minutes or seconds, refer to the man page for `hdparm` (`man hdparm`). This option will only be valid if ⟨*ADJUST_DISK_PERF*⟩ has been set to `yes`. The default setting here is `12`, which equals a time-out of one minute.

APMD_AC_DISK_TIMEOUT="0"
See ⟨*BATTERY_DISK_TIMEOUT*⟩, only that this setting concerns AC power. Default value is `0` for no spindown.

APMD_BATTERY_LOW_SHUTDOWN="0"
When the battery capacity becomes very low, some laptop BIOSes send a "battery low" message. You can then let your machine shut down a few minutes later. Set the number of minutes here. The minumum is 1 minute. A value of `0` switches off this behavior. The default value is `0`.

APMD_SET_CLOCK_ON_RESUME="no"
If you have problems with wrong time settings after a standby or suspend, set ⟨*SET_CLOCK_ON_RESUME*⟩ to `yes`. The kernel time will be set according to the value stored in the GMT variable. Default is `no`.

APMD_SUSPEND_ON_AC="yes"
Set ⟨*SUSPEND_ON_AC*⟩ to `no` to avoid suspend and standby events when your machine is connected to AC power. By default, suspends can occur on either battery or AC power. A suspend requested by the user is executed anyway.

APMD_PCMCIA_SUSPEND_ON_SUSPEND="no"
If PCMCIA is compiled with APM support, cards are normally sus-

pended before your system suspends. If you do not have APM support in PCMCIA, you can let apmd do this job. Default is `no`.

APMD_PCMCIA_EJECT_ON_SUSPEND="no"
PCMCIA cards can be more or less amenable to an APM suspend event. If you have a card that cannot be suspended properly (such as a SCSI card), it should be "ejected" before entering suspend mode. The cards are not physically ejected. Rather, the power to them is turned off via the `cardctl eject` command and is reactivated upon resume. Default value is `no`.

APMD_INTERFACES_TO_STOP=""
If you have a built-in NIC that does not survive a suspend and resume cycle properly, add the interface name to this variable. It will then be shut down before suspend and brought up after resume. Default is "".

APMD_INTERFACES_TO_UNLOAD=""
If it does not help to shut down the network interface via ⟨*APMD_INTERFACES_TO_STOP*⟩, unload the module driving your NIC at suspend and restart the network at resume.

APMD_LEAVE_X_BEFORE_SUSPEND="no"
If your graphic device is not able to return properly from suspend, switch to text console before suspend and return to your X console after resume. Default is `no`.

APMD_LEAVE_X_BEFORE_STANDBY="no"
Sometimes, it is needed for standby. Default is `no`.

APMD_LOCK_X_ON_SUSPEND="no"
If you like apmd to lock your screen before suspend, set this variable to `yes`. If only one X server is running and no one is logged in at any virtual terminal, this can be considered a safe state. Together with an encrypted partition for your data, no one can access your data when your laptop is in this state. Default is `no`.

APMD_STOP_SOUND_BEFORE_SUSPEND="no"
Sometimes the sound modules do not survive a suspend and resume cycle. In this case, everything seems to be OK, but you cannot hear anything. To avoid this, the sound modules can be unloaded before suspend. A reload of these modules will only be done if you use ALSA or OSS. If you use modules from the kernel, they will be reloaded automatically. If you like that, set ⟨*APMD_STOP_SOUND_BEFORE_SUSPEND*⟩ to `alsa`, `oss`, or `kernel`, depending on what type of sound system you are using. To unload all sound modules successfully, all sound applications that are currently using some of them must be killed. Default value is `no`.

APMD_KBD_RATE=""
It might be necessary to reset the key repetition rate and delay. You can set the variables to any numeric value. The program kbdrate will select the nearest possible values to these specified. To use the default values, just leave the variable empty. Default for both is "".

APMD_KBD_DELAY=""

APMD_TURN_OFF_IDEDMA_BEFORE_SUSPEND=""
There are some notebooks that do not resume properly from suspend when the hard disk was in DMA mode. Add every disk here that needs DMA turned off. For `/dev/hda`, set it to `hda`. Several disks are separated by spaces. Default is "".

proxy Proxy settings

PROXY_ENABLED="yes"
Enable the generation of the proxy settings to the profile. This setting allows to turn the proxy on and off while preserving the particular proxy setup.

HTTP_PROXY=""
Some programs (e. g., lynx, arena, or wget) use a proxy server if this environment variable is set. SuSEconfig will set it in `/etc/SuSEconfig/*`. Example: `"http://proxy.provider.com:3128/"` .

FTP_PROXY=""
Proxy for FTP. Example: `"http://proxy.provider.com:3128/"` .

GOPHER_PROXY=""
Proxy for Gopher. Example: `"http://proxy.provider.com:3128/"` .

NO_PROXY="localhost"
Exclude domains or subdomains from proxy use. Example: `"www.me.de, do.main, localhost"` .

security Settings for system security

CHECK_PERMISSIONS="set"
Should SuSEconfig check file permissions using `/etc/permissions`? Value `set` will correct false settings. `warn` produces warnings. Disable this feature with `no`.

PERMISSION_SECURITY="easy local"
In `/etc/permissions.paranoid`, `/etc/permissions.secure`, and `/etc/permissions.easy`, three security levels are predefined.

Enter `easy`, `secure`, or `paranoid`. If you select `paranoid`, some system sevices might not be available anymore. Explicitly enable them, if needed.

Note

/etc/permissions.local and logrotate

When making entries in `/etc/permissions.local`, make sure they do not conflict with any defaults set by the logrotate mechanism. logrotate will overwrite values set in `/etc/permissions.local`. See *Log Files — the Package logrotate* on page 268.

Note

`sendmail` sendmail variables. Use the YaST `mail` module for configuration.

`suseconfig` Settings for SuSEconfig.

`ENABLE_SUSECONFIG="yes"`
Decide whether SuSEconfig should take care of updating the configuration. Do not disable SuSEconfig if you want to consult our Installation Support.

`MAIL_REPORTS_TO="root"`
Select the user to which SuSEconfig should send e-mail reports created during the automatic system administration.

`MAIL_LEVEL="warn"`
Set the variable to `warn` if only important messages should be sent. Set it to `all` if the log files should be mailed, too.

`CREATE_INFO_DIR="yes"`
Set the variable to `yes` if a perl script should be used to generate the file `/usr/share/info/dir` automatically. This file is the index for all info pages.

`CHECK_ETC_HOSTS="yes"`
Defines whether SuSEconfig should check and modify `/etc/hosts`.

`BEAUTIFY_ETC_HOSTS="no"`
Should `/etc/hosts` be sorted by SuSEconfig?

`SORT_PASSWD_BY_UID="no"`
If this variable is set to yes, SuSEconfig sorts your /etc/passwd and /etc/group by "uid" and "gid".

`CWD_IN_ROOT_PATH="no"`
Should the current working directory (".") be in the path of user `root`? For security reasons, this is not recommended. This setting is valid for all users with a "UID" below 100 (system users).

CWD_IN_USER_PATH="yes"
Should the current working directory (".") be in the path for normal users?

HALT_SOUND="no"
Set to `yes` or `quint` to play a quint tone sequence at system halt or reboot or set to `octave` to play octave sound at that occasion.

CREATE_PERLLOCAL_POD="yes"
May SuSEconfig modify your `perllocal.pod`?

UPDATE_GROFF_CONF="yes"
Update `DESC` to get page sizes correct?

GROFF_PAGESIZE=""
If the correct page size cannot be found in your `printcap`, this variable can be set to the following values: `letter`, `legal`, `a4`, or `b5`, supported by both groff and ghostscript

SuSEfirewall2 Activating the firewall. See the README file in package `SuSEfirewall2` and *Masquerading and Firewalls* on page 444.

sysctl System control at the kernel level.

IP_DYNIP="no"
Enable the "dynamic IP patch" at boot?

IP_TCP_SYNCOOKIES="yes"
Enable "syn flood protection"? See `/usr/src/linux/Documentation/Configure.help`.

IP_FORWARD="no"
If the host is supposed to forward to two network interfaces, set this variable to `yes`. This is usually applicable for routers or "masquerading". The script `/etc/init.d/boot.proc` enables IP forwarding with an entry in the `/proc` file system.

DISABLE_ECN="yes"
If you have trouble connecting to some machines on the Internet with your 2.4 kernel but there are no problems with 2.2, this may be due to broken firewalls dropping network packets with the ECN (early congestion notification) flag set. Set this to `yes` to disable ECN at boot.

ENABLE_SYSRQ="no"
If you set this to `yes`, you will have some control over the system even if it crashes, for example, during kernel debugging. Consult `/usr/src/linux/Documentation/sysrq.txt` for further information.

syslog Configuring the syslog daemon.

SYSLOGD_ADDITIONAL_SOCKET_DHCP="/var/lib/dhcp/dev/log"
The contents of this variable are added by the `dhcp-server` package. The file name mentioned here is added using `-a <filename>` as an additional socket via ⟨*SYSLOGD_PARAMS*⟩ when syslogd is started. This additional socket is needed in case syslogd is restarted. Otherwise, a chrooted dhcpd will not be able to continue logging.

SYSLOGD_ADDITIONAL_SOCKET_FROX="/var/lib/frox/dev/log"
The contents of this variable are added by the `frox` package. The file name mentioned here is added using `-a <filename>` as an additional socket via ⟨*SYSLOGD_PARAMS*⟩ when syslogd is started. This additional socket is needed in case syslogd is restarted. Otherwise, a chrooted frox will not be able to continue logging.

SYSLOGD_ADDITIONAL_SOCKET_STUNNEL="/var/lib/stunnel/dev/log"
The contents of this variable are added by the `stunnel` package. The file name mentioned here is added using `-a <filename>` as an additional socket via ⟨*SYSLOGD_PARAMS*⟩ when syslogd is started. This additional socket is needed in case syslogd is restarted. Otherwise, a chrooted stunnel will not be able to continue logging.

KERNEL_LOGLEVEL="1"
Default log level for klogd.

SYSLOGD_PARAMS=""
Parameters for syslogd, for example, `-r -s my.domain.com`.

KLOGD_PARAMS="-2"
Parameters for klogd.

syslog-ng Configuring syslog-ng.

SYSLOG_NG_REPLACE="yes"
Replace the default syslog daemon? If set to `no`, syslog-ng will be started *in addition* to syslog.

SYSLOG_NG_PARAMS=""
Parameters for syslog-ng. Refer to `man 8 syslog-ng` for details.

windowmanager Window manager.

DEFAULT_WM="kde"
Here, set the default window manager, such as `kde`, `gnome`, or `fvwm`.

INSTALL_DESKTOP_EXTENSIONS="yes"
Install the SuSE extensions for new users (theme and additional functions).

KDE_USE_FAM="no"
Should KDE use the fam daemon? It only makes sense on NFS-mounted directories.

KDE_USE_FAST_MALLOC="yes"
Use the improved malloc?

SUSEWM_UPDATE="yes"
Should SuSEconfig.wm create system-wide configuration files for the window managers?

SUSEWM_WM="all"
Space-separated list of window managers for which configuration files should be generated. Valid values are `fvwm`, `fvwm2`, `fvwm95`, `bowman`, `mwm`, `ctwm`, `kwm`, and `all`.

SUSEWM_XPM="yes"
Set ⟨*SUSEWM_XPM*⟩ to `yes` for pixmaps in menus. The package `3dpixms` must be installed.

xntp Starts the "Network Time Protocol (NTP) Daemon" of package `xntp`. Configuration is done in file `/etc/ntp.conf`. Further guidance on this topic can be taken from the XNTP documentation, which is contained in package `xntp-doc`.

XNTPD_INITIAL_NTPDATE="AUTO-2"
A space-separated list of NTP servers to query for current time and date before the local xntpd is started, for example, "`sun.cosmos.com`". Set the value `AUTO` to query all servers and peers configured in `/etc/ntpd.conf`. The new default value is `AUTO-2`, which will query only the first two servers listed in `/etc/ntpd.conf`.

Radio and modem clocks have addresses in the form `127.127.T.U`, where `T` is the clock type and `U` is a unit number in the range `0-3`. Most of these clocks require a serial port or special bus peripheral. The particular device is normally specified by adding a soft link from `/dev/device-U` to the particular hardware device involved, where U correspond to the unit number above. See `/usr/share/doc/packages/xntp/html/refclock.htm`.

ypbind Configuration of a NIS client. The domain name is set in `/etc/defaultdomain`. The server name will be entered in `/etc/yp.conf` directly during configuration with YaST.

YPBIND_OPTIONS=""
Extra options for ypbind.

YPBIND_LOCAL_ONLY="no"
If this option is set, ypbind will only bind to the loopback interface and remote hosts cannot query it.

YPBIND_BROADCAST="no"
If this option is set to `yes`, ypbind will ignore `/etc/yp.conf` and use a broadcast call to find a NIS server in the local subnet. Avoid using this, as it is a big security risk.

YPBIND_BROKEN_SERVER="no"
Set this to `yes` if you have a NIS server in your network, which binds only to high ports over 1024. Since this is a security risk, you should consider replacing the NIS server with another implementation.

ypserv Configuration of a NIS server.

YPPWD_SRCDIR="/etc"
Specify the YP source directory where YP will search the source files for the passwd and group tables. Default is `/etc`

YPPWD_CHFN="no"
Should a user be allowed to change his GECOS field using ypchfn?

YPPWD_CHSH="no"
Should the user be allowed to change his default login shell using ypchsh?

zope Configuration of ZOPE systems.

ZOPE_FTP="yes"
Should Zope be accessible via FTP?

ZOPE_FTP_PORT="8021"
If so, on which port?

ZOPE_HTTP_PORT="8080"
If you run Zope as a stand-alone server, which port should it occupy?

Part IV

Network

Linux in the Network

Linux, really a child of the Internet, offers all the necessary networking tools and features for integration into all types of network structures. An introduction into the customary Linux protocol, TCP/IP, follows. The various services and special features of this protocol are discussed. Network access using a network card can be configured with YaST2. The central configuration files are discussed and some of the most essential tools described. Only the fundamental mechanisms and the relevant network configuration files are discussed in this chapter. The configuration of Internet access with PPP via modem, ISDN, or other connection can be completed with YaST2. It is described in the *User Guide*.

TCP/IP — The Protocol Used by Linux

Linux and other Unix operating systems use the TCP/IP protocol. It is not a single network protocol, but a family of network protocols that offer various services. TCP/IP was developed based on an application used for military purposes and was defined in its present form in an RFC in 1981. RFC stands for "Request for Comments". They are documents that describe various Internet protocols and implementation procedures for the operating system and its applications. Since then, the TCP/IP protocol has been refined, but the basic protocol has remained virtually unchanged.

Tip

The RFC documents describe the setup of Internet protocols. To expand your knowledge about any of the protocols, refer to the appropriate RFC document. They are available online at `http://www.ietf.org/rfc.html`

Tip

The services listed in Table 13.1 are provided for the purpose of exchanging data between two Linux machines via TCP/IP. Networks combined by TCP/IP, comprising a world-wide network are also referred to, in their entirety, as "the Internet."

Protocol	Description
TCP	Transmission Control Protocol: A connection-oriented secure protocol. The data to transmit is first sent by the application as a stream of data then converted by the operating system to the appropriate format. The data arrives at the respective application on the destination host in the original data stream format in which it was initially sent. TCP determines whether any data has been lost during the transmission and that there is no mix-up. TCP is implemented wherever the data sequence matters.

Table 13.1: *continued overleaf...*

UDP	User Datagram Protocol: A connectionless, insecure protocol. The data to transmit is sent in the form of packets already generated by the application. The order in which the data arrives at the recipient is not guaranteed and data loss is a possibility. UDP is suitable for record-oriented applications. It features a smaller latency period than TCP.
ICMP	Internet Control Message Protocol: Essentially, this is not a user-friendly protocol, but a special control protocol that issues error reports and can control the behavior of machines participating in TCP/IP data transfer. In addition, a special echo mode is provided by ICMP that can be viewed using the program ping.
IGMP	Internet Group Management Protocol: This protocol controls the machine behavior when implementing IP multicast. The following sections do not contain more infomation regarding IP multicasting, because of space limitations.

Table 13.1: *Several Protocols in the TCP/IP Protocol Family*

Almost all hardware protocols work on a packet-oriented basis. The data to transmit is packaged in "bundles", as it cannot be sent all at once. This is why TCP/IP only works with small data packets. The maximum size of a TCP/IP packet is approximately sixty-four kilobytes. The packets are normally quite a bit smaller, as the network software can be a limiting factor. The maximum size of a data packet on an ethernet is about fifteen hundred bytes. The size of a TCP/IP packet is limited to this amount when the data is sent over an ethernet. If more data is transferred, more data packets need to be sent by the operating system.

Layer Model

IP (Internet Protocol) is where the insecure data transfer takes place. TCP (Transmission Control Protocol), to a certain extent, is simply the upper layer for the IP platform serving to guarantee secure data transfer. The IP layer itself is, in turn, supported by the bottom layer, the hardware-dependent protocol, such as ethernet. Professionals refer to this structure as the "layer model". See Figure 13.1.

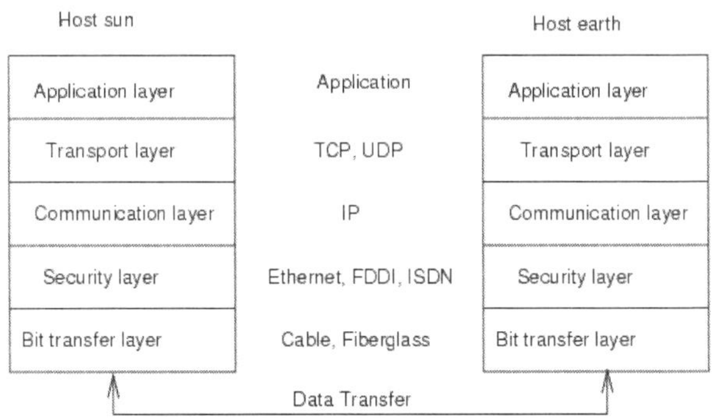

Figure 13.1: *Simplified Layer Model for TCP/IP*

The diagram provides one or two examples for each layer. As you can see, the layers are ordered according to "degrees of abstraction". The lowest layer is very close to the hardware. The uppermost layer, however, is almost a complete abstraction from the hardware. Every layer has its own special function, clarified in the following.

The special functions of each layer are already implicit in their description. For example, the network used (e.g., ethernet) is depicted by the bit transfer and security layers.

- While layer 1 deals with cable types, signal forms, signal codes, and the like, layer 2 is responsible for accessing procedures (which host may send data?) and correcting errors. Layer 1 is called the bit transfer layer. Layer 2 is called security layer
- Layer 3 is the communication layer and is responsible for remote data transfer. The network layer ensures that the data arrives at the correct remote recipient and can be delivered.
- Layer 4, the transport layer, is responsible for application data. The transport layer ensures the data arrives in the correct order and none is lost. The security layer is only there to make sure the data that has arrived is correct. The transport layer protects data from being lost.
- Finally, layer 5 is the layer where data is processed by the application itself.

For every layer to serve its designated function, additional information regarding each layer must be saved in the data packet. This takes place in the header of the packet. Every layer attaches a small block of data, called the protocol header, to the front of each emerging packet. A sample TCP/IP data packet traveling over an ethernet cable is illustrated in Figure 13.2.

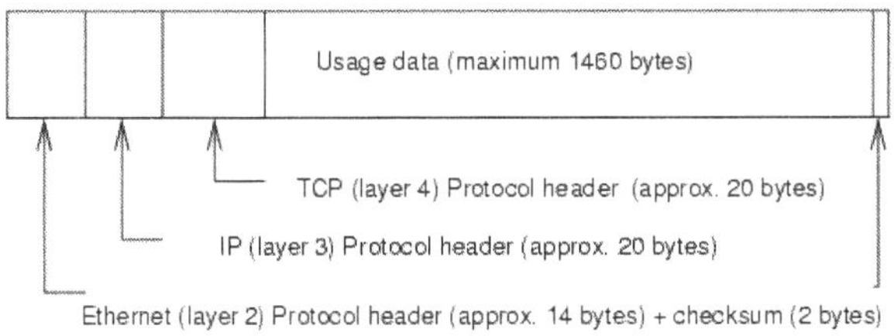

Figure 13.2: *TCP/IP Ethernet Packet*

The proof sum is located at the end of the packet, not at the beginning. This simplifies things for the network hardware. The largest amount of usage data possible in one packet is 1460 bytes in an ethernet network.

When an application sends data over the network, the data passes through each layer, all implemented in the Linux kernel except layer 1: network card. Each layer is responsible for preparing the data so it can be passed to the next layer below. The lowest layer is ultimately responsible for sending the data.

The entire procedure is reversed when data is received. Like the layers of an onion, in each layer the protocol headers are removed from the usage data. Finally, layer 4 is responsible for making the data available for use by the applications at the destination.

In this manner, one layer only communicates with the layer directly above or below it. For applications, it is irrelevant whether data is being transmitted via a 100 MBit/s FDDI network or via a 56-kbit/s modem line. Likewise, it is also irrelevant for the data transfer what data is being sent, as long as it has been properly compressed.

IP Addresses and Routing

IP Addresses

Every computer on the Internet has a unique 32-bit address. These 32 bits (or 4 bytes) are normally written as illustrated in the second row in Table 13.2.

IP Address (binary):	11000000	10101000	00000000	00010100
IP Address (decimal):	192.	168.	0.	20

Table 13.2: *How an IP Address is Written*

In decimal form, the four bytes are written in the decimal number system, separated by periods. The IP address is assigned to a host or a network interface. It cannot be used anywhere else in the world. There are certainly exceptions to this rule, but these play a minimal role in the following passages.

The ethernet card itself has its own unique address: the MAC (media access control) address. It is 48 bits long, internationally unique, and is programmed into the hardware by the network card vendor. There is, however, an unfortunate disadvantage of vendor-assigned addresses — the MAC addresses do not make up a hierarchical system, but are instead more or less randomly distributed. Therefore, they cannot be used for addressing remote machines. The MAC address plays an important role in communication between hosts in a local network and is the main component of the protocol header from layer 2.

The points in IP addresses indicate the hierarchical system. Until the 1990s, the IP addresses were strictly categorized in classes. However, this system has proven to be too inflexible and therefore was discontinued. Now, "classless routing" (or CIDR, Classless Inter Domain Routing) is used.

Netmasks and Routing

Netmasks were conceived for the purpose of informing the host with the IP address `192.168.0.20` of the location of the host with the IP address `192.168.0.1`. To put it simply, the netmask on a host with an IP address defines what is "internal" and what is "external". Hosts located "internally" (professionals say, "in the same subnetwork") respond directly. Hosts located "externally" ("not in the same subnetwork") only respond via a gateway or router. Because every network interface can receive its own IP address, it can get quite complicated.

Before a network packet is sent, the following runs on the computer: the IP address is linked to the netmask via a logical AND, the address of the sending host is likewise connected to the netmask via the logical AND. If there are several network interfaces available, normally all possible sender addresses will be verified. The results of the AND links will be compared. If there are no discrepancies in this comparison, the destination, or receiving

	Binary representation
IP address:192.168.0.20	11000000 10101000 00000000 00010100
Netmask: 255.255.255.0	11111111 11111111 11111111 00000000
Result of the link	11000000 10101000 00000000 00000000
In the decimal system	192. 168. 0. 0
IP address: 213.95.15.200	11010101 10111111 00001111 11001000
Netmask: 255.255.255.0	11111111 11111111 11111111 00000000
Result of the link	11010101 10111111 00001111 00000000
In the decimal system	213. 95. 15. 0

Table 13.3: *Linking IP Addresses to the Netmask*

host, is located in the same subnetwork. Otherwise, it will have to be accessed via a gateway. That means that the more "1" bits are located in the netmask, the fewer hosts can be accessed directly and the more hosts can be reached via a gateway. Several examples are illustrated in Table 13.3.

The netmasks appear, like IP addresses, in decimal form divided by periods. Because the netmask is also a 32-bit value, four number values are written next to each other. Which hosts are gateways or which address domains are accessible over which network interfaces must be entered in the user configurations.

To give another example: all machines connected with the same ethernet cable are usually located in the *same subnetwork* and are directly accessible. When the ethernet is divided by switches or bridges, these hosts can still be reached.

However, the economical ethernet is not suitable for covering larger distances. You will have to transfer the IP packets to another hardware (e. g., FDDI or ISDN). Devices for this transfer are called routers or gateways. A Linux machine can carry out this task. The respective option is referred to as ip_forwarding.

If a gateway has been configured, the IP packet will be sent to the appropriate gateway. This will then attempt to forward the packet in the same manner, from host to host, until it reaches the destination host or the packet's TTL (time to live) has expired.

The base network address	This is the netmask AND any address in the network, as shown in Table 13.3 on the page before under Result. This address cannot be assigned to any hosts.
The broadcast address	This basically says, "Access all hosts in this subnetwork." To generate this, the netmask is inverted in binary form and linked to the base network address with a logical OR. The above example therefore results in 192.168.0.255. This address cannot be assigned to any hosts.
The local host	The address `127.0.0.1` is strictly assigned to the "loopback device" on each host. A connection can be set up to your own machine with this address.

Table 13.4: *Specific Addresses*

As IP addresses must be unique all over the world, you cannot just come up with your own random addresses. There are three address domains to use to set up a private IP-based network. With these, you cannot set up any connections to the rest of the Internet, unless you apply certain tricks, because these addresses cannot be transmitted over the Internet. These address domains are specified in RFC 1597 and listed in Table 13.5.

Network, Netmask	Domain
10.0.0.0, 255.0.0.0	10.x.x.x
172.16.0.0, 255.240.0.0	172.16.x.x - 172.31.x.x
192.168.0.0, 255.255.0.0	192.168.x.x

Table 13.5: *Private IP Address Domains*

Domain Name System

DNS

DNS serves to alleviate the burden of having to remember IP addresses: DNS assists in assigning an IP address to one or more names and assigning a name to an IP address. In Linux, this conversion is usually carried out by a special type of software known as bind. The machine that takes care of this conversion is called a name server.

The names make up a hierarchical system in which each name component is divided by points. The name hierarchy is, however, independent of the IP address hierarchy described above.

Consider a complete name such as `laurent.suse.de`, written in the format `hostname.domain`. A full name, referred to by experts as a "fully qualified domain name" or FQDN for short, consists of a host name and a domain name (*suse.de*), including the top level domain or TLD (*de*).

TLD assignment has become, for historical reasons, quite confusing. For instance, three-letter domain names are used in the USA. In the rest of the world, the two-letter ISO national codes are the standard.

In the early days of the Internet (before 1990), the file `/etc/hosts` was used to store the names of all the machines represented over the Internet. This quickly proved to be impractical in the face of the rapidly growing number of computers connected to the Internet. For this reason, a decentralized database was developed to store the host names in a widely distributed manner. This database, similar to the name server, does not have the data pertaining to all hosts in the Internet readily available, but can dispatch requests to other name servers.

The top of the hierarchy is occupied by "root name servers". These root name servers manage the top level domains. The root name servers are managed by the Network Information Center, or NIC for short. The root name server recognizes the name servers responsible for each top level domain. More information about top level domain NICs is available at `http://www.internic.net`.

For your machine to resolve an IP address, it must recognize at least one name server with an IP address. Configure a name server with the help of YaST2. If you have a modem dial-up connection, you may not need to configure a name server manually at all. The dial-up protocol provides the name server address as the connection is made.

DNS can do more than just resolve host names. The name server also "knows" which host is receiving e-mails for an entire domain, the mail exchanger (MX). The configuration of name server access with SuSE Linux is described in *DNS — Domain Name Service* on page 358.

whois

Closely related to DNS is the protocol whois. With this program, quickly find out who is responsible for any given domain.

IPv6 — The Next Generation's Internet

A New Internet Protocol

Due to the emergence of the WWW (World Wide Web), the Internet has experienced explosive growth with an increasing number of computers communicating via TCP/IP in the last ten years. Since Tim Berners-Lee at CERN (`http://public.web.cern.ch/`) invented the WWW in 1990, the number of Internet hosts has grown from a few thousand to about 100 million.

An IP address "only" consists of 32 bits. Because quite a few IP addresses cannot be used due to organizational circumstances, many IP addresses are lost. The Internet is divided into subnetworks. The number of addresses available in your subnet is the number of bits squared minus two. A subnetwork has, for example, two, six, or fourteen addresses available. To connect 128 hosts to the Internet, for instance, you will need a "Class C" subnetwork with 256 IP addresses, from which only 254 are usable. Two IP addresses are subtracted from the subnetwork — the broadcast address and the base network address.

Configuring a host in the TCP/IP network is relatively complicated. As already discussed, configure the following items on your host: IP address, subnetmask, gateway address (if available), and a name server. You will already have to know this information or receive it from your provider.

Every IP packet contains a proof total that verifies each routing procedure and will have to be recalculated. This is why very fast routers require a lot of processor performance and are more expensive.

Some services have previously been implemented using broadcasts (for example, the Windows network protocol SMB). Hosts for which this service is irrelevant are, however, forced to process the packets and subsequently ignore them. This could lead to problems in high-speed networks.

The successor of the previous IP, IPv6, is a solution to all these problems. The main goal of its development was to expand significantly the rather limited address space, to simplify the configuration of workstations, and to automate them when possible. In this section, IPv4 or IP will be mentioned in reference to the Internet protocol currently used and IPv6 in reference to the new version 6.

IPv6 is defined in more detail in RFC 1752. IPv6 uses 128-bit addresses so features quadrillions of IP addresses, enough for even more general address distribution. This enormous amount of IPv6 addresses allows you to "enlarge" even the smallest subnetwork to 48 bits.

This enables you, then, to use the above mentioned MAC address as an address component. As this address is entirely unique and is strictly defined by the hardware vendor, this will make your host configuration a lot easier. In reality, an EUI-64 token will be consolidated down to the first 64 bits. In doing so, the last 48 bits of the MAC address will be removed and the remaining 24 bits will contain special information on the token type. This also enables the assignment of an EUI-64 token to devices without a MAC address (PPP and ISDN connections).

Furthermore, there has been a new development in IPv6: normally, several IP addresses are assigned to a network interface. This has the advantage that different networks can be made accessible. One of them can be turned into an automatically configured network. Specify the MAC address of the network card and a prefix and you will not need to configure anything else. All hosts in the local network will be accessible right after starting IPv6 ("link-local address").

Moreover, the remaining configuration tasks on a workstation can be carried out automatically to a greater extent. There is a special protocol for this purpose with which workstations can receive an IP address from a router.

All IPv6 supported hosts absolutely require "multicast" support. Multicast can aid several hosts in being accessible at the same time — they do not all have to be set to ("broadcast") or only one to ("unicast"), but, rather, a pair. Which of them that is depends on the application. However, a pair of well-defined multicast groups exists as well, for example, "all name servers multicast group" or "all routers multicast group."

As updating all hosts in the Internet from IPv4 to IPv6 is in no way feasible, there is a compatibility mode. This maps the previous addresses to IPv6 addresses. At the same time, there are mechanisms such as "tunneling" — here, IPv6 packets are sent in the form of IPv4 packets. Of course, it is also possible to convert IPv6 to IPv4. To reach an IPv6 host from a IPv4 host, the IPv6 host absolutely must have an IPv4 compatibility address.

Structure of an IPv6 Address

An IPv6 address, conditional upon 128 bits, is significantly longer than an IPv4 address with its 32 bits. An IPv6 address is consequently 16 bytes long. Due to the size factor, the new IPv6 addresses are written in a different format than the IPv4 addresses used previously. Look at the examples in Table 13.6 on the following page.

As you can see in the table, IPv6 addresses are represented by hexadecimal numbers. The hexadecimal numbers are represented in two-byte segments separated by a colon. Therefore, there can only be a maximum of eight

Local host	::1
IPv4-compatible IPv6 address	::10.10.11.102 (IPv6 supported)
IPv4-mapped IPv6 address	::ffff:10.10.11.102 (IPv6 is not supported)
random address	3ffe:400:10:100:200:c0ff:fed0:a4c3
Link-local address	fe80::10:1000:1a4
Site-local address	fec0:1:1:0:210:10ff:fe00:1a4
Multicast group "All link-local routers"	ff02:0:0:0:0:0:0:2

Table 13.6: *Representation of Various IPv6 Addresses*

groups and seven colons in one address. Zero-bytes in front of a group can be omitted, but not if these are in the middle or at the end of a group. More than four zero-bytes following one another can be skipped by the omission character ::. However, only one omission character is allowed in one address. This omission procedure is technically referred to as *collapsing*. IPv4 compatibility addresses are a specific example of collapsing: here, the IPv4 address is simply attached to the predefined prefix for IPv4 compatibility addresses.

Every part of an IPv6 address has a set meaning. The first bytes comprise a prefix and specify the address type. The middle portion addresses a network or has no meaning. The last part of the address comprises the host segment. Table 13.7 on the next page explains the meaning of some of the more common prefixes.

Prefix (hexadecimal)	Usage
00	IPv4 and IPv4 via IPv6 compatibility addresses. This is an IPv4-compatible address. The IPv6 packet will still need to be converted to an IPv4 packet via an appropriate router. Further special addresses (e. g., loopback devices) are likewise designated this prefix.
First digit 2 or 3	provider-based unicast addresses. As in the previous example, you can be designated a subnetwork in IPv6 from a provider.

Table 13.7: *continued overleaf...*

fe80 to febf	link-local addresses with this prefix cannot be routed and, therefore, cannot be accessed in the same subnetwork.
fec0 to feff	site-local. These addresses can be routed, but only internally within an organization. In this way, these addresses correspond to the previous "private" networks (for example, 10.x.x.x).
ff	multicast IPv6 addresses beginning with ff are multicast addresses.

Table 13.7: *Various IPv6 Prefixes*

As you can already see above, special unicast addresses can get quite long. These can no longer simply be memorized. A functional name server is therefore even more important for IPv6 than for IPv4. Name servers are so important that there is even an autoconfiguration protocol for them.

IPv6 Netmasks

Netmasks are represented by IPv6 in a slightly different way. The categorization of networks in classes is no longer practical, as classless routing is used from the beginning and the small subnetwork can already take up any number of hosts. Because netmasks would get quite long if written out in the previous manner, they will now be written in an entirely different format. The format fec0:1:1:0:210:10ff:fe00:1a4/64 indicates that the last 64 bits make up the host segment and the first 64 bits are the network segment.

To be more precise, the 64 means that the netmask is filled up, as indicated at left, with 1 bits. Therefore, there are 64 one-bits in the netmask. As in IPv4, linking the netmask with the IP address with the logical AND defines whether a host is located in the same or in a different subnetwork.

For More Information About IPv6

Of course, the above overview cannot and is not intended to be a comprehensive introduction to the very extensive topic of IPv6. For a more in-depth introduction in IPv6, refer to `http://www.ipv6.org/`.

Network Integration

Currently TCP/IP is the standard network protocol. All modern operating systems can communicate via TCP/IP. Nevertheless, Linux also supports other network protocols, such as IPX (previously) implemented by Novell Netware or Appletalk used by Macintosh machines. Only the integration of a Linux machine into a TCP/IP network is discussed here. To integrate "exotic" arcnet, token rings, or FDDI network cards, refer to the kernel sources documentation at `/usr/src/linux/Documentation`. For information about network configuration changes made in SuSE Linux version 8.0, read the file `/usr/share/doc/packages/sysconfig/README`.

Preparing

The machine has to have a supported network card. Normally, the network card will already be recognized during installation and the appropriate driver loaded. See if your card has been integrated properly by entering the command `ifstatus eth0`. The output should show the status of the network device eth0.

If the kernel support for the network card is implemented as a module, as is usually the case with the SuSE kernel, the name of the module must be entered as an alias in `/etc/modules.conf`. For example, for the first ethernet card:

```
alias eth0 tulip
```

This will occur automatically if the driver support is started in the linuxrc during the first installation. Otherwise, start it via YaST2 at a later time.

If you are using a hotplug network card (e. g., PCMCIA or USB), the drivers are autodetected when the card is plugged in. No configuration is necessary. Find more information in *Hotplugging Services* on page 221.

Configuration Assisted by YaST2

To configure the network card with YaST2, start the Control Center and select 'Network – Devices' → 'Network Card Configuration'. With 'Add', configure a new network card. With 'Delete', remove it from the configuration. With 'Edit', modify the network card configuration.

Activate the check box 'Hardware' to modify the hardware data for an already configured network card with 'Edit'. This opens the dialog for changing the settings of the network card, shown in Figure 13.3 on the next page.

Normally, the correct driver for your network card is configured during installation and is activated. Therefore, manual hardware parameter settings are only needed if multiple network cards are used or if the network hardware is not automatically recognized. In this case, select 'Add' to specify a new driver module.

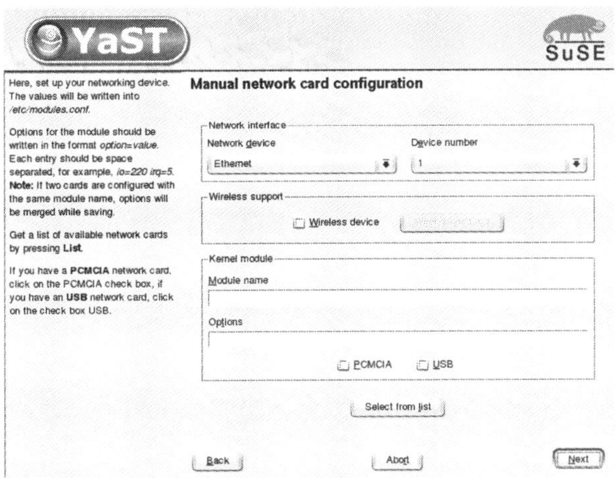

Figure 13.3: Configuring the Hardware Parameters

In this dialog, set the network card type and, for an ISA card, the interrupt to implement and the IO address. For some network drivers, also specify special parameters, such as the interface to use or whether it uses an RJ-45 or a BNC connection. For this, refer to the driver module documentation. To use PCMCIA or USB activate the respective check boxes.

After entering the hardware parameters, configure additional network interface data. Select 'Interface' in the dialog 'Network Base Configuration' to activate the network card and assign it an IP address. Select the card number then click 'Edit'. A new dialog will appear in which to specify the IP address and other IP network data. Find information about assigning addresses to your own network in *TCP/IP — The Protocol Used by Linux* on page 334 and Table 13.5 on page 340. Otherwise, enter the address assigned by your network administrator in the designated fields.

Configure a name server under 'Host Name and Name Server' so the name resolution functions as described in *DNS — Domain Name Service* on page 358. Via 'Routing', set up the routing. Select 'Configuration for Experts' to make advanced settings.

If you are using wireless lan network cards, activate the check box 'Wireless Device'. In the dialog window, set the most important options, like operation mode, network names, and the key for encrypted data transfer.

With that, the network configuration is complete. YaST2 starts SuSEconfig and transfers the settings to the corresponding files (see *Manual Network Configuration* on the next page). For the changes to take effect, the relevant programs must be reconfigured and the required daemons must be restarted. This is done by entering the command `rcnetwork restart`.

Hotplug and PCMCIA

Hotplug network cards, like PCMCIA or USB devices, are managed in a somewhat special way. Normal network cards are fixed components assigned a permanent device name, such as eth0. By contrast, PCMCIA cards are assigned a free device name dynamically on an as-needed basis. To avoid conflicts with fixed network cards, hotplug and PCMCIA services are loaded after the network has been started.

PCMCIA-related configuration and start scripts are located in the directory `/etc/sysconfig/pcmcia`. The scripts will be executed as soon as cardmgr, the PCMCIA Device Manager, detects a newly inserted PCMCIA card — which is why PCMCIA services do not need to be started before the network during boot.

Configuring IPv6

To configure IPv6, you will not normally need to make any changes on the individual workstations. However, the IPv6 support will have to be loaded. Do this most easily by entering the command `modprobe ipv6`.

Because of the autoconfiguration concept of IPv6, the network card is assigned an address in the "link-local" network. Normally, no routing table management takes place on a workstation. The network routers can be queried by the workstation, using the "router advertisement protocol", for what prefix and gateways should be implemented.

The radvd program out of package `radvd` can be used to set up an IPv6 router. This program informs the workstations which prefix to use for the IPv6 addresses and which routers.

To assign a workstation an IPv6 address easily, it is advisable to install and configure the router using the radvd program. The workstations will then automatically receive the IPv6 addresses assigned to them.

Manual Network Configuration

Manual configuration of the network software should always be the last alternative. We recommend using YaST2.

All network interfaces are set up with the script /sbin/ifup. To halt the interface, use ifdown. To check its status, use ifstatus.

If you only have normal, built-in network cards, configure the interfaces by name. With the commands ifup eth0, ifstatus eth0, and ifdown eth0, start, check, or stop the interface eth0. The respective configuration files are stored in /etc/sysconfig/network/ifcfg-eth0. eth0 is the name of the interface and the name of the configuration.

The network can alternatively be configured in relation to the hardware address (MAC address) of a network card. In this case, a configuration file ifcfg-<hardwareaddresswithoutcolon> is used. Use lowercase characters in the hardware address, as displayed by the command ip link (ifconfig shows uppercase letters). If ifup finds a configuration file matching the hardware address, a possibly existing file ifcfg-eth0 will be ignored.

Things are a little more complicated with hotplug network cards. If you do not use one of those cards, skip the following sections and continue reading *Configuration Files* on the following page.

Hotplug network cards are assigned the interface name arbitrarily, so the configuration for one of those cards cannot be stored under the name of the interface. Instead, a name is used that contains the kind of hardware and the connection point. In the following, this name is referred to as the hardware description. ifup has to be called with two arguments — the hardware description and the current interface name. ifup will then determine the configuration that best fits the hardware description.

For example, a laptop with two PCMCIA slots, a PCMCIA ethernet network card and a built-in network card configured as interface eth0 is configured in the following way: The built-in network card is in slot 0 and its hardware description is eth-pcmcia-0. The program cardmgr or the hotplug network script runs the command ifup eth-pcmcia-0 eth1 and ifup searches in /etc/sysconfig/network/ for a file ifcfg-eth-pcmcia-0. If there is no such file, it looks for ifcfg-eth-pcmcia, ifcfg-pcmcia-0, ifcfg-pcmcia, ifcfg-eth1 and ifcfg-eth. The first of these files found by ifup is used for the configuration. To generate a network configuration valid for all PCMCIA network cards in all slots, the configuration file must be named ifcfg-pcmcia. This file would then be used for the ethernet card in slot 0 (eth-pcmcia-0) as well as for a token ring card in slot

1 (tr-pcmcia-1). A configuration depending on the hardware address is treated with higher priority.

YaST2 lists the configurations for hotplug cards and accordingly writes the settings to ifcfg-eth-pcmcia-<number>. To use such a configuration file for all slots, a link ifcfg-eth-pcmcia points to this file. Keep this in mind if you sometimes configure the network with and sometimes without YaST2.

Configuration Files

This section provides an overview of the network configuration files and explains their purpose and the format used.

/etc/sysconfig/network/ifcfg-*

These files contain data specific to a network interface. They may be named after the network interface (ifcfg-eth2), the hardware address of a network card (ifcfg-000086386be3), or the hardware description (ifcfg-usb). If network aliases are used, the respective files are named ifcfg-eth2:1 or ifcfg-usb:1. The script ifup gets the interface name and, if necessary, the hardware description as arguments then searches for the best matching configuration file.

The configuration files contain the IP address (BOOTPROTO="static", IPADDR="10.10.11.214") or the direction to use DHCP (BOOTPROTO="dhcp"). The IP address may also include the netmask (IPADDR="10.10.11.214/16") or the netmask can be specified separately (NETMASK="255.255.0.0"). Refer to the man page for ifup (man ifup) for the complete list of variables.

In addition, all the variables in the files dhcp, wireless, and config can be used in the ifcfg-* files, if a general setting is only to be used for one interface. By using the variables POST_UP_SCRIPT and PRE_DOWN_SCRIPT, individual scripts can be run after starting or before stopping the interface.

/etc/sysconfig/network/config, dhcp, wireless

The file config contains general settings for the behavior of ifup, ifdown, and ifstatus. dhcp contains settings for DHCP and wireless for wireless lan cards. The variables in all three configuration files are commented and can also be used in ifcfg-* files, where they are treated with higher priority.

/etc/hosts

In this file (see File 34), IP addresses are assigned to host names. If no name server is implemented, all hosts to which an IP connection will be set up must be listed here. For each host, a line consisting of the IP address, the fully qualified host name, and the host name (e. g., `earth`) is entered into the file. The IP address has to be at the beginning of the line, the entries divided by blanks and tabs. Comments are always preceeded by the `'#'` sign.

```
127.0.0.1 localhost
192.168.0.1 sun.cosmos.com sun
192.168.0.20 earth.cosmos.com earth
```

File 34: `/etc/hosts`

/etc/networks

Here, network names are converted to network addresses. The format is similar to that of the `hosts` file, except the network names preceed the addresses (see File 35).

```
loopback     127.0.0.0
localnet     192.168.0.0
```

File 35: `/etc/networks`

/etc/host.conf

Name resolution — the translation of host and network names via the *resolver* library — is controlled by this file. This file is only used for programs linked to the libc4 or the libc5. For current glibc programs, refer to the settings in `/etc/nsswitch.conf`. A parameter must always stand alone in its own line. Comments are preceeded by a `'#'` sign. Table 13.8 on the next page shows the parameters available.

order *hosts, bind*	Specifies in which order the services are accessed for the name resolution. Available arguments are (separated by blank spaces or commas): *hosts*: Searches the `/etc/hosts` file *bind*: Accesses a name server

Table 13.8: *continued overleaf…*

	nis: Via NIS
multi *on/off*	Defines if a host entered in /etc/hosts can have multiple IP addresses.
nospoof *on* alert *on/off*	These parameters influence the name server *spoofing*, but, apart from that, do not exert any influence on the network configuration.
trim ⟨*domainname*⟩	The specified domain name is separated from the host name after host name resolution (as long as the host name includes the domain name). This option is useful if only names from the local domain are in the /etc/hosts file, but should still be recognized with the attached domain names.

Table 13.8: *Parameters for /etc/host.conf*

An example for /etc/host.conf is shown in File 36.

```
# We have named running
order hosts bind
# Allow multiple addrs
multi on
```

File 36: */etc/host.conf*

/etc/nsswitch.conf

With the GNU C Library 2.0, the "Name Service Switch" (NSS) became more important. See the man page for nsswitch.conf or, for more details, *The GNU C Library Reference Manual*, Chap. "System Databases and Name Service Switch". Refer to package libcinfo.

In the /etc/nsswitch.conf file, the order of certain data is defined. An example of nsswitch.conf is shown in File 37. Comments are preceeded by '#' signs. Here, for instance, the entry under "database" hosts means that a request is sent to /etc/hosts (files) via DNS (see *DNS — Domain Name Service* on page 358).

```
passwd:     compat
group:      compat

hosts:      files dns
```

```
networks:   files dns

services:   db files
protocols:  db files

netgroup:   files
```

File 37: */etc/nsswitch.conf*

The "databases" available over NSS are listed in Table 13.9. In addition, automount, bootparams, netmasks, and publickey are expected in the near future.

aliases	Mail aliases implemented by sendmail(8). See also the man page for aliases.
ethers	Ethernet addresses.
group	For user groups, used by getgrent(3). See also the man page for group.
hosts	For host names and IP addresses, used by gethostbyname(3) and similar functions.
netgroup	Valid host and user lists in the network for the purpose of controlling access permissions. See also the man page for netgroup.
networks	Network names and addresses, used by getnetent(3).
passwd	User passwords, used by getpwent(3). See also the man page for passwd.
protocols	Network protocols, used by getprotoent(3). See also the man page for protocols.
rpc	"Remote Procedure Call" names and addresses, used by getrpcbyname(3) and similar functions.
services	Network services, used by getservent(3).
shadow	"Shadow" user passwords, used by getspnam(3). See also the man page for shadow.

Table 13.9: *Available Databases via /etc/nsswitch.conf*

The configuration options for NSS databases are listed in Table 13.10 on the following page.

`files`	directly access files, for example, to `/etc/aliases`.
`db`	access via a database.
`nis`	NIS, see also *NIS — Network Information Service* on page 367.
`nisplus`	
`dns`	Only usable by `hosts` and `networks` as an extension.
`compat`	Only usable by `passwd`, `shadow`, and `group` as an extension.
also	It is possible to trigger various reactions with certain lookup results. Details can be found in the man page for `nsswitch.conf`.

Table 13.10: *Configuration Options for NSS "Databases"*

`/etc/nscd.conf`

The nscd (Name Service Cache Daemon) is configured in this file (see the man pages for `nscd` and `nscd.conf`). This effects the data resulting from `passwd`, `groups`, and `hosts`. The daemon must be restarted every time the name resolution (DNS) is changed by modifying the `/etc/resolv.conf` file. Use `rcnscd restart` to restart it.

Caution

If, for example, the caching for `passwd` is activated, it will usually take about fifteen seconds until a newly added user is recognized by the system. By restarting nscd, reduce this waiting period.

Caution

`/etc/resolv.conf`

As is already the case with the `/etc/host.conf` file, this file, by way of the *resolver* library, likewise plays a role in host name resolution. The domain to which the host belongs is specified in this file (keyword search). Also listed is the status of the name server address (keyword name server) to access. Multiple domain names can be specified. When resolving a name that is not fully qualified, an attempt is made to generate one by attaching the individual search entries. Multiple name servers can be made known by entering several lines, each beginning with name server. Comments are preceeded by `'#'` signs.

An example of /etc/resolv.conf is shown in File 38.

```
# Our domain
search cosmos.com

name server 192.168.0.1
```

File 38: /etc/resolv.conf

Some services, like pppd (wvdial), ipppd (isdn), dhcp (dhcpcd and dhclient), pcmcia, and hotplug, modify the file /etc/resolv.conf. To do so, they rely on the script modify_resolvconf.

If the file /etc/resolv.conf has been temporarily modified by this script, it will contain a predefined comment giving information about the service by which it has been modified, about the location where the original file has been backed up, and hints on how to turn off the automatic modification mechanism.

If /etc/resolv.conf is modified several times, the file will include modifications in a nested form. These can be reverted in a clean way even if this reversal takes place in an order different from the order in which modifications where introduced. Services that may need this flexibility include isdn, pcmcia, and hotplug.

If it happens that a service was not terminated in a normal, clean way, modify_resolvconf can be used to restore the original file. Also, on system boot, a check will be performed to see whether there is an uncleaned, modified resolv.conf (e. g., after a system crash), in which case the original (unmodified) resolv.conf will be restored.

YaST2 uses the command modify_resolvconf check to find out whether resolv.conf has been modified and will subsequently warn the user that changes will be lost after restoring the file.

Apart from this, YaST2 will not rely on modify_resolvconf, which means that the impact of changing resolv.conf through YaST2 is the same as that of any manual change. In both cases, changes are made on purpose and with a permanent effect, while modifications requested by the above-mentioned services are only temporary.

/etc/HOSTNAME

Here is the host name without the domain name attached. This file is read by several scripts while the machine is booting. It may only contain one line where the host name is mentioned.

Start-Up Scripts

Apart from the configuration files described above, there are also various scripts that load the network programs while the machine is being booted. This will be started as soon as the system is switched to one of the *multiuser runlevels* (see also Table 13.11).

`/etc/init.d/network`	This script takes over the configuration for the network hardware and software during the system's start-up phase.
`/etc/init.d/inetd`	Starts inetd. This is only necessary if you want to log in to this machine over the network.
`/etc/init.d/portmap`	Starts the portmapper needed for the RPC server, such as an NFS server.
`/etc/init.d/nfsserver`	Starts the NFS server.
`/etc/init.d/sendmail`	Controls the sendmail process.
`/etc/init.d/ypserv`	Starts the NIS server.
`/etc/init.d/ypbind`	Starts the NIS client.

Table 13.11: *Some Start-Up Scripts for Network Programs*

Routing in SuSE Linux

The routing table is set up in SuSE Linux via the configuration files `/etc/sysconfig/network/routes` and `/etc/sysconfig/network/ifroute-*`.

All the static routes required by the various system tasks can be entered in the `/etc/sysconfig/network/routes` file: routes to a host, routes to a host via a gateway, and routes to a network. For each interface that need individual routing, define an additional configuration file: `/etc/sysconfig/network/ifroute-*`. Replace `'*'` with the name of the interface. The entries in the routing configuration files look like this:

```
DESTINATION            GATEWAY NETMASK    INTERFACE [ TYPE ] [ OPTIONS ]
DESTINATION            GATEWAY PREFIXLEN  INTERFACE [ TYPE ] [ OPTIONS ]
DESTINATION/PREFIXLEN  GATEWAY -          INTERFACE [ TYPE ] [ OPTIONS ]
```

To omit GATEWAY, NETMASK, PREFIXLEN, or INTERFACE, write '-' instead. The entries TYPE and OPTIONS may just be omitted.

- The route's destination is in the first column. This column may contain the IP address of a network or host or, in the case of *reachable* name servers, the fully qualified network or host name.
- The second column contains the default gateway or a gateway through which a host or a network can be accessed.
- The third column contains the netmask for networks or hosts behind a gateway. The mask is `255.255.255.255`, for example, for a host behind a gateway.
- The last column is only relevant for networks connected to the local host such as loopback, ethernet, ISDN, PPP, and dummy device. The device name must be entered here.

The following scripts in the directory `/etc/sysconfig/network/scripts/` assist with the handling of routes:

ifup-route for setting up a route

ifdown-route for disabling a route

ifstatus-route for checking the status of the routes

DNS — Domain Name Service

DNS (Domain Name Service) is needed to resolve the domain and host names into IP addresses. In this way, the IP address `192.168.0.20` is assigned to the host name `earth`, for example. Before setting up your own name server, read the general information about DNS in *Domain Name System* on page 340.

Starting the Name Server BIND

The name server BIND is already preconfigured in SuSE Linux, so you can easily start it right after installing the distribution. If you already have a functioning Internet connection and have entered 127.0.0.1 as name server for the local host in `/etc/resolv.conf`, you normally already have a working name resolution without needing to know the DNS of the provider. BIND carries out the name resolution via the root name server, a notably slower process. Normally, the DNS of the provider should be entered with its IP address in the configuration file `/etc/named.conf` under forwarders to ensure effective and secure name resolution. If this works so far, the name server will run as a pure "caching-only" name server. Only when you configure its own zones will it become a proper DNS. A simple example of this can be found under `/usr/share/doc/packages/bind8/sample-config`. However, do not set up any official domains until assigned one by the responsible institution. Even if you have your own domain and it is managed by the provider, you are better off not to use it, as BIND would otherwise not forward any more requests for this domain. The provider's web server, for example, would not be accessible for this domain.

To start the name server, enter `rcnamed start` on the command line (as root). If "done" appears to the right in green, `named`, as the name server process is called, has been started successfully. Test the operability of the name server immediately on the local system with the `host` or `dig` programs. The local host should appear as the default server with the address 127.0.0.1. If this is not the case, `/etc/resolv.conf` possible contains an incorrect name server or this file does not exist at all. For the first test, enter `host 127.0.0.1`, which should always work. If you get an error message, use `rcnamed status` to check if `named` is actually running. If the name server does not start or exhibits faulty behavior, you will usually find the cause in the log file `/var/log/messages`.

If you have a dial-up connection, be sure that BIND8, once it starts, will review the root name server. If it does not manage this because an Internet connection has not been made, this can cause the DNS requests not to be resolved other than for locally-defined zones. BIND9 behaves differently, but requires quite a bit more resources than BIND8.

To implement the name server of the provider or one already running on your network as "forwarder", enter one or more of these in the options section under forwarders. See File 39.

```
options {
        directory "/var/named";
        forwarders { 10.11.12.13; 10.11.12.14; };
        listen-on { 127.0.0.1; 192.168.0.99; };
        allow-query { 127/8; 192.168.0/24; };
        notify no;
       };
```

File 39: *Forwarding Options in* `named.conf`

Adjust the IP addresses to your personal environment.

After options follows the zone, "localhost", "0.0.127.in-addr.arpa", and "." entries. At least entries from "type hint" should exist. Their corresponding files never have to be modified, as they function in their present state. Also, be sure that a ";" follows each entry and that the curly braces are properly set.

If you have made changes to the configuration file `/etc/named.conf` or to the zone files, have BIND reread these files by entering `rcnamed reload`. Otherwise, completely restart the name server with `rcnamed restart`. To stop the name server, enter `rcnamed stop`.

The Configuration File /etc/named.conf

Make all the settings for the name server BIND8 and BIND9 in the `/etc/named.conf` file. The zone data, consisting of the host names, IP addresses, and similar, for the domains to administer are stored in separate files in the `/var/named` directory.

The `/etc/named.conf` is roughly divided into two areas. One is the options section for general settings and the other consists of zone entries for the individual domains. Additional sections for logging and acl type entries can be added. Comment lines begin with a `'#'` sign or `'//'`. A minimalistic `/etc/named.conf` looks like File 40 on the following page.

```
options {
        directory "/var/named";
        forwarders { 10.0.0.1; };
        notify no;
};

   zone "localhost" in {
           type master;
           file "localhost.zone";
   };

   zone "0.0.127.in-addr.arpa" in {
           type master;
           file "127.0.0.zone";
   };

   zone "." in {
           type hint;
           file "root.hint";
   };
```

File 40: *A Basic* `/etc/named.conf`

This example works for both BIND8 and BIND9, because no special options are used that are only understood by one version or the other. BIND9 accepts all BIND8 configurations and makes note of options not implemented at start-up. Special BIND9 options are, however, not supported by BIND8.

Important Configuration Options

directory "/var/named"; specifies the directory where BIND can find the files containing the zone data.

forwarders 10.0.0.1; ; is used to specify the name servers (mostly of the provider) to which DNS requests, which cannot be resolved directly, are forwarded.

forward first; causes DNS requests to be forwarded before an attempt is made to resolve them via the root name servers. Instead of forward first, forward only can be written to have all requests forwarded and none sent to the root name servers. This makes sense for firewall configurations.

listen-on port 53 127.0.0.1; 192.168.0.1; ; tells BIND to which network interface and port to listen. The port 53 specification can be left out, as

53 is the default port. If this entry is completely omitted, BIND accepts requests on all interfaces.

query-source address * port 53; This entry is necessary if a firewall is blocking external DNS requests. This tells BIND to post requests externally from port 53 and not from any of the ports greater than 1024.

allow-query 127.0.0.1; 192.168.1/24; ; defines the networks from which clients can post DNS requests. The /24 at the end is an abbreviated expression for the netmask, in this case, 255.255.255.0.

allow-transfer ! *; ; controls which hosts can request zone transfers. This example cuts them off completely due to the ! *. Without this entry, zone transfers can be requested anywhere without restrictions.

statistics-interval 0; In the absence of this entry, BIND generates several lines of statistical information in `/var/log/messages`. Specifying 0 suppresses these completely. Otherwise the time in minutes can be given here.

cleaning-interval 720; This option defines at which time intervals BIND clears its cache. This triggers an entry in `/var/log/messages` each time it occurs. The time specification is in minutes. The default is 60 minutes.

interface-interval 0; BIND regularly searches the network interfaces for new or no longer existing interfaces. If this value is set to 0, this will not be carried out and BIND will only listen at the interfaces detected at start-up. Otherwise, the interval can be defined in minutes. The default is 60 minutes.

notify no; no prevents other name servers from being informed when changes are made to the zone data or when the name server is restarted.

The Configuration Section "Logging"

What, how, and where archiving takes place can be extensively configured in BIND. Normally, the default settings should be sufficient. File 41 represents the simplest form of such an entry and will completely suppress any logging:

```
logging {

        category default { null; };

};
```

File 41: *Entry to Disable Logging*

Zone Entry Structure

```
zone "my-domain.de" in {
        type master;
        file "my-domain.zone";
        notify no;
};
```

***File 42:** Zone Entry for my-domain.de*

After zone, the name of the domain to administer is specified, my-domain.de, followed by in and a block of relevant options enclosed in curly braces, as shown in File 42. To define a "slave zone", the type is simply switched to slave and a name server is specified that administers this zone as master (but can also be a "slave"), as shown in File 43.

```
zone "other-domain.de" in {
        type slave;
        file "slave/other-domain.zone";
        masters { 10.0.0.1; };
};
```

***File 43:** Zone Entry for other-domain.de*

The options:

type master; master indicates that this zone is administered on this name server. This assumes that your zone file has been properly created.

type slave; This zone is transferred from another name server. Must be used together with masters.

type hint; The zone . of the type hint is used for specification of the root name servers. This zone definition can be left alone.

file "my-domain.zone" or file "slave/other-domain.zone"; This entry specifies the file where zone data for the domain is located. This file is not required by slaves, because its contents is read by another name server. To differentiate master and slave files, the directory `slave` is specified for the slave files.

masters { 10.0.0.1; }; This entry is only needed for slave zones. It specifies from which name server the zone file should be transferred.

allow-update { ! *; }; This options controls external write access, which would allow clients to make a DNS entry — something normally not desirable for security reasons. Without this entry, zone updates are not allowed at all. With the above sample entry, the same would be achieved because ! * effectively bars any clients from such access.

Structure of Zone Files

Two types of zone files are needed. One serves to assign IP addresses to host names and the other does the reverse — supplies a host name for an IP address.

`'.'` has an important meaning in the zone files here. If host names are given without ending with a `'.'`, the zone will be appended. Thus, complete host names specified with a complete domain must end with a `'.'` so the domain is not added to it again. A missing point or one in the wrong place is probably the most frequent cause of name server configuration errors.

The first case to consider is the zone file `world.zone`, responsible for the domain `world.cosmos`, shown in File 44.

```
1. $TTL 2D
2. world.cosmos.  IN SOA      gateway  root.world.cosmos. (
3.                2001040901  ; serial
4.                1D          ; refresh
5.                2H          ; retry
6.                1W          ; expiry
7.                2D )        ; minimum
8.
9.                IN NS       gateway
10.               IN MX       10 sun
11.
12. gateway       IN A        192.168.0.1
13.               IN A        192.168.1.1
14. sun           IN A        192.168.0.2
15. moon          IN A        192.168.0.3
16. earth         IN A        192.168.1.2
17. mars          IN A        192.168.1.3
```

***File 44:** File `/var/named/world.zone`*

Line 1: $TTL defines the standard TTL that applies for all the entries in this file, here 2 days. TTL means *time to live*.

Line 2: The SOA control record begins here:

- The name of the domain to administer is world.cosmos in the first position. This ends with a `'.'`, because otherwise the zone would be appended a second time. Alternatively, a `'@'` can be entered here. Then, the zone would be extracted from the corresponding entry in `/etc/named.conf`.
- After IN SOA is the name of the name server in charge as master for this zone. The name is extended from gateway to gateway.world.cosmos, because it does not end with a `'.'`.
- An e-mail address of the person in charge of this name server will follow. Because the `'@'` sign already has a special significance, `'.'` is entered here instead, for root@world.cosmos, consequently root.world.cosmos..The `'.'` sign at the end cannot be neglected. Otherwise, the zone will still be added here.
- A `'('` follows at the end here, including the following lines up until `')'` into the SOA record.

Line 3: The serial number is an arbitrary number that is increased each time this file is changed. It is needed to inform the secondary name servers (slave servers) of changes. For this, a ten-digit number of the date and run number, written as YYYYMMDDNN, has become the customary format.

Line 4: The refresh rate specifies the time interval at which the secondary name servers verify the zone serial number. In this case, 1 day.

Line 5: The retry rate specifies the time interval at which a secondary name server, in case of error, attempts to contact the primary server again. Here, 2 hours.

Line 6: The expiration time specifies the time frame after which a secondary name server discards the cached data if it has not regained contact to the primary server. Here, it is a week.

Line 7: The minimum time to live states how long the results of the DNS requests from other servers can be cached before they become invalid and must be requested again.

Line 9: The IN NS specifies the name server responsible for this domain. The same is true here that gateway is extended to gateway.world.cosmos because it does not end with a `'.'`. There can be several lines like this — one for the primary and one for each secondary name server. If notify is not set to no in `/etc/named.conf`, all the name servers listed here will be informed of the changes made to the zone data.

Line 10: The MX record specifies the mail server that accepts, processes, and forwards e-mails for the domain world.cosmos. In this example, this is the host sun.world.cosmos. The number in front of the host name is the preference value. If there are multiple MX entries, the mail server with the smallest value is taken first and, if mail delivery to this server fails, an attempt will be made with the next higher value.

Line 12–17: These are now the actual address records where one or more IP addresses are assigned to the host names. The names are listed here without a `'.'`, because they are entered without a domain added and can all be appended with world.cosmos. Two IP addresses are assigned to the host gateway, because it has two network cards.

The pseudodomain in-addr.arpa is used to assist the reverse lookup of IP addresses into host names. This will be appended, for this purpose, to the network components described here in reverse order. 192.168.1 is thus translated into 1.168.192.in-addr.arpa. See File 45.

```
1. $TTL 2D
2. 1.168.192.in-addr.arpa. IN SOA  gateway.world.cosmos.
                                      root.world.cosmos. (
3.                         2001040901      ; serial
4.                         1D              ; refresh
5.                         2H              ; retry
6.                         1W              ; expiry
7.                         2D )            ; minimum
8.
9.                         IN NS           gateway.world.cosmos.
10.
11. 1                      IN PTR          gateway.world.cosmos.
12. 2                      IN PTR          earth.world.cosmos.
13. 3                      IN PTR          mars.world.cosmos.
```

File 45: Reverse Lookup

Line 1: $TTL defines the standard TTL that applies to all entries here.

Line 2: 'Reverse lookup' should be activated with this file for the network 192.168.1.0. Because the zone is called '1.168.192.in-addr.arpa' here, it is, of course, undesirable to add this to the host name. Therefore, these are all entered complete with domain and ending with `'.'`. The rest corresponds to the previous example described for world.cosmos.

Line 3–7: See the previous example for world.cosmos.

Line 9: This line also specifies the name server responsible for this zone. This time, however, the name is entered completely with domain and ending with `'.'`.

Line 11–13: These are the pointer records linked to an IP address at the respective host name. Only the last part of the IP address is entered at the beginning of the line without the last `'.'`. Now, if the zone is appended to this and the .in-addr.arpa is neglected, the entire IP address will be backwards.

In this form, the zone files are usable both for BIND8 and BIND9. Zone transfers between different versions should not normally be an issue.

NIS — Network Information Service

As soon as multiple UNIX systems in a network want to access common resources, it becomes important that all user and group identities are the same for all machines in that network. The network should be transparent to the user: whatever machine a user uses, he will always find himself in exactly the same environment. This is made possible by means of NIS and NFS services. NFS distributes file systems over a network and is discussed in *NFS — Shared File Systems* on page 371.

NIS (Network Information Service) is a database service that enables access to `/etc/passwd`, `/etc/shadow`, and `/etc/group` across a network. NIS can be used for other, more specialized tasks (such as for `/etc/hosts` or `/etc/services`).

NIS Master and Slave Server

For the configuration, select 'NIS Server' from the YaST2 module 'Network — Services'. If no NIS server existed so far in your network, activate 'Create NIS Master Server' in the next screen. If you already have an NIS server (a "master"), you can add a NIS slave server (for example, if you want to configure a new subnetwork). First, the configuration of the master server is described.

If some needed packages are missing, insert the respective CD or DVD as requested to install the packages automatically. Enter the domain name at the top of the configuration dialog, which is shown in Figure 13.4 on the next page. In the check box below, define whether the host should also be an NIS client, enabling users to log in and access data from the NIS server.

If you want to configure additional NIS servers (*slave servers*) in your network afterwards, activate 'Active NIS Slave Server Exists' now. Select 'Fast Map Distribution' to set fast transfer of the database entries from the master to the slave server.

To allow users in your network to change their passwords on the NIS server (with the command `yppasswd`), activate this option. This will activate the check boxes 'Allow Changes of GECOS Field' and 'Allow Changes of Login Shell'. "GECOS" means that the users can also change their names and address settings with the command `ypchfn`. "SHELL" allows users to modify their default shell with the command `ypchsh`.

By clicking 'Other Global Settings...', access a screen, shown in Figure 13.5 on page 369, in which to change the source directory of the NIS server (`/etc` by

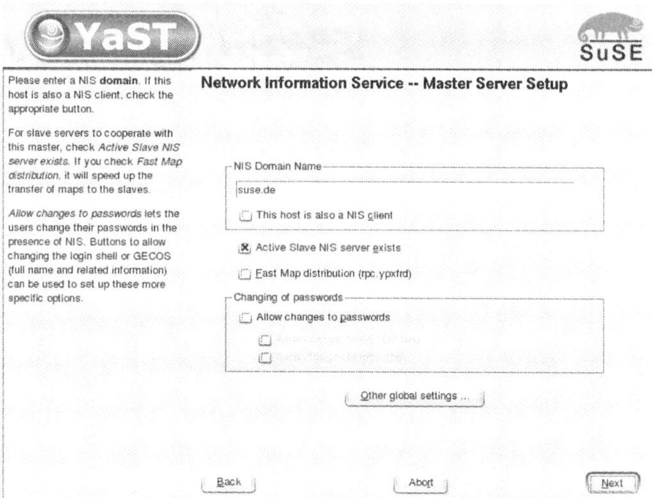

Figure 13.4: *YaST2: NIS Server Configuration Tool*

default). In addition, passwords and groups can be linked here. The setting should be left at 'Yes' so the files (`/etc/passwd` and `/etc/shadow` as well as `/etc/group` and `/etc/gshadow`) can be synchronized. Also determine the smallest user and group ID. Press 'OK' to confirm your settings and return to the previous screen. Click 'Next'.

If you previously enabled 'Active NIS Slave Server Exists', enter the host names used as slaves and click 'Next'. If you do not use slave servers, the slave configuration is skipped and you continue directly to the dialog for the database configuration. Here, specify the *maps*, the partial databases to be transferred from the NIS server to the respective client. The default settings are usually adequate. You should know exactly what you are doing if you modify the settings.

'Next' continues to the last dialog, shown in Figure 13.6 on page 370. Specify from which networks requests can be sent to the NIS server. Normally, this is your internal network. In this case, there should be the following two entries:

```
255.0.0.0 127.0.0.0
0.0.0.0 0.0.0.0
```

The first one enables connections from your own host, which is the NIS server. The second one allows all hosts with access to the same network to send requests to the server.

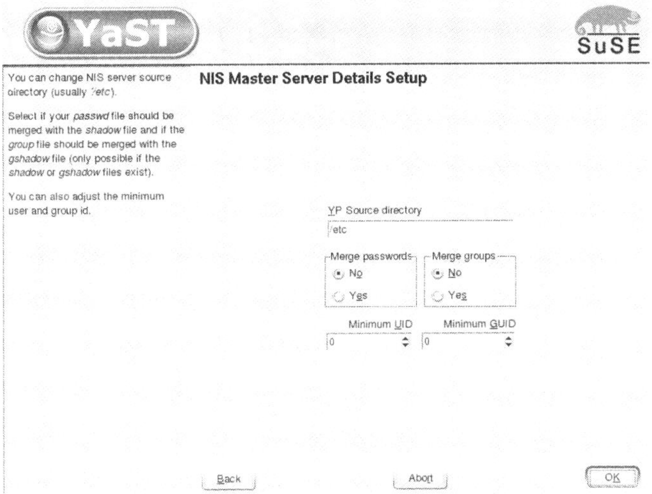

Figure 13.5: *YaST2: Changing the Directory and Synchronizing Files for a NIS Server*

The NIS Client Module of YaST2

This module facilitates the configuration of the NIS client. In the following dialog, first select whether the host has a fixed IP address or gets one via DHCP. DHCP also provides the NIS domain and the NIS server. For further information about DHCP, see *DHCP* on page 375. If a static IP address is used, specify the NIS domain and the NIS server manually.

In addition, you also have the possibility to specify multiple domains with one default domain. Use 'Add' to specify multiple servers including the broadcast function for the individual domains.

In the expert settings, check 'Answer to the Local Host Only', if you do not want other hosts to be able to query which server your client is using. By checking 'Broken Server', no answers from servers on unprivileged ports are accepted. This is recommended for security reasons. For further information, see `man ypbind`.

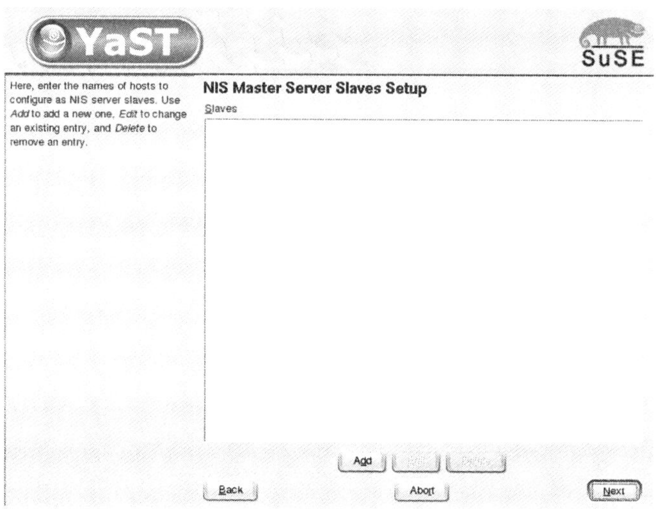

Figure 13.6: *YaST2: Setting Request Permissions for a NIS Server*

NFS — Shared File Systems

As mentioned in *NIS — Network Information Service* on page 367, NFS (together with NIS) makes a network transparent to the user. With NFS, it is possible to distribute file systems over the network. It does not matter at which terminal a user is logged in. He will always find himself in the same environment.

As with NIS, NFS is an asymmetric service. There are NFS servers and NFS clients. A machine can be both — it can supply file systems over the network (export) and mount file systems from other hosts (import). Generally, these are servers with a very large hard disk capacity, whose file systems are mounted by other clients.

Importing File Systems with YaST2

Any user authorized to do so can mount NFS directories from an NFS server into his own file tree. This can be achieved most easily using the YaST2 module 'NFS Client'. Just enter the host name of the NFS server, the directory to import, and the mount point at which to mount this directory locally. All this is done after clicking 'Add' in the first dialog.

Importing File Systems Manually

File systems can easily be imported manually from an NFS server. The only prerequisite is a running RPC port mapper, which can be started by entering the command `rcportmap start` as `root`. Once this prerequisite is met, remote file systems exported on the respective machines can be mounted in the file system just like local hard disks by using the command `mount` with the following syntax:

`mount` ⟨*host*⟩`:`⟨*remote-path*⟩ ⟨*local-path*⟩

If user directories from the machine `sun`, for example, should be imported, the following command can be used:

```
earth:~ #  mount sun:/home /home
```

Exporting File Systems with YaST2

YaST2 enables you to quickly turn any host in your network into an NFS server. In YaST2 select 'Network — Services' → 'NFS Server'.

Next, activate 'Start NFS Server' and click 'Next'. In the upper text field, enter the directories to export. Below, enter the hosts that should have access to them. This dialog is shown in Figure 13.7. There are four options that can be set for each host: ⟨*single host*⟩, ⟨*net groups*⟩, ⟨*wild cards*⟩, and ⟨*IP networks*⟩. A more thorough explanation of these options is provided by the man page for `exports` (`man exports`).

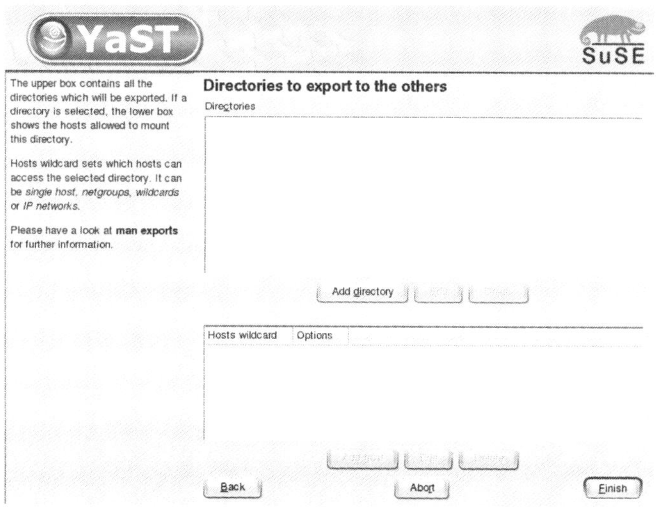

Figure 13.7: Configuring an NFS Server with YaST2

'Exit' completes the configuration.

Exporting File Systems Manually

If you do not want to use YaST, make sure the following systems run on the NFS server:

- RPC portmapper (*rpc.portmap*)
- RPC mount daemon (*rpc.mountd*)
- RPC NFS daemon (*rpc.nfsd*)

For these services to be started by the scripts /etc/init.d/portmap and /etc/init.d/nfsserver when the system is booted, enter the commands `insserv /etc/init.d/nfsserver` and `insserv /etc/init.d/portmap`. After these daemons have been started, the configuration file `/etc/exports` decides which directories should be exported to which machines.

For each directory to export, one line is needed to specify which machines may access that directory with what permissions. All subdirectories of this directory will automatically be exported as well. Authorized machines are usually denoted with their full names (including domain name), but it is possible to use wild cards like `'*'` or `'?'`. If no machine is specified here, any machine is allowed to import this file system with the given permissions.

Permissions of the file system to export are specified in brackets after the machine name. The most important options are:

ro	File system is exported with read-only permission (default).
rw	File system is exported with read-write permission.
root_squash	This makes sure the user `root` of the given machine does not have `root` specific permissions on this file system. This is achieved by assigning user ID `65534` to users with user ID `0` (root). This user ID should be set to `nobody`
no_root_squash	Does not assign user ID `0` to user ID `65534` (default).
link_relative	Converts absolute links (those beginning with `'/'`) to a sequence of `'../'`. This is only useful if the entire file system of a machine is mounted (default).
link_absolute	Symbolic links remain untouched.
map_identity	User IDs are exactly the same on both client and server (default).
map-daemon	Client and server do not have matching user IDs. This tells nfsd to create a conversion table for user IDs. **ugidd** is required for this to work.

Table 13.12: *Permissions for Exported File Systems*

Your `exports` file might look like File 46.

```
#
# /etc/exports
```

```
#
/home            sun(rw)   venus(rw)
/usr/X11         sun(ro)   venus(ro)
/usr/lib/texmf   sun(ro)   venus(rw)
/                earth(ro,root_squash)
/home/ftp        (ro)
# End of exports
```

File 46: `/etc/exports`

File `/etc/exports` is read by mountd. If you change anything in this file, restart mountd and nfsd for your changes to take effect. This can easily be done with `rcnfsserver restart`.

DHCP

The DHCP Protocol

The purpose of the "Dynamic Host Configuration Protocol" is to assign network settings centrally from a server rather than configuring them locally on each and every workstation. A client configured to use DHCP does not have control over its own static address. It is enabled to fully autoconfigure itself according to directions from the server.

One way to use DHCP is to identify each client using the hardware address of its network card (which is fixed in most cases) then supply that client with identical settings each time it connects to the server. DHCP can also be configured so the server assigns addresses to each "interested" host *dynamically* from an address pool set up for that purpose. In the latter case, the DHCP server will try to assign the same address to the client each time it receives a request from it (even over longer periods). This, of course, will not work if there are more client hosts in the network than network addresses available.

With these possibilities, DHCP can make life easier for system administrators in two ways. Any changes (even bigger ones) related to addresses and the network configuration in general can be implemented centrally by editing the server's configuration file. This is much more convenient than reconfiguring lots of client machines. Also it is much easier to integrate machines, particularly new machines, into the network, as they can be given an IP address from the pool. Retrieving the appropriate network settings from a DHCP server can be especially useful in the case of laptops regularly used in different networks.

A DHCP server not only supplies the IP address and the netmask, but also the host name, domain name, gateway, and name server addresses to be used by the client. In addition to that, DHCP allows for a number of other parameters to be configured in a centralized way, for example, a time server from which clients may poll the current time or even a print server.

The following section, gives an overview of DHCP without describing the service in every detail. In particular, we want to show how to use the DHCP server dhcpd in your own network to easily manage its entire setup from one central point.

DHCP Software Packages

Both a DHCP server and DHCP clients are available for SuSE Linux. The DHCP server available is dhcpd (published by the Internet Software Consortium). On the client side, you can choose between two different DHCP client programs: package dhclient (also from ISC) and the "DHCP client daemon" in the package dhcpcd package.

SuSE Linux installs dhcpcd by default. The program is very easy to handle and will be launched automatically on each system boot to watch for a DHCP server. It does not need a configuration file to do its job and should work out of the box in most standard setups. For more complex situations, use the ISC dhclient, which is controlled by means of the configuration file /etc/dhclient.conf.

The DHCP Server dhcpd

The core of any DHCP system is the *dynamic host configuration protocol daemon*. This server "leases" addresses and watches how they are used, according to the settings as defined in the configuration file /etc/dhcpd.conf. By changing the parameters and values in this file, a system administrator can influence the program's behavior in numerous ways.

Look at a basic sample /etc/dhcpd.conf file:

```
default-lease-time 600;          # 10 minutes
max-lease-time 7200;             # 2  hours

option domain-name "kosmos.all";
option domain-name-servers 192.168.1.1, 192.168.1.2;
option broadcast-address 192.168.1.255;
option routers 192.168.1.254;
option subnet-mask 255.255.255.0;

subnet 192.168.1.0 netmask 255.255.255.0
 {
  range 192.168.1.10 192.168.1.20;
  range 192.168.1.100 192.168.1.200;
 }
```

File 47: *The Configuration File /etc/dhcpd.conf*

This simple configuration file should be sufficient to get the DHCP server to assign IP addresses in the network. Make sure a semicolon is inserted at the end of each line, because otherwise dhcpd will not be started.

As you can see, the above sample file can be divided into three sections. The first one defines how many seconds an IP address is "leased" to a requesting host by default (default-lease-time) before it should apply for renewal. The section also includes a statement on the maximum period for which a machine may keep an IP address assigned by the DHCP server without applying for renewal (`max-lease-time`).

In the second part, some basic network parameters are defined on a global level:

- The line `option domain-name` defines the default domain of your network.
- With the entry `option domain-name-servers`, specify up to three values for the DNS servers used to resolve IP addresses into host names (and vice versa). Ideally, configure a name server on your machine or somewhere else in your network before setting up DHCP. That name server should also define a host name for each dynamic address and vice versa. To learn how to configure your own name server, read *DNS — Domain Name Service* on page 358.
- The line `option broadcast-address` defines the broadcast address to be used by the requesting host.
- With `option routers`, tell the server where to send data packets that cannot be delivered to a host on the local network (according to the source and target host address and the subnet mask provided). In most cases, especially in smaller networks, this router will be identical with the Internet gateway.
- With `option subnet-mask`, specify the netmask assigned to clients.

The last section of the file is there to define a network, including a subnet mask. To finish, specify the address range that the DHCP daemon should use to assign IP addresses to interested clients. In our example, clients may be given any address between `192.168.1.10` and `192.168.1.20` as well as `192.168.1.100` and `192.168.1.200`.

After editing these few lines, you should be able to activate the DHCP daemon with the command `rcdhcpd start`. It will be ready for use immediately. You can also use the command `rcdhcpd check-syntax` to perform a brief syntax check. If you encounter any unexpected problems with your configuration — the server aborts with an error or does not return "done" on start — you should be able to find out what has gone wrong by looking for information either in the main system log `/var/log/messages` or on console 10 (Ctrl + Alt + F10).

Hosts with Fixed IP Addresses

As mentioned above, DHCP can also be used to assign a predefined, static address to a specific host for each request. As might be expected, addresses assigned explicitly will always take priority over addresses from the pool of dynamic addresses. Furthermore, a static address will never expire in the way a dynamic address would, for example, if there were not enough addresses available so the server needed to redistribute them among hosts.

To identify a host configured with a *static* address, dhcpd uses the hardware address, which is a globally unique, fixed numerical code consisting of six octet pairs for the identification of all network devices (e.g., `00:00:45:12:EE:F4`).

If the respective lines, like the ones in 48, are added to the configuration file 47 on page 376, the DHCP daemon will assign the same set of data to the corresponding host under all circumstances.

```
host earth {
 hardware ethernet 00:00:45:12:EE:F4;
 fixed-address 192.168.1.21;
}
```

File 48: *Additions to the Configuration File*

The structure of this entry is almost self-explanatory: The name of the respective host (host *host name*) is entered in the first line and the MAC address in the second line. On Linux hosts, this address can be determined with the command `ifstatus` followed by the network device (e.g., eth0). If necessary, activate the network card first: `ifup eth0`. The output should contain something like *link/ether 00:00:45:12:EE:F4*.

In the above example, a host with a network card having the MAC address *00:00:45:12:EE:F4* is assigned the IP address `192.168.1.21` and the host name `earth` automatically. The type of hardware to enter is `ethernet` in nearly all cases, although `token-ring`, which is often found on IBM systems, is also supported.

For More Information

As stated at the beginning of this chapter, these pages are only intended to provide a brief survey of what you can do with DHCP. For more information, the page of the *Internet Software Consortium* on the subject (`http:`

//www.isc.org/products/DHCP/) will prove a good source to read about the details of DHCP, including about version 3 of the protocol, currently in beta testing. Apart from that, you can always rely on the man pages for further help. Try `man dhcpd`, `man dhcpd.conf`, `man dhcpd.leases`, and `man dhcp-options`. Also, several books about *Dynamic Host Configuration Protocol* have been published over the years that take an in-depth look at the topic.

With `dhcpd`, it is even possible to offer a file to a requesting host, as defined with the parameter *filename*, and that this file may contain a bootable Linux kernel. This allows you to build client hosts which do not need a hard disk — they are enabled to load both their operating system and their network data over the network (*diskless clients*), which could be an interesting option for both cost and security reasons. Now add the package `alice` to all this and you can do some really amazing things.

File Synchronization

Today, many people use several computers — one computer at home, one or several computers at the workplace, and possibly a laptop or PDA on the road. Many files are needed on all these computers. You may want to be able work with all computers and modify the files and subsequently have the latest version of the data available on all computers.

Data Synchronization Software

Data synchronization is no problem for computers that are permanently linked by means of a fast network. In this case, use a network file system like NFS and store the files on a server, enabling all hosts to access the same data via the network. This approach is impossible if the network connection is poor or not permanent. When you are on the road with a laptop, you need to keep copies of all needed files on the local hard disk. However, it will then be necessary to synchronize modified files. When you modify a file on one computer, you have to make sure that a copy of the file is updated on all other computers. For occasional copies, this can be done manually with scp or rsync. However, if many files are involved, the procedure can be complicated and requires great care to avoid errors, such as overwriting a new file with an old file.

Caution

Risk of data loss

Before you start managing your data with a synchronization system, you should be well acquainted with the program used and test its functionality. A backup is indispensable for important files.

Caution

The time-consuming and error-prone task of manually synchronizing data can be avoided by using one of the programs that employ various methods to automate this job. The following summaries are merely intended to convey a general understanding of how these programs work and how they can be used. If you plan to use them, read the program documentation.

InterMezzo

The idea of InterMezzo is the implementation of a file system that exchanges files via the network like NFS, but stores local copies on the individual computers, thus ensuring that the files are available even when the network connection is down. The local copies can be edited. All changes are noted in a special log file. When the connection is restored, these changes are automatically forwarded and the files are synchronized. More information about InterMezzo is available in `/usr/share/doc/packages/InterMezzo/InterMezzo-HOWTO.html`, if the package is installed.

Unison

Unison is not a network file system. Rather, the files are simply saved and edited locally. The program Unison can be executed manually to synchronize files. When the synchronization is performed for the first time, a database is created on the two hosts, containing check sums, time stamps, and permissions of the selected files. The next time it is executed, Unison can recognize which files were changed and propose the transmission from or to the other host. Usually all suggestions can be accepted.

CVS

CVS, which is mostly used for managing program source versions, offers the possibility to keep copies of the files on multiple computers. Accordingly, it is also suitable for our purpose.

CVS maintains a central repository on the server, in which not only the files but also changes to files are saved. Changes that are performed locally are committed to the repository and can be retrieved from other computers by means of an update. Both procedures must be initiated by the user.

CVS is very resilient to errors in the event that changes occur on several computers. The changes are merged and, if changes took place in the same lines, a conflict will be reported. When a conflict occurs, the database remains in a consistent state. The conflict is only visible for resolution on the client host.

mailsync

In contrast to the synchronization tools covered in the previous sections, mailsync merely serves the purpose of synchronizing e-mails between mailboxes. The procedure can be applied to local mailbox files as well as to mailboxes on an IMAP server.

Based on the message ID contained in the e-mail header, the individual messages are either synchronized or deleted. Synchronization is possible between individual mailboxes and between mailbox hierarchies.

Determining Factors for Selecting a Program

Client-Server vs. Peer-to-Peer

Two different models are commonly used for distributing data. In the first model, all clients synchronize their files with a central server. The server must be accessible by all clients at least from time to time. This model is used by CVS and InterMezzo.

The other possibility is to let equal hosts synchronize their data among each other. This is the approach Unison uses.

Portability

InterMezzo is a solution that only supports Linux systems at present. In the past, the support was limited to 32-bit little endian architectures (ix86). Due to the migration from the perl-based lento to InterSync, this limitation no longer applies. Nevertheless, caution is needed when synchronizing between different architectures, as this feature has not yet been tested thoroughly. CVS and Unison are also available for many other operating systems, including various Unix and Windows systems.

Interactive vs. Automatic

In InterMezzo, the data synchronization normally occurs automatically in the background as soon as a network connection can be established with the server. Manual intervention is only required when conflicts arise.

In CVS and Unison, the data synchronization is started manually be the user. This enables more control over the data to synchronize and easier conflict handling. On the other hand, if the synchronization intervals are too long, conflicts are more likely to occur.

Speed

Due to their interactive character, Unison and CVS appear to be slower than InterMezzo, which operates in the background. Usually CVS is somewhat faster than Unison.

Conflicts: Incidence and Solution

Conflicts do not occur often in CVS, even if several people work on one large program project. This is because the documents are merged on the basis of individual lines. When a conflict occurs, only one client is affected. Usually conflicts can easily be resolved in CVS.

Unison reports conflicts, allowing the affected files to be excluded from the synchronization. However, changes cannot be merged as easy as in CVS.

Due to the noninteractive character of InterMezzo, conflicts cannot simply be resolved interactively. When conflicts occur, InterSync terminates with an alert message. In this case, the system administrator must intervene and possibly transfer files manually (using rsync or scp) to restore a consistent state.

Selecting and Adding Files

InterMezzo synchronizes the entire file system. Newly added files in the file system automatically appear on the other computers.

Configured in the simplest way possible, Unison synchronizes an entire directory tree. New files appearing in the tree are automatically included in the synchronization.

In CVS, new directories and files must be added explicitly using the command `cvs add`. Thus, the user has more control over the files to synchronize. On the other hand, new files are often overlooked, especially if the question marks in the output of `cvs update` are ignored because of the number of files.

History

An additional feature of CVS is that old file versions can be reconstructed. A brief editing remark can be inserted for each change and the development of the files can easily be traced later based on the content and the remarks. This is a valuable aid for theses and program texts.

Data Volume and Hard Disk Requirements

An adequate amount of free space for all distributed data is required on the hard disks of all involved hosts. CVS requires additional space for the repository on the server. The file history is also stored on the server, requiring even more space. When files in text format are changed, only the modified lines need to be saved. Binary files require additional space amounting to the size of the file every time the file is changed.

GUI

Unison offers a graphical user interface that displays the synchronization procedures Unison wants to perform. Accept the proposal or exclude individual files from the synchronization. In text mode, you can interactively confirm the individual procedures.

Experienced users normally control CVS from the command line. However, graphical user interfaces are available for Linux, such as cervisia, as well as for other operating systems, like wincvs. Many development tools (such as kdevelop) and text editors (such as emacs) provide CVS support. The resolution of conflicts is often much easier with these front-ends.

InterMezzo does not offer that much comfort. On the other hand, normally it does not require any interaction and should simply do its job in the background once it is configured.

User Friendliness

The configuration of InterMezzo is relatively difficult and should only be performed by a system administrator who has some experience with Linux. `root` privileges are required for the configuration. Unison is easy to use and is also suitable for newcomers.

CVS is more difficult to use. Users should understand the interaction between the repository and local data. Changes to the data should first be merged locally with the repository. This is done with the command `cvs update`. Then the data must be sent back to the repository with the command `cvs commit`. If this procedure has been grasped, newcomers will also be able to use CVS with ease.

Security Against Attacks

During transmission, the data should be protected against interception and manipulation. Both Unison and CVS can easily be used via ssh (Secure Shell), providing security against attacks of this kind. Use of CVS or Unison via rsh (Remote Shell) should be avoided and access by way of the CVS "pserver" mechanism in insecure networks is not advisable either.

In InterMezzo, the data synchronization is performed via http. This protocol can easily be intercepted or altered. To increase the level of security, SSL can be used, but this makes the configuration a little bit more difficult. InterMezzo should only be used without SSL in secure, trustworthy networks.

Protection Against Data Loss

CVS looks back on a long record of deployment by developers for the management of program projects and is extremely stable. As the development

	InterMezzo	Unison	CVS	mailsync
C-S/equal	C-S	P2P	C-S	P2P
Portability	Linux(i386)	Lin,Un*x,Win	Lin,Un*x,Win	Lin,Un*x
Interactive	-	x	x	-
Speed	++	-	o	+
Conflicts	-	o	++	+
File selection	File system	Directory	Selection	Mailbox
History	-	-	x	-
Hard disk space	o	o	--	+
GUI	-	+	o	-
Difficulty	-	+	o	o
Attacks	-	+(ssh)	+(ssh)	+(SSL)
Data loss	o	+	++	+

Table 14.1: *Features of the File Synchronization Tools -- = very poor, - = poor or not available, o = medium, + = good, ++ = excellent, x = available*

history is saved, CVS even provides protection against certain user errors, such as the unintentional deletion of a file.

Unison is still relatively new, but boasts a high level of stability. However, it is more sensitive to user errors. Once the synchronization of the deletion of a file has been confirmed, there is no way to restore the file.

Currently, InterMezzo is still in alpha stage. As the files are stored in a separate file system, the probability of a major data loss is relatively low. However, something could go wrong with the file synchronization itself, leaving behind wrecked files. The resilience to user errors is also limited: when a file is deleted locally, the same step is performed on all synchronized hosts. For this reason, backups are strongly recommended.

Introduction to InterMezzo

Architecture

InterMezzo uses a special file system type. The files are stored locally on the hard disks of the individual hosts. One of the file systems available in Linux is used for this purpose, preferably `ext3` or one of the other journaling file systems. Following the preparation of the partition, the file system is mounted with the type `intermezzo`. The kernel loads a module with InterMezzo support and all changes performed in this file system are written to a log file.

Following these preliminary steps, InterSync can be started. This program starts a web server, such as apache, other hosts can access to exchange data. When configuring a client, the name of the server must be specified in InterSync. This server will be contacted. A freely selectable designation for the file system — the "fileset" — is used to identify the file system.

InterSync is the next generation of the older InterMezzo system, which used a perl daemon called lento for the file synchronization. The documentation of InterSync still refers to this older system occasionally. However, this system has been replaced by InterSync. Unfortunately, the module included in standard kernels still supports lento and does not work with InterSync. A newer module is available in the SuSE kernel. For self-compiled kernels, the kernel module should be built with the package `km_intersync`.

The configuration of InterMezzo requires system administrator permissions. As indicated above, the configuration of InterMezzo is relatively difficult and should therefore be performed by an experienced system administrator. The configuration described below does not provide any protective mechanisms. Thus, others can easily intercept and manipulate the data synchronized with InterMezzo. For this reason, the configuration should only take place in a trustworthy environment, such as a wired private network protected by a firewall.

Configuring an InterMezzo Server

One of the hosts, preferably one having a good network connection, is assigned the role of the server. The entire data synchronization traffic traverses this server.

A separate file system must be set up for the data storage. If you do not have a spare partition and do not use LVM, the easiest way is to set up the file system in the form of a "loop device", which enables the use of a file in the local file system as a separate file system.

In the following example, an InterMezzo/ext3 file system with a size of 256 MB is set up in the root directory. The fileset is assigned the designation `fset0`.

```
dd if=/dev/zero of=/izo0 bs=1024 count=262144
mkizofs -r fset0 /izo0 # The warning can be ignored
```

This file system is mounted to `/var/cache/intermezzo`.

```
mount -t intermezzo -ofileset=fset0,loop /izo /var/cache/intermezzo
```

To do this automatically when the system is booted, an entry must be made in the file /etc/fstab. Now InterSync can be configured by customizing /etc/sysconfig/intersync. The following is entered in this file:

```
INTERSYNC_CLIENT_OPTS="--fset=fset0"
INTERSYNC_CACHE=/var/cache/intermezzo
INTERSYNC_PROXY=""
```

Now InterSync can be started with the following command:

```
/etc/init.d/intersync start
```

To do this automatically when the system is booted, the service can be entered in the list of services to start with insserv intersync.

Configuring InterMezzo Clients

The configuration of the clients (one server can serve multiple clients) is virtually the same as that of the server. The only difference is that the name of the server has to be specified in the variable INTERSYNC_CLIENT_OPTS when configuring /etc/sysconfig/intersync:

```
INTERSYNC_CLIENT_OPTS="-fset=fset0 -server=sun.cosmos.com"
```

sun.cosmos.commust be replaced with the network name of the server. If possible, the file systems on all computers should have the same size.

Troubleshooting

As soon as a client is started, changes to files located in the directory /var/cache/intermezzo/ should also be visible on the server and all other clients. If this is not the case, this is usually because no connection can be established to the server or due to a configuration error such as a wrong "fileset" designation. To find the error, analyze the log messages in the system log /var/log/messages. The web server started logs its data to /var/intermezzo-X/. The log file of the kernel, which records changes to the file system, is located in /var/cache/intermezzo/.intermezzo/fset0/kml and can be viewed with kmlprint.

When a conflict occurs, normally one of the InterSync processes is aborted. If the file synchronization is no longer performed, look for indications in the log file and use `/etc/init.d/intersync status` to check if the synchronization service is still active.

If necessary, refer to the package documentation:

```
/usr/share/doc/packages/intersync/
http://www.inter-mezzo.org/
```

Introduction to Unison

Uses

Unison is an excellent solution for synchronizing and transferring entire directory trees. The synchronization is performed in both directions and can be controlled by means of an intuitive graphical front-end. A console version can also be used. The synchronization can be automated so interaction with the user is not required, but experience is necessary.

Requirements

Unison must be installed on the client as well as on the server. In this context, the term *server* refers to a second, remote host (unlike CVS, explained in *CVS* on page 383).

In the following section, Unison is used together with ssh. An ssh client must be installed on the client and an ssh server must be installed on the server.

Using Unison

The approach used by Unison is the association of two directories ("roots") with each other. This association is symbolic — it is not an online connection. In our example, the directory layout is as follows:

Client:	Server:
`\bsphome/dir1`	`/home/geeko/dir2`

You want to synchronize these two directories. The user is known as `newbie`on the client and as `geeko` on the server. The first thing to do is to test if the client-server communication works:

```
unison -testserver /home/tux/dir1 ssh://geeko@server//homes/geeko/dir2
```

The most frequently encountered problems are:

- The Unison versions used on the client and server are not compatible
- The server does not allow SSH connections
- None of the two specified paths exists

If everything works, omit the option `-testserver`.

During the first synchronization, Unison does not yet know the relationship between the two directories and submits suggestions for the transfer direction of the individual files and directories. The arrows in the 'Action' column indicate the transfer direction. A question mark means that Unison is not able to make a suggestion regarding the transfer direction, as both versions were either changed or are new.

The arrow keys can be used to set the transfer direction for the individual entries. If the transfer directions are correct for all displayed entries, simply click "Go".

The characteristics of Unison (e.g., whether to perform the synchronization automatically in clear cases) can be controlled by means of command-line parameters specified when the program is started. The complete list of all parameters can be viewed with `unison --help`.

For each pair, a synchronization log is maintained in the user directory `~/.unison`. Configuration sets such as `~/.unison/example.prefs` can also be stored in this directory:

```
root=/home/foobar/dir1
root=ssh://fbar@server//homes/fbar/dir2
batch=true
```

File 49: *The file* `~/.unison/example.prefs`

To start the synchronization, specify this file as the command-line parameter as in `unison example.prefs`.

More Information

The official documentation of Unison is extremely useful. For this reason, this section merely provides a brief introduction. The complete manual is available at `http://www.cis.upenn.edu/~bcpierce/unison/` and in the SuSE package `unison`.

Introduction to CVS

Uses

CVS is suitable for synchronization purposes if individual files are edited frequently and are stored in a loose file format, such as ASCII text or program source text. The use of CVS for synchronizing data in other formats, such as JPEG files, is possible, but leads to large amounts of data, as all variants of a file are stored permanently on the CVS server. Furthermore, in such cases most of the capabilities of CVS cannot be used.

The use of CVS for synchronizing files is only possible if all workstations can access the same server. In contrast, with the program Unison the data can be passed by host A through the hosts B and C to the server S.

Configuring a CVS Server

The "server" is the place where all valid files are located, including the latest versions of all files. Any stationary workstation can be used as a server. If possible, the data of the CVS should be included in regular backups.

When configuring a CVS server, it might be a good idea to grant the user access to the server via ssh. If the user is known to the server as `newbie`and the CVS software is installed on the server as well as on the client (e.g., notebook), the following environment variables must be set on the client side:

```
CVS_RSH=ssh CVS_ROOT=newbie@server:/serverdir
```

The command `cvs init` can be used to initialize the CVS server from the client side. This needs to be done only once.

Finally, the synchronization must be assigned a name. Select or create a directory on the client that will exclusively contain files to manage with CVS (the directory can also be empty). The name of the directory will also be the name of the synchronization. In our example, we use a directory called `synchome`. Change to this directory and enter the following command to set the synchronization name to `synchome`:

```
cvs import synchome newbie newbie_0
```

Many CVS commands require a comment. For this purpose, CVS starts an editor (the editor defined in the environment variable `$EDITOR` or vi if no editor was defined). The editor call can be circumvented by entering the comment in advance on the command line, such as in the following example:

```
cvs import -m 'this is a test' synchome newbie newbie_0
```

Using CVS

From now on, the synchronization repository can be "checked out" from all hosts:

```
cvs co synchome
```

This creates a new subdirectory `synchome` on the client. To commit your changes to the server, change to the directory `synchome` (or one of its subdirectories) and enter `cvs commit`.

By default, all files (including subdirectories) are committed to the server. To commit only individual files or directories, specify them as in `cvs commit file1 directory1`. New files and directories must be added to the repository before they are committed to the server with a command like `cvs add file1 directory1`. Subsequently, the newly added files and directories can be committed: `cvs commit file1 directory1`.

If you change to another workstation, "check out" the synchronization repository, provided this has not been done during an earlier session at the same workstation (see above).

The synchronization with the server is started with the command `cvs update`. You can also update individual files or directories as in `cvs update file1 directory1`. If you first want to see the difference from the versions stored on the server, use the command `cvs diff`or `cvs diff file1 directory1`. Use `cvs -nq update` to see which files would be affected by an update.

Here are some of the status symbols displayed during an update:

U The local version was updated.

M The local version was modified. If there were changes on the server, it was possible to merge the differences in the local copy.

P The local version was patched with the version on the server.

C The local file conflicts with current version in the repository.

? This file does not exist in the CVS.

The status `M` indicates a locally modified file. Either commit the local copy to the server or remove the local file and run the update again. In this case, the missing file will be retrieved from the server. If you commit a locally modified file and the file was changed and commited before in the same line, you might get a conflict indicated with `C`. In this case look at conflict marks (»> and «<) in the file and decide between the two versions. As this can be a rather unpleasant job, you might decide to abandon your changes, delete the local file, and enter `cvs up` to retrieve the current version from the server.

More Information

This section merely offers a brief introduction to the many possibilities of CVS. Extensive documentation is available at the following URLs:

```
http://www.cvshome.org/
http://www.gnu.org/manual/
```

Introduction to mailsync

Uses

mailsync is mainly suitable for the following three tasks:

- Synchronization of locally stored e-mails with e-mails stored on a server
- Migration of mailboxes to a different format or to a different server
- Integrity check of a mailbox or search for duplicates

Configuration and Use

mailsync distinguishes between the mailbox itself (the "store") and the connection between two mailboxes (the "channel". The definitions of the stores and channels are stored in `~/.mailsync`. The following paragraphs explain a number of store examples.

A simple definition might appear as follows:

```
store saved-messages {
   pat  Mail/saved-messages
prefix  Mail/
}
```

`Mail/` is a subdirectory of the user's home directory that contains e-mail folders, including the folder `saved-messages`. If mailsync is started with

```
mailsync -m saved-messages
```

an index of all messages will be listed in `saved-messages`. If the following definition is made

```
store localdir {
          pat     Mail/*
          prefix  Mail/
}
```

the command `mailsync -m localdir` will cause all messages stored under `Mail/` to be listed. In contrast, the command `mailsync localdir` lists the folder names. The specifications of a store on an IMAP server appear as follows:

```
store imapinbox {
  server  {mail.edu.harvard.com/user=gulliver}
  ref     {mail.edu.harvard.com}
  pat     INBOX
}
```

The above example merely addresses the main folder on the IMAP server. A store for the subfolders would appear as follows:

```
store imapdir {
  server  {mail.edu.harvard.com/user=gulliver}
  ref     {mail.edu.harvard.com}
  pat     INBOX.*
  prefix  INBOX.
}
```

If the IMAP server supports encrypted connections, the server specification should be changed to

```
server  {mail.edu.harvard.com/ssl/user=gulliver}
```

or, if the server certificate is not known, to

```
server {mail.edu.harvard.com/ssl/novalidate-cert/user=gulliver}
```

The prefix will be explained later.

Now the folders under `Mail/` should be connected to the subdirectories on the IMAP server:

```
channel folder localdir imapdir {
        msinfo .mailsync.info
}
```

mailsync uses the `msinfo` file to keep track of the messages that have already been synchronized.

The command `mailsync folder` does the following:

- The mailbox pattern is expanded on both sides
- The prefix is removed from the resulting folder names
- The folders are synchronized in pairs (or created if they do not exist)

Accordingly, the folder `INBOX.sent-mail` on the IMAP server will be synchronized with the local folder `Mail/sent-mail` (provided the definitions explained above exist). The synchronization between the individual folder is performed as follows:

- If a message already exists on both sides, nothing happens
- If the message is missing on one side and is new (not listed in the `msinfo` file), it will be transmitted there
- If the message merely exists on one side and is old (already listed in the `msinfo` file), it will be deleted there (because the message that had obviously existed on the other side was deleted)

To know in advance which messages will be transmitted and which will be deleted during a synchronization, start mailsync with a channel *and* a store:

```
mailsync folder localdir
```

This command produces a list of all messages that are new on the local host as well as a list of all messages that would be deleted on the IMAP side during a synchronization. Similarly, the command

```
mailsync folder imapdir
```

produces a list of all messages that are new on the IMAP side and a list of all messages that would be deleted on the local host during a synchronization.

Possible Problems

In the event of a data loss, the safest method is to delete the relevant channel log file `msinfo`. Accordingly, all messages that only exist on one side will be viewed as new and therefore will be transmitted during the next synchronization.

Only messages with a message ID are included in the synchronization. Messages lacking a message ID are simply ignored, which means they are neither transmitted nor deleted. A missing message ID is usually caused by faulty programs when sending or writing a message.

On certain IMAP servers, the main folder is addressed with `INBOX` and subfolders are addressed with a randomly selected name (in contrast to INBOX and INBOX.name). Therefore, for such IMAP servers, it is not possible to specify a pattern exclusively for the subfolders.

After the successful transmission of messages to an IMAP server, the mailbox drivers (c-client) used by mailsync set a special status flag. For this reason, some e-mail programs, like mutt, are not able to recognize these messages as new. The setting of this special status flag can be disabled with the option `-n`.

More Information

The `README` in `/usr/share/doc/packages/mailsync/`, which is included in the package `mailsync`, provides additional information. In this connection, RFC 2076 "Common Internet Message Headers" is of special interest.

Heterogenous Networks

In addition to connecting to other Linux systems, Linux is also able to connect to Windows and Macintosh computers and communicate over Novell networks. This chapter shows the requirements for and configuration of heterogenous networks.

Samba

With the program Samba, convert a UNIX machine into a file and print server for DOS, Windows, and OS/2 machines. The Samba Project is run by the Samba Team and was originally developed by the Australian Andrew Tridgell.

Samba has now become a fully-fledged and rather complex product. This section presents an overview of its basic functionality. Samba offers plenty of online documentation. Enter `apropos samba` at the command line to display some manual pages or just browse the `/usr/share/doc/packages/samba` directory if Samba is installed for more online documentation and examples. A commented example configuration (`smb.conf.SuSE`) can be found in the `examples` subdirectory.

Samba uses the SMB protocol (Server Message Block) that is based on the NetBIOS services. Due to pressure from IBM, Microsoft released the protocol so other software manufacturers could establish connections to a Microsoft domain network. Samba sets the SMB protocol on top of the TCP/IP protocol, so the TCP/IP protocol must also be installed on all clients.

NetBIOS

NetBIOS is a software interface (API) designed for communication between machines. Here, a name service is provided. It enables machines connected to the net to reserve names for themselves. After reservation, these machines can be addressed by name. There is no central process that checks names. Any machine on the network can reserve as many names as it wants, if the names are not already in use. The NetBIOS interface can now be implemented for different network architectures. An implementation that works relatively closely with network hardware is called NetBEUI, but this is often referred to as NetBIOS. Network protocols implemented with NetBIOS are IPX from Novell (NetBIOS via TCP/IP) and TCP/IP.

The NetBIOS names sent via TCP/IP have nothing in common with the names used in `/etc/hosts` or those defined by DNS. NetBIOS uses its own, completely independent naming convention. However, it is recommended to use names that correspond to DNS host names to make administration easier. This is the default used by Samba.

Clients

All common operating systems, such as Mac OS X, Windows, and OS/2, support the SMB protocol. The TCP/IP protocol must be installed on all computers. Samba provides a client for the UNIX versions. For Linux, there is a file-system kernel module for SMB that allows the integration of SMB resources on the Linux system level.

SMB servers provide hardware space to their clients by means of shares. Here, a share includes a directory and its subdirectories. It is exported by means of a name and can be accessed by its name. The share name can be set to any name — it does not have to be the name of the export directory. A printer is also assigned a name. Clients can access the printer by its name.

Installing and Configuring the Server

If you intent to use Samba as server, install the package `samba`. The services required for Samba can be started with `rcnmb start && rcsmb start` and stopped with `rcsmb stop && rcnmb stop`.

The main configuration file of Samba is `/etc/samba/smb.conf`. This file can be divided into two logical parts. The `[global]` section contains the central and global settings. The `[share]` sections contain the individual file and printer shares. By means of this approach, details regarding the shares can be set differently or globally in the `[global]` section, which enhances the structural transparency of the configuration file.

The following sections provide an overview of some selected parameters.

The global Section

The following parameters of the `[global]` section need some adjustment to match the requirements of your network setup so other machines can access your Samba server via SMB in a Windows environment.

workgroup = TUX-NET This line assigns the Samba server to a work group. Replace `TUX-NET` with an appropriate work group of your networking environment. Your Samba server will appear under its DNS name unless this name has been assigned to any other machine in the net.

If the DNS name is not available, set the server name using `netbiosname=MYNAME`. See `man smb.conf` for more details about this parameter.

os level = 2 This parameter triggers whether your Samba server tries to become LMB "Local Master Browser" for its work group. Choose a very low value to spare the existing Windows net from any disturbances caused by a misconfigured Samba server. More information about this important topic can be found in the files `BROWSING.txt` and `BROWSING-Config.txt` under the `textdocs` subdirectory of the package documentation.

As long as there is no other SMB server present in your network, such as a Windows NT or 2000 server, and the Samba server should keep a list of all systems present in the local environment, set the `os level` to a higher value (for example, `65`). Your Samba server will thus be chosen as LMB for your local network.

When changing this setting, consider carefully how this could affect an existing Windows network environment. A misconfigured Samba server can cause serious problems when trying to become LMB for its work group. Contact your administrator and subject your configuration to some heavy testing either in an isolated network or at a noncritical time of day.

wins support and wins server If your Samba server should integrate into an existing Windows network with a running WINS server, remove the leading semicolon in front of the `wins server` parameter and adjust the IP address to the requirements of your network. If your Windows machines run in separate subnets, they should "see" each other, your Windows network does not have a WINS server running, and your Samba server should become the WINS server, uncomment the line holding the `wins support = yes` parameter. Make sure you activate this setting solely on a Samba server. `wins server` may not be used in this constellation.

Shares

The following examples illustrate how a CD-ROM drive and the user directories (`homes`) are made available to the SMB clients.

```
[cdrom]
```

```
;[cdrom]
;          comment = Linux CD-ROM
;          path = /media/cdrom
;          locking = No
```

File 50: *A CD-ROM Share*

To avoid having the CD-ROM drive accidentally made available, these lines are deactivated with comment marks (semicolons in this case). Remove the semicolons in the first column to share the CD-ROM drive via Samba.

[cdrom] and comment The entry [cdrom] is the name of the share that can be seen by all SMB clients on the net. An additional comment can be added to further describe the share.

path = /media/cdrom path exports the directory /media/cdrom.

By means of a very restrictive default configuration, this kind of share is only made available to the users present on this system. If this share should be made available to everybody, add a line guest ok = yes to the configuration. This setting gives read permissions to anyone on the network. It is recommended to handle this parameter with great care. This applies even more to the use of this parameter in the [global] section.

[homes]
The [home] share is of special importance here. If the user has a valid account and password for the Linux file server and his own home directory, he can be connected to it.

```
[homes]
        comment = Home Directories
        valid users = %S
        browseable = No
        read only = No
        create mask = 0640
        directory mask = 0750
```

***File 51:** homes Share*

[homes] As long as there is no other share using the share name of the user connecting to the SMB server, a share is dynamically generated using the [homes] share directives. The resulting name of the share is identical to the user name.

valid users=%S %S is replaced by the concrete name of the share as soon as a connection has been successfully established. For a [homes] share, this is always identical to the user's name. As a consequence, access rights to a user's share are restricted exclusively to the user.

browseable = No This setting enables the share to be invisible in the network environment.

read only = No By default, Samba prohibits write access to any exported share by means of the read only = Yes parameter. To make a share writeable, set the value read only = No, which is synonymous with writeable = Yes.

`create mask = 0640` Systems that are not based on MS Windows NT do not understand the concept of UNIX permissions, so they cannot assign permissions when creating a file.
The parameter `create mask` defines the access permissions assigned to newly created files. This only applies to writeable shares. In effect, this setting means the owner has read and write permissions and the members of the owner's primary group have read permissions. `valid users = %S` prevents read access even if the group has read permissions. Therefore, if you want the group to have read or write access, the line `valid users = %S` must be deactivated.

Security Levels

The SMB protocol comes from the DOS and Windows world and directly takes into consideration the problem of security. Each share access can be protected with a password. SMB has three possible ways of checking the permissions:

- **Share Level Security:** A password is firmly assigned to a share. Everyone who knows this password has access to that share.
- **User Level Security:** This variation introduces the concept of the user to SMB. Each user must register with the server with his own password. After registering, the server can grant access to individual exported shares dependent on user names.
- **Server Level Security:** To its clients, Samba pretends to be working in User Level Mode. However, it passes all password queries to another User Level Mode Server, which takes care of authentication. This setting expects an additional parameter (`password server =`).

The distinction between share, user, and server level security applies to the entire server. It is not possible to offer individual shares of a server configuration with Share Level Security and others with User Level Security. However, you can run a separate Samba server for each configured IP address on a system.

More information on this subject can be found in the file `textdocs/security_level.txt`. For multiple servers on one system, pay attention to the parameters `interfaces` and `bind interfaces only`.

Tip

For simple administration tasks with the Samba server, there is also the program swat. It provides a simple web interface with which to configure the Samba server conveniently. In a web browser, open `http://localhost:901` and log in as user `root`. swat is also activated in the files `/etc/inetd.conf` and `/etc/services`. More information about swat can be found in its man page.

Tip

Samba as Login Server

In networks where predominantly Windows clients are found, it is often preferable that users may only register with a valid account and password. This can be brought about with the help of a Samba server. In a Windows-based network, this task is handled by a Windows NT server configured as a Primary Domain Controller (PDC). The entries that must be made in the `[global]` section of `smb.conf` are shown in File 52.

```
[global]
 workgroup = TUX-NET
 domain logons = Yes
 domain master = Yes
```

File 52: *Global Section in smb.conf*

If encrypted passwords are used for verification purposes — the default settings in maintained MS Windows 9x versions, MS Windows NT 4.0 from service pack 3, and all later products — the Samba server must be able to handle these. The entry `encrypt passwords = yes` in the `[global]` section enables this functionality. In addition, it is necessary to prepare user accounts and passwords in an encryption format that conforms with Windows. This is done with the command `smbpasswd -a name`. Because, in accordance with the Windows NT domain concept, the computers themselves need a domain account, this is created with the following commands:

```
useradd machinename\$
smbpasswd -a -m machinename
```

File 53: *Setting up a Machine Account*

With the useradd command, a dollar sign is added. The command smbpasswd inserts this automatically when the parameter -m is used. The commented configuration example (/usr/share/doc/packages/Samba/examples/smb.conf.SuSE) contains settings that automate this task.

```
add user script = /usr/sbin/useradd -g machines \
                  -c "NT Machine Account" -d \
                  /dev/null -s /bin/false %m\$
```

***File 54:** Automated Setup of a Machine Account*

For the authentication method selected in this example, all user data is stored in /etc/samba/smbpasswd. To store your user data on an LDAP server, go to 'YaST' → 'System' → '/etc/sysconfig Editor' → 'Network Services' → 'Samba' then modify the parameter SAMBA_SAM to ldap. Finally, execute SuSEconfig -module samba.

Installing Clients

Clients can only access the Samba server via TCP/IP. NetBEUI and NetBIOS via IPX cannot be used with Samba.

Windows 9x and ME

Windows 9x and ME already have built-in support for TCP/IP. However, this is not installed as the default. To add TCP/IP, go to 'Control Panel' → 'System' and choose 'Add' → 'Protocols' → 'TCP/IP from Microsoft'. After rebooting your Windows machine, find the Samba server by double-clicking the desktop icon for the network environment.

Tip

To use a printer on the Samba server, install the standard or Apple-PostScript printer driver from the corresponding Windows version. It is best to link this to the Linux printer queue, which accepts Postscript as input format.

Tip

Optimization

`socket options` is one possible optimization provided with the sample configuration that ships with your Samba version. Its default configuration refers to a local ethernet network. For additional information about `socket options`, refer to the section "socket options" in the man page for `smb.conf` (`man smb.conf`) and to the man page for `socket` (`man 7 socket`). Additional information is provided in `textdocs/Speed.txt` and `textdocs/Speed2.txt`.

The standard configuration in `/etc/samba/smb.conf` is designed to provide useful settings based on the default settings of the Samba team. However, a ready-to-use configuration is not possible, especially in view of the network configuration and the work group name. The commented sample configuration `examples/smb.conf.SuSE` contains information that will be helpful for the adaption to local requirements.

Tip

The Samba team offers `textdocs/DIAGNOSIS.txt`, which is a step-by-step guide to check your configuration.

Tip

Netatalk

With the package `netatalk`, obtain a high-performance file and print server for MacOS clients. With it, access data on a Linux machine from a Macintosh or print to a connected printer. Netatalk is a suite of Unix programs that run on kernel-based DDP (Datagram Delivery Protocol) and implement the AppleTalk protocol family (ADSP, ATP, ASP, RTMP, NBP, ZIP, AEP, and PAP).

AppleTalk is, in effect, an equivalent to the more familiar TCP (Transmission Control Protocol). It has counterparts to many TCP/IP-based services, including services for resolving host names and time synchronization. For example, the command `aecho` (AEP, AppleTalk Echo Protocol) is used instead of `ping` (ICMP ECHO_REQUEST, Internet Control Message Protocol).

The three daemons described below are normally started on the server:

- atalkd ("AppleTalk Network Manager") that somewhat correlates with the programs ifconfig and routed
- afpd (AppleTalk Filing Protocol daemon), which provides an interface for Macintosh clients to Unix file systems
- papd (Printer Access Protocol daemon), which makes printers available in the (AppleTalk) network.

Of course, you can export server directories not only via Netatalk, but also, at the same time, via Samba for Windows clients (see *Clients* on page 400) and via NFS (see *NFS — Shared File Systems* on page 371), which is very useful in heterogeneous network environments. This centralizes the management of data backup and user permissions on the Linux server.

There are some important details to consider when using Netatalk:

- Due to Macintosh client restrictions, the user passwords on the server cannot be longer than eight characters.
- Macintosh clients cannot access Unix files with names longer than 31 characters.
- File names may not contain colons (`':'`) because they serve as path name separators in MacOS.

Configuring the File Server

In the default configuration, Netatalk is already fully functional as a file server for home directories of the Linux system. To use the extended features, define some settings in the configuration files. These are located in the /etc/atalk directory.

All configuration files are pure text files. Text that follows a hash mark '#' (comments) and empty lines can be disregarded.

Configuring the Network — atalkd.conf

Define, in /etc/atalk/atalkd.conf, over which interfaces services are provided. This is usually eth0, which means that it suffices if the only value entered here is eth0. In the example file that comes with Netatalk, this is the case. Enter additional interfaces to use several network cards at the same time. When the server is started, it will search the network for already existing zones and servers and modify the corresponding lines by entering the set AppleTalk network addresses. You will then find a line such as

```
eth0 -phase 2 -net 0-65534 -addr 65280.57
```

at the end of the file. To make more complex configurations, find examples for this in the configuration file. Find documentation about additional options in the manual page of afpd.

Defining File Servers — afpd.conf

The afpd.conf file contains definitions for how your file server appears on MacOS machines as an item under the 'Chooser' dialog. As is the case with the other configuration files, these also contain detailed comments explaining the wide variety of options.

If you do not change anything here, the default server will simply be started and displayed with the host name in the 'Chooser'. Therefore, you do not necessarily need to enter anything. However, you can give additional file servers a variety of names and options here, for instance, to provide a specific "guest server" where everybody can save files as "guest",

```
"Guest server" -uamlist uams_guest.so
```

Define a server that denies guests access, but which is only accessible for users who already exist in the Linux system with:

```
"Font server" -uamlist uams_clrtxt.so,uams_dhx.so
```

This behavior is controlled by the option `uamlist`, followed by a list of authentication modules to use, separated by commas. If you do not provide this option, all procedures are active by default.

An AppleShare server not only provides its services by default via AppleTalk, but also ("encapsulated") via TCP/IP. The default port is 548. Assign dedicated ports to additional AppleShare servers (on the same machine) if these should also run via TCP. The availability of the service via TCP/IP enables access to the server even over non-AppleTalk networks, such as the Internet.

In this case, the syntax would read:

```
"Font server" -uamlist uams_clrtxt.so,uams_dhx.so -port 12000
```

The AppleShare server, set to the port 12000, then appears in the network with the name "Font server" and will not allow guest access. In this way, it is also accessible via TCP/IP routers.

The file `AppleVolumes.default` (described in detail below) defines which directories located on the server are made available by each AppleShare server as network *volumes*. Define other files containing unique descriptions for each AppleShare server using the option `-defaultvol`, such as with (in one line):

```
"Guest server" -uamlist uams_guest.so -defaultvol
/etc/atalk/AppleVolumes.guest
```

Further options are explained in the `afpd.conf` file itself.

Directories and Access Permissions — `AppleVolumes.default`

Here, define directories to export. The access permissions are defined via the customary Unix user and group permissions. This is configured in the `AppleVolumes.default` file.

Along with `AppleVolumes.default`, additional files can be created, such as `AppleVolumes.guest`, used by some servers (by giving the option `-defaultvol` in the `afpd.conf` file — see previous section).

Note

Here, the syntax has partially changed. Take this into consideration if you are updating this version from a previous one. For example, it is now `allow:` instead of `access=` (a typical symptom would be if, instead of the drive descriptions, you were to see a display of the drive options on the Mac clients in the 'Chooser'.) Because the new files are created with the `.rpmnew` endings during an update, it is possible that your previous settings may no longer function as a result of the modified syntax. Create backups of your configuration files, copy your old configurations from them into your new files, then rename these files to the proper names. This way, you will benefit from the current comments contained in the configuration files, which provide a detailed explanation of the diverse options.

Note

The syntax

```
/usr/local/psfonts "PostScript Fonts"
```

indicates that the Linux directory `/usr/local/psfonts` located in the root directory is available as an AppleShare volume with the name "PostScript Fonts".

Options are separated by a space and attached to the end of a line. A very useful option is the access restriction:

```
/usr/local/psfonts "PostScript Fonts" allow:User1,@group0
```

which restricts access to the volume "PostScript Fonts" to the user "User1" and all members of the group "group0". The users and groups entered here must be known to the Linux system. Likewise, explicitly deny users access with `deny:User2`.

These restrictions only apply to access via AppleTalk and not to the normal access rights users have if they can log in to the server itself.

Netatalk maps the customary Resource Fork of MacOS files to `.AppleDouble` directories in the Linux file system. Using the `noadouble` option, set these directories to be created only when they are actually needed. Syntax:

```
/usr/local/guests "Guests" options:noadouble
```

Additional options and features can be found in the explanations included in the file itself.

The tilde ('~') in this configuration file stands for the home directory for each and every user on the server. This way, every user can easily access his home directory without each one being defined explicitly here. The example file installed already includes a tilde, which is why Netatalk makes the home directory available by default as long as you do not modify anything in this file.

afpd also searches for a file `Applevolumes` or `.Applevolumes` in the home directory of a user logged on to the system. Entries in this file supplement the entries in the server files `AppleVolumes.system` and `AppleVolumes.default` to enable individual type and creator file specifications and to access specific directories. These entries are extensions and do not allow access for the user for whom access permission is denied from the server side.

The `netatalk.pamd` file is used, via PAM (pluggable authentication modules), for authentication purposes. Using PAM is, however, irrelevant in this context.

File Specifications — `AppleVolumes.system`

In the `AppleVolumes.System` file, define which customary MacOS type and creator specifications are assigned to certain file endings. An entire series of default values are already predefined. If a file is displayed by a generic white icon, there is not yet an entry for it in this file. If you encounter a problem with a text file belonging to another system, which cannot be opened properly in MacOS or vice versa, check the entries there.

Configuring the Print Server

A laserwriter service is made available by configuring the `papd.conf` file. The printer must be already functioning locally via lpd, so configure a printer as described in Chapter *Printer Operation* on page 141 you can print a text file locally using the command `lpr file.txt`, the first step has been successfully completed.

You do not necessarily need to enter anything in `papd.conf` if a local printer is configured in Linux, because print jobs can simply be forwarded to the print daemon `lpd` without additional specifications. The printer registers itself in the AppleTalk network as Laserwriter. You can, however, extend your printer entries by referring to File 55.

```
Printer_Reception:pr=lp:pd=/etc/atalk/kyocera.ppd
```

File 55: `papd.conf`

This causes the printer named Printer_Reception to appear as a 'Chooser' item. The corresponding printer description file is usually provided by the vendor. Otherwise, refer to the file `Laserwriter` located in the 'System Extensions' folder. However, when using this file you often cannot use all of the printer's features.

Starting the Server

The server can be started at system boot time via its "init script" or manually with `rcatalk start`. The init script is located at `/etc/init.d/atalk`.

The actual starting of the server takes place in the background. It takes about a minute until the AppleTalk interfaces are set up and responsive. Check for the status as shown in the following (all servers are running if `OK` is reported three times):

```
earth:~ #  rcatalk status
Checking for service atalk:OKOKOK
```

From a Mac running MacOS, check for AppleTalk activation, choose 'Filesharing', then double-click 'AppleShare'. The names of the servers should then appear in the window. Double-click a server and log in. It should then be possible to access a shared volume.

The procedure is a bit different for AppleShare servers configured to use TCP only (and no DDP). To connect, press the 'Server IP address' button and enter the respective IP address. If necessary, append the port number, separated by a colon (`':'`).

Additional Information

To take full advantage of all the options netatalk offers, read the corresponding manual pages. Find them by entering the command `rpm -qd netatalk`. The `/etc/atalk/netatalk.conf` file is not used in our netatalk version, so disregard it.

Helpful URLs:

- `http://netatalk.sourceforge.net/`
- `http://www.umich.edu/~rsug/netatalk/`
- `http://thehamptons.com/anders/netatalk/`
- `http://cgi.zettabyte.net/fom-serve/netatalk/cache/1.html`

We do not currently recommend trying to access an AppleShare file system hosted on a Macintosh from a Linux machine. Software is available, but it is in early development stages. For more information, refer to `http://www.panix.com/~dfoster/afpfs/`.

Netware Emulation with MARSNWE

The Netware emulator MARSNWE can easily replace the file and print services of a Novell Netware 2.2 or 3.11 server. It can also be used in this manner as an IPX router. However, it does not offer the features of newer Netware versions, such as NDS (Netware Directory Services). Workstations running DOS or Windows already configured to access a Netware 2.2, 3.11, or 3.12 server can use the Linux server with the Netware emulator MARSNWE as a server without having to change the configuration much. Administration is best taken care of in Linux, because Novell system administration applications can only be utilized under certain conditions and have licensing issues as well.

Starting the Netware Emulator MARSNWE

MARSNWE in SuSE Linux can be started immediately after installation, because it is already preconfigured for initial testing. The required IPX support on the part of the kernel is available as a loadable kernel module and is automatically loaded by the start script. The IPX interface is automatically set up by MARSNWE. At this point, the network number and the protocol to use will both be read from the extensively commented configuration file `/etc/nwserv.conf`. MARSNWE is started via the command `rcnwe start`. The `done` message to the right of the screen in green indicates that MARSNWE has been successfully started. Use `rcnwe status` to check whether the Netware emulator is running. Halt it with `rcnwe stop`.

The Configuration File /etc/nwserv.conf

The configuration options are summarized in enumerated sections. Every configuration line starts with the number of the corresponding section. Only sections 1 to 22 are relevant here. Not all numbers are used, however. Most of the time, the following sections are enough for the configuration:

1 Netware Volumes

2 Server Name

4 IPX Network

13 User Names

21 Printers

After modifying the configuration, MARSNWE must be restarted with the command `rcnwe restart`.

The configuration options in detail:

Volumes (Section 1):

```
1     SYS     /usr/local/nwe/SYS/     kt     711 600
```

Here, the volumes to export are defined. Every line begins with the section number (here 1), followed by the volume name and the server directory path. In addition, various options can be specified represented by specific letters and a UMASK for the generation of both directories and files. If a UMASK is not specified, the default value from Section 9 is used. The volume for SYS is already entered. To avoid problems with uppercase and lowercase letters in the file names, it is recommended to use the k option, so all the file names will be converted to lowercase letters.

Server Name (Section 2):

```
2     MARS
```

This specification is optional. The host name will be used by default.

Internal Network Number (Section 3):

```
3     auto
```

The internal network number is generated from the network card's MAC address if auto is specified here. This setting is usually retained.

IPX Configuration (Section 4):

```
4     0x0      *       AUTO            1
4     0x22     eth0    ethernet_ii     1
```

Here, the Netware network number is specified as well as to which network interface using which protocol the bind should be made. The first example sets up everything automatically, while the second binds the network number 0x22 to the network card eth0 with the frame type Ethernet-II. If you have several network cards and enter all these with different network numbers, IPX will be routed between them.

Create Mode (Section 9):

```
9    0751    0640
```

Enters the default permission with which directories and files are created.

GID and GID with minimal permissions (Section 10, 11):

```
10   65534
11   65534
```

Group ID and user ID for users not logged in. Here nogroup and nobody.

Supervisor Login (Section 12):

```
12   SUPERVISOR      root
```

The supervisor is mapped to user `root`.

User Logins (Section 13):

```
13   LINUX           linux
```

Netware users are assigned to Linux users. A static password can optionally be entered here.

Automatic User Mapping (Section 15):

```
15   0       top-secret
```

If `1` is specified here instead of `0`, Linux logins will automatically be made available as Netware logins. In this case, the password is "top-secret".

Printer Queues (Section 21):

```
21   LP       -       lpr -
```

The first parameter LP is the name of the Netware printer. Second, the name of the spool directory can be given. The print command is listed last.

Print Server (Section 22):

```
22   PS_NWE  LP_PS   1
```

Printers can be defined here that are accessed over the pserver by the package ncpfs.

Access to Netware Servers and Their Administration

The package ncpfs is a collection of small programs that can be used to administer a Netware 2.2 or 3.11 server from Linux, mount Netware volumes, or manage printers. To access Netware servers newer than version 4, the bindery emulation and IPX must be enabled on them.

The following programs are available. Refer to the man pages for their functions:

nwmsg	ncopy	ncpmount	ncpumount
nprint	nsend	nwauth	nwbocreate
nwbols	nwboprops	nwborm	nwbpadd
nwbpcreate	nwbprm	nwbpset	nwbpvalues
nwdir	nwdpvalues	nwfsctrl	nwfsinfo
nwfstime	nwgrant	nwpasswd	nwpurge
nwrevoke	nwrights	nwsfind	nwtrustee
nwtrustee2	nwuserlist	nwvolinfo	pqlist
pqrm	pqstat	pserver	slist

ncpmount, for example, is an essential program used to mount volumes from a Netware server in Linux. In turn, ncpumount is used to unmount them. package ncpfs contains tools for configuring the IPX protocol and IPX routing:

```
ipx_cmd
ipx_configure
ipx_interface
ipx_internal_net
ipx_route
```

With ipx_configure and ipx_interface, configure the the network card's IPX. If you already have MARSNWE running, however, it will take care of this configuration automatically.

IPX Router with ipxrip

Another package for converting Linux into an IPX router is package `ipxrip`. Usually, it is not needed, because an IPX router can be configured with MARSNWE or the tools from package `ncpfs`.

Internet

A lot could be written about the Internet, but most applications just work "out of the box" after configuring Internet access with YaST. Therefore, this chapter only focuses on more interesting aspects: the configuration of the smpppd (SuSE Meta PPP-Daemon), the manual configuration of ADSL access in case problems arise with the YaST2 configuration, and the configuration of the Squid proxy.

The smpppd as Dial-up Assistant

Program Components for the Internet Dial-Up

Most home users do not have a dedicated line connecting them to the Internet. Rather, they use dial-up connections. Depending on the dial-up method (ISDN or DSL), the connection is controlled by the ipppd or the pppd. Basically, all that needs to be done to go online is to start these programs correctly.

If you have a flat-rate connection that does not generate any additional costs for the dial-up connection, simply start the respective daemon. Control the dial-up connection with a KDE applet or a command-line interface. If the Internet gateway is not the host you are using, you might want to control the dial-up connection by way of a network host.

This is where smpppd is involved. It provides a uniform interface for auxiliary programs and acts in two directions: first, it programs the required pppd or ipppd and controls its dial-up properties. Second, it makes various providers available to the user programs and transmits information about the current status of the connection. As smpppd can also be controlled by way of the network, it is suitable for controlling dial-up connections to the Internet from a workstation in a private subnetwork.

Configuring the smpppd

The connections provided by smpppd are automatically configured by YaST. The actual dial-up programs kinternet and cinternet are also preconfigured. Manual settings are only required to configure additional features of the smpppd, such as remote control.

The configuration file of smpppd is `/etc/smpppd.conf`. By default, it does not enable remote control. The most important options of this configuration file are as follows:

open-inet-socket = `<yes|no>` To control smpppd via the network, this option must be set to `yes`. The port on which the smpppd will listen is `3185`. If this parameter is set to `yes`, the parameters `bind-address`, `host-range`, and `password` should also be set accordingly.

bind-address = `<ip>` If a host has several IP addresses, this parameter can be used to determine by which IP address smpppd should accept connections.

host-range = <min ip> <max ip> The parameter host-range can be used to define a network range. Hosts whose IP addresses are within this range are granted access to smpppd. All hosts not within this range are denied access.

password = <password> By assigning a password, limit the clients to authorized hosts. As this is a plain-text password, you should not overrate the security it provides. If no password is assigned, all clients are entitled to access smpppd.

More information about smpppd is available in the man page for smpppd (man 8 smpppd) and the man page for smpppd.conf (man 5 smpppd.conf).

Configuring kinternet and cinternet for Remote Use

The programs kinternet and cinternet can be used locally as well as for controlling a remote smpppd. cinternet is the the command-line counterpart of the graphical kinternet. To prepare these utilities for use with a remote smpppd, edit the configuration file /etc/smpppd-c.conf manually or using kinternet. This file only uses three options:

server = <server> Here, specify the host on which the smpppd runs. If this host is the same as the default gateway of the host, it is sufficient to set the gateway-fallback to yes.

gateway-fallback = <yes|no> If no server was specified and there is no local smpppd, this option, which is enabled by default, causes a search for an smpppd on the default gateway.

password = <password> Insert the password selected for smpppd.

If the smpppd is active, you can now try to access it. This can be done with the command cinternet --verbose --interface-list. If you experience difficulties at this point, refer to the man page for smpppd-c.conf (man 5 smpppd-c.conf) and the man page for cinternet (man 8 cinternet).

Configuring an ADSL or T-DSL Connection

Default Configuration

Currently, SuSE Linux supports DSL connections that work with the point-to-point over ethernet protocol (PPPoE) used by most major providers. If you are not sure what protocol is used for your DSL connections, ask your provider. If you have a single-user workstation with a graphical interface, the DSL connection should be set up with the YaST2 modules ADSL or T-DSL.

1. The `ppp` and `smpppd` packages must be installed. It is best to use YaST2 for this purpose.
2. Configure your network card with YaST2. Do not activate dhcp, but set a fixed IP address instead, such as `192.168.2.22`.
3. The parameters set with the DSL module of YaST2 will be saved in the file `/etc/sysconfig/network/providers/provider0`. In addition, there are configuration files for the smpppd (SuSE meta ppp daemon) and its front-ends kinternet and cinternet. For information, refer to `man smpppd`.
4. If necessary, start the network with the command `rcnetwork start` and the smpppd with the command `rcsmpppd start`.
5. On a system without a graphical user interface, use the commands `cinternet -start` and `cinternet -stop` to establish or terminate a connection. On a graphical user interface, this can be done with kinternet. This program is started automatically in KDE if you used YaST2 to set up DSL. Click the gear icon in the control panel. Select 'Communication/Internet' → 'Internet Tools' → 'kinternet'. A plug icon will appear in the control panel. Start the connection by clicking it once and, by clicking it again, terminate the connection.

DSL Connection by Dial-on-Demand

Dial-on-demand means that the connection will automatically be set up when the user goes online, for example, when visiting a web site in a browser or when sending an e-mail. After a certain amount of idle time when no data is sent or received, the connection will automatically be dropped. Because the dial-up connection via PPPoE, the protocol for ADSL, is very fast, it seems as if it were a dedicated line to the Internet.

Using dial-on-demand, however, really only makes sense if you have a flat-rate connection. If you use it but are charged for time online, make sure tthere are no interval processes, such as a cronjob, periodically establishing a connection. This could get quite expensive.

Although a permanent online connection would also be possible using a DSL flat-rate connection, there are certain advantages to having a connection that only exists for a short amount of time when needed:

- Most providers drop the connection after a certain period of time.
- A permanent connection can be considered as a drain on resources (e. g., IP addresses).
- Being online permanently is a security risk, because hackers may be able to comb the system systematically for vulnerable areas. A system that is only accessible over the Internet when necessary and is always changing IP addresses is significantly more difficult to attack.

Dial-on-demand can be enabled using YaST2 (also refer to the *User Guide*). Alternatively, set it up manually:

Set the parameter DEMAND="yes" in the `/etc/sysconfig/network/providers/provider0` file then define an idle time via the variable IDLETIME="60". This way, an unused connection will be dropped after sixty seconds.

Proxy Server: Squid

The following chapter describes how caching web sites assisted by a proxy server works and what the advantages of using proxy servers are. The most popular proxy cache for Linux and UNIX platforms is Squid. The chapter discusses its configuration, the specifications required to get it running, how to configure the system to do transparent proxying, how to gather statistics about the cache's use with the help of programs like Calamaris and cachemgr, and how to filter web contents with squidGuard.

About Proxy Caches

Squid acts as a proxy cache. It behaves like an agent that receives requests from clients, in this case web browsers, and passes them to the specified server. When the requested objects arrive at the agent, it stores a copy in a disk cache. Benefits arise when different clients request the same objects: these will be served directly from the disk cache, much faster than obtaining them from the Internet and, at the same time, saving overall bandwidth for the system.

Tip

Squid covers a wide range of features, including intercommunicating hierarchies of proxy servers to divide the load, defining strict access control lists to all clients accessing the proxy, and, with the help of other applications, allowing or denying access to specific web pages. It also can obtain statistics about the most visited web sites, user usage of the Internet, and others.

Tip

Squid is not a generic proxy. It proxies normally only between HTTP connections. It does also support the protocols FTP, Gopher, SSL, and WAIS, but it does not support other Internet protocols, such as Real Audio, news, or videoconferencing. Because Squid only supports the UDP protocol to provide communication between different caches, many other multimedia programs will not be supported.

Some Facts About Cache Proxying

Squid and Security

It is also possible to use Squid together with a firewall to secure internal networks from the outside using a proxy cache. The firewall denies all clients access to external services except Squid. All web connections must be established by way of the proxy.

If the firewall configuration includes a DMZ, set the proxy there. In this case, it is important that all computers in the DMZ send their log files to hosts inside the secure network. The possibility of implementing a "transparent" proxy is covered in *Transparent Proxy Configuration* on page 435.

Multiple Caches

Several proxies can be configured in such a way that objects can be exchanged between them, thus reducing the total system load and increasing the chances of finding an object already existing in the local network. It enables the configuration of cache hierarchies so a cache is able to forward object requests to sibling caches or to a parent cache. It can get objects from another cache in the local network or directly from the source.

Choosing the appropriate topology for the cache hierarchy is very important, because we do not want to increase the overall traffic on the network. For example, in a very large network, it is possible to configure a proxy server for every subnetwork and connect it to a parent proxy, connected in its turn to the proxy cache from the ISP. All this communication is handled by ICP (Internet Cache Protocol) running on top of the UDP protocol. Data transfers between caches are handled using HTTP (Hyper Text Transmission Protocol) based on TCP.

To find the most appropriate server from which to get the objects, one cache sends an ICP request to all sibling proxies. These will answer the requests via ICP responses with a HIT code if the object was detected or a MISS if it was not. If multiple HIT responses were found, the proxy server will decide which server to download depending on factors such as which cache sent the fastest answer or which one is closer. If no satisfactory responses have been sent, the request will be sent to the parent cache.

Tip

To avoid duplication of objects in different caches in our network, other ICP protocols are used, such as CARP (Cache Array Routing Protocol) or HTCP (HyperText Cache Protocol). The more objects maintained in the network, the greater the possibility of finding the desired one.

Tip

Caching Internet Objects

Not all objects available in the network are static. There are a lot of dynamically generated CGI pages, visitor counters, and encrypted SSL content documents. Objects like this are not cached because they will have changed each time they are accessed.

The question remains as to how long all the other objects stored in the cache should stay there. To determine this, all objects in the cache are assigned one of three states.

Web and proxy servers find out the status of an object by adding headers to these objects, such as "Last modified" or "Expires" and the corresponding date. Other headers specifying that objects must not be cached are used as well.

Objects in the cache are normally replaced, due to a lack of free hard disk space, using algorithms such as LRU (Last Recently Used). It consists of first replacing the less requested objects.

System Requirements

The most important thing is to determine the maximum load the system will have to bear. It is, therefore, important to pay more attention to the load picks, because these might be more than four times the day's average. When in doubt, it would be better to overestimate the system's requirements, because having Squid working close to the limit of its capabilities could lead to a severe loss in the quality of the service. The following sections point to the system factors in order of significance.

Hard Disks

Speed plays an important role in the caching process, so this factor deserves special attention. In hard disks, this parameter is described as "random seek time", measured in milliseconds. As a rule of thumb, the lower this value, the better.

Size of the Disk Cache

It depends on a few factors. In a small cache, the probability of a HIT (finding the requested object already located there) will be small, because the cache is easily filled so the less requested objects will be replaced by newer ones. On the other hand, if `1 GB` is available for the cache and the users only surf `10 MB` a day, it will take more than one hundred days to fill the cache.

Probably the easiest way to determine the needed cache size is to consider the maximum transfer rate of our connection. With a `1 Mbit/s` connection, the maximum transfer rate will be `125 KB/s`. If all this traffic ends up in the cache, in one hour it will add up to `450 MB` and, assuming that all this traffic is generated in only 8 working hours, it will reach `3.6 GB` in one day. Because the connection was not used up to its maximum capacity, assume that the total amount of data going through the cache is about `2 GB`. In the example, to keep all the browsed data of *one* day in the cache, `2 GB` of disk space is required for Squid. Summing up, Squid tends to read and write smaller blocks from or to the disk, making it more important how fast it detects these objects on the disk than having a fast disk.

RAM

The amount of memory required by Squid directly correlates to the number of objects in the cache. Squid also stores cache object references and frequently requested objects in the main memory to speed up retrieval of this data. The memory is up to one million times faster than a hard disk. Compare the seek time of a hard disk, about 10 milliseconds, with the 10 nanoseconds access time of the newer RAM memories.

It is very important to have more than enough memory for the Squid process, because system performance will be dramatically reduced if it must be swapped to disk. The cachemgr.cgi tool can be used for the cache memory management. This tool is introduced in *cachemgr.cgi* on page 438.

CPU

Squid is not a program that requires intensive CPU usage. The load of the processor is only increased while the contents of the cache are being loaded or checked. Using a multiprocessor machine does not increase the performance of the system. To increase efficiency, it is better to buy faster disks or add more memory.

Some examples of configured systems running Squid are available at `http://wwwcache.ja.net/servers/squids.html`.

Starting Squid

Squid is already preconfigured in SuSE Linux, so you can start it easily right after installation. A prerequisite for a smooth start is an already configured network, at least one name server and, of course, Internet access. Problems can arise if a dial-up connection is used with dynamic DNS configuration. In cases such as this, at least the name server should be clearly entered, because Squid will not start if it does not detect a DNS server in the `/etc/resolv.conf`.

To start Squid, enter `rcsquid start` at the command line as `root`. For the initial start-up, the directory structure must first be defined in `/var/squid/cache`. This is done by the start script `/etc/init.d/squid` automatically and can take a few seconds or even minutes. If `done` appears to the right in green, Squid has been successfully loaded. Test Squid's functionality on the local system by entering `localhost` and `Port 3128` as proxy in the browser. To allow all users to access Squid and thus the Internet, change the entry in the configuration file `/etc/squid/squid.conf` from `http_access deny all` to `http_access allow all`. However, in doing so, consider that Squid is made completely accessible to anyone by this action. Therefore, define ACLs that control access to the proxy. More on this is available in *Options for Access Controls* on page 433.

If you have made changes in the configuration file /etc/squid/squid.conf, instruct Squid to load the changed file. Do this by entering rcsquid reload or restart Squid with rcsquid restart. With rcsquid status, determine whether the proxy is running. Use rcsquid stop to halt Squid. The latter can take a while, because Squid waits up to half a minute (shutdown_lifetime option in /etc/squid/squid.conf) before dropping the connections to the clients then will still need to write its data to the disk. Terminating Squid with kill or killall can lead to the destruction of the cache, which will then have to be fully removed to restart Squid.

If Squid dies after a short period of time, although it has seemingly been started successfully, it can be the result of a faulty name server entry or a missing /etc/resolv.conf file. The cause of the start failure would then be logged by Squid in the /var/squid/logs/cache.log file.

If Squid should be loaded automatically when the system boots, reset the entry START_SQUID=no to START_SQUID=yes in the /etc/sysconfig/squid file.

An uninstall of Squid will remove neither the cache or the log files. Manually delete the /var/cache/squid directory.

Local DNS Server

Setting up a local DNS server, such as BIND8 or BIND9, makes absolute sense even if the server does not manage its own domain. It will then simply act as a "caching-only DNS" and will also be able to resolve DNS requests via the root name server without requiring any special configuration. If you enter this in the /etc/resolv.conf with the IP address 127.0.0.1 for localhost, Squid will detect a valid name server when it starts up. Configuring a name server is discussed in *DNS — Domain Name Service* on page 358. It is sufficient, however, to install the package and to boot it. The name server of the provider should be entered in the configuration file /etc/named.conf under forwarders along with its IP address. If you have a firewall running, even if it is just personal-firewall, make sure the DNS requests will be sent.

The Configuration File /etc/squid/squid.conf

All Squid proxy server settings are made in the /etc/squid/squid.conf file. To start Squid for the first time, no changes will be necessary in this file, but external clients will initially be denied access. The proxy needs to be made available for the localhost, usually with 3128 as port. The options are extensive and therefore provided with ample documentation and examples in the preinstalled /etc/squid/squid.conf file. Nearly all entries begin with a # sign (the lines are commented out) and the relevant specifications can be found at the end of the line. The given values almost always correlate with the default values, so removing the comment signs without changing any of the parameters actually has little effect in most cases. It is better to leave the sample as it is and reinsert the options along with the modified parameters in the line below. In this way, easily interpret the default values and the changes.

Note

Update from Version 2.4 to Version 2.5
Following an update of Squid from version 2.4 to version 2.5, the cache of Squid must be deleted, as the directory structure was changed.

Note

If you have updated from an earlier Squid version, it is recommended to edit the new /etc/squid/squid.conf and only apply the changes made in the previous file. If you try to implement the old squid.conf again, run a risk that the configuration will no longer function, because options are sometimes modified and new changes added.

General Configuration Options (Selection)

http_port 3128 This is the port where Squid listens for client requests. The default port is 3128, but 8080 is also common. If desired, specify several port numbers separated by blank spaces.

cache_peer <hostname> <type> <proxy-port> <icp-port> Here, enter a parent proxy as "parent", for example, or use that of the provider. As <hostname>, the name and IP address of the proxy to use are entered and, as <type>, parent. For <proxy-port>, enter the port number that is also specified by the operator of the parent for use in the browser, usually 8080. Set the <icp-port> to 7 or 0 if the ICP port of the parent is not known and its use is irrelevant to the provider. In addition, default and no-query should be specified after the port numbers to strictly prohibit the use of the ICP protocol. Squid will then behave like a normal browser as far as the provider's proxy is concerned.

cache_mem 8 MB This entry defines the amount of memory Squid can use for the caches. The default is 8 MB.

cache_dir ufs /var/cache/squid/ 100 16 256 The entry cache_dir defines the directory where all the objects are stored on disk. The numbers at the end indicate the maximum disk space in MB to use and the number of directories in the first and second level. The `ufs` parameter should be left alone. The default is `100 MB` occupied disk space in the `/var/cache/squid` directory and creation of 16 subdirectories inside it, each containing 256 more subdirectories. When specifying the disk space to use, leave sufficient reserve disk space. Values from a minimum of fifty to a maximum of eighty percent of the available disk space make the most sense here. The last two numbers for the directories should only be increased with caution, because too many directories can also lead to performance problems. If you have several disks that share the cache, enter several `cache_dir` lines.

cache_access_log /var/log/squid/access.log path for log messages

cache_log /var/log/squid/cache.log path for log messages

cache_store_log /var/log/squid/store.log path for log messages

These three entries specify the paths where Squid logs all its actions. Normally, nothing is changed here. If Squid is experiencing a heavy usage burden, it might make sense to distribute the cache and the log files over several disks.

emulate_httpd_log off If the entry is set to `on`, obtain readable log files. Some evaluation programs cannot interpret this, however.

client_netmask 255.255.255.255 With this entry, mask the logged IP addresses in the log files to hide the clients' identity. The last digit of the IP address will be set to zero if you enter `255.255.255.0` here.

ftp_user Squid@ With this, set the password Squid should use for the anonymous FTP login. It can make sense, however, to specify a valid e-mail address here, because some FTP servers can check these for validity.

cache_mgr webmaster An e-mail address to which Squid sends a message if it unexpectedly crashes. The default is `webmaster`.

logfile_rotate 0 If you run `squid -k rotate`, Squid can rotate secured log files. The files will be enumerated in this process and after reaching the specified value, the oldest file at that point will be overwritten. This value here normally stands for `0` because archiving and deleting log files in SuSE Linux is carried out by a cronjob found in the configuration file `/etc/logrotate/squid`.

append_domain <domain> With `append_domain`, specify which domain to append automatically when none is given. Usually, your own domain is entered here, so entering `www` in the browser accesses your own web server.

forwarded_for on If you set the entry to `off`, Squid will remove the IP address and the system name of the client from the HTTP requests.

negative_ttl 5 minutes; negative_dns_ttl 5 minutes Normally, you do not need to change these values. If you have a dial-up connection, however, the Internet may, at times, not be accessible. Squid will make a note of the failed requests then refuse to issue new ones, although the Internet connection has been reestablished. In a case such as this, change the `minutes` to `seconds` then, after clicking `Reload` in the browser, the dial-up process should be reengaged after a few seconds.

never_direct allow <acl_name> To prevent Squid from taking requests directly from the Internet, use the above command to force connection to another proxy. This must have previously been entered in `cache_peer`. If `all` is specified as the `<acl_name>`, force all requests to be forwarded directly to the `parent`. This might be necessary, for example, if you are using a provider that strictly stipulates the use of its proxies or denies its firewall direct Internet access.

Options for Access Controls

Squid provides an intelligent system that controls access to the proxy. By implementing ACLs, it can be configured easily and comprehensively. This involves lists with rules that are processed sequentially. ACLs must be defined before they can be used. Some default ACLs, such as `all` and `localhost`, already exist. After defining an ACL, implement it, for example, in conjunction with `http_access`.

acl <acl_name> <type> <data> An ACL requires at least three specifications to define it. The name `<acl_name>` can be chosen arbitrarily. For `<type>`, select from a variety of different options which can be found in the `ACCESS CONTROLS` section in the `/etc/squid/squid.conf` file. The specification for `<data>` depends on the individual ACL type and can also be read from a file, for example, via host names, IP addresses, or URLs. The following are some simple examples:

```
acl mysurfers srcdomain .my-domain.com
acl teachers src 192.168.1.0/255.255.255.0
```

```
acl students src 192.168.7.0-192.168.9.0/255.255.255.0
acl lunch time MTWHF 12:00-15:00
```

http_access allow <acl_name> http_access defines who is allowed to use the proxy and who can access what on the Internet. For this, ACLs must be given. localhost and all have already been defined above, which can deny or allow access via deny or allow. A list containing any number of http_access entries can be created, processed from top to bottom, and, depending on which occurs first, access will be allowed or denied to the respective URL. The last entry should always be http_access deny all. In the following example, the localhost has free access to everything while all other hosts are denied access completely.

```
http_access allow localhost
http_access deny all
```

Another example, where the previously-defined ACLs are used. The group teachers always has access to the Internet. The group students only gets access Monday to Friday during lunch time.

```
http_access deny localhost
http_access allow teachers
http_access allow students lunch time
http_access deny all
```

The list with the http_access entries should only be entered, for the sake of readability, at the designated position in the /etc/squid/squid.conf file. That is, between the text

```
# INSERT YOUR OWN RULE(S) HERE TO ALLOW ACCESS FROM YOUR
# CLIENTS
```

and the last

```
http_access deny all
```

redirect_program /usr/bin/squidGuard With this option, a redirector, such as squidGuard, which is able to block unwanted URLs, can be specified. Internet access can be individually controlled for various user groups with the help of proxy authentication and the appropriate ACLs. squidGuard is a package in and of itself that can be separately installed and configured.

authenticate_program /usr/sbin/pam_auth If users must be authenticated on the proxy, a corresponding program, such as pam_auth, can be specified here. When accessing pam_auth for the first time, the user will see a login window where the user name and password must be entered. In addition, an ACL is still required so only clients with a valid login can use the Internet:

```
acl password proxy_auth REQUIRED

http_access allow password
http_access deny all
```

The `REQUIRED` after `proxy_auth` can be replaced with a list of permitted user names or with the path to such a list.

ident_lookup_access allow <acl_name> With this, have an ident request run for all ACL-defined clients to find each user's identity. If you apply `all` to the `<acl_name>`, this will be valid for all clients. Also, an ident daemon must be running on all clients. For Linux, install the pidentd package for this purpose. For Windows, there is free software available to download from the Internet. To ensure that only clients with a successful ident lookup are permitted, a corresponding ACL also needs to be defined here:

```
acl identhosts ident REQUIRED

http_access allow identhosts
http_access deny all
```

Here, too, replace the `REQUIRED` with a list of permitted user names. Using `ident` can slow down the access time quite a bit, because ident lookups will be repeated for each request.

Transparent Proxy Configuration

The usual way of working with proxy servers is the following: the web browser sends requests to a certain port in the proxy server and the proxy provides these required objects, whether they are in its cache or not. When working in a real network, several situations may arise:

- For security reasons, it is recommended that all clients use a proxy to surf the Internet.
- All clients must use a proxy whether they are aware of it or not.
- The proxy in a network is moved, but the existing clients should retain their old configuration.

In all these cases, a transparent proxy may be used. The principle is very easy: the proxy intercepts and answers the requests of the web browser, so the web browser receives the requested pages without knowing from where they are coming. This entire process is done transparently, hence the name.

Kernel Configuration

First, make sure the proxy server's kernel has support for transparent proxying. Kernel modules change sometimes from version to version. Check the current state in the Transparent Proxy mini-howto installed in your SuSE Linux system at `/usr/share/doc/howto/en/html/mini/TransparentProxy-3.html` or online at the Linux Documentation Project web page (`http://www.tldp.org/HOWTO/mini/TransparentProxy-3.html`).

Configuration Options in /etc/squid/squid.conf

The options to activate in the `/etc/squid/squid.conf` file to get the transparent proxy up and running are:

- httpd_accel_host virtual
- httpd_accel_port 80 # the port number where the actual HTTP server is located
- httpd_accel_with_proxy on
- httpd_accel_uses_host_header on

Firewall Configuration with SuSEfirewall2

Now redirect all incoming requests via the firewall with help of a port forwarding rule to the Squid port.

To do this, use the SuSE-provided tool SuSEfirewall2. Its configuration file can be found in `/etc/sysconfig/SuSEfirewall2`. Again, the configuration file consists of well-documented entries. Even to set only a transparent proxy, you must configure some firewall options In our example:

- Device pointing to the Internet: FW_DEV_EXT="eth1"
- Device pointing to the network: FW_DEV_INT="eth0"

Set ports and services (see /etc/exports) on the firewall being accessed from untrusted networks such as the Internet. In this example, only web services are offered to the outside:

FW_SERVICES_EXT_TCP="www"

Define ports or services (see /etc/exports) on the firewall to be accessed from the secure network, both TCP and UDP services:

FW_SERVICES_INT_TCP="domain www 3128"

FW_SERVICES_INT_UDP="domain"

This allows accessing web services and Squid (whose default port is 3128).

The service "domain" specified before stands for DNS. This service is commonly used. Otherwise, simply take it out of the above entries and set the following option to no:

FW_SERVICE_DNS="yes"

The most important option is number 15:

```
#
# 15.)
# Which accesses to services should be redirected to a localport
# on the firewall machine?
#
# This can be used to force all internal users to surf via your
# squid proxy, or transparently redirect incoming webtraffic to
# a secure webserver.
#
# Choice: leave empty or use the following explained syntax of
# redirecting rules, separated by a space.
# A redirecting rule consists of 1) source IP/net,
# 2) destination IP/net, 3) original destination port and
# 4) local port to redirect the traffic to, separated by a colon,
# e.g. "10.0.0.0/8,0/0,80,3128 0/0,172.20.1.1,80,8080"
#
```

File 56: *Option 15 der Firewallkonfiguration*

The comments above show the syntax to follow. First, the IP address and the netmask of the "internal networks" accessing the proxy firewall. Second, the

IP address and the netmask to which these clients "send" their requests. In the case of web browsers, specify the networks 0/0, a wild card that means "to everywhere". After that, enter the "original" port to which these requests are sent and, finally, the port to which all these requests are "redirected". As Squid supports more protocols than HTTP, redirect requests from other ports to our proxy, such as FTP (port 21), HTTPS, or SSL (port 443). The example uses the default port 3128. If there are more networks or services to add, they only need to be separated by a single blank character in the corresponding entry.

FW_REDIRECT_TCP="192.168.0.0/16,0/0,80,3128 192.168.0.0/16,0/0,21,3128"

FW_REDIRECT_UDP="192.168.0.0/16,0/0,80,3128 192.168.0.0/16,0/0,21,3128"

To start the firewall and the new configuration with it, change an entry in the `/etc/sysconfig/SuSEfirewall2` file. The entry START_FW must be set to "yes".

Start Squid as shown in *Starting Squid* on page 429. To check if everything is working properly, check the Squid logs in `/var/log/squid/access.log`.

To verify that all ports are correctly configured, perform a port scan on the machine from any computer outside your network. Only the web services port (80) should be open. To scan the ports with `nmap`, the command syntax is `nmap -O IP_address`.

Squid and Other Programs

In the following, see how other applications interact with Squid. `cachemgr.cgi` enables the system administrator to check the amount of memory needed for caching objects. squidGuard filters web pages. Calamaris is a report generator for Squid.

cachemgr.cgi

The cache manager (cachemgr.cgi) is a CGI utility for displaying statistics about the memory usage of a running Squid process. It is also a more convenient way to manage the cache and view statistics without logging the server.

Setup

First, a running web server on your system is required. To check if Apache is already running, type, as `root`, `rcapache status`.

If a message like this appears:

```
Checking for service httpd: OK
Server uptime: 1 day 18 hours 29 minutes 39 seconds
```

Apache is running on your machine. Otherwise, type `rcapache start` to start Apache with the SuSE Linux default settings. The last step to set it up is to copy the file `cachemgr.cgi` to the Apache directory `cgi-bin`:

```
cp /usr/share/doc/packages/squid/scripts/cachemgr.cgi
/srv/www/cgi-bin/
```

Cache Manager ACLs in /etc/squid/squid.conf

There are some default settings in the original file required for the cache manager:

```
acl manager proto cache_object
acl localhost src 127.0.0.1/255.255.255.255
```

With the following rules:

```
http_access allow manager localhost
http_access deny manager
```

the first ACL is the most important, as the cache manager tries to communicate with Squid over the cache_object protocol.

The following rules assume that the web server and Squid are running on the same machine. If the communication between the cache manager and Squid originates at the web server on another computer, include an extra ACL as in File 57.

```
acl manager proto cache_object
acl localhost src 127.0.0.1/255.255.255.255
acl webserver src 192.168.1.7/255.255.255.255 # webserver IP
```

File 57: *Access Rules*

Then add the rules as in File 58.

```
http_access allow manager localhost
http_access allow manager webserver
http_access deny manager
```

File 58: *Access Rules*

Configure a password for the manager for access to more options, like closing the cache remotely or viewing more information about the cache. For this, configure the entry cachemgr_passwd with a password for the manager and the list of options to view. This list appears as a part of the entry comments in `/etc/squid/squid.conf`.

Restart Squid every time the configuration file is changed. This can easily be done with `rcsquid reload`.

Viewing the Statistics

Go to the corresponding web site:
`http://webserver.example.org/cgi-bin/cachemgr.cgi`

Press 'continue' and browse through the different statistics. More details for each entry shown by the cache manager is in the Squid FAQ at `http://www.squid-cache.org/Doc/FAQ/FAQ-9.html`

squidGuard

This section is not intended to go through an extensive configuration of squidGuard, only to introduce it and give some advice for using it. For more in-depth configuration issues, refer to the squidGuard web site at `http://www.squidguard.org`.

squidGuard is a free (GPL), flexible, and fast filter, redirector, and access controller plug-in for Squid. It lets you define multiple access rules with different restrictions for different user groups on a Squid cache. squidGuard uses Squid's standard redirector interface.

squidGuard can be used for the following:

- limit the web access for some users to a list of accepted or well-known web servers or URLs
- block access to some listed or blacklisted web servers or URLs for some users
- block access to URLs matching a list of regular expressions or words for some users
- redirect blocked URLs to an "intelligent" CGI-based info page
- redirect unregistered users to a registration form
- redirect banners to an empty GIF

- have different access rules based on time of day, day of the week, date, etc.
- have different rules for different user groups
- and much more

Neither squidGuard or Squid can be used to:

- Edit, filter, or censor text inside documents
- Edit, filter, or censor HTML-embedded script languages, such as JavaScript or VBscript

Using squidGuard

Install the package `squidGuard`. Edit a minimal configuration file `/etc/squidguard.conf`. There are plenty of configuration examples in `http://www.squidguard.org/config/`. Experiment later with more complicated configuration settings.

The following step is to create a dummy "access denied" page or a more or less intelligent CGI page to redirect Squid if the client requests a blacklisted web site. Using Apache is strongly recommended.

Now, tell Squid to use squidGuard. Use the following entry in the `/etc/squid.conf` file:

redirect_program /usr/bin/squidGuard

There is another option called redirect_children configuring how many different "redirect" (in this case squidGuard) processes are running on the machine. squidGuard is fast enough to cope with lots of requests (squidGuard is quite fast: 100,000 requests within 10 seconds on a 500MHz Pentium with 5900 domains, 7880 URLs, total 13780).

Therefore, it is not recommended to set more than 4 processes, because this may lead to an unnecessary increase of memory for the allocation of these processes.

redirect_children 4

Last, have Squid read its new configuration by running `rcsquid reload`. Now, test your settings with a browser.

Cache Report Generation with Calamaris

Calamaris is a Perl script used to generate reports of cache activity in ASCII or HTML format. It works with native Squid access log files. The Calamaris home page is located at `http://Calamaris.Cord.de/`

The use of the program is quite easy. Log in as `root`, then enter:

```
cat access.log.files | calamaris [options] > reportfile
```

It is important when piping more than one log file that the log files are chronologically ordered with older files first.

The various options are:

-a normally used for the output of available reports

-w an HTML report

-l a message or logo in the header of the report

More information about the various options can be found with `man calamaris`.

A typical example is:

```
cat access.log.2 access.log.1 access.log | calamaris -a -w \
 >/usr/local/httpd/htdocs/Squid/squidreport.html
```

This puts the report in the directory of the web server. Apache is required to view the reports.

Another powerful cache report generator tool is SARG (Squid Analysis Report Generator). More information about this can be found in the relevant Internet pages at `http://web.onda.com.br/orso/` .

More Information about Squid

Visit the home page of Squid at `http://www.squid-cache.org/`. Here, find the Squid User Guide and a very extensive collection of FAQs on Squid.

There is a Mini-Howto regarding transparent proxies in the package `howtoen` under `/usr/share/doc/howto/en/mini/TransparentProxy.gz` .

In addition, mailing lists are available for Squid at `squid-users@squid-cache.org`. The archive for this is located at: `http://www.squid-cache.org/mail-archive/squid-users/`

Security in the Network

Masquerading, firewall, and Kerberos constitute the basis for a secure network, enabling control of the data traffic. The Secure Shell (SSH) allows users to log in to remote hosts by way of an encrypted connection. The information in this chapter provides a basis for securing a network and working securely in the network with these tools.

Masquerading and Firewalls

Because of its outstanding network capabilities, Linux is frequently used as a router operating system for dial-up or dedicated lines. *Router*, in this case, refers to a host with multiple network interfaces that transmits any packets not destined for one of its own network interfaces to another host communicating with it. This router is often called a gateway. The packet filtering mechanism provided by the Linux kernel allows precise control over which packets of the overall traffic are transferred.

In general, defining the exact rules for a packet filter requires at least some experience on the part of the administrator. For the less experienced user, SuSE Linux includes a separate package, package `SuSEfirewall2`, intended to make it easier to set up these rules. SuSEfirewall2 is highly configurable, making it a good choice for a more complex packet filtering setup.

With this packet filter solution, a Linux machine can be used as a router with masquerading to link a local network through a dial-up or dedicated connection where only one IP address is visible to the outside world. Masquerading is accomplished by implementing rules for packet filtering.

Caution

This chapter only describes standard procedures that should work well in most situations. Although every effort has been made to provide accurate and complete information, no guarantee is included. SuSE cannot be responsible for the success or failure of your security measures. We do appreciate your criticism and comments. Although you might not receive a direct answer from us, rest assured that suggestions for improvement will be taken seriously.

Caution

Masquerading Basics

Masquerading is the Linux-specific form of NAT (Network Address Translation). The basic principle is not very complicated: Your router has more than one network interface, typically a network card and a separate interface to the Internet (e.g., an ISDN interface). While this interfaces links with the outside world, the remaining ones are used to connect this router with the other hosts in your network. For example, the dial-up is conducted via ISDN and the network interface is `ippp0`. Several hosts in your local network are connected to the network card of your Linux router, in this example, `eth0`.

Hosts in the network should be configured to send packets destined outside the local network to this gateway.

Note

Make sure both the broadcast addresses and the network masks are the same for all the hosts when configuring your network.

Note

When one of the hosts sends a packet destined for an Internet address, this packet is sent to the network's default router. The router needs to be configured to actually forward such packets. SuSE Linux does not enable this with a default installation for security reasons. Set the variable `IP_FORWARD`, defined in the file `/etc/sysconfig/sysctl`, to `IP_FORWARD=yes`. The forwarding mechanism is enabled after rebooting or issuing the command `echo 1 > /proc/sys/net/ipv4/ip_forward`.

The router has only one IP address visible from the outside, such as the IP address of the connected ISDN interface. The source address of transmitted packets must be replaced with the router's address to enable reply. The target host only knows your router, not hosts in your internal network. Your internal host disguises itself behind the router, which is why the technique is called "masquerading."

The router, as the destination of any reply packets, must identify the incoming packets, change the target address to the intended recipient, and forward it to that host in the local network. The identification of packets belonging to a connection handled by a masquerading router is done with the help of a table kept in the kernel of your router while connected. By using the `ipchains` and the `iptables` commands, the superuser (`root`) can view these tables. Read the man pages for these commands for detailed instructions. For the identification of single masqueraded connections, the source and target addresses, the port numbers, and the protocols involved are relevant. A router is capable of hiding many thousand connections per internal host simultaneously.

With the routing of inbound traffic depending on the masquerading table, there is no way to open a connection to an internal host from the outside. For such a connection, there would be no entry in the table because it is only created if an internal host opens a connection with the outside. In addition, any established connection is assigned a status entry in the table and this entry cannot be used by another connection. A second connection would require another status record. As a consequence of all this, you might experience some problems with a number of applications, such as ICQ, cucme, IRC (DCC, CTCP), Quake, and FTP (in PORT mode). Netscape, as well as the standard FTP program and many others, uses the PASV mode. This passive mode is much less problematic as far as packet filtering and masquerading is concerned.

Firewalling Basics

"Firewall" is probably the most widely used term to describe a mechanism to control the data traffic between two networks and to provide and manage the link between networks. There are various types of firewalls, which mostly differ in regard to the abstract level on which traffic is analyzed and controlled. Strictly speaking, the mechanism described in this section is called a "packet filter." Like any other type of firewall, a packet filter alone does not guarantee full protection from all security risks. A packet filter implements a set of rules related to protocols, ports, and IP addresses to decide whether data may pass. This blocks any packets that, according to the address or destination, are not supposed to reach your network. Packets sent to the telnet service of your hosts on port 23, for example, should be blocked, while you might want people to have access to your web server and therefore enable the corresponding port. A packet filter will not scan the contents of any packets as long as they have legitimate addresses (e. g., directed to your web server). Thus, packets could attack your CGI server, but the packet filter would let them through.

A more effective, but more complex mechanism is the combination of several types of systems, such as a packet filter interacting with an application gateway or proxy. In this case, the packet filter rejects any packets destined to disabled ports. Only packets directed to the application gateway are accepted. This gateway or proxy pretends to be the actual client of the server. In a sense, such a proxy could be considered a masquerading host on the protocol level used by the application. One example for such a proxy is Squid, an HTTP proxy server. To use Squid, the browser must be configured to communicate via the proxy, so any HTTP pages requested would be served from the proxy cache rather than directly from the Internet. As another example, the SuSE proxy suite (package `proxy-suite`) includes a proxy for the FTP protocol.

The following section focuses on the packet filter that comes with SuSE Linux. For more information and links, read the Firewall HOWTO included in package `howtoen`. If this package is installed, read the HOWTO with `less /usr/share/doc/howto/en/Firewall-HOWTO.gz`.

SuSEfirewall2

The configuration of SuSEfirewall2 requires a certain degree of experience and understanding. The documentation of SuSEfirewall2 is available in `/usr/share/doc/packages/SuSEfirewall2`.

The configuration can be performed with YaST (see *Configuration with YaST* on page 449) or manually in the file `/etc/sysconfig/SuSEfirewall2`, which is well commented.

Manual Configuration

The following paragraphs provide step-by-step instructions for a successful configuration. For each configuration item, find a note specifying whether it is relevant for firewalling or for masquerading. Aspects related to the DMZ (or "demilitarized zone") are not covered here.

If your requirements are strictly limited to masquerading, only fill out items marked *masquerading*.

- First, use the YaST2 runlevel editor to enable SuSEfirewall2 in your runlevel (3 or 5 most likely). It sets the symlinks for the SuSEfirewall2_* scripts in the `/etc/init.d/rc?.d/` directories.
- FW_DEV_WORLD (firewall, masquerading): The device linked to the Internet, such as `eth0` or `ippp0`.
- FW_DEV_INT (firewall, masquerading): The device linked to the internal, "private" network. Leave this blank if there is no internal network and the firewall is supposed to protect only the one host.
- FW_ROUTE (firewall, masquerading): If you need the masquerading function, enter `yes` here. Your internal hosts will not be visible to the outside, because their private network addresses (e. g., `192.168.x.x`) are ignored by Internet routers.

  For a firewall without masquerading, only set this to `yes` to allow access to the internal network. Your internal hosts need to use officially registered IPs in this case. Normally, however, you should *not* allow access to your internal network from the outside.
- FW_MASQUERADE (masquerading): Set this to `yes` if you need the masquerading function. It is more secure to have a proxy server between the hosts of the internal network and the Internet.

- FW_MASQ_NETS (masquerading): Specify the hosts or networks to masquerade, leaving a space between the individual entries. For example, FW_MASQ_NETS="192.168.0.0/24 192.168.10.1".
- FW_PROTECT_FROM_INTERNAL (firewall): Set this to `yes` to protect your firewall host from attacks originating in your internal network. Services will only be available to the internal network if explicitly enabled. See also FW_SERVICES_INTERNAL_TCP and FW_SERVICES_INTERNAL_UDP.
- FW_AUTOPROTECT_GLOBAL_SERVICES (firewall): This should normally be `yes`.
- FW_SERVICES_EXTERNAL_TCP (firewall): Enter the services that should be available, for example, `"www smtp ftp domain 443"` . Leave this blank for a workstation at home that is not intended to offer any services.
- FW_SERVICES_EXTERNAL_UDP (firewall): Leave this blank if you do not run a name service that should be made available to the outside. Otherwise, enter the ports to use.
- FW_SERVICES_INTERNAL_TCP (firewall): This defines the services available to the internal network. The notation is the same as for external TCP services, but, in this case, refers to the *internal* network.
- FW_SERVICES_INTERNAL_UDP (firewall): See above.
- FW_TRUSTED_NETS (firewall): Specify the hosts you *really* trust ("trusted hosts"). Note, however, that these also need to be protected from attacks.

  `"172.20.0.0/16 172.30.4.2"` means that all hosts with an IP address beginning with `172.20.x.x` and the host with the IP address `172.30.4.2` are allowed to pass information through the firewall.
- FW_SERVICES_TRUSTED_TCP (firewall): Here, specify the port addresses that may be used by the trusted hosts. For example, to grant them access to all services, enter `1:65535`. Usually, it is sufficient to enter `ssh` as the only service.
- FW_SERVICES_TRUSTED_UDP (firewall): Just like above, but for UDP ports.
- FW_ALLOW_INCOMING_HIGHPORTS_TCP (firewall): Set this to `ftp-data` if you intend to use normal (active) FTP services.

- FW_ALLOW_INCOMING_HIGHPORTS_UDP (firewall): Set this to `dns` to use the name servers registered in `/etc/resolv.conf`. If you enter `yes` here, all high ports will be enabled.
- FW_SERVICE_DNS (firewall): Enter `yes` if you run a name server that should be available to external hosts. At the same time, enable port 53 under FW_TCP_SERVICES_*.
- FW_SERVICE_DHCLIENT (firewall): Enter `yes` here if you use dhclient to assign your IP address.
- FW_LOG_* (firewall): Specify the firewall's logging activity. For normal operation, it is sufficient to set FW_LOG_DENY_CRIT to `yes`.
- FW_STOP_KEEP_ROUTING_STATE (firewall): Insert `yes` if you have configured your dial-up procedure to work automatically via diald or ISDN (dial-on-demand).

Now that you have configured SuSEfirewall2, do not forget to test your setup (for example, with `telnet` from an external host). Have a look at `/var/log/messages`, where you should see something like:

```
Feb  7 01:54:14 www kernel: Packet log: input DENY eth0
PROTO=6 129.27.43.9:1427 195.58.178.210:23 L=60 S=0x00
I=36981 F=0x4000 T=59 SYN (#119)
```

Configuration with YaST

The YaST menus for the graphical configuration can be accessed from the YaST Control Center. Select 'System and Users' → 'Firewall'. The configuration is divided in four sections:

Basic Settings Specify the interfaces to protect. To protect an individual host to which no internal network is connected, just specify the interface facing the Internet. If an internal network is connected to your system, the interface facing the network must also be specified. Exit this dialog with 'Next'.

Services You only need this option to use your system to offer services accessible from the Internet (web server, mail server, etc.). Activate the respective check boxes or use the 'Expert...' button to enable services by way of their port numbers (listed in `/etc/services`). If you are not going to use your host as a server, press 'Next' to exit this dialog without making any changes.

Features Here you can select the main features of your firewall:

- 'Allow traceroute' assists you in checking the routing to your firewall.
- 'Forward Traffic and Do Masquerading' protects hosts in the internal network against the Internet — all Internet services seem to be used by your firewall, while the internal hosts remain invisible.
- 'Protect All Running Services' indicates that network access to TCP and UDP services of the firewall is denied entirely. This does not affect the services explicitly made available in the preceding step.
- 'Protect from Internal Network' Only the released firewall services are available for *internal* hosts. As it is not possible to make services available here, deactivate this option to grant access from the internal network.

Upon completion of the feature configuration, exit this dialog with 'Next'.

Logging Determine the scope of logging for your firewall. Before you activate the 'Logging options', consider that these log files produce a great amount of output. The configuration of the logging function is the final step of the firewall configuration. Exit the dialog with 'Next' and confirm the following message to activate the firewall.

SSH — Secure Shell, the Safe Alternative

In these times of increasing networks, accessing a remote system also becomes more common. Regardless of the activity, the person accessing the system must be authenticated.

Most users should know by now that the user name and password are only intended for individual use. Strict confidence pertaining to personal data is usually guaranteed between the employer, computer center, or service provider. However, the ongoing practice of authenticating and transferring data in clear text form is a frightening phenomenon. Most directly affected are the commonly used services Post Office Protocol (POP) for retrieving mail and telnet for logging in on remote systems. Using these methods, user information and data considered sensitive, such as the contents of a letter or a chat via the talk command, travel openly and unsecured over the network.

This encroaches on the user's privacy and leaves such access methods open to misuse. Usually, this misuse occurs by accessing one system to attack another or to obtain administrator or root permissions.

Any device involved in data transfer or operating on the local network, such as firewall, router, switch, mail servers, or workstations, can also access the data. There are laws prohibiting such behavior, but it is difficult to detect.

The SSH software provides the necessary protection. Complete authentication, usually user name and password, as well as the communication is encrypted. Even here, snatching the transferred data is possible, but the contents cannot be deciphered by intruders without the key. This enables secure communication via unsafe networks, such as the Internet. SuSE Linux provides the package OpenSSH.

The OpenSSH Package

SuSE Linux installs the package OpenSSH by default. The programs ssh, scp, and sftp are then available as alternatives to telnet, rlogin, rsh, rcp, and ftp.

The ssh Program

Using the ssh program, it is possible to log in to remote systems and work interactively. It replaces both telnet and rlogin. The symbolic name slogin points to ssh. For example, it is possible to log in to the host `sun` with the command `ssh sun`. The host then prompts for the password on `sun`.

Following successful authentication, work from the command line there or use interactive applications. If the local user name is different from the remote user name, log in using a different login name with `ssh -l augustine sun` or `ssh augustine@sun`.

Furthermore, ssh offers the option of running commands on another system, as does rsh. In the following example, we will run the command `uptime` on the host `sun` and create a directory with the name `tmp`. The program output will be displayed on the local terminal of the host `earth`.

```
newbie@earth:~ >  ssh sun"uptime; mkdir tmp"

newbie@sun's password:
1:21pm up 2:17, 9 users, load average:  0.15, 0.04, 0.02
```

Quotation marks are necessary here to send both instructions with one command. It is only by doing this that the second command is likewise executed on `sun`.

scp — Secure Copy

scp copies files to a remote machine. It is the secure and encoded substitute for rcp. For example, `scp MyLetter.tex sun:` copies the file `MyLetter.tex` from the machine `earth` to the machine `sun`. To give a different user name, use the `username@machine` format.

After the correct password is entered, scp starts the data transfer and shows a series of stars, gradually marking the progress from left to right. In addition, the estimated time of arrival will be shown in the right margin. All output can be suppressed by giving the option `-q`.

scp also provides a recursive copying feature for entire directories. `scp -r src/ sun:backup/` copies the entire contents of the directory `src/` including all subdirectories to the machine `sun` in the subdirectory `backup/`. If this subdirectory does not exist yet, it will be created automatically.

Via the option `-p`, scp leaves the time stamp of the files unchanged. `-C` compresses the data transfer. This minimizes the data volume to be transferred, but creates heavier burden on the processor.

sftp — Secure File Transfer

Instead of scp, sftp can be used for secure file transfer. During the session, sftp provides many of the commands used by ftp. This may be an advantage over scp, especially when transferring data for which the file names are unknown.

The SSH Daemon (sshd) — Server-Side

To work with the SSH client programs ssh and scp, a server, the SSH daemon, has to be running in the background. This waits for its connections on TCP/IP port 22.

The daemon generates three key pairs when starting for the first time. The key pairs consist of a private and a public key. Therefore, this procedure is referred to as public key–based. To guarantee the security of the communication via SSH, only the system administrator can see the private key files. The file permissions are restrictively defined by the default setting. The private keys are only required locally by the SSH daemon and must not be given to anyone else. The public key components (recognizable by the name extension `.pub`) are sent to the communication partner and are readable for all users.

A connection is initiated by the SSH client. The waiting SSH daemon and the requesting SSH client exchange identification data comparing the protocol and software versions and preventing connection to the wrong port. Since a child process of the original SSH daemon replies to the request, several SSH connections can be made simultaneously.

The SSH protocol is available in two versions, 1 and 2, for the communication between SSH server and SSH client. When using SSH with version 1, the server sends its public host key and a server key, regenerated by the SSH daemon every hour. Both allow the SSH client to encrypt a freely chosen session key then send it to the SSH server. The SSH client also tells the server which encryption method (cipher) to use.

SSH in version 2 does not require a server key. A Diffie-Helman algorithm is employed instead for exchanging the keys.

The private host and server keys absolutely necessary for decoding the session key cannot be derived from the public parts. Only the SSH daemon contacted can decrypt the session key using its proprietary keys (see `man /usr/share/doc/packages/openssh/RFC.nroff`). This initial connection phase can be watched closely using the SSH client program's error search option `-v`. Version 2 of the SSH protocol is used by default, which however can be overridden to use version 1 of the protocol with the `-1` switch. By storing all public host keys after initial contact in `~/.ssh/known_hosts` on the client side, so-called "man-in-the-middle" access attempts can be prevented. SSH servers that try to fraudulently use names and IP addresses of others will be exposed by a clear indicator. They will either be noticed due to a wrong host key which differs from `~/.ssh/known_hosts` or they cannot decipher the session key in the absence of an appropriate private counterpart.

It is recommended to securely archive the private and public keys stored in `/etc/ssh/` externally. In this way, key modifications can be detected and the old ones can be used again after a new installation. This spares users the unsettling warning. If it is verified that, despite the warning, it is indeed the correct SSH server, the existing entry regarding this system will have to be removed from `~/.ssh/known_hosts`.

SSH Authentication Mechanisms

Now the actual authentication will take place, which, in its simplest form, consists of entering a password as mentioned above. The goal of SSH was to introduce a secure software that is also easy to use. As it is meant to replace rsh and rlogin programs, SSH must also be able to provide an authentication method good for daily use. SSH accomplishes this by way of another key pair generated by the user. The SSH package also provides a help program, ssh-keygen, for this. After entering `ssh-keygen -t rsa` or `ssh-keygen -t dsa`, the key pair will be generated and you will be prompted for the base file name in which to store the keys:

```
Enter file in which to save the key (/home/newbie/.ssh/id_rsa):
```

Confirm the default setting and answer the request for a passphrase. Even if the software suggests an empty passphrase, a text from ten to thirty characters is recommended for the procedure described here. Do not use short and simple words or phrases. Confirm by repeating the passphrase. Subsequently, you will see where the private and public keys are stored, in our example, the files `id_rsa` and `id_rsa.pub`.

```
Enter same passphrase again:  Your identification has been
saved in /home/newbie/.ssh/id_rsa Your public key has been
saved in /home/newbie/.ssh/id_rsa.pub.  The key fingerprint is:
79:c1:79:b2:e1:c8:20:c1:89:0f:99:94:a8:4e:da:e8 newbie@sun
```

Use `ssh-keygen -p -t rsa` or `ssh-keygen -p -t dsa` to change your old passphrase.

Copy the public key component (`id_rsa.pub` in our example) to the remote machine and save it there at the location `~/.ssh/authorized_keys2`. You will be asked to authenticate yourself with your passphrase the next time you establish a connection. If this does not occur, verify the location and contents of these files.

In the long run, this procedure is more troublesome than giving your password each time. Therefore, the SSH package provides another tool, the ssh-agent, which retains the private keys for the duration of an X session. The entire X session will be started as a child process of ssh-agents. The easiest way to do this is to set the variable `usessh` at the beginning of the `.xsession` file to `yes` and log in via a display manager such as KDM or XDM. Alternatively, enter ssh-agent startx.

Now you can use `ssh` or `scp` as usual. If you have distributed your private key as described above, you are no longer prompted for your password. Take care of terminating your X session or locking it with a password-protection, for instance xlock.

All the relevant changes which resulted from the introduction of version 2 of the SSH protocol have also been documented in the file `/usr/share/doc/packages/openssh/README.SuSE`.

X, Authentication, and Other Forwarding Mechanisms

Beyond the previously described security-related improvements, ssh also simplifies the use of remote X applications. If you run `ssh` with the option `-X`, the DISPLAY variable will automatically be set on the remote machine and all X output will be exported to the remote machine over the existing ssh connection. At the same time, X applications started remotely and locally viewed with this method cannot be intercepted by unauthorized persons.

By adding the option `-A`, the ssh-agent authentication mechanism will be carried over to the next machine. This way, you can work from different machines without having to enter a password, but only if you have distributed your public key to the destination hosts and properly saved it there.

Both mechanisms are deactivated in the default settings, but can be permanently activated at any time in the system-wide configuration file `/etc/ssh/sshd_config` or the user's `~/.ssh/config`.

ssh can also be used to redirect TCP/IP connections. With `ssh -L 25:sun:25 sun`, the SMTP and POP3 port is redirected through ssh. Here, each connection directed to "`earth` port 25", SMTP is redirected to the SMTP port on `sun` via an encrypted channel. This is especially useful for those using SMTP servers without SMTP-AUTH or POP-before-SMTP features. From any arbitrary location connected to a network, e-mail can be transferred to the "home" mail server for delivery. In a similar manner, the command `ssh -L 110:sun:110 sun` forwards all port 110 and POP3 requests on `earth` to the POP3 port of `sun`.

Both examples must be carried out by user `root`, because the connection is made to privileged local ports. E-mail is sent and retrieved by normal users in an existing SSH connection. The SMTP and POP3 host must be set to `localhost` for this.

Additional information can be found in the manual pages for each of the programs described above and also in the files under `/usr/share/doc/packages/openssh`.

Network Authentication — Kerberos

An open network provides no means to ensure that a workstation can identify its users properly except the usual password mechanisms. In common installations, the user must enter the password each time a service inside the network is accessed. Kerberos provides an authentication method with which a user must register once and is then trusted in the complete network for the rest of the session. To have a secure network, the following requirements must be met:

- Have all users prove their identity for each desired service and make sure no one can take the identity of someone else.
- Make sure each network server also proves its identity. If you do not, an attacker might be able to impersonate the server and obtain sensitive information transmitted to the server. This concept is called "mutual authentication", because the client authenticates to the server and vice versa.

Kerberos helps you meet the above requirements by providing strongly encrypted authentication. The following shows how this is achieved. Only the basic principles of Kerberos are discussed here. For detailed technical instruction, refer to the documentation provided with your implementation of Kerberos.

Note

The original Kerberos was designed at the MIT. Besides the MIT Kerberos, there exist several other implementations of Kerberos. SuSE Linux ships with a free implementation of Kerberos 5, the Heimdal Kerberos 5 from KTH. Because the following text covers features common to all versions, the program itself is referred to as Kerberos as long as no Heimdal-specific information is presented.

Note

Kerberos Terminology

The following glossary will help you cope with Kerberos terminology.

credential Users or clients need to present some kind of credentials that authorize them to request services. Kerberos knows two kinds of credentials — tickets and authenticators.

ticket A ticket is a per-server credential used by a client to authenticate at a server from which it is requesting a service. It contains the name of the server, the client's name, the client's Internet address, a time stamp, a lifetime, and a random session key. All this data is encrypted using the server's key.

authenticator Combined with the ticket, an authenticator is used to prove that the client presenting a ticket is really the one it claims to be. An authenticator is built of the client's name, the workstation's IP address, and the current workstation's time all encrypted with the session key only known to the client and the server from which it is requesting a service. An authenticator can only be used once, unlike a ticket. A client can build an authenticator itself.

principal A Kerberos principal is unique entity (a user or service) to which it can assign a ticket. A principal consists of the following components:

- **primary** — the first part of a the principal, which can be the same as your user name in the case of a user.
- **instance** — some optional information characterizing the primary. This string is separated from the primary by a `/`.
- **realm** — this specifies your Kerberos realm. Normally, your realm is your domain name in uppercase letters.

mutual authentication Kerberos ensures that both client and server can be sure of each others identity. They will share a (session) key, which they can use to communicate securely.

session key Session keys are temporary private keys generated by Kerberos. They are known to the client and used to encrypt the communication between the client and the server for which it requested and received a ticket.

replay Almost all messages passed on in a network can be eavesdropped, stolen, and resent. In Kerberos context, this would be most dangerous if an attacker manages to obtain your request for a service containing your ticket and authenticator. He could then try to resend it ("replay") and to impersonate you. However, Kerberos implements several mechanisms to deal with that problem.

server or service "Service" is used when we talk of a specific action to perform. The process behind this action is referred to as a "server".

How Kerberos Works

Kerberos is often called a third party trusted authentication service, which means all its clients trust Kerberos's judgment of another client's identity. Kerberos keeps a database of all its users and their private keys.

To ensure Kerberos is worth all the trust put in it, run both the authentication and ticket-granting server on a dedicated machine. Make sure only the administrator can access this machine physically and over the network. Reduce the (networking) services run on it to the absolute minimum — do not even run sshd.

First contact Your first contact with Kerberos is quite similar to any login procedure at a normal networking system. Enter your user name. This piece of information and the name of the ticket-granting service are sent to the authentication server (Kerberos). If the authentication server knows about your existence, it will generate a (random) session key for further use between your client and the ticket-granting server. Now the authentication server will prepare a ticket for the ticket-granting server. The ticket contains the following information — all encrypted with a session key only the authentication server and the ticket-granting server know:

- the names both of the client and the ticket-granting server
- the current time
- a lifetime assigned to this ticket
- the client's IP address
- the newly-generated session key

This ticket is then sent back to the client together with the session key, again in encrypted form, but this time the private key of the client is used. This private key is only known to Kerberos and the client, because it is derived from your user password. Now that the client has received this response, you are prompted for your password. This password is converted into the key that can decrypt the package sent by the authentication server. The package is "unwrapped" and password and key are erased from the workstation's memory. As long as the lifetime given to the ticket used to obtain other tickets does not expire, your workstation can prove your identity.

Requesting a service To request a service from any server in the network, the client application needs to prove its identity to the server. Therefore, the application generates an authenticator. An authenticator consists of the following components:

- the client's principal
- the client's IP address

- the current time
- a checksum (chosen by the client)

All this information is encrypted using the session key that the client has already received for this special server. The authenticator and the ticket for the server are sent to the server. The server uses its copy of the session key to decrypt the authenticator, which gives him all information needed about the client requesting its service to compare it to that contained in the ticket. The server checks if the ticket and the authenticator originate from the same client.

Without any security measures implemented on the server side, this stage of the process would be an ideal target for replay attacks. Someone could try to resend a request stolen off the net some time before. To prevent this, the server will not accept any request with a time stamp and ticket received previously. In addition to that, a request with a time stamp differing too much from the time the request is received can be ignored.

Mutual authentication Kerberos authentication can be used in both directions. It is not only a question of the client being the one it claims to be. The server should also be able to authenticate itself to the client requesting its service. Therefore, it sends some kind of authenticator itself. It adds one to the checksum it received in the client's authenticator and encrypts it with the session key, which is shared between it and the client. The client takes this response as a proof of the server's authenticity and they both start cooperating.

Ticket-granting — getting into contact with all servers Tickets are designed to be used for one server at a time. This implies that you have to get a new ticket each time you request another service. Kerberos implements a mechanism to obtain tickets for individual servers. This service is called the "ticket-granting service". The ticket-granting service is a service just like any other service mentioned before, so uses the same access protocols that have already been outlined. Any time an application needs a ticket that has not already been requested, it contacts the ticket-granting server. This request consists of the following components:

- the requested principal
- the ticket-granting ticket
- an authenticator

Like any other server, the ticket-granting server now checks the ticket-granting ticket and the authenticator. If they are considered valid, the ticket-granting server builds a new session key to be used between the original client and the new server. Then the ticket for the new server is built, containing the following information:

- the client's principal
- the server's principal
- the current time
- the client's IP address
- the newly-generated session key

The new ticket is assigned a lifetime, which is the lesser of the remaining lifetime of the ticket-granting ticket and the default for the service. The client receives this ticket and the session key, which are sent by the ticket-granting service, but this time the answer is encrypted with the session key that came with the original ticket-granting ticket. The client can decrypt the response without requiring the user's password when a new service is contacted. Kerberos can thus acquire ticket after ticket for the client without bothering the user more than once at login time.

Compatibility to Windows 2000 Windows 2000 contains a Microsoft implementation of Kerberos 5. As SuSE Linux makes use of the Heimdal implementation of Kerberos 5, find useful information and guidancc in the Heimdal documentation. See *For More Information* on the next page.

Users' View of Kerberos

Ideally, a user's one and only contact with Kerberos happens during login at his workstation. The login process includes obtaining a ticket-granting ticket. At logout, a user's Kerberos tickets are automatically destroyed, which hinders anyone else from impersonating this user when not logged in. The automatic destruction of tickets can lead to a somewhat awkward situation when a user's login session lasts longer than the maximum lifespan given to the ticket-granting ticket (a reasonable setting is ten hours). However, the user can get a new ticket-granting ticket by running kinit. Enter the password password again and Kerberos obtains access to desired services without additional authentication. Those interested in a list of all the tickets silently acquired for them by Kerberos should run klist.

Here is a short list of some applications that use Kerberos authentication. These applications can be found under `/usr/lib/heimdal/bin`. They all have the full functionality of their common UNIX and Linux brothers plus the additional bonus of transparent authentication managed by Kerberos:

- telnet, telnetd
- rlogin
- rsh, rcp, rshd
- popper, push
- ftp, ftpd
- su
- imapd
- pine

You no longer have to type your password for using these applications because Kerberos has already proven your identity. ssh — if compiled with Kerberos support — can even forward all the tickets acquired for one workstation to another one. If you use ssh to log in to another workstation, ssh makes sure the encrypted contents of the tickets are adjusted to the new situation. Simply copying tickets between workstations is not sufficient as the ticket contains workstation specific information (the IP address). XDM and KDM offer Kerberos support, too. Read more about the Kerberos network applications in the *Kerberos V5 UNIX User's Guide* at `http://web.mit.edu/kerberos/www/krb5-1.2/krb5-1.2.5/doc/user-guide_toc.html`.

For More Information

SuSE Linux contains a free implementation of Kerberos called Heimdal. Its documentation is installed along with the package `heimdal` under `/usr/share/doc/packages/heimdal/doc/heimdal.info`. It is also available at the project's home page at `http://www.pdc.kth.se/heimdal/`

This is the official site of the MIT Kerberos is `http://web.mit.edu/kerberos/www/`. There, find links to any other relevant resource concerning Kerberos.

A "classical" dialog pointing out the principles of Kerberos is available at `http://web.mit.edu/kerberos/www/dialogue.html`. It is a less technical but still comprehensive read.

The paper at `ftp://athena-dist.mit.edu/pub/kerberos/doc/usenix.PS` gives quite an extensive insight to the basic principles of Kerberos without being too difficult to read. It also provides a lot of opportunities for further investigation and reading about Kerberos.

These links provide a short introduction to Kerberos and answer many questions regarding Kerberos installation, configuration, and administration:
`http://web.mit.edu/kerberos/www/krb5-1.2/krb5-1.2.5/doc/user-guide_toc.html`
`http://www.lns.cornell.edu/public/COMP/krb5/install/install_toc.html`
`http://web.mit.edu/kerberos/www/krb5-1.2/krb5-1.2.5/doc/admin_toc.html`
The official Kerberos FAQ is available at `http://www.nrl.navy.mil/CCS/people/kenh/kerberos-faq.html`.

The book *Kerberos — A Network Authentication System* by Brian Tung (ISBN 0-201-37924-4) offers extensive information.

Installing and Administering Kerberos

This section covers the installation of the Heimdal Kerberos implementation as well as some aspects of administration. This section does, however, assume that you are familiar with the basic concepts of Kerberos (see also *Network Authentication — Kerberos* on page 455).

Choosing the Kerberos Realms

The "domain" of a Kerberos installation is called a realm and is identified by a name, such as `FOOBAR.COM` or simply `ACCOUNTING`. Kerberos is case-sensitive, so `foobar.com` is actually a different realm than `FOOBAR.COM`. Use the case you prefer. It is common practice, however, to use uppercase realm names.

It is also a good idea to use your DNS domain name (or a subdomain, such as `ACCOUNTING.FOOBAR.COM`). As shown below, your life as an administrator can be much easier if you configure your Kerberos clients to locate the KDC and other Kerberos services via DNS. To do so, it is helpful if your realm name is a subdomain of your DNS domain name.

Unlike the DNS name space, Kerberos is not hierarchical. You cannot set up a realm named `FOOBAR.COM`, have two "subrealms" named `DEVELOPMENT` and ACCOUNTING underneath it, and expect the two subordinate realms to somehow inherit principals from FOOBAR.COM. Instead, you would have three separate realms for which you would have to configure "crossrealm" authentication for users from one realm to interact with servers or other users from another realm.

For the sake of simplicity, assume you are setting up just one realm for your entire organization. Setting up crossrealm authentication is described in Tung (1999), for instance. For the remainder of this section, the realm name SAMPLE.COM is used in all examples.

Setting up the KDC Hardware

The first thing required to use Kerberos is a machine that will act as the Key Distribution Center, or KDC for short. This machine holds the entire Kerberos user database with passwords and all information.

The KDC is the most important part of your security infrastructure — if someone breaks into it, all user accounts and all of your infrastructure protected by Kerberos is compromised. An attacker with access to the Kerberos database can impersonate any principal in the database. Tighten security for this machine as much as possible:

- Put the server machine into a physically secured location, such as a locked server room to which only a very few people have access.
- Do not run any network applications on it except the KDC. This includes servers and clients — for instance, the KDC should not import any file systems via NFS or use DHCP to retrieve its network configuration.

  It is probably a good approach to install a minimal system first, then check the list of installed packages and remove any unneeded packages. This includes servers, such as inetd, portmap, and cups, as well as anything X11-based. Even installing an SSH server should be considered a potential security risk.

  No graphical login is provided on this machine as an X server is a potential security risk. Kerberos provides its own administration interface.
- Configure /etc/nsswitch.conf to use only local files for user and group lookup. Change the lines for passwd and group to look like this:

```
passwd:         files
group:          files
```

Edit the `passwd`, `group`, `shadow`, and `gshadow` files in `/etc` and remove the lines that start with a + character (these are for NIS lookups).

Also consider disabling DNS lookups, because there is a potential risk involved. If there is a security bug in the DNS resolver library, an attacker might be able to trick the KDC into performing a DNS query that triggers this bug. To disable DNS lookups, simply remove `/etc/resolv.conf`.

- Disable all user accounts except root's account by editing `/etc/shadow` and replacing the hashed passwords with `*` or `!` characters.

Clock Synchronization

To use Kerberos successfully, make sure all system clocks within your organization are synchronized within a certain range. This is important because Kerberos protects against "replayed" credentials. An attacker might be able to observe Kerberos credentials on the network and reuse them to attack the server. Kerberos employs several defenses to prevent this. One of them is that it puts time stamps into its tickets. A server receiving a ticket with a time stamp that is not the current time rejects the ticket.

Of course, Kerberos will allow a certain leeway when comparing time stamps. However, computer clocks can be very inaccurate in keeping time — it is not unheard of for PC clocks to lose or gain half an hour over the course of a week. For this reason, configure all hosts on the network to synchronize their clocks with a central time source.

A simple way to do so is by installing an NTP time server on one machine and have all clients synchronize their clocks with this server. Do this either by running an NTP daemon in client mode on all these machines or by running `ntpdate` once a day from all clients (this solution will probably work for a small number of clients only). The KDC itself needs to be synchronized to the common time source as well. Because running an NTP daemon on this machine would be a security risk, it is probably a good idea to do this by running ntpdate via a cron entry. NTP configuration itself is beyond the scope of this section. For more information, refer to the NTP documentation included in your installed system under `/usr/share/doc/packages/xntp-doc`.

It is also possible to adjust the maximum deviation Kerberos allows when checking time stamps. This value (called "clock skew") can be set via the `krb5.conf` file as described in *Adjusting the Clock Skew* on page 470.

Log Configuration

By default, the Kerberos daemons running on the KDC host log information to the syslog daemon. To keep an eye on what your KDC is doing, process these log files regularly, scanning for unusual events or potential problems. Either do this by running a log scanner script on the KDC host itself or by copying these files from the KDC to another host with `rsync`. Forwarding all log output via syslogd's log forwarding mechanisms is not recommended, because information traverses the network unencrypted.

Installing the KDC

This section covers the initial installation of the KDC, including creation of an administrative principal.

Installing the RPMs

Before you can start, install the Kerberos software. On the KDC, install the `heimdal` and `heimdal-lib` RPMs:

```
earth:~ #  rpm -ivh heimdal-0*.rpm heimdal-lib-0*.rpm
```

Setting the Master Key

Your next step is to initialize the database where Kerberos keeps all information on principals. First, set the database master key, which is used to protect the database from accidental disclosure, in particular when it is backed up to a tape. The master key is derived from a pass phrase and is stored in a file called the stash file. This is so you do not need to type in the password every time the KDC is restarted. Make sure you choose a good pass phrase, such as a sentence from a book opened at a random page.

When you make tape backups of the Kerberos database (`/var/heimdal/heimdal.db`), do not back up the stash file (which is in `/var/heimdal/m-key`). Otherwise, everyone able to read the tape could also decrypt the database. Therefore, it is also a good idea to keep a copy of the pass phrase in a safe or some other secure location, because you will need it when restoring your database from backup tape after a crash.

To set the master key, run kstash without arguments and enter the pass phrase twice:

```
earth:~ #  kstash
```

```
Master key:<enter pass phrase>
Verifying password - Master key:<enter pass phrase again>
```

Creating the Realm

Finally, create entries for your realm in the Kerberos database. Run kadmin utility with the -l option as shown. This option tells kadmin to access the database locally. By default, it will try to contact the Kerberos admin service over the network. At this stage, this will not work because it is not running yet.

Now, tell kadmin to initialize your realm. It will ask you a number of questions in return. It is best to accept the default settings offered by kadmin initially:

```
earth:~ #  kadmin -l
```

```
kadmin> init SAMPLE.COM
Realm max ticket life [unlimited]: <press return>
Realm max renewable ticket life [unlimited]: <press return>
```

To verify that it did anything, use the list command:

```
kadmin> list *
default@SAMPLE.COM
kadmin/admin@SAMPLE.COM
kadmin/hprop@SAMPLE.COM
kadmin/changepw@SAMPLE.COM
krbtgt/SAMPLE.COM@SAMPLE.COM
changepw/kerberos@SAMPLE.COM
```

This shows that there are now a number of principals in the database. All of these are for internal use by Kerberos.

Creating a Principal

Next, create two Kerberos principals for yourself: one "normal" principal for your everyday work and one for administrative tasks relating to Kerberos. Assuming your login name is `newbie`, proceed as follows:

```
earth:~ #  kadmin -l


kadmin> add newbie
Max ticket life [1 day]: <press return>
Max renewable life [1 week]: <press return>
Principal expiration time [never]: <press return>
Password expiration time [never]: <press return>
Attributes []: <press return>
newbie@SAMPLE.COM's Password: <type password here>
Verifying password: <re-type password here>
```

Accepting the defaults by pressing Enter is okay. Choose a good password, however.

Next, create another principal named `newbie/admin` by typing `add newbie/admin` at the `kadmin` prompt. The `admin` suffixed to your user name is a "role". Later, use this role when administering the Kerberos database. A user can have several roles for different purposes. Roles are basically completely different accounts with similar names.

Starting the KDC

Start the KDC daemons. This includes kdc itself (the daemon handling user authentication and ticket requests), kadmind (the server performing remote administration), and kpasswddd (handling user's password change requests). To start the daemon manually, enter:

```
earth:~ #  rckdc start


Starting kdc                  done
```

Also make sure KDC is started by default when the server machine is rebooted. This is done with the command `insserv kdc`.

Configuring Kerberos Clients

When configuring Kerberos, there are basically two approaches you can take — static configuration via the /etc/krb5.conf file or dynamic configuration via DNS. With DNS configuration, Kerberos applications try to locate the KDC services via DNS records. With static configuration, add the host names of your KDC server to krb5.conf (and update the file whenever you move the KDC or reconfigure your realm in other ways).

DNS-based configuration is generally a lot more flexible and the amount of configuration work per machine is a lot less. However, it requires that your realm name is either the same as your DNS domain or a subdomain of it.

Configuring Kerberos via DNS also creates a minor security issue — an attacker can seriously disrupt your infrastructure through your DNS (by shooting down the name server, by spoofing DNS records, etc). However, this amounts to a denial of service at most. A similar scenario applies to the static configuration case unless you enter IP addresses in krb5.conf instead of host names.

Static Configuration

One way to configure Kerberos is to edit the configuration file /etc/krb5.conf. The file installed by default contains various sample entries. Erase all of these entries before starting. krb5.conf is made up of several sections, each introduced by the section name included in brackets like [this].

To configure your Kerberos clients, add the following stanza to krb5.conf (where kdc.sample.com is the host name of the KDC):

```
[libdefaults]
        default_realm = SAMPLE.COM

[realms]
        SAMPLE.COM = {
                kdc = kdc.sample.com
                kpasswd_server = kdc.sample.com
                admin_server = kdc.sample.com
        }
```

The default_realm line sets the default realm for Kerberos applications. If you have several realms, just add another statement to the [realms] section.

Also add a statement to this file that tells applications how to map host names to a realm. For instance, when connecting to a remote host, the

Kerberos library needs to know in which realm this host is located. This must be configured in the [domain_realms] section:

```
[domain_realm]
        .sample.com = SAMPLE.COM
        www.foobar.com = SAMPLE.COM
```

This tells the library that all hosts in the sample.com DNS domains are in the SAMPLE.COM Kerberos realm. In addition, one external host named www.foobar.com should also be considered a member of the SAMPLE.COM realm.

DNS-Based Configuration

DNS-based Kerberos configuration makes heavy use of SRV records (see *(RFC2052) A DNS RR for specifying the location of services* at http://www.ietf.org). These records are not supported in earlier implementations of the BIND name server. At least BIND version 8 is required for this.

The name of a SRV record, as far as Kerberos is concerned, is always in the format _service._proto.realm, where realm is the Kerberos realm. Domain names in DNS are case insensitive, so case-sensitive Kerberos realms break down when using this configuration method. _service is a service name (different names are used when trying to contact the KDC or the password service, for example). _proto can be either _udp or _tcp, but not all services support both protocols.

The data portion of SRV resource records consists of a priority value, a weight, a port number, and a host name. The priority defines the order in which hosts should be tried (lower values indicate a higher priority). The weight is there to support some sort of load balancing among servers of equal priority. You will probably never need any of this, so it is okay to set these to zero.

Heimdal Kerberos currently looks up the following names when looking for services:

_kerberos This defines the location of the KDC daemon (the authentication and ticket granting server). Typical records look like this:

```
_kerberos._udp.SAMPLE.COM.   IN   SRV    0 0 88 kdc.sample.com.
_kerberos._tcp.SAMPLE.COM.   IN   SRV    0 0 88 kdc.sample.com.
```

_kpasswd This describes the location of the password changing server. Typical records look like this:

```
_kpasswd._udp.SAMPLE.COM.    IN   SRV    0 0 464 kdc.sample.com.
```

Because kpasswdd does not support TCP, there should be no _tcp record.

_kerberos-adm This describes the location of the remote administration service. Typical records look like this:

```
_kerberos-adm._tcp.SAMPLE.COM. IN  SRV    0 0 749 kdc.sample.com.
```

Because kadmind does not support UDP, there should be no _udp record.

As with the static configuration file, there is a mechanism to inform clients that a specific host is in the SAMPLE.COM realm, even if it is not part of the sample.com DNS domain. This can be done by attaching a TXT record to _keberos.hostname, as shown here:

```
_keberos.www.foobar.com.  IN TXT "SAMPLE.COM"
```

Adjusting the Clock Skew

The "clock skew" is the tolerance for accepting tickets with time stamps that do not exactly match the host's system clock. Usually, the clock skew is set to 300 seconds, or 5 minutes. This means a ticket can have a time stamp somewhere between 5 minutes ago and 5 minutes in the future from the server's point of view.

When using NTP to synchronize all hosts, you can reduce this value to about one minute. The clock skew value can be set in /etc/krb5.conf like this:

```
[libdefaults]
        clockskew = 120
```

Remote Kerberos Administration

To be able to add and remove principals from the Kerberos database without accessing the KDC's console directly, you have to tell the Kerberos administration server which principals are allowed to do what. Do this by editing the file /var/heimdal/kadmind.acl (ACL is an abbreviation for Access Control List). The ACL file allows you to specify privileges with a fine degree of control. For details, refer to the man page for kadmind (man 8 kadmind).

Right now, just grant yourself the privilege to do anything you want with the database by putting the following line into the file:

```
newbie/admin              all
```

Replace the user name `newbie` with your own. You then have to restart the KDC for the change to take effect.

Using `kadmin` Remotely

You should now be able to perform Kerberos administration tasks remotely using the kadmin tool. First, obtain a ticket for your admin role and use that ticket when connecting to the kadmin server:

```
earth:newbie # kinit newbie/admin

newbie/admin@SAMPLE.COM's Password: <enter password>

earth:newbie # /usr/sbin/kadmin

kadmin> privs
change-password, list, delete, modify, add, get
```

Using the privs command, verify which privileges you have. The list shown above is the full set of privileges.

As an example, modify the principal `newbie`:

```
kadmin> mod newbie
Max ticket life [1 day]:2 days
Max renewable life [1 week]:
Principal expiration time [never]:2003-01-01
Password expiration time [never]:
Attributes []:
```

This changes the maximum ticket life time to two days and sets the expiration date for the account to January 1, 2003.

Basic `kadmin` Commands

Here is a brief list of kadmin commands. For more information, refer to the man page for `kadmin` (`man 8 kadmin`).

add ⟨*principal*⟩ add a new principal

modify *⟨principal⟩* edit various attributes of a principal, such as maximum ticket life time and account expiration date

delete *⟨principal⟩* remove a principal from the database

rename *⟨principal⟩* *⟨newname⟩* renames a principal to *⟨newname⟩*

list *⟨pattern⟩* list all principals matching the given pattern. Patterns work much like the shell globbing patterns: `list newbie*` would list `newbie` and `newbie/admin` in our example.

get *⟨principal⟩* display detailed information about the principal

passwd *⟨principal⟩* changes a principal's password

At all stages, help is available by typing ? and Enter, including prompts printed by commands, such as modify or add.

The `init` command used when initially creating the realm (as well as a few others) is not available in remote mode. To create a new realm, go to the KDC's console and use kadmin in local mode (using the `-l` command line option). The same is true for dumping and restoring the KDC database using the `dump`, `load`, and `merge` commands.

Creating Kerberos Host Principals

In addition to making sure every machine on your network knows which Kerberos realm it is in and what KDC to contact, create a "host principal" for it. So far, only user credentials have been discussed. However, Keberized services usually need to authenticate themselves to the client user, too. Therefore, special "host principals" must be present in the Kerberos database for each host in the realm.

The naming convention for host principals is `host/`*⟨hostname⟩*`@`*⟨REALM⟩*, where *⟨hostname⟩* is the host's fully qualified host name. Host principals are almost like user principals, but not quite. The main difference between a user principal and a host principal is that the key of the former is protected by a password — when a user obtains a ticket-granting ticket from the KDC, he needs to type his password so Kerberos can decrypt the ticket. Obviously, it would be quite inconvenient for the system administrator if he had to obtain new tickets for the SSH daemon every eight hours or so.

Instead, the key required to decrypt the initial ticket for the host principal is extracted by the administrator from the KDC once and stored in a local file called the "keytab". Services such a the SSH daemon read this key and use it to obtain new tickets automatically when needed. The default keytab file resides in /etc/krb5.keytab.

To create a host principal for machine.sample.com, type the following into your kadmin session:

```
earth:~ #  kinit newbie/admin

newbie/admin@SAMPLE.COM's Password: <type password>

earth:~ #  kadmin add -r host/machine.sample.com

Max ticket life [1 day]:
Max renewable life [1 week]:
Principal expiration time [never]:
Password expiration time [never]:
Attributes []:
```

Instead of setting a password for the new principal, the -r flag tells kadmin to generate a random key. We can do this here because we do not want any user interaction for this principal. It is a server account for the machine.

Finally, extract the key and store it in the local keytab file /etc/krb5.keytab. This file is owned by the superuser, so you must be root to execute the next command:

```
earth:~ #  ktutil get host/machine.sample.com
```

When completed, make sure you destroy the admin ticket obtained via kinit above with kdestroy.

Enabling PAM Support for Kerberos

SuSE Linux comes with a PAM module named pam_krb5, which supports Kerberos login and password update. This module can be used by applications, such as console login, su, and graphical login applications like KDM, where the user presents a password and would like the authenticating application to obtain an initial Kerberos ticket on his behalf. To enable users to update their Kerberos password transparently through the standard passwd utility (rather than having to run the kpasswd program), add pam_krb5 to the PAM configuration of passwd as well. The pam_krb5 module was specifically **not** designed for network services that accept Kerberos tickets as part of user authentication — that is an entirely different story.

In all cases, edit the PAM configuration files of those service to which to add Kerberos support. The following applications can make use of `pam_krb5`. Their corresponding PAM configuration files are also listed.

```
login                     /etc/pam.d/login
su                        /etc/pam.d/su
kdm, gdm, xdm             /etc/pam.d/xdm
xlock                     /etc/pam.d/xlock
passwd                    /etc/pam.d/passwd
```

Using pam_krb5

You can use `pam_krb5` in two ways, depending on whether you want to make your KDC the primary authentication method and use passwords from the traditional password databases as a fallback only or if you want to keep the traditional databases as primary source and just want to use `pam_krb5` to obtain Kerberos tickets for those users with principals in the KDC. The latter approach is especially useful while migrating from some other authentication mechanism to Kerberos.

As Kerberos will only do the authentication, you still need a mechanism to distribute the remaining account information, such as the uid and home directory. One such mechanism is LDAP. Using NIS for this is not an option, because Linux does not currently support any Kerberos security mechanisms for RPC network services.

Optional pam_krb5

In this mode, the primary authentication is with the existing authentication framework, such as user entries in the `/etc/passwd` file or a NIS database. The only difference is that, in addition, if there is a Kerberos principal associated with the user, `pam_krb5` will try to obtain a ticket on behalf of the user, using the password previously supplied.

Consider the PAM configuration file for su, for instance, which contains these lines for the `auth` service:

```
auth     sufficient     pam_rootok.so
auth     required       pam_unix.so      nullok
```

These two lines tell the PAM library that, when authenticating the user, it should first call the `pam_rootok` module. If this module indicates success (which it does when the calling user is the root user), the su request should be accepted without further authentication requests. Otherwise, PAM will proceed and call the pam_unix module, which performs the "traditional" authentication by prompting the user for a password, hashing it, and comparing it to the hashed password of the target user account.

To add optional Kerberos support, add another line after this one, which looks like this:

```
auth     optional       pam_krb5.so      try_first_pass \
                                         missing_keytab_ok \
                                         ccache=SAFE \
                                         putenv_direct
```

This will invoke the pam_krb5 module and ignore any errors flagged by it (for example, when it was unable to obtain a ticket for the user). With this setup, the password is always checked against password entries in the original authentication framework.

For other services, the changes made to the PAM configuration file are similar. It is usually best to add the pam_krb5 line after the one that calls pam_unix or pam_unix2.

Using pam_krb5 for Primary Authentication

If you have migrated all users to Kerberos, you can use pam_krb5 as the primary authentication mechanism and fall back to the local password file if there is an error, for instance, because there is no principal for this user or the KDC is down. With this setup, you would have all user accounts in the Kerberos database by default and the fallback to the local password file exists only for accounts like root.

The following example shows how to change /etc/pam.d/su to accomplish this (note the additional use_first_pass argument to the pam_unix module):

```
auth     sufficient     pam_rootok.so
auth     sufficient     pam_krb5.so     missing_keytab_ok \
                                                ccache=SAFE \
                                                putenv_direct
auth     required       pam_unix.so     use_first_pass nullok
```

This change inserts pam_krb5 before the pam_unix module and declares it as sufficient, which means PAM will return if pam_krb5 indicates success and skip starting pam_unix. If it fails, however, it will continue and fall back to pam_unix.so.

However, not all applications can be changed as easily as su. The PAM file for login (at least those few lines related to authentication) follows:

```
auth    requisite       pam_unix2.so    nullok
auth    required        pam_securetty.so
auth    required        pam_nologin.so
auth    required        pam_env.so
auth    required        pam_mail.so
```

Insert a line for `pam_krb5` before `pam_unix2` and, in the case of success, skip the latter but continue with the other modules. This is somewhat more complicated, as shown here:

```
auth    [success=1 default=ignore] \
                        pam_krb5.so     missing_keytab_ok \
                                        ccache=SAFE \
                                        putenv_direct
auth    requisite       pam_unix2.so    nullok
        ... rest as above ...
```

This will make PAM skip one module (`pam_unix2`) if `pam_krb5` indicates success. Any other return value is ignored and `pam_unix2` is invoked as before.

Password Updates with pam_krb5

When using Kerberos, there are usually two ways users can update their password — through the kpasswd utility (which is for Kerberos passwords only) or by having the system administrator add the `pam_krb5` module to the `passwd` configuration.

To do so, change `/etc/pam.d/passwd` to look like this:

```
auth     required       pam_krb5.so
account  required       pam_unix2.so
password required       pam_pwcheck.so  nullok
password required       pam_krb5.so
password required       pam_unix2.so    nullok use_first_pass use_authtok
session  required       pam_unix2.so
```

If you use a directory service such as LDAP, but do not keep the user passwords in LDAP anymore (it is not a good idea to keep these passwords in LDAP when you have Kerberos), change the PAM `passwd` configuration to look like this:

```
auth     required       pam_krb5.so
account  required       pam_unix2.so
password required       pam_pwcheck.so  nullok
password required       pam_krb5.so     nopasswdverify
session  required       pam_unix2.so
```

Configuring SSH for Kerberos Authentication

OpenSSH supports Kerberos authentication in both protocol version 1 and 2. In version 1, there are special protocol messages to transmit Kerberos tickets. Version 2 does not use Kerberos directly anymore, but relies on "GSSAPI", the General Security Services API. This is a programming interface that is not specific to Kerberos — it was designed to hide the peculiarities of the underlying authentication system, be it Kerberos, a public-key authentication system like SPKM, or others. The GSSAPI library included in SuSE Linux supports only Kerberos, however.

To use sshd with Kerberos authentication, edit `/etc/ssh/sshd_config` and set the following options:

```
# These are for protocol version 1
KerberosAuthentication yes
KerberosTgtPassing yes
# These are for version 2
GSSAPIAuthentication yes
GSSAPIKeyExchange yes
```

Then restart your SSH daemon using `rcsshd restart`.

To use Kerberos authentication with protocol version 2, enable it on the client-side as well. Do this either in the system-wide configuration file `/etc/ssh/ssh_config` or on a per-user level by editing `~/.ssh/config`. In both cases, add the option `GSSAPIAuthentication yes`.

You should now be able to connect using Kerberos authentication. Use `klist` to verify you have a valid ticket, then connect to the SSH server. To force SSH protocol version 1, specify option `-1` on the command line.

```
earth:newbie #  ssh earth.sample.com


Last login: Fri Aug  9 14:12:50 2002 from zamboni.sample.com
Have a lot of fun...


earth:newbie #
```

Using LDAP and Kerberos

When using Kerberos, one way to distribute the user information (such as user ID, groups, home directory, etc.) in your local network is to use LDAP. This requires a strong authentication mechanism that prevents packet spoofing and other attacks. One solution is to use Kerberos for LDAP communication, too.

OpenLDAP implements most authentication flavors through SASL, the Simple Authentication Session Layer. SASL is basically a network protocol designed for authentication. The SASL implementation used in SuSE Linux is cyrus-sasl, and supports a number of different authentication flavors. Kerberos authentication is performed through GSSAPI (General Security Services API). By default, the SASL plugin for GSSAPI is not installed. Install it manually with `rpm -ivh cyrus-sasl-gssapi-*.rpm`.

To enable Kerberos binding to the OpenLDAP server, create a principal `ldap/earth.sample.com` and add that to the keytab:

```
earth:~ # kadmin add -r ldap/earth.sample.com
earth:~ # ktutil get ldap/earth.sample.com
```

By default, the LDAP server slapd will run as user and group `ldap`, while the keytab file is readable by `root` only. Therefore, either change the LDAP configuration so the server runs as `root` or make the keytab file readable by group `ldap`.

To run slapd as root, edit `/etc/sysconfig/openldap`. Disable the `OPENLDAP_USER` and `OPENLDAP_GROUP` variables by putting a comment character in front of them.

To make the keytab file readable by group LDAP, execute

```
earth:~ # chgrp ldap /etc/krb5.keytab
earth:~ # chmod 640 /etc/krb5.keytab
```

Neither solution is perfect. However, at the moment it is not possible to configure OpenLDAP to make it use a separate keytab file.

Finally, restart the LDAP server using `rcldap restart`.

Using Kerberos Authentication with LDAP

You should now be able to use tools, such as ldapsearch, with Kerberos authentication automatically.

```
earth:~ # ldapsearch -b ou=People,dc=suse,dc=de '(uid=newbie)'
```

```
SASL/GSSAPI authentication started
SASL SSF: 56
SASL installing layers
[...]

# newbie, People, suse.de
dn: uid=newbie,ou=People,dc=suse,dc=de
uid: newbie
cn: Olaf Kirch
[...]
```

As you can see, ldapsearch prints a message that it started GSSAPI authentication. The next message is admittedly very cryptic, but it shows that the "Security Strength Factor" (SSF for short) is 56. (The value 56 is somewhat arbitrary. Most likely it was chosen because this is the number of bits in a DES encryption key.) What this tells you is that GSSAPI authentication was successful and that encryption is being used to provide integrity protection and confidentiality of the LDAP connection. If there are several SASL mechanisms that could be used, you can force `ldapsearch` to use GSSAPI by adding `-Y GSSAPI` to the command line options.

In Kerberos, authentication is always mutual. This means that not only have you authenticated yourself to the LDAP server, but also the LDAP server authenticated itself to you. In particular, this means communication is with the desired LDAP server, rather than some bogus service set up by an attacker.

Kerberos Authentication and LDAP Access Control

Now, allow each user to modify the login shell attribute of their LDAP user record. Assuming you have a schema where the LDAP entry of user `joe` is located at `uid=joe,ou=people,dc=suse,dc=de`, set up the following access controls in `/etc/openldap/slapd.conf`:

```
# This is required for things to work _at all_
access to dn.base="" by * read
# Let each user change their login shell
access to dn="*,ou=people,dc=suse,dc=de" attrs=loginShell
       by self write
# Every user can read everything
access to *
       by users read
```

The second statement gives authenticated users write access to the loginShell attribute of their own LDAP entry. The third statement gives all authenticated users read access to the entire LDAP directory.

There is one minor piece of the puzzle missing, which is how the LDAP server can find out that the Kerberos user joe@SAMPLE.COM corresponds to the LDAP distinguished name uid=joe,ou=people,dc=suse,dc=de. This sort of mapping must be configured manually using the saslExpr directive. In our example, add the following to slapd.conf:

```
saslRegexp
        uid=(.*),cn=GSSAPI,cn=auth
        uid=$1,ou=people,dc=example,dc=com
```

To understand how this works, you need to know that when SASL authenticates a user, OpenLDAP will form a distinguished name from the name given to it by SASL (such as joe) and the name of the SASL flavor (GSSAPI). The result would be uid=joe,cn=GSSAPI,cn=auth.

If a saslRegexp has been configured, it will check the DN formed from the SASL information using the first argument as a regular expression. If this regular expression matches, the name will be replaced with the second argument of the saslRegexp statement. The placeholders $1 will be replaced with the substring matched by the (.*) expression.

More complicated match expressions are possible. If you have a more complicated directory structure or a schema where the user name is not part of the DN, you can even use search expressions to map the SASL DN to the user DN.

Security and Confidentiality

Basic Considerations

One of the main characteristics of a Linux or UNIX system is its ability to handle several users at the same time (multiuser) and to allow these users to perform several tasks (multitasking) on the same computer simultaneously. Moreover, the operating system is network transparent. The users often do not know whether the data and applications they are using are provided locally from their machine or made available over the network.

With the multiuser capability the respective data of different users must be stored separately. Security and privacy need to be guaranteed. "Data security" was already an important issue, even before computers could be linked through networks. Just like today, the most important concern was the ability to keep data available in spite of a lost or otherwise damaged data medium, a hard disk in most cases.

This chapter is primarily focused on confidentiality issues and on ways to protect the privacy of users, but it cannot be stressed enough that a comprehensive security concept should always include procedures to have a regularly updated, workable, and tested backup in place. Without this, you could have a very hard time getting your data back — not only in the case of some hardware defect, but also if the suspicion arises that someone has gained unauthorized access and tampered with files.

Local Security and Network Security

There are several ways of accessing data:

- Personal communication with people who have the desired information or access to the data on a computer
- directly from the console of a computer (physical access)
- over a serial line
- using a network link

In all these cases, a user should be authenticated before accessing the resources or data in question. A web server might be less restrictive in this respect, but you still would not want it to disclose all your personal data to any surfer out there.

In the list above, the first case is the one where the highest amount of human interaction is involved, such as when you are contacting a bank employee and are required to prove that you are the person owning that bank account. Then you will be asked to provide a signature, a PIN, or a password to prove that you are the person you claim to be. In some cases, it might be possible to elicit some intelligence from an informed person just by mentioning known bits and pieces here and there to win the confidence of that person by using clever rhethoric. The victim could be led to gradually reveal more information, maybe without even becoming aware of it. Among hackers, this is called "social engineering". You can only guard against this by educating people and by dealing with language and information in a conscious way. Before breaking into computer systems, attackers often try to target receptionists, service people working with the company, or even family members. In many cases, such an attack based on social engineering will only be discovered at a much later time.

A person wanting to obtain unauthorized access to your data could also use the traditional way and try to get at your hardware directly. Therefore, the machine should be protected against any tampering so that no one can remove, replace, or cripple its components. This also applies to backups and even any network cable or the power cord. Likewise, secure the boot procedure, as there are some well-known key combinations which invoke special reactions during booting. Protect yourself against this by setting passwords for the BIOS and the bootloader.

Serial terminals connected to serial ports are still used in many places. Unlike network interfaces, they do not rely on a network protocol to communicate with the host. A simple cable or an infrared port is used to send plain characters back and forth between the devices. The cable itself is the weakest point of such a system: with an older printer connected to it, it is easy to record anything that runs over the wires. What can be achieved with a printer can also be accomplished in other ways, depending on the effort that goes into the attack.

Reading a file locally on a host requires other access rules than opening a network connection with a server on a different host. There is a distinction between local security and network security. The line is drawn where data has to be put into packets to be sent somewhere else.

Local Security

Local security starts with the physical environment in the location where the computer is running. Set up your machine in a place where security is in line with your expectations and needs.

The main goal of "local security" is to keep users separate from each other, so that no user can assume the permissions or the identity of another. This is a general rule to be observed, but it is especially true for the user `root` who holds the supreme power on the system. User `root` can take on the identity of any other local user without being prompted for the password and read any locally stored file.

Passwords

On a Linux system, passwords are, of course, *not* stored as plain text and the text string entered is not simply matched with the saved pattern. If this were the case, all accounts on your system would be compromised as soon as someone got access to the corresponding file. Instead, the stored password is encrypted and, each time it is entered, is encrypted again and the two encrypted strings are compared. Naturally, this will only work if the encrypted password cannot be reverse-computed into the original text string. This is actually achieved by a special kind of algorithm, also called "trapdoor algorithm," because it only works in one direction. An attacker who has obtained the encrypted string will not be able to get your password by simply applying the same algorithm again. Instead, it would be necessary to test all the possible character combinations until a combination is found which looks like your password when encrypted. As you can imagine, with passwords eight characters long, there are quite a number of possible combinations to calculate.

In the seventies, it was argued that this method would be more secure than others due to the relative slowness of the algorithm used, which took a few seconds to encrypt just one password. In the meantime, however, PCs have become powerful enough to do several hundred thousand or even millions of encryptions per second. Because of this, encrypted passwords should not be visible to regular users (`/etc/shadow` cannot be read by normal users). It is even more important that passwords are not easy to guess, in case the password file becomes visible due to some error. Consequently, it is not really useful to "translate" a password like "tantalise" into "t@nt@1ls3".

Replacing some letters of a word with similar looking numbers is not safe enough. Password cracking programs which use dictionaries to guess words also play with substitutions like that. A better way is to make up a word with no common meaning, something which only makes sense to you personally, like the first letters of the words of a sentence or the title of a book, such as "The Name of the Rose" by Umberto Eco. This would give the following safe password: "TNotRbUE9". By contrast, passwords like "beerbuddy" or "jasmine76" are easily guessed even by someone who has only some casual knowledge about you.

The Boot Procedure

Configure your system so it cannot be booted from a floppy or from CD, either by removing the drives entirely or by setting a BIOS password and configuring the BIOS to allow booting from a hard disk only. Normally, a Linux system will be started by a boot loader, allowing you to pass additional options to the booted kernel. This is crucial to your system's security. Not only does the kernel itself run with root permissions, but it is also the first authority to grant root permissions at system start-up. Prevent others from using such parameters during boot by setting an additional password in `/etc/lilo.conf` (see *Booting and Boot Managers* on page 71).

File Permissions

As a general rule, always work with the most restrictive privileges possible for a given task. For example, it is definitely not necessary to be `root` to read or write e-mail. If the mail program has a bug, this bug could be exploited for an attack which will act with exactly the permissions of the program when it was started. By following the above rule, minimize the possible damage.

The permissions of the more than 200,000 files included in a SuSE distribution are carefully chosen. A system administrator who installs additional software or other files should take great care when doing so, especially when setting the permission bits. Experienced and security-conscious system administrators always use the `-l` option with the command `ls` to get an extensive file list, which allows them to detect any wrong file permissions immediately. An incorrect file attribute does not only mean that files could be changed or deleted. These modified files could be executed by `root` or, in the case of configuration files, that programs could use such files with the permissions of `root`. This significantly increases the possibilities of an attacker. Attacks like this are called cuckoo eggs, because the program (the egg) is executed (hatched) by a different user (bird), just like a cuckoo tricks other birds into hatching its eggs.

A SuSE Linux system includes the files `permissions`, `permissions.easy`, `permissions.secure`, and `permissions.paranoid`, all in the directory `/etc`. The purpose of these files is to define special permissions, such as world-writable directories or, for files, the setuser ID bits, which means the corresponding program will not run with the permissions of the user that has launched it, but with the permissions of the file owner, `root` in most cases. An administrator may use the file `/etc/permissions.local` to add his own settings. To define which of the above files is used by SuSE's configuration programs to set permissions accordingly use the submenu 'Security' in YaST2. To learn more about the topic, read the comments in `/etc/permissions` or consult the manual page of `chmod` (`man chmod`).

Buffer Overflows and Format String Bugs

Special care must be taken whenever a program is supposed to process data that can or could be changed by a user, but this is more of an issue for the programmer of an application than for regular users. The programmer has to make sure that his application will interpret data in the correct way, without writing them into memory areas that are too small to hold them. Also, the program should hand over data in a consistent manner, using the interfaces defined for that purpose.

A "buffer overflow" can happen if the actual size of a memory buffer is not taken into account when writing to that buffer. There are cases where this data (as generated by the user) uses up some more space than what is available in the buffer. As a result, data is written beyond the end of that buffer area, which, under certain circumstances, makes it possible that a program will execute program sequences influenced by the user (and not by the programmer), rather than just processing user data. A bug of this kind may have serious consequences, in particular if the program is being executed with special privileges (see Section *File Permissions* on the preceding page).

"Format string bugs" work in a slightly different way, but again it is the user input which could lead the program astray. In most cases, these programming errors are exploited with programs executed with special permissions — setuid and setgid programs — which also means that you can protect your data and your system from such bugs by removing the corresponding execution privileges from programs. Again, the best way is to apply a policy of using the lowest possible privileges (see Section *File Permissions* on the facing page).

Given that buffer overflows and format string bugs are bugs related to the handling of user data, they are not only exploitable if access has been given to a local account. Many of the bugs that have been reported can also be exploited over a network link. Accordingly, buffer overflows and format string bugs should be classified as being relevant for both local and network security.

Viruses

Contrary to what some people will tell you, there *are* viruses that run on Linux. However, the viruses that are known were released by their authors as "proof of concept" to prove that the technique works as intended. None of these viruses have been spotted "in the wild" so far.

Viruses would not be able to survive and spread without a host on which they could live. In our case, the host would be a program or an important storage area of the system, such as the master boot record, which needs to be writable for the program code of the virus. Owing to its multiuser capability, Linux can restrict write access to certain files, especially important with system files. Therefore, if you did your normal work with `root` permissions, you would increase the chance of the system being infected by a virus. By contrast, if you follow the principle of using the lowest possible privileges as mentioned above, chances of getting a virus are slim.

Apart from that, you should never rush into executing a program from some Internet site that you do not really know. SuSE's RPM packages carry a cryptographic signature as a digital label that the necessary care was taken to build them. Viruses are a typical sign that the administrator or the user lacks the required security awareness, putting at risk even a system that should be highly secure by its very design.

Viruses should not be confused with worms which belong to the world of networks entirely. Worms do not need a host to spread.

Network Security

Network security is important for protecting from an attack originating in the network. The typical login procedure requiring a user name and a password for user authentication is a local security issue. However, in the particular case of logging in over a network, we need to differentiate between both security aspects. What happens until the actual authentication is network security and anything that happens afterwards is local security.

X Window System and X11 Authentication

As mentioned at the beginning, network transparency is one of the central characteristics of a UNIX system. X11, the windowing system of UNIX operating systems, can make use of this feature in an impressive way. With X11, it is basically no problem to log in at a remote host and start a graphical program that will then be sent over the network to be displayed on your computer.

For an X client to be displayed remotely using our X server, the latter is supposed to protect the resource managed by it (i. e. the display) from unauthorized access. In more concrete terms, certain permissions must be given to the client program. With the X Window System, there are two ways to do this, called host-based access control and cookie-based access control. The former relies on the IP address of the host where the client is supposed to run. The program to control this is `xhost`. `xhost` enters the IP address of a legitimate client into a tiny database belonging to the X server. However, relying on IP addresses for authentication is not very secure. For example, if there were a second user working on the host sending the client program, that user would have access to the X server as well — just like someone stealing the IP address. Because of these shortcomings, we will not describe this authentication method in more detail here, but you can learn about it from `man xhost`.

In the case of cookie-based access control, a character string is generated which is only known to the X server and to the legitimate user, just like an ID card of some kind. This cookie (the word goes back not to ordinary cookies, but to Chinese fortune cookies which contain an epigram) is stored on login in the file `.Xauthority` in the user's home directory and is available to any X Window client wanting to use the X server to display a window. The file `.Xauthority` can be examined by the user with the tool `xauth`. If you were to rename `.Xauthority` or if you deleted the file from your home directory by accident, you would not be able to open any new windows or X clients. Read more about X Window security mechanisms in the man page of `Xsecurity` (`man Xsecurity`).

`ssh` (secure shell) can be used to completely encrypt a network connection and forward it to an X server transparently without the encryption mechanism being perceived by the user. This is also called X forwarding. X forwarding is achieved by simulating an X server on the server side and setting a DISPLAY variable for the shell on the remote host. Further details about `ssh` can be found in Section *SSH — Secure Shell, the Safe Alternative* on page 450.

Caution

If you do not consider the host where you log in to be a secure host, do not use X forwarding. With X forwarding enabled, an attacker could authenticate via your ssh connection to intrude on your X server and sniff your keyboard input, for instance.

Caution

Buffer Overflows and Format String Bugs

As discussed on on page 484, buffer overflows and format string bugs should be classified as issues concerning both local and network security. As with the local variants of such bugs, buffer overflows in network programs, when successfully exploited, are mostly used to obtain `root` permissions. Even if that is not the case, an attacker could use the bug to gain access to an unprivileged local account to exploit any other vulnerabilities which might exist on the system.

Buffer overflows and format string bugs exploitable over a network link are certainly the most frequent form of remote attacks in general. Exploits for these — programs to exploit these newly-found security holes — are often posted on the security mailing lists. They can be used to target the vulnerability without knowing the details of the code. Over the years, experience has shown that the availability of exploit codes has contributed to more secure operating systems, obviously due to the fact that operating system makers were forced to fix the problems in their software. With free software, anyone has access to the source code (SuSE Linux comes with all available source codes) and anyone who finds a vulnerability and its exploit code can submit a patch to fix the corresponding bug.

DoS — Denial of Service

The purpose of this kind of attack is to force down a server program or even an entire system, something which could be achieved by various means: overloading the server, keeping it busy with garbage packets, or exploiting a remote buffer overflow.

Often a DoS attack is done with the sole purpose of making the service disappear. However, once a given service has become unavailable, communications could become vulnerable to so-called "man-in-the-middle attacks" (sniffing, TCP connection hijacking, spoofing) and DNS poisoning.

Man in the Middle: Sniffing, Hijacking, Spoofing

In general, any remote attack performed by an attacker who puts himself between the communicating hosts is called a "man-in-the-middle attack". What almost all types of man-in-the-middle attacks have in common is that the victim is usually not aware that there is something happening. There are many possible variants, for example, the attacker could pick up a connection request and forward that to the target machine himself. Now the victim has unwittingly established a connection with the wrong host, because the other end is posing as the legitimate destination machine.

The simplest form of a man-in-the-middle attack is called "sniffer" — the attacker is "just" listening to the network traffic passing by. As a more complex attack, the "man in the middle" could try to take over an already established connection (hijacking). To do so, the attacker would have to analyze the packets for some time to be able to predict the TCP sequence numbers belonging to the connection. When the attacker finally seizes the role of the target host, the victims will notice this, because they get an error message saying the connection was terminated due to a failure. The fact that there are protocols not secured against hijacking through encryption, which only perform a simple authentication procedure upon establishing the connection, makes it easier for attackers.

"Spoofing" is an attack where packets are modified to contain counterfeit source data, mostly the IP address. Most active forms of attack rely on sending out such fake packets — something that, on a Linux machine, can only be done by the superuser (`root`).

Many of the attacks mentioned are carried out in combination with a DoS. If an attacker sees an opportunity to abruptly bring down a certain host, even if only for a short time, it will make it easier for him to push the active attack, because the host will not be able to interfere with the attack for some time.

DNS poisoning

DNS poisoning means that the attacker corrupts the cache of a DNS server by replying to it with spoofed DNS reply packets, trying to get the server to send certain data to a victim who is requesting information from that server. Many servers maintain a trust relationship with other hosts, based on IP addresses or host names. The attacker will need a good understanding of the actual structure of the trust relationships between hosts to dusguise itself as one of the trusted hosts. Usually, the attacker analyzes some packets received from the server to get the necessary information. The attacker often needs to target a well-timed DoS attack at the name server as well. Protect yourself by using encrypted connections that are able to verify the identity of the hosts to which to connect.

Worms

Worms are often confused with viruses, but there is a clear difference between the two. Unlike viruses, worms do not need to infect a host program to live. Rather, they are specialized to spread as quickly as possible on network structures. The worms that appeared in the past, such as Ramen, Lion, or Adore, make use of well-known security holes in server programs like `bind8` or `lprNG`. Protection against worms is relatively easy. Given that some time will elapse between the discovery of a security hole and the moment the worm hits your server, there is a good chance that an updated version of the affected program will be available on time. Of course, that is only useful if the administrator actually installs the security updates on the systems in question.

Some General Security Tips and Tricks

Information: To handle security competently, it is important to keep up with new developments and to stay informed about the latest security issues. One very good way to protect your systems against problems of all kinds is to get and install the updated packages recommended by security announcements as quickly as possible. SuSE security announcements are published on a mailing list to which you can subscribe by following the link `http://www.suse.de/security`. The list `suse-security-announce@suse.de` is a first-hand source of information regarding updated packages and includes members of SuSE's security team among its active contributors.

The mailing list `suse-security@suse.de` is a good place to discuss any security issues of interest. Subscribe to it under the URL as given above for `suse-security-announce@suse.de`.

bugtraq@securityfocus.com is one of the best-known security mailing lists worldwide. We recommend reading this list, which receives between 15 and 20 postings per day. More information can be found at http://www.securityfocus.com.

The following is a list of rules which you may find useful in dealing with basic security concerns:

- According to the rule of using the most restricive set of permissions possible for every job, avoid doing your regular jobs as root. This reduces the risk of getting a cuckoo egg or a virus and protects you from your own mistakes.
- If possible, always try to use encrypted connections to work on a remote machine. Use ssh (secure shell) to replace telnet, ftp, rsh, and rlogin.
- Avoid using authentication methods based on IP addresses alone.
- Try to keep the most important network-related packages up-to-date and subscribe to the corresponding mailing lists to receive announcements on new versions of such programs (bind, sendmail, ssh, etc.). The same should apply to software relevant to local security.
- Change the /etc/permissions file to optimize the permissions of files crucial to your system's security. If you remove the setuid bit from a program, it might well be that it cannot do its job anymore in the way it is supposed to. On the other hand, consider that, in most cases, the program will also have ceased to be a potential security risk. You might take a similar approach with world-writable directories and files.
- Disable any network services you do not absolutely require for your server to work properly. This will make your system safer. Open ports, with the socket state LISTEN, can be found with the program netstat. As for the options, we suggest that you use netstat -ap or netstat -anp. The -p option allows you to see which process is occupying a port under which name.

  Compare the netstat results with those of a thorough port scan done from outside your host. An excellent program for this job is nmap, which not only checks out the ports of your machine, but also draws some conclusions as to which services are waiting behind them. However, port scanning may be interpreted as an aggressive act, so do not do this on a host without the explicit approval of the administrator. Finally, remember that it is important not only to scan TCP ports, but also UDP ports (options -sS and -sU).

- To monitor the integrity of the files of your system in a reliable way, use the program `tripwire`, available on the SuSE Linux distribution. Encrypt the database created by `tripwire` to prevent someone from tampering with it. Furthermore, keep a backup of this database available outside your machine, stored on an external data medium not connected to it by a network link.

- Take proper care when installing any third-party software. There have been cases where a hacker had built a trojan horse into the tar archive of a security software package, which was fortunately discovered very quickly. If you install a binary package, have no doubts about the site from which you downloaded it.

  Note that SuSE's RPM packages are gpg-signed. The key used by SuSE for signing reads as follows:

  ID:9C800ACA 2000-10-19 SuSE Package Signing Key <build@suse.de>

  Key fingerprint = 79C1 79B2 E1C8 20C1 890F 9994 A84E DAE8 9C80 0ACA

  The command `rpm --checksig package.rpm` shows whether the checksum and the signature of an uninstalled package are correct. Find the key on the first CD of the distribution and on most key servers worldwide.

- Check your backups of user and system files regularly. Consider that if you do not test whether the backup will work, it might actually be worthless.

- Check your log files. Whenever possible, write a small script to search for suspicious entries. Admittedly, this is not exactly a trivial task. In the end, only you can know which entries are unusual and which are not.

- Use `tcp_wrapper` to restrict access to the individual services running on your machine, so you have explicit control over which IP addresses can connect to a service. For further information regarding `tcp\_wrappers`, consult the manual page of `tcpd` and `hosts\_access` (`man 8 tcpd`, `man hosts_access`).

- Use SuSEfirewall to enhance the security provided by `tcpd` (tcp_wrapper).

- Design your security measures to be redundant: a message seen twice is much better than no message at all.

Using the Central Security Reporting Address

If you discover a security-related problem (please check the available update packages first), write an e-mail to `security@suse.de`. Please include a detailed description of the problem and the version number of the package concerned. SuSE will try to send a reply as soon as possible. You are encouraged to pgp encrypt your e-mail messages. SuSE's pgp key is as follows:

ID:3D25D3D9 1999-03-06 SuSE Security Team <security@suse.de>

Key fingerprint = 73 5F 2E 99 DF DB 94 C4 8F 5A A3 AE AF 22 F2 D5

This key is also available for download from: `http://www.suse.de/security`

Part V

Appendixes

File Systems in Linux

Linux supports a number of different file systems. This chapter presents a brief overview of the most popular Linux file systems, elaborating on their design concept, advantages, and fields of application. Some additional information about LFS ("Large File Support") in Linux is also provided.

Glossary

metadata A file system internal data structure that assures all the data on disk is properly organized and accessible. Essentially, it is "data about the data." Almost every file system has its own structure of metadata, which is partly why the file systems show different performance characteristics. It is of major importance to maintain metadata intact, because otherwise the whole data on the file system could become inaccessible.

inode Inodes contain various information about a file, including size, number of links, date, and time of creation, modification, and access, as well as pointers to the disk blocks where the file contents are actually stored.

journal In the context of a file system, a journal is an on-disk structure containing a kind of log where the file system stores what it is about to change in the file system's metadata. "Journaling" greatly reduces the recovery time of a Linux system because it obsoletes the lengthy search process that checks the whole file system at system start-up. Instead, only the journal is replayed.

Major File Systems in Linux

Unlike two or three years ago, choosing a file system for a Linux system is no longer a matter of a few seconds ("Ext2 or ReiserFS?"). Kernels starting from 2.4 offer a variety of file systems from which to choose. The following is an overview of how those file systems basically work and which advantages they offer.

It is very important to bear in mind that there may be no file system that best suits all kinds of applications. Each file system has its particular strengths and weaknesses, which have to be taken into account. Even the most sophisticated file system cannot substitute for a reasonable backup strategy, however.

The terms "data integrity" or "data consistency", when used in this chapter, do not refer to the consistency of the user space data (the data your application writes to its files). Whether this data is consistent must be controlled by the application itself.

Ext2

The origins of Ext2 go back to the early days of Linux history. Its predecessor, the Extended File System, was implemented in April 1992 and integrated in Linux 0.96c. The Extended File System underwent a number of modifications and, as Ext2, became the most popular Linux file system for years. With the creation of journaling file systems and their astonishingly short recovery times, Ext2 became less important.

A brief summary of Ext2's strengths might help you to understand why it was — and in some areas still is — the favorite Linux file system of many a Linux user.

Solidity Being quite an "old-timer", Ext2 underwent many improvements and was heavily tested. This may be the reason why people often refer to it as "rock-solid". After a system outage when the file system could not be cleanly unmounted, e2fsck starts to analyze the file system data. Metadata is brought into a consistent state and pending files or data blocks are written to a designated directory (called `lost+found`). In contrast to journaling file systems, e2fsck analyzes the entire file system and not just the recently modified bits of metadata. This takes significantly longer than checking the log data of a journaling file system. Depending on file system size, this procedure can take half an hour or more. Therefore, you would not choose Ext2 for any server that needs high availability. Yet, as Ext2 does not maintain a journal and uses significantly less memory, it is sometimes faster than other file systems.

Easy upgradability The code Ext2 is the strong foundation on which Ext3 could become a highly-acclaimed next-generation file system. Its reliability and solidity were elegantly combined with the advantages of a journaling file system.

Ext3

Ext3 was designed by Stephen Tweedie. In contrast to all other "next-generation" file systems, Ext3 does not follow a completely new design principle. It is based on Ext2. These two file systems are very closely related to each other. An Ext3 file system can be easily built on top of an Ext2 file system. The most important difference between Ext2 and Ext3 is that Ext3 supports journaling.

Summed up, Ext3 has three major advantages to offer:

Easy and highly reliable file system upgrades from Ext2 As Ext3 is based on the Ext2 code and shares its on-disk format as well as its metadata format, upgrades from Ext2 to Ext3 are incredibly easy. Unlike transitions to other journaling file systems, such as ReiserFS, JFS, or XFS, which can be quite tedious (making backups of the whole file system and recreating it from scratch), a transition to Ext3 is a matter of minutes. It is also very safe, as the recreation of an entire file system from scratch might not work flawlessly. Considering the number of existing Ext2 systems that await an upgrade to a journaling file system, you can easily figure out why Ext3 might be of some importance to many system administrators. Downgrading from Ext3 to Ext2 is as easy as the upgrade. Just perform a clean unmount of the Ext3 file system and remount it as an Ext2 file system.

Reliability and performance Other journaling file systems follow the "metadata-only" journaling approach. This means your metadata will always be kept in a consistent state but the same cannot be automatically guaranteed for the file system data itself. Ext3 is designed to take care of both metadata and data. The degree of "care" can be customized. Enabling Ext3 in the `data=journal` mode offers maximum security (i.e., data integrity), but can slow down the system as both metadata and data are journaled. A relatively new approach is to use the `data=ordered` mode, which ensures both data and metadata integrity, but uses journaling only for metadata. The file system driver collects all data blocks that correspond to one metadata update. These blocks are grouped as a "transaction" and will be written to disk before the metadata is updated. As a result, consistency is achieved for metadata and data without sacrificing performance. A third option to use is `data=writeback`, which allows data to be written into the main file system after its metadata has been committed to the journal. This option is often considered the best in performance. It can, however, allow old data to reappear in files after crash and recovery while internal file system integrity is maintained. Unless you specify something else, Ext3 is run with the `data=ordered` default.

ReiserFS

Officially one of the key features of the 2.4 kernel release, ReiserFS has been available as a kernel patch for 2.2.x SuSE kernels since SuSE Linux version 6.4. ReiserFS was designed by Hans Reiser and the Namesys development team. ReiserFS has proven to be a powerful alternative to the old Ext2. Its key assets are better disk space utilization, better disk access performance, and faster crash recovery. However, there is a minor drawback: ReiserFS pays great care to metadata but not to the data itself. Future generations of ReiserFS will include data journaling (both metadata and actual data are written to the journal) as well as ordered writes.

ReiserFS's strengths, in more detail, are:

Better disk space utilization In ReiserFS, all data is organized in a structure called B*-balanced tree. The tree structure contributes to better disk space utilization as small files can be stored directly in the B*tree leaf nodes instead of being stored elsewhere and just maintaining a pointer to the actual disk location. In addition to that, storage is not allocated in chunks of 1 or 4 kB, but in portions of the exact size needed. Another benefit lies in the dynamic allocation of inodes. This keeps the file system more flexible than traditional file systems, like Ext2, where the inode density has to be specified at file system creation time.

Better disk access performance For small files, you will often find that both file data and "stat_data" (inode) information are stored next to each other. They can be read with a single disk IO operation, meaning that only one access to disk is required to retrieve all the information needed.

Fast crash recovery Using a journal to keep track of recent metadata changes makes a file system check a matter of seconds, even for huge file systems.

JFS

JFS, the "Journaling File System" was developed by IBM. The first beta version of the JFS Linux port reached the Linux community in the summer of 2000. Version 1.0.0 was released in 2001. JFS is tailored to suit the needs of high throughput server environments where performance is the ultimate goal. Being a full 64-bit file system, JFS supports both large files and partitions, which is another reason for its use in server environments.

A closer look at JFS shows why this file system might prove a good choice for your Linux server:

Efficient journaling JFS follows a "metadata only" approach like ReiserFS. Instead of an extensive check, only metadata changes generated by recent file system activity get checked, which saves a great amount of time in recovery. Concurrent operations requiring multiple concurrent log entries can be combined into one group commit, greatly reducing performance loss of the file system through multiple write operations.

Efficient directory organization JFS holds two different directory organizations. For small directories, it allows the directory's content to be stored directly into its inode. For larger directories, it uses B^+trees, which greatly facilitate directory management.

Better space usage through dynamic inode allocation For Ext2, you have to define the inode density in advance (the space occupied by management information), which restricted the maximum number of files or directories of your file system. JFS spares you these considerations — it dynamically allocates inode space and frees it when it is no longer needed.

XFS

Originally intended as file system for their IRIX OS, SGI started XFS development back in the early 1990s. The idea behind XFS was to create a high-performance 64-bit journaling file system to meet the extreme computing challenges of today. XFS is very good at manipulating large files and performs well on high-end hardware. However, you will find a drawback even in XFS. Like ReiserFS, XFS takes a great deal of care of metadata integrity, but less of data integrity.

A quick review of XFS's key features explains why it may prove a strong competitor for other journaling file systems in high-end computing.

High scalability through the use of allocation groups At creation time of an XFS file system, the block device underlying the file system is divided into eight or more linear regions of equal size. Those are referred to as "allocation groups". Each allocation group manages its own inodes and free disk space. Practically, allocation groups can be seen as "file systems in a file system." As allocation groups are rather independent of each other, more than one of them can be addressed by the kernel simultaneously. This feature is the key to XFS's great scalability. Naturally, the concept of independent allocation groups suits the needs of multiprocessor systems.

High performance through efficient management of disk space Free space and inodes are handled by B^+ trees inside the allocation groups. The use of B^+ trees greatly contributes to XFS's performance and scalability. A feature truly unique to XFS is "delayed allocation". XFS handles allocation by breaking the process into two pieces. A pending transaction is stored in RAM and the appropriate amount of space is reserved. XFS still does not decide where exactly (speaking of file system blocks) the data should be stored. This decision is delayed until the last possible moment. Some short-lived temporary data may never make its way to disk, because it may be obsolete at the time XFS decides where to actually save it. Thus XFS increases write performance and reduces file system fragmentation. Because delayed allocation results in less frequent write events than in other file systems, it is likely that data loss after a crash during a write is more severe.

Preallocation to avoid file system fragmentation Before writing the data to the file system, XFS "reserves" (preallocates) the free space needed for a file. Thus, file system fragmentation is greatly reduced. Performance is increased as the contents of a file will not be distributed all over the file system.

Some Other Supported File Systems

Table A.1 on the next page summarizes some other file systems supported by Linux. They are supported mainly to ensure compatibility and interchange of data with different kinds of media or foreign operating systems.

`cramfs`	*Compressed ROM file system*: A compressed read-only file system for ROMs.
`hpfs`	*High Performance File System*: the IBM OS/2 standard file system — only supported in read-only mode.
`iso9660`	Standard file system on CD-ROMs.
`minix`	This file system originated from academic projects on operating systems and was the first file system used in Linux. Nowadays, it is used as a file system for floppy disks.
`msdos`	*fat*, the file system originally used by DOS, is today used by various operating systems.
`ncpfs`	file system for mounting Novell volumes over networks.
`nfs`	*Network File System*: Here, data can be stored on any machine in a network and access may be granted via a network.

***Table A.1:** continued overleaf...*

`smbfs`	*Server Message Block*: used by products such as Windows to enable file access over a network.
`sysv`	Used on SCO UNIX, Xenix, and Coherent (commercial UNIX systems for PCs).
`ufs`	Used by BSD, SunOS, and NeXTstep. Only supported in *read-only* mode.
`umsdos`	*UNIX on MSDOS*: applied on top of a normal `fat` file system. Achieves UNIX functionality (permissions, links, long file names) by creating special files.
`vfat`	*Virtual FAT*: extension of the `fat` file system (supports long file names).
`ntfs`	*Windows NT file system*, read-only.

Table A.1: *File System Types in Linux*

Large File Support in Linux

Originally, Linux supported a maximum file size of 2 GB. This was enough before the explosion of multimedia and as long as no one tried to manipulate huge databases on Linux. Becoming more and more important for server computing, the kernel and C library were modified to support file sizes larger than 2 GB when using a new set of interfaces that applications must utilize. Nowadays, (almost) all major file systems offer LFS support, allowing you to perform high-end computing.

Table A.2 on the facing page offers an overview of the current limitations of Linux files and file systems for Kernel 2.4.

File System	File Size Limit [Byte]	File System Size [Byte]
Ext2 or Ext3 (1 kB block size)	2^{34} (16 GB)	2^{41} (2 TB)
Ext2 or Ext3 (2 kB block size)	2^{38} (256 GB)	2^{43} (8 TB)
Ext2 or Ext3 (4 kB block size)	2^{41} (2 TB)	2^{44} (16 TB)

Ext2 or Ext3 (8 kB block size) (systems with 8 kB pages (like Alpha))	2^{46} (64 TB)	2^{45} (32 TB)
ReiserFS 3.5	2^{32} (4 GB)	2^{44} (16 TB)
ReiserFS 3.6 (Linux 2.4)	2^{60} (1 EB)	2^{44} (16 TB)
XFS	2^{63} (8 EB)	2^{63} (8 EB)
JFS (512 Bytes block size)	2^{63} (8 EB)	2^{49} (512 TB)
JFS (4 kB block size)	2^{63} (8 EB)	2^{52} (4 PB)
NFSv2 (client side)	2^{31} (2 GB)	2^{63} (8 EB)
NFSv3 (client side)	2^{63} (8 EB)	2^{63} (8 EB)

Table A.2: *Maximum Sizes of File Systems*

Note

Linux Kernel Limits

Table A.2 describes the limitations regarding the on-disk format. The following kernel limits (kernel version 2.4.x) exist:

- *32-bit systems:* The maximum size of any file or block device is limited to 2 TB. Using LVM to combine several block devices allows you to handle larger file systems.
- *64-bit systems:* File and file system sizes are limited to 2^{63} (8 EB). This limit may not yet be reached due to a lack of hardware driver support.

Note

For More Information

Each of the file system projects described above maintains its own home page where you can find mailing list information as well as further documentation and FAQs.

```
http://e2fsprogs.sourceforge.net/
http://www.zipworld.com.au/~akpm/linux/ext3/
http://www.namesys.com/
```

`http://oss.software.ibm.com/developerworks/opensource/jfs/`
`http://oss.sgi.com/projects/xfs/`

A comprehensive multipart tutorial on Linux file systems can be found at *IBM developerWorks*:

`http://www-106.ibm.com/developerworks/library/l-fs.html`

For a comparison of the different journaling file systems in Linux, look at Juan I. Santos Florido's article at *Linuxgazette*: `http://www.linuxgazette.com/issue55/florido.html`.

Those interested in an in-depth analysis of LFS in Linux should try Andreas Jaeger's LFS site: `http://www.suse.de/~aj/linux_lfs.html`.

Access Control Lists in Linux

This chapter provides a brief summary of the background and functions of POSIX ACLs for Linux file systems. Learn how the traditional permission concept for file system objects can be expanded with the help of ACLs (*Access Control Lists*) and which advantages this concept provides.

Advantages of ACLs

Note

POSIX ACLs

The term "POSIX ACL" suggests that this is a true POSIX (*Portable Operating System Interface*) standard. However, the respective draft standards POSIX 1003.1e and POSIX 1003.2c have been withdrawn. The implementation of file system ACLs as described in this chapter is based on the contents of these two documents, which can be viewed at the following URL:

`http://wt.xpilot.org/publications/posix.1e/`

Note

Traditionally, a file object in Linux is associated with three sets of permissions. These sets assign read (`r`), write (`w`), and execute (`x`) permissions for the three user groups file owner, group, and other. Nine bits are used to determine the characteristics of all objects in a Linux file system. Additionally, the *set user id*, *set group id*, and *sticky* bits can be set for special cases.

This lean concept is fully adequate for most practical cases. However, for more complex scenarios or advanced applications, system administrators formerly had to use a number of tricks to circumvent the limitations of the traditional permission concept.

ACLs can be used for situations that require an extension of the traditional file permission concept. They allow the assignment of permissions to individual users or groups even if these do not correspond to the owner or his group.

Access Control Lists are a feature of the Linux kernel and are currently supported by ReiserFS, Ext2, Ext3, JFS, and XFS. Using ACLs, complex scenarios can be realized without implementing complex permission models on the application level.

The advantages of ACLs are clearly evident in situations such as the replacement of a Windows server by a Linux server. Some of the connected workstations may continue to run under Windows even after the migration. The Linux system offers file and print services to the Windows clients with Samba. As Samba supports ACLs, user permissions can be configured both on the Linux server and in Windows with a graphical user interface (only Windows NT and later). With winbindd, it is even possible to assign permissions to users that only exist in the Windows domain without any account on the Linux server. On the server side, edit the Access Control Lists using getfacl and setfacl.

Definitions

User class The conventional POSIX permission concept uses three *classes* of users for assigning permissions in the file system: the owner, the owning group, and other users. Three permission bits can be set for each user class, giving permission to read (`r`), write (`w`), and execute (`x`). An introduction to the user concept in Linux is provided in the *User Guide* in the chapter *Working with the Shell*.

Access ACL The user and group access permissions for all kinds of file system objects (files and directories) are determined by means of access ACLs.

Default ACL Default ACLs can only be applied to directories. They determine the permissions a file system object inherits from its parent directory when it is created.

ACL entry Each ACL consists of a set of ACL entries. An ACL entry contains a type (see Table B.1 on the following page), a qualifier for the user or group to which the entry refers, and a set of permissions. For some entry types, the qualifier for the group or users is undefined.

Handling ACLs

The following section explains the basic structure of an ACL and its various characteristics. The interrelation between ACLs and the traditional permission concept in the Linux file system is briefly demonstrated by means of several figures. Two examples show how you can create your own ACLs using the correct syntax. In conclusion, find information about the way ACLs are interpreted by the operating system.

Structure of ACL Entries

Basically, ACLs can be divided into two classes: A *minimum* ACL merely comprises the entries for the types owner, owning group, and other, which corresponds to the conventional permission bits for files and directories. An *extended* ACL exceeds this concept. It must contain a *mask* entry and may contain several entries for the *named user* and *named group* types. Table B.1 on the next page provides a brief summary of the various available types of ACL entries.

Type	Text Form
owner	`user::rwx`
named user	`user:name:rwx`
owning group	`group::rwx`
named group	`group:name:rwx`
mask	`mask::rwx`
other	`other::rwx`

Table B.1: *ACL Entry Types*

The permissions defined in the entries *owner* and *other* are always effective. Except for the *mask* entry, all other entries (*named user*, *owning group*, and *named group*) can be either effective or masked. If permissions exist in one of the above-mentioned entries as well as in the mask, they are effective. Permissions contained only in the mask or only in the actual entry are not effective. The example in Table B.2 demonstrates this mechanism.

Entry Type	Text Form	Permissions
named user	`user:jane:r-x`	`r-x`
mask	`mask::rw-`	`rw-`
	effective permissions:	`r--`

Table B.2: *Masking Access Permissions*

ACL Entries and File Mode Permission Bits

The smooth interaction of applications supported by ACL and those using the conventional concept can only be ensured if all ACL configurations are workable in the old concept.

This means that each of the three sets of permission bits (*owner*, *group*, and *other*) must be mapped to corresponding ACL entries.

Figure B.1 on the next page and Figure B.2 on the facing page illustrate the two cases of a minimum ACL and an extended ACL. The figures are structured in three blocks — the left block shows the type specifications of the ACL entries, the center block displays an example ACL, and the right block shows the respective permission bits according to the conventional permission concept as displayed by `ls -l`.

In both cases, the *owner class* permissions are mapped to the ACL entry *owner*. The mapping of *other class* permissions to the respective ACL entry is also constant. However, the mapping of the *group class* permissions varies.

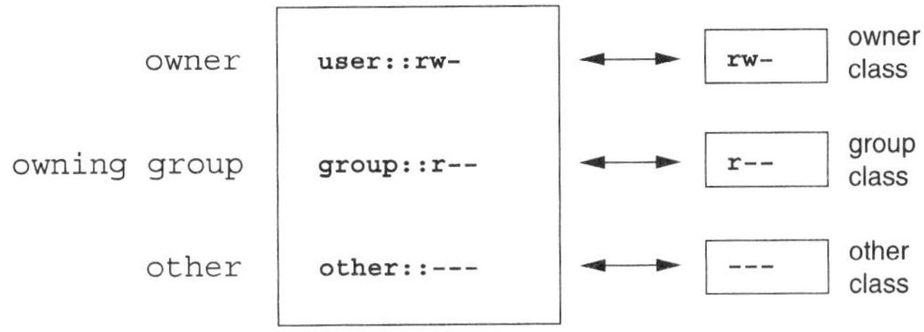

Figure B.1: *Minimum ACL: ACL Entries Compared to Permission Bits*

In the case of a minimum ACL — without *mask* entry — the *group class* permissions are mapped to the ACL entry *owning group*. This is shown in Figure B.1.

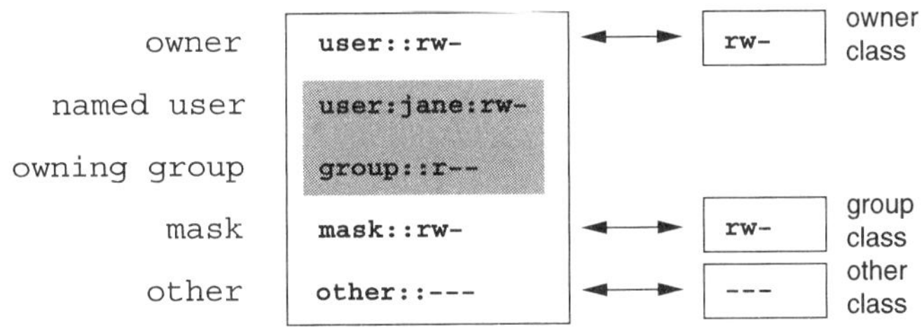

Figure B.2: *Extended ACL: ACL Entries Compared to Permission Bits*

In the case of an extended ACL — with *mask* entry — the *group class* permissions are mapped to the *mask* entry. This is shown in Figure B.2.

This mapping approach ensures the smooth interaction of applications with ACL support and those without ACL support. The access permissions that were assigned by means of the permission bits represent the upper limit for all other "fine adjustments" made by means of ACLs. All permissions not reflected here were either not set in the ACL or are not effective. If permission bits are changed, this is also reflected in the respective ACL and vice versa.

A Directory with Access ACL

The handling of access ACLs is demonstrated in three steps by means of the following example:

- Creating a file system object (a directory in this case)
- Modifying the ACL
- Using masks

1. Before you create the directory, use the `umask` command to determine which access permissions should be masked from the outset:

   ```
   earth:~ #  umask 027
   ```

   The owner has all access permissions (read, write, execute) (`rwx`), the group does not have write access (`r-x`). All other users are denied all kinds of access (`---`).

   ```
   earth:~ #  mkdir mydir
   ```

   After creating the `mydir` directory with the permissions set by `umask`, use the following command to check if all permissions were assigned correctly:

   ```
   earth:~ #  ls -dl mydir
   drwxr-x--- ...  tux project3 ...  mydir
   ```

2. Check the initial state of the ACL and insert a new user entry and a new group entry.

   ```
   earth:~ #  getfacl mydir

   # file: mydir
   # owner: tux
   # group: project3
   user::rwx
   group::r-x
   other::---
   ```

   The output of `getfacl` precisely reflects the mapping of permission bits and ACL entries as described in *ACL Entries and File Mode Permission Bits* on page 508. The first three output lines display the name, owner, and owning group of the directory. The next three lines contain the three ACL entries *owner*, *owning group*, and *other*. In fact, in the case of this minimum ACL, the `getfacl` command does not produce any information you could not have obtained with `ls`.

Your first modification of the ACL is the assignment of read, write, and execute permissions to an additional user `jane` and an additional group `djungle`.

```
earth:~ #  setfacl -m user:jane:rwx,group:djungle:rwx mydir
```

The option `-m` prompts `setfacl` to modify the existing ACL. The following argument indicates the ACL entries to modify (several entries are separated by commas). The final part specifies the name of the directory to which these modifications should be applied.

Use the `getfacl` command to take a look at the resulting ACL.

```
earth:~ #  getfacl mydir

# file: mydir
# owner: tux
# group: project3
user::rwx
user:jane:rwx
group::r-x
group:djungle:rwx
mask::rwx
other::---
```

In addition to the entries initiated for the user `jane` and the group `djungle`, a *mask* entry has been generated. This *mask* entry is set automatically to reduce all entries in the *group class* to a common denominator. Furthermore, `setfacl` automatically adapts existing *mask* entries to the settings modified, provided you do not deactivate this feature with `-n`. *mask* defines the maximum effective access permissions for all entries in the *group class*. This includes: *named user*, *named group*, and *owning group*. Thus, the *mask* entry corresponds to the *group class* permission bits that would be displayed by `ls -dl mydir` as described in *ACL Entries and File Mode Permission Bits* on page 508.

```
earth:~ #  ls -dl mydir

drwxrwx---+ ...  tux project3 ...  mydir
```

As expected, the *group class* permission bits now reflect the *mask* entry.

Additionally, the first column of the output contains a +, which points to an *extended* ACL.

3. According to the output of the ls command, the permissions for the *mask* entry include write access. Traditionally, permission bits of this kind would indicate that the *owning group* (here: project3) also has write access to the directory mydir. However, the effective access permissions for the *owning group* are defined as the intersection of the permissions defined for the *owning group* and *mask* — r-x in our example (see Table B.2 on page 508). Nothing changed here even after the addition of the ACL entries.

   Edit the *mask* entry with setfacl or chmod.

```
earth:~ #  chmod g-w mydir
earth:~ #  ls -dl mydir

drwxr-x---+ ... tux project3 ... mydir

earth:~ #  getfacl mydir

# file: mydir
# owner: tux
# group: project3
user::rwx
user:jane:rwx           # effective: r-x
group::r-x
group:djungle:rwx       # effective: r-x
mask::r-x
other::---
```

   After having used the chmod command to disable the write access from the *group class* bits, the output of the ls command is sufficient to see that the *mask* bits were adjusted with chmod. This is even more evident from the output of getfacl. getfacl adds comments for all entries whose effective permission bits do not correspond to those originally set, as they are filtered by the *mask* entry. Of course, you can use chmod to restore the original state at any time:

```
earth:~ #  chmod g+w mydir
earth:~ #  ls -dl mydir

drwxrwx---+ ... tux project3 ... mydir
```

```
earth:~ # getfacl mydir

# file: mydir
# owner: tux
# group: project3
user::rwx
user:jane:rwx
group::r-x
group:djungle:rwx
mask::rwx
other::---
```

A Directory with a Default ACL

Directories can be equipped with a special kind of ACL — a default ACL. The default ACL defines the access permissions all objects under this directory inherit when they are created. A default ACL affects subdirectories as well as files.

Effects of a Default ACL

Basically, the permissions in a default ACL are handed down in two ways:

- A subdirectory inherits the default ACL of the parent directory both as its own default ACL and as an access ACL.
- A file inherits the default ACL as its own access ACL

All system calls that create file system objects use a `mode` parameter that defines the access permissions for the newly created file system object:

- If the parent directory does not have a default ACL, an intersection of the permissions defined in the `mode` parameter and those in the current `umask` is formed and assigned to the object.
- If a default ACL exists for the parent directory, the permission bits are determined according to the intersection of the value of the `mode` parameter and the permissions defined in the default ACL and assigned to the object.

Application of Default ACLs

The following three examples show the main operations for directories and default ACLs:

- Creating a default ACL for an existing directory
- Creating a subdirectory in a directory with default ACL
- Creating a file in a directory with default ACL

1. Add a default ACL to the existing directory `mydir`:

   ```
   earth:~ #  setfacl -d -m group:djungle:r-x mydir
   ```

   The option `-d` of the `setfacl` command prompts `setfacl` to perform the following modifications (option `-m`) in the default ACL.

   Take a closer look at the result of this command:

   ```
   earth:~ #  getfacl mydir

   # file: mydir
   # owner: tux
   # group: project3
   user::rwx
   user:jane:rwx
   group::r-x
   group:djungle:rwx
   mask::rwx
   other::---
   default:user::rwx
   default:group::r-x
   default:group:djungle:r-x
   default:mask::r-x
   default:other::---
   ```

   `getfacl` returns both the access ACL and the default ACL. All lines that begin with `default` form the default ACL. Although you merely executed the `setfacl` command with an entry for the `djungle` group for the default ACL, `setfacl` automatically copied all other entries from the access ACL to form a valid default ACL. Default ACLs do not have a direct effect on access permissions, they only come into play when file system objects are created. When handing down the permissions, only the default ACL of the parent directory is taken into consideration.

2. In the next example, use `mkdir` to create a subdirectory in `mydir`, which will "inherit" the default ACL.

```
earth:~ #  mkdir mydir/mysubdir
earth:~ #  getfacl mydir/mysubdir

# file: mydir/mysubdir
# owner: tux
# group: project3
user::rwx
group::r-x
group:djungle:r-x
mask::r-x
other::---
default:user::rwx
default:group::r-x
default:group:djungle:r-x
default:mask::r-x
default:other::---
```

As expected, the newly-created subdirectory `mysubdir` has the permissions from the default ACL of the parent directory. The access ACL of `mysubdir` is an exact reflection of the default ACL of `mydir`, just as the default ACL that this directory will hand down to its subordinate objects.

3. Use `touch` to create a file in the `mydir` directory:

```
earth:~ #  touch mydir/myfile
earth:~ #  ls -l mydir/myfile

-rw-r-----+ ... tux project3 ... mydir/myfile

earth:~ #  getfacl mydir/myfile

# file: mydir/myfile
# owner: tux
# group: project3
user::rw-
group::r-x          # effective:r--
group:djungle:r-x   # effective:r--
mask::r--
other::---
```

Important in this example: `touch` passes on `mode` with the value `0666`, which means that new files are created with read and write permissions for all user classes, provided no other restrictions exist in `umask` or in the default ACL (see *Effects of a Default ACL* on page 513).

If effect, this means that all access permissions not contained in the `mode` value are removed from the respective ACL entries. Although no permissions were removed from the ACL entry of the *group class*, the *mask* entry was modified to mask permissions not set via `mode`.

This approach ensures the smooth interaction of applications, such as compilers, with ACLs. You can create files with restricted access permissions and subsequently mark them as executable. The `mask` mechanism makes sure that the respective users and groups are assigned the permissions they are granted in the default ACL.

The ACL Check Algorithm

The following section provides brief information on the check algorithm applied to all processes or applications before they are granted access to an ACL-protected file system object. As a basic rule, the ACL entries are examined in the following sequence: *owner*, *named user*, *owning group* or *named group*, and *other*. The access is handled in accordance with the entry that best suits the process; permissions do not accumulate.

Things are more complicated if a process belongs to more than one group and would potentially suit several *group* entries. An entry is randomly selected from the suitable entries with the required permissions. It is irrelevant which of the entries triggers the final result "access granted". Likewise, if none of the suitable *group* entries contains the correct permissions, a randomly selected entry triggers the final result "access denied".

Outlook

As described in the preceding sections, ACLs can be used to implement very complex permission scenarios that fully meet modern applications. The traditional permission concept and ACLs can be combined in a smart manner.

However, some important applications still lack ACL support. Except for the star archiver, there are no backup applications that guarantee the full preservation of ACLs during a backup. Editors and file managers (such as

Konqueror) continue to cause problems for administrators and users who try to use ACLs correctly. Currently, most of these applications do not offer any ACL support. If, for example, a file with an access ACL is modified in an editor, the backup mode of the editor used will determine whether or not the access ACL is preserved following the modification:

- If the editor writes the changes to the original file, the access ACL will be preserved.
- If the editor saves the updated contents to a new file that is subsequently renamed to the old file name, the ACLs may be lost, unless the editor supports ACLs.

Although the basic file commands (`cp`, `mv`, `ls`, etc.) already support ACLs, presently ACLs are lost when copying files with the file manager Konqueror. The more applications support ACLs, the more it will be possible to exploit the great potential of this feature.

Tip

Additional information
Detailed information about ACLs is available at the following URLs:

`http://sdb.suse.de/en/sdb/html/81_acl.html`
`http://acl.bestbits.at/`

and in the man page for `getfacl` (`man 1 getfacl`), the man page for `acl` (`man 5 acl`), and the man page for `setfacl` (`man 1 setfacl`).

Tip

Manual Page of e2fsck

E2FSCK(8) E2FSCK(8)

NAME
e2fsck - check a Linux second extended file system

SYNOPSIS
e2fsck [-pacnyrdfvstFSV] [-b superblock] [-B blocksize] [-l|-L bad_blocks_file] [-C fd] [-j external-journal] [device

DESCRIPTION
e2fsck is used to check a Linux second extended file system (e2fs). E2fsck also supports ext2 filesystems countaining a journal, which are also sometimes known as ext3 filesystems.

device is the special file corresponding to the device (e.g /dev/hdc1).

OPTIONS
-a This option does the same thing as the -p option. It is provided for backwards compatibility only; it is suggested that people use -p option whenever possible.

-b superblock
Instead of using the normal superblock, use an alternative superblock specified by superblock. This option is normally used when the primary superblock has been corrupted. The location of the backup superblock is dependent on the filesystem's blocksize. For filesystems with 1k blocksizes, a backup superblock can be found at block 8193; for filesystems with 2k blocksizes, at block 16384; and for 4k blocksizes, at block 32768.

Additional backup superblocks can be determined by using the mke2fs program using the -n option to print out where the superblocks were created. The -b option to mke2fs, which specifies blocksize of the filesystem must be specified in order for the superblock locations that are printed out to be accurate.

If an alternative superblock is specified and the filesystem is not opened read-only, e2fsck will make sure that the primary superblock is updated appropriately upon completion of the filesystem check.

-B blocksize

Normally, e2fsck will search for the superblock at various different block sizes in an attempt to find the appropriate block size. This search can be fooled in some cases. This option forces e2fsck to only try locating the superblock at a particular blocksize. If the superblock is not found, e2fsck will terminate with a fatal error.

-c

This option causes e2fsck to run the badblocks(8) program to find any blocks which are bad on the filesystem, and then marks them as bad by adding them to the bad block inode.

-C

This option causes e2fsck to write completion information to the specified file descriptor so that the progress of the filesystem check can be monitored. This option is typically used by programs which are running e2fsck. If the file descriptor specified is 0, e2fsck will print a completion bar as it goes about its business. This requires that e2fsck is running on a video console or terminal.

-d

Print debugging output (useless unless you are debugging e2fsck).

-f

Force checking even if the file system seems clean.

-F

Flush the filesystem device's buffer caches before beginning. Only really useful for doing e2fsck time trials.

-j external-journal

Set the pathname where the external-journal for this filesystem can be found.

-l filename

```
        Add the blocks listed  in  the  file  specified  by
        filename  to the list of bad blocks.  The format of
        this file is the same as the one generated  by  the
        badblocks(8) program.
 -L filename
        Set  the  bad  blocks list to be the list of blocks
        specified by filename.  (This option is the same as
        the  -l  option,  except  the  bad  blocks  list is
        cleared before the blocks listed in  the  file  are
        added to the bad blocks list.)

 -n     Open the filesystem read-only, and assume an answer
        of 'no' to all questions.  Allows e2fsck to be used
        non-interactively.   (Note:  if  the  -c, -l, or -L
        options are specified in addition to the -n option,
        then  the  filesystem will be opened read-write, to
        permit the bad-blocks list to be updated.  However,
        no other changes will be made to the filesystem.)

 -p     Automatically  repair  ("preen")  the  file  system
        without any questions.

 -r     This option does nothing at  all;  it  is  provided
        only for backwards compatibility.

 -s     This  option  will byte-swap the filesystem so that
        it is using  the  normalized,  standard  byte-order
        (which  is i386 or little endian).  If the filesys-
        tem is already in the standard  byte-order,  e2fsck
        will take no action.

 -S     This  option will byte-swap the filesystem, regard-
        less of its current byte-order.

 -t     Print timing statistics for e2fsck.  If this option
        is  used  twice,  additional  timing statistics are
        printed on a pass by pass basis.

 -v     Verbose mode.

 -V     Print version information and exit.

 -y     Assume an answer of 'yes' to all questions;  allows
        e2fsck to be used non-interactively.

EXIT CODE
       The exit code returned by e2fsck is the sum of the follow-
       ing conditions:
            0    - No errors
            1    - File system errors corrected
            2    - File system errors corrected, system should
                   be rebooted if file system was mounted
            4    - File system errors left uncorrected
```

```
       8    - Operational error
       16   - Usage or syntax error
       128  - Shared library error

SIGNALS
       The following signals have the following effect when  sent
       to e2fsck.

       SIGUSR1
              This  signal  causes  e2fsck  to start displaying a
              completion bar.  (See discussion of the -C option.)

       SIGUSR2
              This signal causes e2fsck to stop displaying a com-
              pletion bar.

REPORTING BUGS
       Almost any piece of software will have bugs.  If you  man-
       age  to find a filesystem which causes e2fsck to crash, or
       which e2fsck is unable to repair, please report it to  the
       author.

       Please include as much information as possible in your bug
       report.  Ideally, include a  complete  transcript  of  the
       e2fsck  run,  so I can see exactly what error messages are
       displayed.  If you have a writeable filesystem  where  the
       transcript can be stored, the script(1) program is a handy
       way to save the output of e2fsck to a file.

       It is also useful to send the output of dumpe2fs(8).  If a
       specific  inode  or inodes seems to be giving e2fsck trou-
       ble, try running the debugfs(8) command and send the  out-
       put  of the stat(1u) command run on the relevant inode(s).
       If the inode is a directory, the debugfs dump command will
       allow  you to extract the contents of the directory inode,
       which can sent to me after being first run  through  uuen
       code(1).

       Always  include  the full version string which e2fsck dis-
       plays when it is run, so I know which version you are run-
       ning.

AUTHOR
       This  version  of  e2fsck  was  written  by  Theodore Ts'o
       &lt;tytso@mit.edu&gt;.

SEE ALSO
       mke2fs(8), tune2fs(8), dumpe2fs(8), debugfs(8)


E2fsprogs version 1.25    September 2001               E2FSCK(8)
```

Manual Page of reiserfsck

```
REISERFSCK(8)                                          REISERFSCK(8)


NAME
       reiserfsck - check a Linux Reiserfs file system

SYNOPSIS
       reiserfsck  [  -afprVy  ]  [  --check  |  --fix-fixable  |
       --rebuild-sb | --rebuild-tree | --clean-attributes ] [  -j
       |  --journal-device  device ] [ --no-journal-available ] [
       -z | --adjust-file-size ] [ -S | --scan-whole-partition  ]
       [  -l  |  --logfile  filename  ]  [  -n | --nolog ] [ -q |
       --quiet ] device

DESCRIPTION
       Reiserfsck searches for a Reiserfs filesystem on a device,
       replays  any  necessary transactions, and either checks or
       repairs the file system.

       device is the special file corresponding to the device  or
              partition  (e.g /dev/hdXX for IDE disk partition or
              /dev/sdXX for SCSI disk partition).

OPTIONS
       --check
              This default action checks file system  consistency
              and reports but does not repair any corruption that
              it finds. This option may be used  on  a  read-only
              file  system  mount.  The --check option exits with
              status 0 to indicate that no corruption was  found.
              Otherwise, reiserfsck returns 1 to indicate corrup
              tion that can be fixed with --fix-fixable and 2  to
              indicate corruption that requires --rebuild-tree.

       --fix-fixable
              This  option  recovers  certain kinds of corruption
```

that do not require rebuilding the entire file sys tem tree (--rebuild-tree). Normally you only need this option if the --check option reports "corrup tion that can be fixed with --fix-fixable". This includes: zeroing invalid data-block pointers, cor recting st_size and st_blocks for directories, and deleting invalid directory entries.

--rebuild-sb
: This option recovers the superblock on a Reiserfs partition. Normally you only need this option if mount reports "read_super_block: can't find a reis erfs file system" and you are sure that a Reiserfs file system is there.

--rebuild-tree
: This option rebuilds the entire file system tree using leaf nodes found on the device. Normally you only need this option if the --check option reports "corruption that can be fixed only during --rebuild-tree". You are strongly encouraged to make a backup copy of the whole partition before attempting the --rebuild-tree option.

--clean-attributes
: This option cleans reserved fields of Stat-Data items.

--journal-device device , -j device
: This option supplies the device name of the current file system journal. This option is required when the journal resides on a separate device from the main data device (although it can be avoided with the expert option --no-journal-available).

--adjust-file-size, -z
: This option causes reiserfsck to correct file sizes that are larger than the offset of the last discov ered byte. This implies that holes at the end of a file will be removed. File sizes that are smaller than the offset of the last discovered byte are corrected by --fix-fixable.

--logfile filename, -l filename
: This option causes reiserfsck to report any corrup tion it finds to the specified log file rather than stderr.

--nolog, -n
: This option prevents reiserfsck from reporting any kinds of corruption.

--quiet, -q

```
              This  option prevents reiserfsck from reporting its
              rate of progress.

       -a, -p These options are usually passed by fsck -A  during
              the  automatic  checking  of /etc/fstab partitions.
              For compatibility, these options simply cause reis
              erfsck  to  print  information  about the specified
              file system.  No checks are performed.  When it  is
              set  - reiserfsck assumes that it is called by fsck
              -A, provides some information about  the  specified
              filesystem and exits.

       -V     This  option  prints  the reiserfsprogs version and
              exit.

       -r, -p, -y
              These options are ignored.

       -V, -f prints version and exits

EXPERT OPTIONS
       DO NOT USE THESE OPTIONS UNLESS  YOU  KNOW  WHAT  YOU  ARE
       DOING.  WE  ARE  NOT  RESPONSIBLE  IF  YOU LOSE DATA AS A
       RESULT OF THESE OPTIONS.

       --no-journal-available
              This option allows reiserfsck to proceed  when  the
              journal device is not available. This option has no
              effect when the journal is located on the main data
              device.  NOTE:  after  this  operation you must use
              reiserfstune to specify a new journal device.

       --scan-whole-partition, -S
              This option causes --rebuild-tree to scan the whole
              partition, not only used space on the partition.

EXAMPLE OF USING
       1. You think something may be wrong with a reiserfs parti
       tion on /dev/hda1 or you would  just  like  to  perform  a
       periodic disk check.

       2.  Run  reiserfsck --check --logfile check.log /dev/hda1.
       If reiserfsck --check exits with  status  0  it  means  no
       errors were discovered.

       3.  If reiserfsck --check exits with status 1 (and reports
       about fixable corruptions) it means that  you  should  run
       reiserfsck  --fix-fixable --logfile fixable.log /dev/hda1.

       4. If reiserfsck --check exits with status 2 (and  reports
       about  fatal  corruptions)  it  means that you need to run
       reiserfsck --rebuild-tree.  If reiserfsck --check fails in
       some  way  you  should also run reiserfsck --rebuild-tree,
```

```
       but we also encourage you to submit this as a bug  report.

       5. Before running reiserfsck --rebuild-tree, please make a
       backup of the whole partition before proceeding. Then  run
       reiserfsck --rebuild-tree --logfile rebuild.log /dev/hda1.

       6. If the --rebuild-tree step fails or  does  not  recover
       what you expected, please submit this as a bug report. Try
       to provide as much information as possible and we will try
       to help solve the problem.

EXIT CODE
       reiserfsck uses the following exit codes:
            0      - No errors
            1      - File system errors corrected
            2      - File system errors corrected, system should
                     be rebooted if file system was mounted
            4      - File system errors left uncorrected
            8      - Operational error
            16     - Usage or syntax error

AUTHOR
       This  version  of  reiserfsck  has  been written by Vitaly
       Fertman   <vitaly@namesys.com>   and   Vladimir   Saveliev
       <vs@namesys.com>.

BUGS
       There  are  likely  to be some bugs. Please report bugs to
       the ReiserFS mail-list <reiserfs-list@namesys.com>.

TODO
       Faster recovering, signal handling,  i/o  error  handling,
       return reasonable exit codes, etc.

SEE ALSO
       mkreiserfs(8), debugreiserfs(8), reiserfstune(8)


Reiserfsprogs-3.6.2        January 2002             REISERFSCK(8)
```

The GNU General Public License

GNU General Public License

Foreword

The licenses for most software are designed to take away your freedom to share and change it. By contrast, the *GNU General Public License* is intended to guarantee your freedom to share and change free software — to make sure the software is free for all its users. This *General Public License* applies to most of the *Free Software Foundation's* software and to any other program whose authors commit to using it. (Some other *Free Software Foundation* software is covered by the *GNU Library General Public License* instead.) You can apply it to your programs, too.

When we speak of *"free" software*, we are referring to freedom, not price. Our General Public Licenses are designed to make sure that you have the freedom to distribute copies of free software (and charge for this service if you wish), that you receive source code or can get it if you want it, that you can change the software or use pieces of it in new free programs; and that you know you can do these things.

To protect your rights, we need to make restrictions that forbid anyone to deny you these rights or to ask you to surrender the rights. These restrictions translate to certain responsibilities for you if you distribute copies of the software, or if you modify it.

For example, if you distribute copies of such a program, whether gratis or for a fee, you must give the recipients all the rights that you have. You must make sure that they, too, receive or can get the source code. And you must show them these terms so they know their rights.

We protect your rights with two steps: (1) copyright the software, and (2) offer you this license which gives you legal permission to copy, distribute and/or modify the software.

Also, for each author's protection and ours, we want to make certain that everyone understands that there is no warranty for this free software. If the software is modified by someone else and passed on, we want its recipients to know that what they have is not the original, so that any problems introduced by others will not reflect on the original authors' reputations.

Finally, any free program is threatened constantly by software patents. We wish to avoid the danger that redistributors of a free program will individually obtain patent licenses, in effect making the program proprietary. To prevent this, we have made it clear that any patent must be licensed for everyone's free use or not licensed at all.

The precise terms and conditions for copying, distribution and modification follow.

GNU General, Public License

Terms and Conditions for Copying, Distribution and Modification

0. This License applies to any program or other work which contains a notice placed by the copyright holder saying it may be distributed under the terms of this *General Public License.* The "Program", below, refers to any such program or work, and a *work based on the Program* means either the Program or any derivative work under copyright law: that is to say, a work containing the Program or a portion of it, either verbatim or with modifications and/or translated into another language. (Hereinafter, translation is included without limitation in the term "modification".) Each licensee is addressed as "you".

Activities other than copying, distribution and modification are not covered by this License; they are outside its scope. The act of running the Program is not restricted, and the output from the Program is covered only if its contents constitute a work based on the Program (independent of having been made by running the Program). Whether that is true depends on what the Program does.

1. You may copy and distribute verbatim copies of the Program's source code as you receive it, in any medium, provided that you conspicuously and appropriately publish on each copy an appropriate copyright notice and disclaimer of warranty; keep intact all the notices that refer to this License and to the absence of any warranty; and give any other recipients of the Program a copy of this License along with the Program.

You may charge a fee for the physical act of transferring a copy, and you may at your option offer warranty protection in exchange for a fee.

2. You may modify your copy or copies of the Program or any portion of it, thus forming a work based on the Program, and copy and distribute such modifications or work under the terms of Section 1 above, provided that you also meet all of these conditions:

a) You must cause the modified files to carry prominent notices stating that you changed the files and the date of any change.

b) You must cause any work that you distribute or publish, that in whole or in part contains or is derived from the Program or any part thereof, to be licensed as a whole at no charge to all third parties under the terms of this License.

c) If the modified program normally reads commands interactively when run, you must cause it, when started running for such interactive use in the most ordinary way, to print or display an announcement including an appropriate copyright notice and a notice that there is no warranty (or else, saying that you provide a warranty) and that users may redistribute the program under these conditions, and telling the user how to view a copy of this License. (Exception: if the Program itself is interactive but does not normally print such an announcement, your work based on the Program is not required to print an announcement.)

These requirements apply to the modified work as a whole. If identifiable sections of that work are not derived from the Program, and can be reasonably considered independent and separate works in themselves, then this License, and its terms, do not apply to those sections when you distribute them as separate works. But when you distribute the same sections as part of a whole which is a work based on the Program, the distribution of the whole must be on the terms of this License, whose permissions for other licensees extend to the entire whole, and thus to each and every part regardless of who wrote it.

Thus, it is not the intent of this section to claim rights or contest your rights to work written entirely by you; rather, the intent is to exercise the right to control the distribution of derivative or collective works based on the Program.

In addition, mere aggregation of another work not based on the Program with the Program (or with a work based on the Program) on a volume of a storage or distribution medium does not bring the other work under the scope of this License.

3. You may copy and distribute the Program (or a work based on it, under Section 2) in object code or executable form under the terms of Sections 1 and 2 above provided that you also do one of the following:

a) Accompany it with the complete corresponding machine–readable source code, which must be distributed under the terms of Sections 1 and 2 above on a medium customarily used for software interchange; or,

b) Accompany it with a written offer, valid for at least three years, to give any third party, for a charge no more than your cost of physically performing source distribution, a complete machine–readable copy of the corresponding source code, to be distributed under the terms of Sections 1 and 2 above on a medium customarily used for software interchange; or,

c) Accompany it with the information you received as to the offer to distribute corresponding source code. (This alternative is allowed only for noncommercial distribution and only if you received the program in object code or executable form with such an offer, in accord with Subsection b above.)

The source code for a work means the preferred form of the work for making modifications to it. For an executable work, "complete source code" means all the source code for all modules it contains, plus any associated interface definition files, plus the scripts used to control compilation and installation of the executable. However, as a special exception, the source code distributed need not include anything that is normally distributed (in either source or binary form) with the major components (compiler, kernel, and so on) of the operating system on which the executable runs, unless that component itself accompanies the executable.

If distribution of executable or object code is made by offering access to copy from a designated place, then offering equivalent access to copy the source code from the same place counts as distribution of the source code, even though third parties are not compelled to copy the source along with the object code.

4. You may not copy, modify, sublicense, or distribute the Program except as expressly provided under this License. Any attempt otherwise to copy, modify, sublicense or distribute the Program is void, and will automatically terminate your rights under this License. However, parties who have received copies, or rights, from you under this License will not have their licenses terminated so long as such parties remain in full compliance.

5. You are not required to accept this License, since you have not signed it. However, nothing else grants you permission to modify or distribute the Program or its derivative works. These actions are prohibited by law if you do not accept this License. Therefore, by modifying or distributing the Program (or any work based on the Program), you indicate your acceptance of this License to do so, and all its terms and conditions for copying, distributing or modifying the Program or works based on it.

6. Each time you redistribute the Program (or any work based on the Program), the recipient automatically receives a license from the original licensor to copy, distribute or modify the Program subject to these terms and conditions. You may not impose any further restrictions on the recipients' exercise of the rights granted herein. You are not responsible for enforcing compliance by third parties to this License.

7. If, as a consequence of a court judgment or allegation of patent infringement or for any other reason (not limited to patent issues), conditions are imposed on you (whether by court order, agreement or otherwise) that contradict the conditions of this License, they do not excuse you from the conditions of this License. If you cannot distribute so as to satisfy simultaneously your obligations under this License and any other pertinent obligations, then as a consequence you may not distribute the Program at all. For example, if a patent license would not permit royalty–free redistribution of the Program by all those who receive copies directly or indirectly through you, then the only way you could satisfy both it and this License would be to refrain entirely from distribution of the Program.

If any portion of this section is held invalid or unenforceable under any particular circumstance, the balance of the section is intended to apply and the section as a whole is intended to apply in other circumstances.

It is not the purpose of this section to induce you to infringe any patents or other property right claims or to contest validity of any such claims; this section has the sole purpose of protecting the integrity of the free software distribution system, which is implemented by public license practices. Many people have made generous contributions to the wide range of software distributed through that system in reliance on consistent application of that system; it is up to the author/donor to decide if he or she is willing to distribute software through any other system and a licensee cannot impose that choice.

This section is intended to make thoroughly clear what is believed to be a consequence of the rest of this License.

8. If the distribution and/or use of the Program is restricted in certain countries either by patents or by copyrighted interfaces, the original copyright holder who places the Program under this License may add an explicit geographical distribution limitation excluding those countries, so that distribution is permitted only in or among countries not thus excluded. In such case, this License incorporates the limitation as if written in the body of this License.

9. The *Free Software Foundation* may publish revised and/or new versions of the *General Public License* from time to time. Such new versions will be similar in spirit to the present version, but may differ in detail to address new problems or concerns.

Each version is given a distinguishing version number. If the Program specifies a version number of this License which applies to it and "any later version", you have the option of following the terms and conditions either of that version or of any later version published by the *Free Software Foundation.* If the Program does not specify a version number of this License, you may choose any version ever published by the *Free Software Foundation.*

10. If you wish to incorporate parts of the Program into other free programs whose distribution conditions are different, write to the author to ask for permission. For software which is copyrighted by the *Free Software Foundation,* write to the *Free Software Foundation*; we sometimes make exceptions for this.

Our decision will be guided by the two goals of preserving the free status of all derivatives of our free software and of promoting the sharing and reuse of software generally.

No Warranty

11. Because the program is licensed free of charge, there is no warranty for the program, to the extent permitted by applicable law. Except when otherwise stated in writing the copyright holders and/or other parties provide the program "as is" without warranty of any kind, either expressed or implied, including, but not limited to, the implied warranties of merchantability and fitness for a particular purpose. The entire risk as to the quality and performance of the program is with you. Should the program prove defective, you assume the cost of all necessary servicing, repair or correction.

12. In no event unless required by applicable law or agreed to in writing will any copyright holder, or any other party who may modify and/or redistribute the program as permitted above, be liable to you for damages, including any general, special, incidental or consequential damages arising out of the use or inability to use the program (including but not limited to loss of data or data being rendered inaccurate or losses sustained by you or third parties or a failure of the program to operate with any other programs), even if such holder or other party has been advised of the possibility of such damages.

End of Terms and Conditions

How to Apply These Terms to Your New Programs

If you develop a new program, and you want it to be of the greatest possible use to the public, the best way to achieve this is to make it free software which everyone can redistribute and change under these terms.

To do so, attach the following notices to the program. It is safest to attach them to the start of each source file to most effectively convey the exclusion of warranty; and each file should have at least the "copyright" line and a pointer to where the full notice is found.

> *one line to give the program's name and a brief idea of what it does.*
> Copyright (C) 19*yy* *name of author*
> This program is free software; you can redistribute it and/or modify it under the terms of the GNU General Public License as

> published by the Free Software Foundation; either version 2 of the License, or (at your option) any later version.
>
> This program is distributed in the hope that it will be useful, but WITHOUT ANY WARRANTY; without even the implied warranty of MERCHANTABILITY or FITNESS FOR A PARTICULAR PURPOSE. See the GNU General Public License for more details.
>
> You should have received a copy of the GNU General Public License along with this program; if not, write to the Free Software Foundation, Inc., 675 Mass Ave, Cambridge, MA 02139, USA.

Also add information on how to contact you by electronic and paper mail.

If the program is interactive, make it output a short notice like this when it starts in an interactive mode:

> Gnomovision version 69, Copyright (C) 19*yy* *name of author*
>
> Gnomovision comes with ABSOLUTELY NO WARRANTY; for details type 'show w'. This is free software, and you are welcome to redistribute it under certain conditions; type 'show c' for details.

The hypothetical commands `show w` and `show c` should show the appropriate parts of the General Public License. Of course, the commands you use may be called something other than `show w` and `show c`; they could even be mouse–clicks or menu items — whatever suits your program.

You should also get your employer (if you work as a programmer) or your school, if any, to sign a "copyright disclaimer" for the program, if necessary. Here is a sample; alter the names:

> Yoyodyne, Inc., hereby disclaims all copyright interest in the program 'Gnomovision' (which makes passes at compilers) written by James Hacker.
>
> *Signed by Ty Coon*, 1 April 1989
>
> Ty Coon, President of Vice

This *General Public License* does not permit incorporating your program into proprietary programs. If your program is a subroutine library, you may consider it more useful to permit linking proprietary applications with the library. If this is what you want to do, use the *GNU Library General Public License* instead of this License.

Bibliography

1 **Almesberger 1994** ALMESBERGER, Werner: *LILO User's guide*, 1994. – (see file /usr/doc/lilo/user.dvi)

2 **Bailey 1997** BAILEY, Edward C.: *Maximum RPM*. Red Hat, 1997. – (ISBN 1-888172-78-9)

3 **Cameron und Rosenblatt 1991** CAMERON, Debra ; ROSENBLATT, Bill: *Learning GNU Emacs*. O'Reilly & Associates, Inc., 1991. – (ISBN 0 937175-84-6)

4 **Chapman und Zwicky 1996** CHAPMAN ; ZWICKY: *Einrichten von Internet Firewalls. Sicherheit im Internet gewährleisten*. O'Reilly & Associates, Inc., 1996. – (ISBN 3-930673312)

5 **Cheswick und Bellovin 1996** CHESWICK, William R. ; BELLOVIN, Steven M.: *Firewalls und Sicherheit im Internet*. Addison Wesley GmbH, 1996. – (ISBN 3-89319-875-x)

6 **Costales u. a. 1993** COSTALES, Bryan ; ALLMAN, Eric ; RICKERT, Neil: *sendmail*. O'Reilly & Associates, Inc., 1993. – (ISBN 1-56592-056-2)

7 **Dawson v2.8, 07 Jan 1995** DAWSON, Terry: *Linux NET-2/NET-3 HOWTO*, v2.8, 07 Jan 1995. – (see file /usr/doc/howto/NET-2-HOWTO)

8 **Fang u. a. 1993** FANG, Chin ; CROSSON, Bob ; RAYMOND, Eric S.: *The Hitchhiker's Guide to X386/XFree86 Video Timing (or, Tweaking your Monitor for Fun and Profit)*, 1993. – (see file /usr/X11/lib/X11/doc/VideoModes.doc)

9 **Frisch 1993** FRISCH, Æleen: *Essential System Administration*. O'Reilly & Associates, Inc., 1993. – (ISBN 0-937175-80-3)

10 **Garfinkel und Spafford 1993** GARFINKEL, Simson ; SPAFFORD, Gene: *Practical UNIX Security*. O'Reilly & Associates, Inc., 1993. – (ISBN 0-937175-72-2)

11 **Gilly 1992** GILLY, Daniel: *UNIX in a nutshell: System V Edition*. O'Reilly & Associates, Inc., 1992. – (ISBN 1-56592-001-5)

12 **Goossens u. a. 1993** GOOSSENS, Michel ; MITTELBACH, Frank ; SAMARIN, Alexander: *The LaTeX Companion*. Addison Wesley GmbH, 1993. – (ISBN 3-54199-8)

13 **Grieger 1994** GRIEGER, W.: *Wer hat Angst vorm Emacs?* Addison Wesley GmbH, 1994. – (ISBN 3-89319-620-X)

14 **Herold 1992** HEROLD, H.: *UNIX Grundlagen*. Addison Wesley GmbH, 1992. – (ISBN 3-89319-542-8)

15 **Hetze u. a. 1996** HETZE, Sebastian ; HOHNDEL, Dirk ; MÜLLER, Martin ; KIRCH, Olaf: *Linux Anwenderhandbuch*. 6. LunetIX Softfair, 1996. – (ISBN 3-929764-05-9)

16 **Hoffmann 1997** HOFFMANN, Erwin: EMail-Gateway mit qmail. In: *iX* 12 (1997), S. 108ff

17 **Hunt 1995** HUNT, Craig: *TCP/IP Netzwerk Administration*. O'Reilly & Associates, Inc., 1995. – (ISBN 3-930673-02-9)

18 **Kienle 1995** KIENLE, Micheal: TIS: Toolkit für anwendungsorientierte Firewall-Systeme. In: *iX* 8 (1995), S. 140ff

19 **Kirch 1995** KIRCH, Olaf: *LINUX Network Administrator's Guide*. O'Reilly & Associates, Inc., 1995. – (ISBN 1-56592-087-2)

20 **Kofler 1995** KOFLER, M.: *Linux*. Addison Wesley GmbH, 1995. – (ISBN 3-89319-796-6)

21 **Kopka 1994** KOPKA, Helmut: *LaTeX-Einführung*. Addison Wesley GmbH, 1994. – (ISBN 3-89319-664-1)

22 **Kunitz 1995** KUNITZ, Ulrich: Sicherheit fast kostenlos: Einrichtung eines kostenlosen Firewall-Systems. In: *iX* 9 (1995), S. 176ff

23 **Lamb 1990** LAMB, Linda: *Learning the vi Editor*. O'Reilly & Associates, Inc., 1990. – (ISBN 0-937175-67-6)

24 **Lamport 1994** LAMPORT, Leslie: *LaTeX User's Guide and Reference Manual*. Addison Wesley GmbH, 1994. – (ISBN 0-201-52983-1)

25 **Leffler 1996a** LEFFLER, Sam: *HylaFAX Home Page.* `http://www.vix.com/hylafax/:` , 1996

26 **Leffler 1996b** LEFFLER, Sam: *TIFF Software.* `http://www-mipl.jpl.nasa.gov/~ndr/tiff/:` , 1996

27 **O'Reilly und Todino 1992** O'REILLY, Tim ; TODINO, Grace: *Manging UUCP and Usenet.* O'Reilly & Associates, Inc., 1992. – (ISBN 0-937175-93-5)

28 **Perlman 1994** PERLMAN, G.: *Unix For Software Developers.* Prentice-Hall, 1994. – (ISBN 13-932997-8)

29 **Pugh 1994** PUGH, K.: *UNIX For The MS-DOS User.* Prentice-Hall, 1994. – (ISBN 13-146077-3)

30 **Scheiderer 1998** SCHEIDERER, Jürgen: Sicherheit Kostenlos - Firewall mit Linux. In: *iX* 12 (1998)

31 **Schoonover und Bowie 1992** SCHOONOVER, M. ; BOWIE, J.: *GNU Emacs.* Addison Wesley GmbH, 1992. – (ISBN 0-201-56345-2)

32 **Stoll 1998** STOLL, Clifford: *Kuckucksei; Die Jagd auf die deutschen Hacker, die das Pentagon knackten.* Fischer-TB.-Vlg., 1998. – (ISBN 3596139848)

33 **The XFree86™-Team 1996** THE XFREE86™-TEAM: *XF86Config(4/5) - Configuration File for Xfree86™*, 1996. – Manual-Page zu XFree86™

34 **Todino u. a. 1993** TODINO, Grace ; STRANG, John ; PEEK, Jerry: *Learning the UNIX operating system.* O'Reilly & Associates, Inc., 1993. – (ISBN 1-56592-060-0)

35 **Tung 1999** TUNG, Brian: *Kerberos: A Network Authentication System.* Fischer-TB.-Vlg., 1999. – (ISBN 0-201-37924-4)

36 **User Guide 2003** *SuSE Linux: User Guide.* 2. Nuremberg : SuSE Linux AG, 2003

37 **Welsh 1994** WELSH, Matt: *Linux Installation and Getting Started.* 2. SuSE Linux AG, 1994. – (ISBN 3-930419-03-3)

38 **Welsh und Kaufman 1995** WELSH, Matt ; KAUFMAN, Lars: *Running Linux.* O'Reilly & Associates, Inc., 1995. – (ISBN 1-56592-100-3)

Index

C

L

M

T

U

V

Notice

Notice

Notice

Notice

Notice